ARIEL SHARON

ARIEL SHARON

A LIFE

NIR HEFEZ AND
GADI BLOOM

*Translated from the Hebrew
by Mitch Ginsburg*

RANDOM HOUSE NEW YORK

Published in the United States by Random House,
an imprint of The Random House Publishing Group,
a division of Random House, Inc., New York.

RANDOM HOUSE and colophon are registered
trademarks of Random House, Inc.

LIBRARY OF CONGRESS CATALOGING-IN-PUBLICATION DATA
Hefez, Nir.
[Ro'eh. English]
Ariel Sharon: a life / Nir Hefez and Gadi Bloom; translated from the Hebrew
by Mitch Ginsburg
p. cm.
ISBN 1-4000-6587-9
1. Sharon, Ariel.   2. Generals—Israel—Biography.   3. Prime ministers—
Israel—Biography.   4. Statesmen—Israel—Biography.   5. Israel—Politics
and government.   I. Bloom, Gadi.   II. Title.
DS126.6.S42H4413 2006
956.9405'4092—dc22   2006049144
[B]

Printed in the United States of America on acid-free paper

www.atrandom.com

246897531

FIRST EDITION

Title page photo © Ziv Koren
Maps © Avigdor Orgad
Book design by Carole Lowenstein

For our loved ones:

Allegria and Leon Bloom,
Osnat and Chanoch Bloom,
and Pazit Ben Nun

Sara and El-Ami Hefez,
Noam and Omer Hefez,
and Orit Hefez

CONTENTS

INTRODUCTION

The Sharon Code

On a cold Wednesday night in early January 2006, Prime Minister Ariel Sharon, seventy-eight years of age, sat in his Sycamore Ranch home amid the desolate beauty of the northern Negev. Only four months had passed since he had redrawn Israel's borders, uprooting his historic allies, the settlers, from the entire Gaza Strip and four West Bank settlements. The general election was three months away. All polls put Sharon and Kadima, the new party he had founded, well ahead of the competition.

But not all was well with Sharon. A mild stroke had hospitalized him for twenty-four hours the week before. Cardiac catheterization and the formal transfer of power to Vice Prime Minister Ehud Olmert were planned for the following day. Suddenly he felt pain in his chest. His son Gilad, living on the ranch with his wife and three children, summoned the prime minister's personal physician, Dr. Shlomo Segev, who determined that Sharon needed immediate hospital care.

Sharon was alert during the hour-and-fifteen-minute race to the hospital, but just minutes before the ambulance reached the hospital's gates, his condition took a sharp turn for the worse. He lost the ability to speak and slipped out of consciousness. At 10:56 P.M., Sharon was wheeled into the trauma unit at Hadassah University Medical Center's Ein Kerem Hospital and hidden behind a curtain. Concerned citizens and edgy TV crews were kept at bay. The doctors knew immediately that the prime minister had suffered a devastating stroke.

Sharon was sedated and connected to life support. Intracranial bleeding was discovered. At 12:10 A.M. he was brought to the operating table in critical condition. The nation of Israel held its breath and crossed its fingers. The man who personified heroism to some and malice to others—who had been influencing the fate of the country since his heroic and disastrous reprisal raids in 1953, who had been exiled from Israeli political life following the upheavals of the Lebanon War and the massacres in the Sabra and Shatilla refugee camps—had become the most popular prime minister in Israel's history. Much like another awful night, November 4, 1995, when Prime Minister Yitzhak Rabin was gunned down, the country huddled around its fallen leader, awaiting word of his fate.

Sharon's sudden exit from the political stage has cast Israel's future in a nebulous light. Israeli citizens had come to see Sharon as a wise and paternal leader, giving him tremendous license to shape the final borders of the state, relying on him to capitulate when warranted and stand firm when necessary. Suddenly they felt fatherless, like a flock without a shepherd.

What brought Ariel Sharon—a staunch right-wing politician, the most reviled character in the Arab world, and the greatest proponent of Jewish settlement in the occupied territories—to reverse his views late in life and withdraw from Gaza and four northern West Bank settlements, uprooting twenty-four Jewish communities?

In October 1979, six months after Egypt and Israel pledged peace at the White House, an Israeli government vehicle with civilian plates boarded an Egyptian ferry on the arid Asian side of the Suez Canal. As the boat cut across the narrow strip of water, the workers on board easily recognized the rotund man with the flowing white hair in the back of the sedan. They knew him as the most notorious of all Israeli generals, Ariel Sharon, "Arik" to one and all—the man who six years earlier had crossed the same canal at the head of a column of tanks, winning the pivotal battle in the Sinai campaign of the Yom Kippur War. He was now in Egypt on official, if covert, business as Israel's minister of agriculture.

This was the first time Ariel Sharon had been invited to tread on Arab soil. Over the course of three decades, he had visited often—at the head of small commando teams and war parties. The invitation was extended by Dr. Muhammad Daoud, the Egyptian minister of agriculture. They were to discuss Egyptian water and irrigation systems. But it was clear that the Israeli general's true host was Egyptian president Anwar Sadat. The two had a private dinner together at the presidential palace on Sharon's second night in Cairo.

Sadat, having researched the likes and dislikes of the Israeli minister, met the man with an abundance of food. He was served thin slices of choice beef immediately upon arrival, but later, as the president, and primarily the minister, dug into a king's banquet, the talk turned from food to diets to water. Egypt's water sources lay near the Sudanese border. Sharon peppered Sadat with questions. He was the son of a cash-strapped agronomist who had grown up in an isolated farming village ringed by hostile Arab towns, and had later acquired one of the biggest cattle ranches in the country; Israel's water sources were never far from his mind. Suddenly, President Sadat clapped his hands twice, summoning a servant.

The man brought Sadat a topographical map of Egypt. The president spread the giant map across the floor, and the two got down on their knees as Sadat, speaking in English, traced Egypt's water sources with his finger, explaining as he went. When they got up off the floor, Sadat told Sharon he would lend him his private plane, *Mister 20,* for a daylong tour of the water sources. Sharon boarded along with Eli Landau, his assistant and confidant at the agricultural ministry. The two were flown to the border region, where they were taken on a tour of the Aswan Dam.

Not far from the dam, the two Israeli guests toured the temple of Abu Simbel. The shrine, built by Ramses II in the thirteenth century BCE, was erected in honor of ancient Egypt's megalomaniacal pharaoh, the supposed enslaver of Moses and the Hebrews. Hieroglyphics engraved on the temple's towering sandstone pillars caught Sharon's eye. He examined them for several minutes and then asked Landau: "What do you think, will they write something like that about me?" "Depends what you do, Arik," Landau replied.

● ● ●

Sharon's influence over Israeli and Middle Eastern affairs, for better and for worse, was pivotal. Few world leaders have as riveting and contentious a life history as Arik Sharon. Perhaps no other contemporary leader's personal history is as tightly woven with that of his nation as is Sharon's with that of the State of Israel. The history of the man and that of the fifty-eight-year-old country are inseparable.

Sharon fought in Israel's War of Independence, easily shouldering the singular stress of leading men into battle. He was wounded and left for dead. During the War of Attrition, he assembled Israel's first special forces team—the wild, unruly, and daring Unit 101. In 1956, during the Suez War, he led the paratroopers into the Sinai Desert, where they suffered heavy—and some say avoidable—casualties. In 1967, during the Six Day War, he commanded the assault on the Abu Ageila fortress, a battle still studied in military academies around the world.

Sharon crossed the Suez Canal in the 1973 Yom Kippur War, changing the course of that conflict; he founded the Likud Party; he led the withdrawal of Israeli citizens from Sinai, as demanded by the peace deal between Israel and Egypt; and he knew immense personal tragedy. His first wife, his childhood love, Margalit, was killed in a car accident. His first son, Gur, was wounded by an accidental rifle discharge, and died in his arms. Years later, his second wife, Lily, Margalit's younger sister, died after a long struggle with cancer. Their relationship was one of the great love stories of Israeli public life.

Above all, three episodes will determine Sharon's epitaph in the book of Jewish history: the Lebanon War, which he led in June 1982; the settlement movement in Gaza and the West Bank, which he championed for thirty years; and the "Disengagement," the withdrawal of all Israeli settlers from the Gaza Strip and four isolated West Bank settlements, which he presided over from the prime minister's seat.

The last of the three historic moves—the uprooting of sixty-five hundred people from their homes and the destruction of twenty-four settlements—tore the Israeli public in half. During July and August 2005, the country was painted—in dress, billboards, hand-held signs, car antennas—in two colors: orange for those opposing the withdrawal, and blue for those in favor. The success of the withdrawal seems likely to determine Sharon's place in history. Will he be remembered as the first Israeli leader to take the bold step of uprooting settlements in the West Bank and the Gaza Strip, finalizing Israel's permanent borders and laying the groundwork for peace with the Palestinians after 150 years of warfare? Or will he be remembered as the man responsible for the bloody Lebanon War, the demise of the settlement movement, and the establishment of a Palestinian state that serves as a hothouse for terrorism, an eternal enemy?

Analysts, politicians, journalists, military officers, academics, lawyers, and the Israeli public all grapple with the question of how Sharon reached the dramatic decision to disengage from Gaza and raze twenty-four settlements to the ground. That question cannot be answered without delving into the fascinating and stormy life of the former prime minister. This book unravels the story of that life, which is interwoven with the story of the founding and growth of the State of Israel. In piecing together the puzzle of Arik Sharon, the mystery of the Disengagement becomes clear.

Over the past three years, as we researched and wrote this book, we pored over thousands of documents and spoke with hundreds of people who knew Sharon in different periods of his life. We did not, however, speak with Sharon or his sons, preferring to write from an unbiased perspective.

A number of characteristics comprise what might be called the Sharon code. First and foremost, Sharon possessed unusual, almost inhuman, courage. As a child raised in a spartan home, he developed an almost unnatural immunity to fear. Soldiers and officers who served with him in battle all testify that enemy fire left Sharon unaffected. He walked upright, impervious, his calm spreading through the ranks. Sharon's unassailable courage extended to his civilian life. He did not care what people said about him, was never afraid of making mistakes, and never hesitated to roll the dice.

A second piece of the puzzle is his resilience. No matter how dire the predicament, Ariel Sharon would never fly the white flag of surrender. Most people capitulate or crumble in the face of public failure or personal tragedy; Sharon was different. As opposed to Prime Minister Menachem Begin, who lived out his days in self-imposed exile after the Lebanon War, or Lt. Gen. David Elazar, the Israel Defense Forces' chief of staff during the 1973 Yom Kippur War, who never recovered from the damning Agranat Commission's report of his service, Sharon never allowed himself to sink into despair: not when he was left for dead on the battlefield at Latrun, lying flat on his back and staring at the hazy sky; not when he was forced out of the army; not when the Kahan Commission essentially removed him from his position as defense minister after the massacre in the Palestinian refugee camps of Sabra and Shatilla. Failure was constructive for Sharon. He would draw up a set of lessons and proceed—certain of victory in the next round.

A third key to understanding the Sharon puzzle is his willingness to think and act outside the box so long as his conclusions corresponded to his sense of justice. This characteristic is one of the main reasons that Arik Sharon, from an early age, found himself at the heart of so many controversies. His unbridled tenacity got him into trouble from the time he was a young officer. In October 1953, Sharon, the commander of Unit 101, led his men on a reprisal raid in Jordan. Tasked with the retributive mission of destroying houses, his men killed dozens of women, children, and elderly people who cowered unnoticed in the dark corners of their homes. David Ben-Gurion, the prime minister at the time, claimed ignorance of the raid once he learned of its disastrous results. Three years later, in 1956, Sharon received permission to insert a surveillance team into the fortified Mitla Pass in the Sinai Desert; he sent in a heavily armed unit, embroiling the paratroopers in one of the Israel Defense Forces' most costly battles.

He was again charged with overstepping his bounds during the 1973 Yom Kippur War, pushing relentlessly to cross the Suez Canal. In Lebanon, nine years later, he again went too far when he led the IDF on a charge into Beirut. In September 2000, his visit to the Temple Mount—the epicenter of Arab-Jewish tension in Israel—heralded the start of the second, "al-Aqsa," intifada. In the thirty-eight years of Israeli settlement in the Gaza Strip and the West Bank, Sharon spurred settlers to grab land illegally. His unwavering certainty in himself, coupled with his determination to proceed in the face of formidable obstacles, is why he is known in his country as "the Bulldozer."

Fourth, Arik Sharon, always able to read the winds of change, had a long history of equivocation. It is not difficult to find quotes from him in favor of and in opposition to the same issue. Sharon was for and then against a Palestinian state, a security wall, a national referendum, and the forced withdrawal of settlers from the Gaza Strip and the West Bank. He favored reprisal during the first Gulf War, when Yitzhak Shamir was prime minister, and opposed it during the second Gulf War, when he occupied the same seat. He was opposed to a unilateral withdrawal from Gaza when Amram Mitzna of the Labor Party proposed it, and in favor of it after he won the 2003 elections. In 1987, Shimon Peres suggested withdrawing from Gaza in the early days of the first intifada; at the time, Sharon called Peres's proposal "unreasonable."

Sharon's history of equivocations evolved from three separate aspects of his character. First, he was not motivated by a firm ideology, certainly not in the religious sense of the word. His guiding light was always security. His creed, in its barest form: "Maximum security for Jews." That creed required different measures at different times.

Next, Sharon liked to be in charge, the final arbiter. His love of power, in our view, repeatedly dictated his stance on issues of national importance. Over the years, as a second-tier minister in Likud-led governments, exiled from the most important foreign policy and security decisions, he often took a reactionary stance against his own party's leader; once he was brought into the fold, however, his opinions became more malleable. For instance, in October 1998, all Prime Minister Binyamin Netanyahu had to do to convert Sharon from a staunch opponent of the Wye Plantation Agreement to a firm backer was to change his title: Foreign Minister

Ariel Sharon accepted what Infrastructure Minister Ariel Sharon would not.

Finally, Ariel Sharon viewed honesty pragmatically, as a commodity rather than an ideal. David Ben-Gurion, Israel's first prime minister and defense minister, was Sharon's primary advocate during his years in uniform, admiring his courage and his unconventional thought. But Ben-Gurion was bedeviled by Sharon's tendency to bend the truth.

A fifth trait is Sharon's intuition. Arik was blessed with an acute ability to read his opponent's weaknesses. His emotional compass could pinpoint a person's fears, desire, and hidden motivations. Over his many years as a politician, he expanded his abilities from the micro to the macro, often sensing the feelings and fears of the people. When stuck in a tight corner, he knew how to manipulate public opinion, spinning it at will.

Soldiers, officers, politicians, friends and foes, allies and adversaries all agree that Sharon was uniquely charismatic. Sharon, says Shimon Kahaner (Katcha), one of the celebrated soldiers of the 101st and a steadfast friend, "always used his head, but when we were in a tight spot and everyone was stressed out, his calm was like a lifeline. He never asked us to do anything he hadn't done. He always went first. His leadership qualities were absolute. A leader is someone who can convince you that what he wants is exactly what you want, that the two of you strive for the exact same thing. Sharon is the maestro in that regard. That's the secret to his strength and his ability to influence so many people's fate."

Despite these traits, it is still, to a certain degree, incredible that Arik Sharon became the "shepherd" of the people of Israel. Sharon never seemed slated for greatness. Unlike other Zionist leaders—Yitzhak Rabin, Moshe Dayan, Yigal Allon, Shimon Peres—who hailed from the ruling party's elite, Sharon spent his early years working the land with his impoverished parents. His father, Samuel Scheinerman, an agronomist, wished nothing more for his son than to study agriculture and continue to cultivate the family's land. Sharon was proud of his roots as a farmer and took a personal interest in his cattle, sheep, and goats. His office secretaries knew the drill: When a call came from the ranch announcing the birth of a calf, a kid, or a lamb, Sharon had to be told about it immediately, and the information had to include the weight and name of the newborn and the condition of the mother—even if it meant sending a note to the prime minister in the middle of a tense cabinet meeting. In this regard, Sharon was in good company. The great leaders of the Jewish people had all been shepherds—Abraham, Isaac, Jacob, Moses, King David.

Sharon's flock of supporters grew over time. With each promotion in the military, from commander of the paratroopers to division commander to general in the 1967 war, he was surrounded by soldiers willing to follow him blindly. Even then, his supporters were certain that Sharon was destined to lead the country. After the Lebanon War—a campaign many considered unwarranted and unnecessary—some turned their backs, but the core group stood by him, supporting him during his exile at Sycamore Ranch. That type of fervent allegiance is unprecedented in Israeli public life. All leaders have loyalists and backers, but only with Sharon did the relationship come to seem more like that of a guru with his worshippers—or a shepherd with his flock.

Many of his supporters never regretted their unflinching loyalty to the guru. Some received jobs in the public sector; others used his connections to further their business interests. But with all due respect to his supporters and friends, many of whom are immensely talented, they have never played a role as great as that of his family members—Lily Sharon, who participated in each of his important decisions and frequently decided who would be allowed to get close to her husband; his son Omri, the family's "foreign minister," the unofficial voice of his father; and Gilad, his youngest son, the introverted "interior minister," handling the family's financial matters and often plotting political strategy.

Sharon is Israeli politics' uncrowned king of scandals. No other prime minister has come close to his level of questionable involvements. He faced criminal investigation for three major scandals: the Greek Island affair, the Annex Research affair, and the Cyril Kern affair. The first two investigations were closed on the recommendation of Israel's attorney general—although he did concede that he had been dangerously close to indicting the prime minister. Sharon's oldest son, Omri, the Likud primaries campaign manager in 1999, has been convicted of keeping false corporate records, providing false testimony, and violating political fundraising laws. His sentence of nine months' jail time, nine months' suspended sentence, and a 300,000-shekel fine awaits appeal. The Cyril Kern affair, involving loans and payments that crossed four continents, is still in the hands of the International Crime Unit of the Israeli police.

This seemingly improper and unethical behavior is not new. Sharon's name has been featured in articles, state comptrollers' reports, and attorney generals' rulings for years. He has been blamed for conflict of interest, nepotism, and more.

It is important to note that each of his questionable endeavors has been investigated, and Arik Sharon was never brought before a criminal court nor convicted of a crime. His record remains clean despite the years in public office and the multitudes who have watched his every move.

One major accusation leveled at Sharon is that the true motivation for the Disengagement was to remove family scandals from the public agenda. According to this thesis, Sharon's openness to territorial compromise with the Palestinians—which was based entirely on the prime minister's ability to bend the will of his own party—hinged on his need for cover from the law. His reasoning, they claim, was that a standing prime minister would never be indicted in the midst of a historic peace settlement. Member of the Knesset (MK) Zvi Hendel of the National Union Party, whose constituents are mostly settlers and their sympathizers, has said derisively, "The Disengagement will go as far as the criminal investigations go."

Our opinion is that it is unlikely that the police investigations into the Sharon family's affairs were his primary motivation in pushing for the withdrawal; after all, he had announced in September 2001 that he was willing to grant the Palestinians a state in the Gaza Strip and the West Bank. Moreover, he later acquiesced to the terms of the Bush Road Map, which requires far deeper concessions than the withdrawal, including a freeze on building in the West Bank, the end of "the occupation that began in 1967," a "fair solution" to the predicament of the Palestinian refugees, and a "negotiated resolution of the status of Jerusalem." Sharon also has a track record of carrying out forced evacuations: In 1982, as defense minister, he presided over the destruction of all of the settlements in the Sinai Peninsula, even though he had pushed to settle those areas as OC Southern Command ten years earlier.

Still, it is hard to dismiss the feeling that the police investigations played a role in the timing of Sharon's decision to go public with his Disengagement Plan. The proximity of the two events arouses suspicion. Sharon unveiled his plan on February 2, 2004, only seven days after the newly sworn-in attorney general, Menachem Mazuz, stated that his decision on whether to indict Sharon in the Greek Island affair was imminent. Sharon's announcement came just three days before the International Crime Unit showed up to question him at his official residence in Jerusalem, and two weeks after it became known that State Prosecutor Edna Arbel had recommended he be indicted. The ground beneath his feet was burning. Yet from the second of February, when it became clear that Sharon was serious about evacuating settlements, the heat from the press died down, and a virtual flock of journalists, many of whom lean to the left ideologically, began to fall in step behind the once-ostracized shepherd.

What, then, brought Sharon to the dramatic reversal in his political convictions, pushing him to disengage not only from his historic allies—the settlers—but also from his supporters in the Likud Central Committee? The answer, in our opinion, is linked to Sharon's rare introspective moment at the foot of the temple of Abu Simbel in October 1979. At seventy-seven, Ariel Sharon was the richest prime minister in Israel's history, with an estimated family fortune of over ten million dollars. All that remained for him to accomplish was to secure his place in history.

In the thirties, when Sharon was still a child in Kfar Malal, he used to look out on the hostile villages surrounding his home, and his father would tell him, "Always go see what lies over the next hill." Throughout his years in uniform and in government, he passed that advice on hundreds of times. His motto was always to climb the mountain and see what lies beyond. His metaphorical ascent to the top of the hill, to the ideal vantage point, took sixty years. Only when he summited—when he was voted in as prime minister in February 2001—was he able to see what lay over the next hill. Only then could he see where to lead the flock.

The fantastic story of Ariel Sharon's life has in all likelihood run its course. In any case, the following sixty chapters embody what Samuel Scheinerman used to tell his young son when he tired of the Sisyphean task of field work under the blazing sun: "Look back," Samuel would tell young Arik, "and see how much you've done already."

ARIEL SHARON

CHAPTER 1

The Battle of Latrun

PRIME MINISTER ARIEL SHARON WAS A NUMBINGLY DULL ORATOR. His tone was nasal and monotonous, he fumbled with his glasses as he spoke, and he always read from the page, his voice bobbing up and down like a distant boat in a soft sea. The hand gestures meant to inflect his words with emotion were frequently a beat late. History, from the lips of Sharon, needed to be listened to carefully, lest it slip by undetected.

On September 23, 2001, Sharon, seventy-three, obese yet agile, climbed onto the podium in the Latrun amphitheater and addressed a group of teachers. They grasped the historical significance of his speech. Sharon had just announced his agreement, in principle, to the founding of a Palestinian state west of the Jordan River, making him the first prime minister from the right-wing Likud Party to publicly concede the West Bank to the Palestinians. "Israel," Sharon said as the sun set behind him, "wants to give the Palestinians what no else ever has: the opportunity to establish a state of their own. No one—not the Turks, nor the English, nor the Egyptians, nor the Jordanians—has ever given them this chance before."

It was no coincidence that Ariel Sharon made this declaration at the tank corps' monument to the fallen, in Latrun. Sharon chose Latrun as the burial ground for an ideology that he had upheld for thirty years, agreeing, against the wishes of the Likud Central Committee and virtually his entire electoral base, to initiate the founding of a Palestinian state just a few hundred yards from the spot where he had nearly lost his life.

As he spoke, his mind wandered fifty-three years back in time, to one of the Israel Defense Forces' worst embarrassments—the

Battle of Latrun. He recalled how he had lain flat on his back, half a mile from where he now stood in a starched shirt and tie, blood pouring out of his stomach, his will to live ebbing. Pictures from his past flashed through his mind: the bullet slicing his stomach; the armed Palestinian villagers pillaging and murdering his downed soldiers; the oppressive heat; the flies; the clouds of gnats that descended on his open wounds; the evacuation he barely survived.

That battle played a major role in shaping the ideology of a man who would become one of the world's most influential leaders. In the Battle of Latrun, Sharon emerged as an unflappable and fearless warrior. Over a lifetime of crises—military, political, and personal—he would often recall the moment he was allowed to "rise from the dead" at Latrun. In his darkest moments he could always return there to draw the strength necessary to rise, Phoenix-like, from the ashes.

The Battle of Latrun began on the night of May 24, 1948, ten days after Israel's first prime minister, David Ben-Gurion, declared the establishment of the State of Israel, drawing an all-out attack by seven neighboring nations. During the first days of war, the Jordanian Legion surrounded Jerusalem, cutting the city's hundred thousand Jewish residents off without food, water, medicine, or weapons. The Jordanian Arab Legion's 4th Battalion, bolstered by armed Palestinian fighting gangs, had taken control of the Arab city of Latrun, the nearby Trappist monastery, the Crusader fort Le Toron des Chevaliers, and the square stone building that had served the British as police headquarters during their mandate in Palestine. As in the Middle Ages, the Crusader fort dominated the western route to Jerusalem, completing the siege. On May 23, the Jordanians strengthened their forces, adding the 2nd Battalion to the troops already in place. The overpowering force kept Jerusalem beyond Jewish reach. Numerous convoys were destroyed as they rumbled up the first ridge on the way to the capital, nine miles west.

Ben-Gurion was determined to break the blockade. The military maneuver aimed at opening a corridor to Jerusalem was named "Operation Bin-Nun," after the biblical Joshua, the son of Nun, who led the Jews into Canaan and prevailed in a battle over the Amorites in the same region. The hastily assembled 7th Brigade—a unit that had been put together only a week before and consisted of un-trained Holocaust survivors marched straight from the boats to the battlefield—was given the mission. Since many of them had rarely fired a weapon before, their brigade was reinforced by the 32nd Infantry Battalion, a battle-hardened unit from the Alexandroni Bri-gade. The commander of Platoon 1, Company B, of the 32nd Bat-talion was Arik Scheinerman (later and better known to the world as Ariel Sharon), just twenty years old.

Scheinerman's arm was in a cast. He had broken it in a car ac-cident a short time before, but had decided nonetheless to lead Platoon 1. His decision to participate in the battle may have been influenced by rumors floating through the ranks that the battle for Latrun would be won with ease. Men under the command of Chaim Weizmann, later the president of Israel, issued intelligence reports stating that Latrun was being held by several hundred armed but unorganized Palestinian villagers. But beyond the view of the Israeli troops, one thousand Bedouin soldiers from the Arab Legion, armed with mortars, artillery, armored vehicles, hundreds of heavy machine guns, and thousands of rifles, lay in wait. The in-telligence failure would lead to one of the bloodiest battles of the War of Independence.

Toward evening on May 24, four companies, two from the 7th Brigade and two from the 32nd Battalion, organized their gear in the Hulda "Forest," a small patch of eucalyptus trees next to Kib-butz Hulda. Ya'akov Bugin, a young soldier from Kfar Pinnes who had been transferred to Arik's platoon a few days before the battle, remembers their morale-boosting trip to Hulda from their perma-nent base in Pardaisiya via the newly conquered Arab city of Jaffa. "Arik sat down on the bus and I remember looking at him admir-ingly," recalls Bugin, who had not yet even been introduced to his new commanding officer. "I was seventeen years old at the time, an age when I was looking for heroes and role models, and Arik defi-nitely had a heroic look to him. His body was sturdy and healthy, his face was childlike; I remember sitting behind him on the bus and thinking, 'He reminds me of a Roman emperor.'"

The Israeli force's communications officer, Ted Arison, later the owner of Carnival Cruise Lines and the wealthiest Jew in the world, scurried through the troops looking for spare transceiver batteries. He was not alone in his search for vital gear. Many soldiers lacked canteens, uniforms, and boots. There were not enough rifles and ammunition to go around. The engineering and artillery corps were nowhere to be found. At the last minute, the operations chief of the IDF general staff, Yigal Allon, tried to persuade Ben-Gurion to delay the battle, telling him that the 7th Brigade was ill suited to the task of liberating Jerusalem. Ben-Gurion, fearing for the lives of the capital's Jewish citizens and dreading the possibility of the holy city's falling in its entirety, refused to delay for more than twenty-four hours.

Arik Scheinerman spent the hours leading up to the battle lying on his stomach in an olive grove, storing energy for what was sure to be a sleepless night. He was already an accomplished military leader, brave, conscientious, and sincere beyond his years, with a habit of collecting himself in solitude. He watched as the 7th Brigade's new recruits hopped off the backs of a convoy of trucks. Ram Oren, in his book *Latrun*, published a letter Arik Scheinerman wrote to his parents:

> My platoon and I are lazing in an olive grove, passing the heat of the day, thinking pre-battle thoughts, blending with the water-smoothed stones and the earth, feeling part and parcel of the land: a rooted feeling, a feeling of a home-land, of belonging, of ownership. Suddenly a convoy of trucks stopped next to us and unloaded new, foreign-looking recruits. They looked slightly pale, and were wearing sleeveless sweaters, gray pants, and striped shirts. A stream of languages filled the air, names like Herschel and Yazek, Jan and Maitek were thrown around. They stuck out against the backdrop of olives, rocks, and yellowing grains. They'd come to us through blocked borders, from Europe's death camps. I watched them. Watched them strip, watched their white bodies. They tried to find fitting uniforms, and fought the straps on their battle jackets as their new commanders helped them get suited up. They did this

in silence, as though they had made their peace with fate. Not one of them cried out: "Let us at least breathe the free air after the years of terrible suffering." It is as if they'd come to the conclusion that this is one final battle for the future of the Jewish people.

As Arik Scheinerman and his men filled canteens and magazines, the commanders of Operation Bin-Nun huddled together in a nearby cabin and reviewed their battle plans. The 32nd Battalion's two companies were to take the Trappist monastery, the Crusader fort, the British police building, the Arab village of Latrun, and the nearby Hill 315. The 72nd Battalion of the 7th Brigade was to take the fortified ridge to the east of the village. The two-pronged attack would ensure total control of the route to Jerusalem.

It was a simple plan in theory, but on the ground, problems began to multiply: The bus scheduled to take the soldiers to the drop-off point was late; a backup platoon of infantrymen and an artillery unit of 155mm guns were no-shows; the 32nd's battalion commander, hobbled by a chronic lack of sleep and food and general war-weariness, fainted on the spot. He was replaced by future chief of the general staff Chaim Laskov.

Ya'akov Bugin recalls:

As evening came they brought our company, Company B, together and told us that the goal of the mission was to take the French fort and the Arab village of Latrun and open the road to Jerusalem. Arik, the platoon commander, gave the briefing. He hung a map on one of the trees and revealed the details of the plan. By ten at night we were on the buses, but we just sat there for over three hours. We were wound tight with tension. Only at one in the morning did the order to move out toward Latrun come down. The entire time on the bus Arik sat in silence, in his own shell.

The fruitless hope that the artillery unit and the backup platoon would arrive were the cause of the delay. After the order to move out, the first bus in the convoy bungled the navigation and wasted more precious hours of darkness. The soldiers finally dis-

embarked at two-thirty in the morning near an old British deten-
tion center, where leaders of the pre-state fighting units had been
imprisoned. Asher Levi, Company B's commander, led his men in
single file. A treacherous silence surrounded them. Higher up on
the ridge, on top of the old fort, Jordanian lookouts kept their commanders well informed of all Israeli troop movements.

It was just before four in the morning. Black gave way to blue
and then to a clear dawn just beyond the fortified hills of Latrun.
Asher Levi told the commander of the lead platoon, Arik Scheinerman, that they were at the point where their paths diverged.
Sharon led his thirty-six-man platoon down into a streambed and
toward the hills of Latrun. Walking point, he could make out the
houses of the Arab village and the shape of the fort and the
monastery in the early morning light. The monks' vineyard was all
that stood between his men and the monastery. At four-thirty they
were given the order: Charge!

The moment is lodged in Ya'akov Bugin's mind:

All of a sudden, a lethal burst of fire was leveled at us. It
was massive, planned, and orchestrated, and coming from
different angles. The fire caught our platoon, which was
first, on a vulnerable stretch. I remember bullets and shells
flying through us like raindrops. The whole slope was like
a firing range. Suddenly I was thrown to the ground. I felt
dizziness, heat, chills, and a deafening ringing. I'd caught a
bullet in the chin and I closed my eyes and waited for the
end. To my good fortune a man named Rami, from [the
town of] Magdiel, Arik's deputy, crawled to me under fire
along with a medic. The two of them bandaged me, and
then Rami dragged me down the hill, under a barrage of
fire. I noticed that the rest of the company had retreated
and taken cover behind the hill; only we, Arik's platoon,
were caught on the exposed slope. We galloped down the
hill. Arik found a little fold in the contours of the valley
where we could hide from the ceaseless fire. Only later did
we realize that it was a death trap.

Rami and I were heading toward the fold in the earth

where Arik and the rest of the platoon had taken cover, but the Jordanians were lining us up like sitting ducks. A bullet hit Rami and killed him. I ran like a wild man, zigzagging across the slope as the Jordanians fired at me from all directions. I'd already dropped my rifle, so I ran with my hand on my jaw, keeping the bandage in place. A bullet slammed into my shoulder, in through the front and out the back. Another bullet charred the skin on my neck. As I ran, Arik kept calling to me from the fold in the valley. "Run!" he yelled. "Don't stop running!"

Somehow I made it to cover in the valley, where I learned that there were many more injured. From where I lay, next to the other injured soldiers, I watched Arik in action. His radio had been smashed and ruined by a bullet, so he had no way to communicate with the rest of the company. We were completely adrift. The Arabs were firing at us from the monastery and the surrounding hills, actually sniping right at our heads. Now and again another person would go down. We pressed ourselves into the valley walls, grabbing bushes and vines with our fingernails. It went on like that for hours. We consoled ourselves with the fact that the Jordanians couldn't storm into the valley with the rest of our company positioned behind a hill, returning fire.

As daylight came and the morning went on, the situation went from bad to worse. We couldn't lift our heads, and we had only four uninjured soldiers. Arik was one of them. Eventually the Arab soldiers started to try and sneak into the valley through the vineyards. Arik placed a lookout in that direction and each time they attempted to come in we opened fire. Since we were completely surrounded we didn't think there was any chance of retreat during the daylight hours. Our only hope was to wait until night and creep out under the cover of darkness. The midday heat was brutal and the sun beat down on us mercilessly. We had not eaten since the day before and the water in our canteens was long gone. Clouds of gnats descended on us, especially on the blood-soaked wounded.

At around one-thirty in the afternoon there was a sudden silence. The fire died down on both sides. We were sure IDF reinforcements had arrived. I remember Arik gave an order to prepare to storm the monastery in order to reestablish the offensive as soon as the reinforcements showed up. The silence only lasted a few minutes. Arik, to his profound shock, saw that our company had been replaced by the Arab Legion. He understood immediately that the force that had been covering us, preventing the enemy from storming into the valley and slaughtering us, had retreated: We were alone. That was the reason for the silence. Our guys had abandoned us on the battlefield.

A few moments later we found ourselves surrounded by Arab Legion soldiers and bands of armed Palestinian peasants, who advanced on us from above from all sides, unobstructed. We fired at them but our bullets were like drops in the sea. They were close to us, maybe only a few hundred yards away, when Arik roared: "Retreat!"

There was a wheat field three hundred yards from the valley. Our plan was to run there as fast as we could and hide between the rows of crops. The problem was getting across the open country between our position and the field. One by one we tried to make our way. Many were shot and killed. Arik was hit in the stomach as he ran. I knew that if I remained lying in the open ground, I'd be done for. The Arabs tended to murder and rob the wounded. I dragged myself centimeter by centimeter to the field of grain. I was lucky to even get there.

As soon as I made it to the field I began pushing my way through the tall stalks of wheat in a stance that was somewhere between a crawl and a walk. Suddenly I saw a discarded tommy gun on the ground. I recognized the weapon immediately—only Arik had that type of firepower in our platoon. I picked it up and thought to myself: "I'll just bring this back to Arik and he'll love me forever." I know it sounds strange, but at that time my thinking revolved around Arik's reaction when I gave him back his gun. I was downright eager for the moment. Exhausted, I dragged that gun a few yards, until I had to drop it back down in the field. On either side of me, not more than a few dozen yards away, I could hear the joy in the voices of the Arabs as they looted the bodies of the dead. I could hear them shooting the wounded and laughing.

I continued crawling through the field, when suddenly I heard moaning from a patch of stalks. I crawled close and saw Arik, on his back, eyes open, looking at the sky, soaked in blood. I stopped next to him. As soon as I saw him, lying in his own blood, I felt a miraculous surge of strength. My fears, pains, and hunger all vanished. I tried to help him up, but Arik muttered: "Run, escape, save yourself." But I insisted. I didn't listen to him. And although he didn't allow me to touch him because of the pain, I tried to help him up, just as his deputy, Rami, had done for me a few hours earlier, until a Jordanian bullet killed him. Together, combining our strength, we proceeded.

During those fateful minutes, Ya'akov Bugin had no idea that moments earlier another soldier from their platoon had found Sharon in the same position. The soldier, a native of one of the Jewish villages near Sharon's home, had known him since they were children. He leaned over his officer and friend, staring at him. Sharon said, years later, that his old friend looked at the wound in his stomach, looked back at him for a few more seconds, and then continued on his way. Several minutes later, perhaps propelled by guilt, the soldier returned to his side, looked at him long and hard, parted with him in silence, and headed off again. He did not return. Sharon later claimed to hold no grudge, as the man was simply fleeing death.

Bugin chose a different course of action:

We had no choice but to stand tall and walk through the field in full view of the armed Palestinian peasants. Once we stood up, we could see the Arabs shooting our wounded right beside us. They saw us, but luckily they were too busy looting the bodies to raise their weapons and kill the two miserable, bleeding soldiers limping past. They were so busy competing with one another over who snatched more watches and wallets that they couldn't be bothered by us. I remember one of their faces clearly: a villager with a beard. They were all around us in the field, close enough to touch. All they would have had to do to kill us is raise their weapons to their shoulders. They wouldn't even have had to run. That's how Arik and I made our way through the field, surrounded by Arabs, until we slowly distanced ourselves. We were lucky that Arik knew the area well and that he had binoculars, which helped us find the area for wounded soldiers.

We walked like that for hours, at a frightfully slow pace, weary and in pain. The fields around were burning, set on fire by mortar rounds, which meant we had to keep on climbing up and over stone terraces. It was very hard for Arik to make it over the wobbly stone walls. Each time we had to go over one of the terraces he'd lean on my shoulders and I'd push him over the top. We hardly said a word the entire time; I'd been shot in the jaw and couldn't speak or drink. We were desperately thirsty. At one point Arik found some foul water, which may even have been urine. He told me to drink, but I couldn't, so he drank alone.

The entire way, as we limped through the fields, scores of Israeli wounded passed us by. Not one of them stopped to help me carry Arik. Every once in a while, when an artillery round would land near us, Arik would say: "Leave me, save yourself." But I didn't leave him. In my heart I'd reached a conclusion: I would not let this man die.

CHAPTER 2

Georgian Roots

RAIN PELTED THE COASTAL PLAIN OF BRITISH-RULED PALESTINE ON February 26, 1928, tapping out an unsettling rhythm against the tin roof of the nursery as Vera Scheinerman bore her second child, Ariel. The following day, the newborn, already known as Arik, was brought home to join his sister, Dita, in the Scheinermans' leaky shack. For once, the severe Scheinerman home in Kfar Malal erupted in unrestrained celebration.

Samuel Scheinerman, an agronomist by training, set up Arik's crib in the living room, previously occupied by the family's two cows. Seven days later, a small circle of friends congregated at their home for Arik's circumcision. The ceremony was brief. As soon as it ended, Vera and Samuel went back to work on their two-and-a-half-acre farm.

Kfar Malal was deceptively lush. Residents of the nearby town, Kfar Saba, used to call the moshav Kfar Umlal (Village of Misery). The sun cooked the wooden shacks in summer and the coastal winds blew through gaping walls in winter. Samuel Scheinerman, learned in many arts, lacked talent with a hammer and nails. The shack wheezed and shuddered through many storms.

Kfar Malal, the first cooperative farm established by the Jewish National Fund (JNF), was situated on swampland and sand. The villagers scraped by, growing beans, sweet potatoes, and peanuts. During their first years as farmers, the Scheinerman family lived in poverty: Samuel and Vera knew hunger.

Samuel Scheinerman's infatuation with the Holy Land had begun in 1910, when his father, Mordechai, brought the family to Palestine. Mordechai Scheinerman was one of the leaders of the Zionist Party in Brest Litovsk, Russia, teaching a regular Hebrew class and attending the first World Zionist Congress in Basel in 1897. Several years later he helped Ze'ev Dov Begin, father of future prime minister Menachem Begin, smash the door of the local synagogue in protest of the rabbi's refusal to hold a memorial service for the father of Zionism, Theodore Herzl. Six years after Herzl's death, Mordechai Scheinerman, his wife, and their four children boarded a rickety sea craft called *Walnut Shell* and set sail for the port city of Jaffa, Palestine. They settled in Rehovot, where Mordechai took a position as a teacher.

Two years of hardship in the malarial promised land sufficed. Mordechai and his family, still determined to help found a Jewish state in Palestine but unable to continue living there, returned to Russia. Soon thereafter, Mordechai fell ill, his dreams of return dashed. His son Samuel, however, soaked up his father's Zionist vigor and set his mind to returning.

The Scheinerman family left Brest Litovsk in 1914 with the outbreak of World War I, leading an itinerant lifestyle for months until they settled in Tbilisi, Georgia. Mordechai Scheinerman, an intellectual, made sure his son was well versed in the classic texts, Jewish philosophy, and the Torah. By the end of high school, Samuel had a firm command of French, Hebrew, German, and Latin.

Mindful of the fact that his father had failed to survive as a teacher in Palestine, Samuel enrolled in agronomy studies at the University of Tbilisi, hoping to secure his future as a farmer in the budding Jewish *yishuv*. During his time at the university he met Vera Schneeroff, an attractive medical student, and fell in love. Vera, one of eight siblings, grew up in Belarus, in the small Christian village of Mohilov, where her father was a successful timber merchant. The Schneeroffs were the village's only Jews.

Despite the rising tide of anti-Semitism in the area, the Schneeroff family, unobservant but very much Jewish, maintained strong ties with their neighbors. The pogroms of 1905 and 1906 spread through the Caucasus region but left the Schneeroffs untouched. Nonetheless, Vera was affected by the family's isolation from other Jews and by her strict home life. Although a small, wispy woman, she was confident, unflinchingly tough, and tenacious. Samuel Scheinerman was drawn to her strength, and thought she would be able to weather the hardships of pioneer life in Palestine.

In early 1921, as the Red Army advanced through Georgia, Samuel and Vera prepared to flee the Silk Road city of Tbilisi. As a Zionist activist and one of the heads of the Workers of Zion, a movement that helped Jewish students emigrate to Palestine, Samuel feared that the Red Army's control of the city would lead to his arrest. Vera did not share his Zionist ideology. She pressed Samuel often about his convictions, asking why he insisted on supporting Zionism while the Communist Revolution, spreading through the region, promised equality for all.

One night in the spring of 1921, Samuel showed up late for a Hebrew lecture. As he approached the building, he saw dozens of Communist revolutionaries dragging Jews out of the hall. He knew they would be jailed and sent to labor camps in the far north, if not marched straight to the firing squad. Shaken, Samuel ran home and urged Vera to marry him so that they could run away together. Vera, an excellent student nearing her fourth year of medical school, agreed to his frenzied proposal. For Samuel, who had received his degree in agronomy weeks before, the timing was fortuitous. They married and prepared to flee the country. Samuel took few things with him, but was careful to include his *kinjal* (a sharp local knife) and his violin.

The newlywed couple caught a train to the Black Sea port of Baku. On a rainy day in February 1922, with the sea and Vera in equally tempestuous moods, the young couple arrived in Jaffa. Samuel stood on the boat's deck, riveted. Vera, much like Herzl, was shaken by the desolate view. She left the boat last. Looking at the bleak sand dunes beyond the pier, she understood that a steady diet of drudgery and hardship lay in store for her. Samuel, an emotional idealist, had, on the other hand, no notion of the travails that awaited them.

The Scheinermans were part of the Third Aliyah, a wave of Jewish immigration that brought forty thousand Jews to Palestine from 1919 to 1923. Two events served as catalysts: the Balfour

Declaration—a document stating that "His Majesty's Government views with favor the establishment in Palestine of a national home for the Jewish people" (the first official recognition of Palestine as the Jewish homeland)—and the October 1917 Russian Revolution. At first, the October Revolution promised emancipation for Russia's long-suffering Jewry. But during the subsequent Russian Civil War, the Zionist movement was deemed illegal, and anti-Semitic pogroms spread through 160 towns and cities, killing tens, if not hundreds, of thousands of Jews.

Vera and Samuel Scheinerman docked in Jaffa two years after the San Remo Conference of 1920, where the victorious parties of the First World War, reaffirming the Sykes-Picot Agreement, divided up the old Ottoman lands of the Middle East. Palestine was given to the British Crown, with the understanding that a Jewish state would eventually be founded on that territory, without infringing on "the civil and religious rights of existing non-Jewish communities in Palestine."

Vera, unlike many of her enthusiastic peers, did not speak Hebrew or Yiddish. Her only means of communicating in Palestine was in Russian. She clung to the hope of completing her studies, even imagining earning a degree from the esteemed American University of Beirut. That notion died, slowly and painfully, as she came to know the cultural and intellectual desert that was post–World War I Palestine. The hinterlands, where Jewish pioneers tilled the soil as a means of redemption from years of urban toil in Europe, left her bitter to her dying day. Vera never spoke publicly about her great disappointment, but her demeanor suggested emotional barrenness. Arik, close to his mother despite her austerity, recognized and accepted her grief in his youth.

A person close to Sharon, who does not wish to be identified, explains:

> Vera had a very lucid mind and a sharp tongue. Arik admired her throughout her life. He never skipped his regular meetings with her, even in adulthood, when he held important and stressful positions in the army and govern-

ment. He'd always mellow while speaking with Vera and listen to every word she said. She had an opinion about everything. It was plain that she held enormous influence over him. The visits were of a son coming to see his dear mother, and to the observer it was obvious that Arik got a lot out of those conversations. He really seemed to need them.

The Scheinermans' first stop in Palestine was the experimental agricultural farm in Ben Shemen, where Samuel found a job. Even with his firm command of Hebrew, Samuel had a hard time on the farm, as the agricultural knowledge he brought with him from Tbilisi, on the banks of the Kura River, did not apply to the arid land of Zion. Samuel realized that he had to "revolutionize" his agronomy. They went to Mikve Yisrael, an agricultural school, so that he could learn about the soil and climate in Palestine.

They lived there for a year, as Samuel learned agriculture anew. Conditions were harsh. The Scheinermans were barely able to feed themselves. During that year, Vera came to understand that she would never be a doctor, and that she had traded a life of luxury in her parents' home for a life of struggle. She yearned for her cultured friends and family and was mired in a deep melancholy.

With his studies complete, Samuel wanted to move to Kibbutz Ein Harod, where they would at least be assured of square meals. Vera objected, certain that the communal lifestyle of a kibbutz would be intolerable. They both detested the marriage of Communism and Zionism. Vera believed that one's immediate family had to be protected at all costs. In his parents' home, Sharon would learn that familial solidarity was all-important.

Samuel, eager to please Vera, proposed an agricultural village, where they could work the land but live privately. The young couple had no money, and Vera adamantly refused to ask her parents for financial assistance. The only land they could afford was in remote Kfar Malal—a moshav that one year earlier had been sacked by Arab villagers. Vera was neither pleased with the location nor fervently opposed to it, which was good enough for Samuel. Samuel even sensed expectation awakening in his wife. He tried to lift her spirits further by telling her that the moshav was a mere eighteen miles north of Tel Aviv, close enough for them to go to town now and again.

Vera and Samuel rented a horse and wagon for the day, threw in their few belongings, and set out for Kfar Malal. At the time, the moshav was still called Ein Chai (Spring of Life). Samuel would soon see why locals had fun with that name too, changing it to Ain Chai (No Life). They presented themselves at the moshav's office and were led to an overgrown field, the only plot they could afford.

The land was scarred by World War I trenches. There was no running water and no electricity. They lived in a tent until they built their own home: a lopsided shack. With a roof over their heads, they set to the backbreaking work of clearing the field. Vera was unhappy, but she devoted herself heart and soul to the work of survival.

The Scheinermans soon learned that although their land had been purchased by the JNF, a nearby Bedouin tribe claimed it as their own. They fought a long and often dangerous battle over land rights with the tribe. Eventually, the leaders of the al-Qishik tribe gave up. Ariel Scheinerman would be born on land cleared of Palestinian Bedouins.

In August 1929, a year and a half after Arik was born, riots erupted throughout Palestine. A group of six thousand Jews marked the Ninth of Av, a fast day commemorating the destruction of the temple, with a pilgrimage to the Western Wall, Judaism's holiest site, chanting, "This wall is ours." On Friday, August 23, a Muslim mob, incensed by their religious leaders' claims that the Jews were preparing to take over Muslim holy sites, charged through Jerusalem's Old City, killing 17 people. In Hebron, 60 of the 600 Jews in the city were slaughtered. Mobs moved from house to house, looting, burning, and murdering. All told, 133 Jews were killed and 230 injured. Vera Scheinerman spent the nights of that terrible week in the cowshed with Arik and Dita and the rest of the village's women and children, hiding from the neighboring Bedouin tribe.

Vera never forgot that dark night, listening to the sound of the

men as they patrolled around the women and children. She repeated the tale to her children many times, stressing the meager
amount of ammunition at their disposal and their vulnerability to
a possible attack.

It took Vera and Samuel a year and a half to get the farm running. In those early years, the sum total of the Scheinermans' pos-
sessions were their scarred land, a horse, a donkey, and three cows.
Every few days, Samuel, *kinjal* on his belt, would take the horse
and the wagon down to the river for water. Vera milked the cows,
fed the animals, and worked alongside Samuel in the field.

Samuel Scheinerman offered his services to those in need of
an accredited agronomist. Slowly he built a client base. At times he
had to go as far as Turkey in order to make a wage. When he was
away, the former medical student plowed the fields, planted orange
trees and tobacco, tended the chickens, milked the cows, and
watched the two children alone. Her day started before the sun
rose and ended well into the night. She slept with a loaded rifle beside her.

The old-timers in Kfar Malal remember Vera's fortitude. Some
recall how she would work in the field with strips of leather tied
around her feet. When asked why she didn't wear shoes, she said
she didn't want to ruin her only pair. She would sprinkle water on
her skin as she worked in order to make sure her hands didn't dry
up or blister. If anyone wanted to hear, she would complain bitterly
about the agricultural life she was forced to lead.

In September 1985, years after her husband's death, Vera, still
living on the same land, spoke with Yigal Sarna of the daily newspaper *Hadashot* and revealed some of the tension in her home during those early days. "My husband tied me to Zionism against my
will. Poor thing, I made his life very difficult then," she said.

The adults would sit down to dinner after a long day in the
field, and Arik, supposedly asleep, would listen to their conversation. There was a feeling of togetherness, but rarely any levity. As a
child, Arik understood his mother's deep despondency, even recognizing that the root of her melancholy lay in her menial work in the
fields.

Vera hid a scalpel and several medical textbooks in her house.

As a child, Arik often felt his mother's physical proximity offset by her emotional distance. She sent scores of letters to her parents in Tbilisi, her friends in Baku, her sister in Tashkent, and her brothers in Paris, Istanbul, and Germany. At times, overcome with sadness, Vera would lock herself in her room for a full day and write letters. Samuel, who called those days "letter days," accepted her behavior with understanding and calmed his rattled son.

CHAPTER 3

The Outsiders

SAMUEL SCHEINERMAN, A LIBERAL INTELLECTUAL WHO DESPISED anything remotely related to socialism or communism, was a strange bird in Kfar Malal. In fact, all of the Scheinermans stood out in the moshav, where nearly every resident was a card-carrying Laborite. The founders of the moshav congregated regularly for town hall–style meetings, where they voted on issues of the day and bickered over all things political. Samuel Scheinerman, an ideological outsider with vociferous opinions, was disliked for his haughtiness.

Scheinerman did not even grow the same crops as his neighbors, attempting, unsuccessfully at first, to grow avocados, clementines, and cotton. He made things worse by refusing to sell his produce along with the rest of the moshav (to the Tnuva Cooperative, which sold Jewish produce in bulk throughout Palestine). Instead, Scheinerman sold the fruits of his soil independently, even hawking his wares on the side of the road. Samuel Scheinerman augmented his income by working outside the village as an agronomist, further straining his relations with the community.

Samuel Scheinerman was a talented painter and gifted violinist. Even in the worst of times he painted pastorals in watercolor, read Russian poetry, and sang Zionist ballads in his mellow tenor voice. Musicians would stop by to play with him, lulling the young Arik to sleep with the sounds of classical music. Scheinerman's music partners came from the surrounding villages, since, as far as he was concerned, his neighbors' cultural tastes ended at the henhouse. Even today, more than seven decades later, long after Samuel Scheinerman has passed away, the old-timers in Kfar Malal remain bitter. "Samuel was proud as a rooster," says Yossef

Margalit, a next-door neighbor and childhood friend of Sharon's who has remained in the moshav ever since.

"Samuel," Margalit says, "was a well-educated aristocrat. He always thought he knew better than everyone else. Arik really looked up to him. He'd wait in awe for his father to come home, but Vera would threaten him: 'Wait till you see what your father will do to you if you don't do your homework.' "

Margalit does not dismiss the effects of the family's ostracism. "Arik really took his father's quarrels with the rest of the village to heart," he says.

> Even as a child he identified with his father's suffering. There's no doubt that his parents' rift with the rest of the moshav—and there really was an all-out battle here—played a big role in shaping Arik's personality. Their house felt like it was under siege. There was a terrible loneliness in the home and a sense that they were surrounded by enemies. Arik took the struggle to heart. He saw and heard how his father was ostracized and how the whole campaign against them only made Vera's suffering that much worse.

The Scheinermans, as opposed to the other moshav members, fenced their yard and grew a small orchard at the front of their house, which served as a barrier. Shortly thereafter, a general meeting was called, and the members voted in favor of an ordinance requiring all families to designate a percentage of their land for the founding of a new neighboring village, Ramat Ha'shavim. The Scheinermans were dead set against the decision. As soon as the moshav's planning committee stretched a few strands of wire across the Scheinermans' land, marking the area allotted for the new village, Vera began planning a clandestine raid.

That same night, Samuel Scheinerman stayed in the city for work. Seizing on his absence, Vera conducted a quick reconnaissance of the area and decided to take action. After dark she left her two toddlers in bed, pulled on a pair of boots, grabbed a rifle and a pair of pliers, and ran the mile and a half to the vineyard. Her heart was pounding. She sprinted out of concern for her children, alone in the family shack. When she reached the vineyard, she cut the demarcation wires in five different spots, collapsing the two-mile-long fence. She raced home and found her two children fast asleep, unaware. The mission had gone smoothly.

Sharon heard the fence-sabotage story many times in his youth and kept it close to heart as an adult, relaying it to his own children as a parable. To Sharon, his mother's militant action symbolized an uncompromising stand, a battle for borders, and a sense of enterprise and initiative. In six decades of public service, in uniform and out, Sharon would replicate his mother's behavior time and again.

The following day, Vera Scheinerman asked the contractor to put the fence back up, on land beyond her property. The contractor agreed, enraging the other members of the moshav. From that point on, the acrimony only grew in intensity. Samuel Scheinerman decided that the family needed a sentry at the gate of the house to guard their crops. He would chase after kids who were caught sneaking into the family plot to steal fruit.

Vera and Samuel Scheinerman were devoted parents who gave their children all they could, but both were introverts who found it difficult to express their feelings. While it may have been hard growing up in such a restrained household—hugs and kisses were not freely dispensed in the Scheinerman home—Sharon felt his parents' affection in other ways. Vera and Samuel placed tremendous importance on the virtues of determination and willpower, taking pains to etch those traits into their children. In Kfar Malal, a moshav of hard-working, cash-strapped farmers, none of the families could compete with the indefatigable resolve of the Scheinermans.

When Arik was four years old, the Scheinermans' trusted donkey threw him from its back. He landed headfirst on a sharp rock; blood poured down his face. Vera Scheinerman scooped him up in her arms and took off running through the fields for the nearby town of Kfar Saba. She didn't take him to the clinic right there in Kfar Malal, even though they would certainly have given him medical attention.

The path to Kfar Saba stretched for two and a half miles. As Vera ran, holding Arik and whispering soothing words, evening fell across the fields and the neighboring Arab villages. They reached Dr. Vogel's house after dark. Sharon remembered his childhood trauma well, recalling his mother knocking on Dr. Vogel's door. He could envision the doctor, a friend of Vera's and a particularly caring physician who treated Arab patients pro bono, approaching them with a flashlight in hand, leading them into her house, and bandaging him in silence.

Once he had been treated, the two of them headed back home through the deserted, moonlit fields. Arik was calm, certain his mother would protect him. The late-night dash to Kfar Saba and his mother's refusal to seek medical help in the neighborhood clinic taught Arik a memorable lesson: Principles are to be protected even if it means putting your life on the line. One year later, at age five, Arik's father gave him a dagger for his birthday. The weapon made a deep impression on the child; he later noted its role in shaping the warrior aspect of his personality.

For his sixth birthday, Samuel bought Arik a violin, which he never quite mastered. Yet despite his ineptitude as a musician, the violin, he said, kindled in him a lifelong love for music and also enhanced his capacity for concentration, which served him well when taking weighty decisions. Sharon always noted the dagger and the violin, received one after the other, on his fifth and sixth birthdays, as the two poles planted in his personality.

His beautiful sister, Dita, a distant and introverted girl, excelled at the violin and in school, two areas in which Arik struggled. The Scheinermans foresaw a future in the academy for their daughter, and a future of soil-tilling for their son. Although they never expressed these thoughts in front of their children, Arik was well aware of their mediocre aspirations for him. In a home that prized learning and culture, this took a toll on the child, who coasted through elementary school, neither excelling nor failing.

The Scheinermans had the first radio in Kfar Malal. Sharon's peers still remember how their parents used to sneak onto the Scheinermans' property, sit under the windowsill, and listen to the music box. Yossef Margalit observed them from his window. "That radio," he says, "was custom-made by Arik's uncle, Samuel's sister's husband, an engineer and an inventor," who later moved to France and invented a taxi radio that made him a millionaire. From there he moved to the United States and, as a firm believer in Greater Israel, always contributed to Arik's political campaigns.

Neither the radio nor the violin lessons did anything to bridge the chasm between the Scheinerman family and the rest of the moshav. Sharon's parents saw the divide as purely ideological. They were certain that it had nothing to do with Samuel's maddening behavior. Despite the tension, Samuel paved the way agriculturally for the rest of the moshav. He was the first to grow peanuts and sweet potatoes, and the only member of the moshav to prefer goats to cows.

Samuel believed in the Zionist dream of rebuilding the Jewish nation in its ancestral home, but he did not share the majority opinion of his neighbors, many of whom were immigrants from Eastern Europe and firm believers in communal agriculture and socialism. Samuel was an individualist, disdainful of their ideals, and was seen as a Revisionist and a capitalist, an infidel worthy of scorn and exclusion.

The divide deepened after Chaim Arlozorov, a Labor leader, was shot and killed on the Tel Aviv waterfront on June 16, 1933. Samuel lashed out against those who insinuated that Revisionist Zionists were responsible. Like many right-wing party members, Samuel was convinced the murder had been the work of Arab assassins.

Arik, at only five and a half years old, was aware of the storm whipped up between his father and the other members of the moshav over the still-unsolved Arlozorov affair. As time passed and the storm died down, the stigma only worsened: The Scheinermans were no longer mere Revisionists; they were fanatics.

Years later, Sharon gave three reasons for his family's outsider status in Kfar Malal: a principled argument over personal freedom and the will of the majority; his family's refusal to hand over part of their land; and their refusal to accept that Arlozorov had been killed by Jewish assassins. But ultimately Sharon felt that his parents' predicament was the result of their inherent dissimilarity to the other farmers in Kfar Malal.

Samuel Scheinerman wanted to leave the moshav and start a new life elsewhere. All he needed was a fair price for his land. The negotiations with the moshav, rather than settling the issue, were a source of further acrimony and tension. The moshav leaders hired an appraiser for the Scheinerman farm, who made a list of their earthly belongings: one shack, one mule, one wagon, two cows, one old plow, one new plow, a vineyard, three-quarters of an acre of watermelons, fourteen Australian casuarina trees, three wooden barrels, and 140 chicks.

The appraisal left Samuel irate: The house and the land were deemed equal in value to the sum total of the Scheinerman family's debt to the moshav. If the family wished to leave, they would do so almost empty-handed. Samuel demanded an additional 150 liroth* from the moshav in damages; in exchange for his immediate departure, they offered him 50. The negotiations fell through, and the tension between the Scheinerman family and the rest of the moshav reached new heights.

Samuel ran his farm from afar and made his living in other people's orchards. His average earnings grew to 204 liroth annually, four times greater than the average family income on the moshav. Not long after Samuel Scheinerman decided to remain in Kfar Malal, the family's orchard, with all of its unusual crops, burst into full bloom, further enraging his neighbors.

Samuel Scheinerman, at this tense moment, placed fierce guard dogs around his home. The animals enhanced Arik's sense of the importance of strength. He learned from his parents that independence, initiative, inventiveness, and determination pay off in the long run, much like Samuel Scheinerman's exceptional crops, which were ridiculed and then envied. More than anything else, Arik learned, as a result of his experience as an outsider, how to persevere and emerge victorious even when desperately outnumbered.

*The lira was the former Israeli pound.

CHAPTER 4

An Average Student

THE BALANCE OF POWER WAS CLEAR TO ARIK: IT WAS HE AND HIS FAM-
ily against the world. For respite, Arik would retreat to the barn,
where he could think alone and listen to the soothing sound of the
rain.

Arik went to the local county school in Kfar Malal. The Yossef
Aharonovitz School educated children from the nearby agricultural villages of Yarkona, Ganei Am, and Ramat Ha'shavim. His
classmates and teachers recall a pudgy, wholly unexceptional
child. "I don't think you could say that Arik excelled at anything,"
recalls his classmate Binyamin Toren. "He was the most average
student imaginable."

In December 2000 Sharon told *Al Ha'sharon,* a weekly newspaper, about a particularly embarrassing moment:

> It happened during the first grade graduation play. I had
> one line. I was playing the role of chalk. I was holding some
> kind of box of chalk. The stage was made of a row of desks
> and there were sheets instead of curtains. Then the curtain
> came up. I had no more than six words to say but . . .
> whoops, I can't remember a thing. I had a total blackout. It
> was something else.

He went home, cried, and, despite his mother's pleas, refused to
leave his room for two days.

That was an unusual episode for Sharon. As a child and an
adult, he rarely lost his poise under the spotlight. Feeling a deep
sense of responsibility at an early age, he would always hurry home
from school to help his parents in the fields, while his schoolmates
looked on and played. At age eight he began picking oranges and
loading them onto the family's horse-drawn wagon.

In the evenings he would play with the other kids. Their meeting place was just opposite the Scheinerman house, in a boggy patch of sand. Their favorite game was called "sand bombs." "One of the kids would bring a newspaper," explains the Scheinermans' neighbor, Yossef Margalit, "then we'd fill it up with chunks of wet sand and throw it at each other. Arik was an expert bomb maker, without doubt the village champion. That was his favorite game when we were little."

There were other games—footraces, crawling on felled timber, dodgeball, and swimming in the irrigation tanks—but Arik never took part in them. Arik was busy. His father often instructed him to stand guard in the family orchard, looking out for thieves and vandals.

Yossef Margalit remembers seeing Arik, at age ten, lying at the edge of the family orchard, keeping watch. "His father taught him to be a fighter," he says. "Arik wasn't scared of doing guard duty, even though it meant staying quiet, in the dark, all alone. On the contrary, it was obvious that the task made him feel like a hero. You could just tell that pleasing his father, being brave in his eyes, was everything to him." One night, while lying on the ground, dagger in his hand, Arik saw shadows in the orchard. He recognized his father and understood that he was watching over him. He never mentioned the episode to his father.

At ten, Arik joined the Labor-Zionist Hanoar Haoved Vehalomed youth movement. While others treated the gatherings as a game, Arik took the whole affair with grave sincerity. Soon he was picked to assist the leader, Yossef Golomb. He acted as a kind of enforcer. When the other kids acted up, Arik would set them straight, raising his voice and his fists. Not all of the children appreciated his approach. Binyamin Toren says, "I was in the same class as Arik and in the same youth movement. I don't remember him as a very likable child. He used to come to our meetings with a martial-arts stick. All the kids thought it was a bit strange. They asked him why he needed the stick. He said it was in case they saw jackals . . . but we saw a jackal once every two years or so, at most."

The Jewish farmers were wary of their Palestinian neighbors.

The August 1929 riots were part of the school curriculum and spoken of in every Jewish home. In 1936, the security situation worsened with the outbreak of the Great Arab Revolt. Arik listened closely to his father's militaristic opinions. In his autobiography, *Warrior,* he recalls taking the bus to Jerusalem with his mother and looking out the window, searching the fields for Abu Jilda, a wanted Arab terrorist.

At home, Samuel always had a sidearm tucked into his belt. Even Vera took target practice now and again. When he left the house, Samuel would hide the pistol, illegal under British law, in the barn and retrieve it when he came home, much to Arik's delight and fascination.

Samuel escaped two attempts on his life. Once, Arab gunmen damaged the irrigation lines and waited in hiding for him to come and fix them, but Scheinerman spotted them before he bent down to work. On another occasion, he was ambushed on his way home from an orchard he managed.

In defending the village from Arab terrorists, the Scheinermans entered the consensus. Arik's security tasks made him feel that he belonged. The mediocre son of outsiders excelled at last. "In matters of security," one of his old classmates says, "we were all together. When we needed to fight terrorism, the Scheinermans and the rest of the moshav united."

Even Vera, who was certainly not motivated by a deep belief in the justness of Zionism, allied herself with the cause. As soon as he could read, Arik began reading the *Davar* newspaper to her during breakfast. His father would pick out the articles about internal Jewish strife and worry that the Jewish yishuv in Palestine might split into two warring groups. Throughout his political career, Sharon kept his father's fears in mind. After the mass protests against the Lebanon War, Sharon repeatedly stated, at all public gatherings, that Jewish solidarity was the key to Israeli fortitude and security.

In 1941, at the age of thirteen, Arik graduated from elementary school and enrolled at the prestigious Geulah High School in Tel

Aviv, where, after years of social confinement in Kfar Malal, he was at last free of the yoke of his parents' ideology. The decision to send their son to high school, let alone in Tel Aviv, was novel in Kfar Malal. Most children went to work in the fields upon graduation from elementary school. Agriculture, as a way of life, was far more important than academic studies. The early Zionist Laborites saw the pursuit of learning as a leisure activity for bourgeois capitalists and the bookish Jews of old. The Scheinerman family disagreed. They too foresaw an agricultural life for their son, but they placed supreme importance on their children's education.

Geulah High School was private and pricey, and Arik there found himself a country boy among urban elites. His classmates knew nothing of his formative experiences. Few of them had broken soil. They were interested in the security situation, his area of expertise. During recess they debated the pros and cons of the different youth movements.

For Arik the change was bliss, even though he now had to wake up in the dark and work in the fields before taking the bus to school. He would get off at the Tel Aviv Central Bus Station and walk two kilometers, pocketing the change he'd been given for the bus so that he could buy a falafel sandwich and fruit juice in Mugrabi Square. Both he and Dita were immaculately dressed, even compared to the city kids.

Arik continued to be the most ordinary of students. He coasted through school, unperturbed by his 70 average. Years later, when asked to recall high school memories, he chose the following:

> I studied at Geulah because my sister had received a scholarship. Coming to the city liberated me from all of the things happening on the moshav. One day my homeroom teacher praised me for something I'd written on a test. I got up in front of everyone and said: "I have to admit that that specific passage on the test, I copied." She praised me even more.

Mordechai Horvitz, husband of folksinger Naomi Shemer, remembers Arik well:

We were in the same class. I could see the uniqueness in Arik already in his school days. He was ordinary, didn't stand out, but there was something very strong in him that was unusual for kids. In 1985, when no one believed he could bounce back from the blows he'd taken after the Lebanon War, I was interviewed in the paper as a child-hood friend. Back then I said there are great moments in his future. It wasn't prophecy. I just knew Arik personally. As someone who watched him grow up in school and then suddenly, amazingly, witnessed the change in him when he went to fight in the War of Independence, it was obvious to me that this person was capable of great things.

Those good years for Arik were nerve-racking for the Jewish yishuv in Palestine. In September 1939, World War II broke out. One year later, Hitler was at the height of his power. In June 1940, France surrendered to Nazi Germany and lost its hold on Syria and Lebanon. Iraq threw off English control in April 1941. During that same month, Germany seized control of Greece and Crete. The Nazis were at the gates of the Middle East. Erwin Rommel, commander of the famous Afrika Korps, battled the British in the desert to the south of Palestine. Italian warplanes attacked Tel Aviv and Haifa, igniting gasoline tanks. The smoke was visible from Kfar Malal. The Jewish yishuv lived in constant fear: If Rommel emerged victorious in the desert, he would be unchallenged on his path to Palestine. Many able-bodied males volunteered to fight in the different branches of the British armed forces and with other Allied nations.

Arik joined the Gadna, a paramilitary youth battalion, and transformed himself during this period. While his friends from the moshav remembered a chubby, unremarkable kid, he was now, with the military a part of his life, a commanding young man. Arik excelled in all facets of paramilitary training—the night maneuvers, the hand-to-hand combat, the long hours of crawling, the knot tying, and the stick fighting.

Yossef Margalit, Arik's friend from Kfar Malal, remembers the metamorphosis: "From his first day in the Gadna, he changed. All of a sudden, with no warning at all, we discovered a totally different Arik. He became a serious young man who was determined and knew what he wanted of himself. Even his face grew serious. It was as if he had swapped [his old self for] the divine imprint he had been given."

CHAPTER 5

In Uniform

NOT LONG AFTER HE ENTERED THE YOUTH CORPS, ARIK SCHEINER-
man, now fourteen, along with other standout cadets, joined the
Haganah, the yishuv's main martial force. Late one night, local
leaders of the Labor-Zionist militia summoned him to an orchard
outside his village. One at a time the boys passed behind a curtain,
took a pistol and a Bible in their hands, and swore allegiance to the
cause.

It did not take long for Scheinerman's instructors to realize
that he had more to offer than most, and he was soon drafted into
an elite youth unit in the Signal Corps. Of all the junior units, only
the signalers learned how to fire air guns, clean rifles, and wield
knives. On their first mission they carried notes to the Haganah's
watchmen. After that, most of their operations involved the rather
unclandestine purchase of cigarettes for their commanders.

Scheinerman's peers in Kfar Malal took their underground service in the Haganah, which was entered into without parental consent, very seriously, but none matched Scheinerman's dedication
and sincerity. In the evenings he would go running around the village at a feverish pace, improving his aerobic fitness. During hand-
to-hand combat drills, he volunteered first and often.

At one point in their training, an instructor from the Jewish
Settlement Police arrived and taught them to fire automatic weapons and throw grenades. Like all members of the British-backed
police squad, he had sworn allegiance to the king of England but,
under penalty of incarceration, worked with the illegal Haganah
forces, preparing them for the day the British folded their flag. The
settlement police were the only Jews in Palestine legally allowed to
carry a weapon. At night, they would use those weapons to train
young recruits like Scheinerman.

The signalers spent many nights trudging through rocky river-beds and up the steep, terraced slopes of the Shomron region, learning to read topography and navigate at night. Their routes took them close to the local Arab villages, where they learned the lay of the land. Scheinerman was gifted at translating the squiggly contour lines of the map to the terrain, understanding at a glance the shape of the hills and the curves of the rivers. He thrived on field maneuvers.

Scheinerman stood out during the training course, exhibiting a natural charisma, but, to his commanders' dismay, also showing the first signs of an independent streak that would become legendary. His instructors asked him to smuggle firearms from one village to another, a major violation of British law. Mindful of the fact that the instructors couldn't compel him to commit criminal acts, he flat-out refused. At seventeen, after three years of training, Scheinerman graduated from the leadership course and took a position as a Gadna youth instructor.

A cadet of Scheinerman's, Avner Yitzhar, recalled an exercise at

> a fourteen-foot-high Tnuva factory in the moshav. During one of our training drills Arik instructed us to jump off the roof. Everyone jumped, but we weren't sure if Arik, who was already more than pudgy, would leap. But he not only jumped, he took a running start and landed properly. It was a drill in overcoming fear, and he was one of the few who didn't know what fear was.

Yossef Margalit says that "as soon as Arik became an instructor, everyone treated him differently. Despite his age, they treated him like a commander."

In the summer of 1945, after graduating from high school and completing his Bagrut matriculation exams, Scheinerman, along with several high school friends, joined the Haganah's underground Squad Leader Training School. He was a tough, aggressive soldier. His temperament and physique, as well as the tacit approval of authority figures, strengthened the young commander's firm belief in the might of the fist.

The physically demanding squad leader training was held out

in the open stretches of creased and cracked desert near Kibbutz Rehuma, some ten miles east of Gaza. In order to get to the base, Scheinerman took the bus to Kibbutz Negba and transferred to an Arab Gaza-bound bus. He got off in the middle of nowhere, as instructed, and waited for a ride to come and take him to the secret training grounds.

In the seclusion of the desert, the Haganah could detect British patrols from miles away. They fired rifles without fear of being caught. Yet this time, the physical strain of the course and the desolate yellow-and-sage desert left Scheinerman yearning for his home in Kfar Malal. Homesickness might explain the mediocre marks he received after two months of crawling through sand and thorns. He felt betrayed by his scores, but with war looming, his instructors made it clear that the Haganah would need stellar and subpar commanders alike.

After the course, Scheinerman returned to the farm to weigh his options. He could either join the Palmach, the Haganah's crack fighting force, or follow his father's wishes and stay in the moshav. Samuel Scheinerman believed that the Palmach had betrayed the underground operatives of the Etzel and the Lehi—the Jewish Revisionist-Zionist forces in Palestine who lived underground and employed terrorist methods in their battle against the British. Scheinerman decided to continue his clandestine work with the Haganah and forgo the Palmach for the time being. As a company commander, he soon made a name for himself as an especially demanding trainer at the Mosensohn Agricultural Institute near Kfar Malal.

In 1947, on the eve of war, Arik was working on the family farm. All thoughts of joining the Palmach had been put aside months before when his father was diagnosed with a heart condition. The fate of the farm rested on Arik's shoulders. His parents enrolled him in the country's premier agricultural school, in Rehovot. Arik Scheinerman may well have pursued an agricultural degree, tilling his father's soil in anonymity, had the United Nations vote in favor of partition, on November 29, 1947, not triggered an all-out war.

CHAPTER 6

Love and War

Love, too, found Scheinerman in the fields. One clear day, as he picked oranges, he noticed a girl from the Mosensohn School in the neighboring orchard. He looked up at her and, unlike all previous crushes, felt something different: love at first sight.

For the next hour he watched the girl through the citrus trees. Too embarrassed to approach her, he decided to arrange a meeting as soon as possible. The Mosensohn School was mostly for children who had come to Palestine from Europe without their parents. The faculty kept the students under close watch and locked the doors after dark. As a well-connected Gadna company commander, Scheinerman asked around, found out her name, and sent word that he'd like to meet her. Margalit Zimmerman accepted.

Their first date was a cloak-and-dagger affair. On the agreed-upon evening, Arik cut a hole in the school's perimeter fence and the sixteen-year-old Margalit crawled through. They sat in the nearby fields and talked. She told him that she was from Romania and that her parents had stayed behind with her two youngest siblings. She and a younger sister, Lily, had come to Palestine a year before to join their older brothers. Arik and Margalit spoke for hours, and many clandestine dates followed. Only after several months did the two begin to see each other during the day. Immediately, their relationship became the talk of the school and the moshav.

At first, Gadna commanders were not sure about the propriety of the affair between the brawny instructor and the young student. But once they saw how the two complemented each other—Arik was introverted, rugged, and ambitious; she was opinionated, dainty, and content to let life come to her—they gave the relationship their blessing.

During the spring of 1947, however, the two saw less and less of each other. Jewish-Arab tension swelled as eleven members of the U.N. Special Committee on Palestine toured the land in an attempt to solve the Jewish-Arab conflict in the area. Arab groups took advantage of their presence and increased the frequency of terror attacks on Jewish settlements. Scheinerman spent many nights on patrol, far from his new love.

Arik's love for "Gali" and his desire to be with her as often as possible led him repeatedly to request a continuation of his tenure at the school. In the end, though, he was forced to leave the Mosensohn School and join the Shai, the Haganah's National Information Service, a precurser to the Mossad. His first job was to remove all public posters of the Etzel and the Lehi—forebears of the Likud Party, which he would eventually form.

Scheinerman also joined the Jewish Settlement Police. At his induction ceremony, he purposely barked out a mouthful of garbled syllables to the British officer who stood opposite him. After the ceremony, he told the other Jewish officers he would never swear allegiance to a foreign power. For the rest of his life, he took pomp, ceremony, and symbolism very seriously, unusual for an Israeli. (It was no surprise that Sharon later refused to shake Yasser Arafat's hand, while Yitzhak Rabin, Shimon Peres, Binyamin Netanyahu, and Ehud Barak, who equally reviled the man, agreed to.)

Scheinerman, working undercover as a military intelligence officer and openly as a member of the police force, no longer lived on the fringe of society. The ugly duckling of Kfar Malal had become a swan: He was dating a beautiful girl, and was widely praised by his superiors. But maturation came at a price. The favor he found in his father's eyes dimmed as he continued his efforts on behalf of the Haganah, hanging posters that made Samuel cringe. Samuel Scheinerman wanted his son to follow in his footsteps, and yet Arik, like so many of the children of the Jewish European immigrants in Palestine, embarked on a new path in the new land. These Palestine-born, and later Israeli, children were known as Sabras, a metaphor that alludes to the coarse exterior and sweet interior of the native cactus fruit.

In the fall of 1947, a few weeks before the historic U.N. decision to end the British Mandate in Palestine and partition the land into two states, Scheinerman participated in his first real mission. He and a few other Haganah members were tasked with sending a message to the son of a Bedouin chieftain. Abu Qishik's son was believed to be behind much of the terrorist activity in the area. The Haganah squad would deter them from any further criminal behavior by stealing the sheikh's son's most valued possession, his bright red car. Scheinerman led the operation.

He learned the target's driving routine and set up an ambush at a secluded bend in the road through an orange grove. As the car slowed for the turn, Scheinerman and his team jumped in front of the car. Abu Qishik's son hit the brakes and ran away as soon as he saw the motley crew. Scheinerman set out after him, chasing him through the grove for a few hundred yards to no avail. Arik Scheinerman's first mission ended with him and his fellow recruits driving their stolen booty to an old barn, away from the prying eyes of the British police.

As winter approached, the number of Haganah missions increased. On November 29, 1947, Scheinerman was at home, sitting around the radio with his parents, counting out the votes for and against the partition of Palestine at the U.N. General Assembly. Thirty-three nations voted in favor of ending the British Mandate and instituting two separate states, thirteen opposed, and ten abstained. Scheinerman flew out of the house to join the erupting celebrations. That night the residents of the village saw a side of him they hadn't known: The introvert was running through the crowds shouting with glee. At one point, he burst into a friend's house and woke him up with a homemade stun grenade.

The celebrations were brief. The following day, November 30, 1947, Palestinian Arabs announced a three-day general strike, which led to the riots that inaugurated what Israelis call the War of Independence and Arabs refer to as al-Naqba (the Disaster). The British confiscated weapons and hindered the Haganah's ability to act as an army before leaving the country in May 1948. From that first morning of autonomy in November, Scheinerman began to thirst for a command position. The Haganah set up ten new

brigades of combat soldiers. In early December 1947, Scheinerman assumed command of a squad in the Alexandroni Brigade.

Other soldiers took naturally to his command. Walking at the
head of a formation, Scheinerman felt, for the first time, the surge
of excitement that comes with the burden of command. The fact
that the other soldiers depended on his acumen bolstered his confidence. Determined not to let his men down, he forced himself to
excel.

Scheinerman swelled with pride each time he came back to the
village and caught the admiring stares of his soldiers' parents, the
same people who had ostracized his family. Now everyone greeted
him with open arms and invitations. His proudest moment came
early one morning when he returned to Kfar Malal after a successful night mission and bumped into his father. Samuel, in the midst
of his morning chores, nearly saluted his son.

As an eternal outsider in the reborn Jewish homeland, Samuel
must also have felt a pang of jealousy toward his son. Samuel took
his feud with his neighbors to his grave. When he died, in 1956, he
left a will that reiterated all of the old grievances. He specified that
he refused to be taken to his final resting spot in Kfar Malal's
hearse.

In his later years, ostracism was compounded by personal woe.
Dita, his firstborn, left for America. The stunning girl was shunned
by her peers and spent most of her time studying. Her father doted
on her and blamed himself for her departure.

In 1941, Samuel was hospitalized. Dita, still in high school,
visited her father and made a profound impression on Dr. Shmuel
Mandel. At the time, Mandel, a ladies' man, was in the middle of
his surgical residency. He fell in love with the striking teenager immediately, and she responded in kind. The two were married in
front of a handful of people in the Scheinerman home in Kfar
Malal. At the end of the restrained ceremony, the new couple flew
to New York, where Dita began working as an interior designer and
Shmuel as a pediatrician in a neighborhood clinic in Brooklyn.
Samuel, Vera, and Arik were vehemently opposed to Dita's *yerida*—
a derogatory term for emigration from Israel that connotes a spiritual descent. Once she left, her family ties withered. Years later the

couple tried to return to Israel, taking up residence in Ramat Gan, but Dr. Mandel could not find a suitable position, and they returned to New York for good.

In the 1970s, when Vera's health started to decline, Dita asked her to divide the Kfar Malal property so that she could build a house on the second plot. Unable to secure permission from the Israel Land Authority, Vera kept all the land in her name.

On July 15, 1987, several months before her death, Vera Scheinerman signed her will in the presence of Dov Weisglass, later Prime Minister Sharon's chief of staff. She wrote:

> After a thorough investigation it has become clear to me that it is legally and agriculturally impossible to divide the land into two plots; therefore, in order to ensure that the farm stay active, I have decided to bequeath it to one of my grandsons, Arik's oldest son. My daughter will be properly compensated. This was a difficult decision: My love for my children, Arik and Dita, is equal, yet this is the only possible solution I could find.

Vera left the contents of the house and most of her money and valuables to her son. Out of an inheritance of an estimated half a million dollars, Dita received $25,000. Vera explained:

> I do not mean to convey my love for my daughter with this sum; my love for her cannot be learned from money, but I do wish to include her in my passing. The sum to be given to my daughter, Yehudit Mandel, was determined by considering that my son, Ariel Sharon, has been assisting me from January 1984 on, keeping the farm in working order, supporting me financially, and paying for home assistance, which has cost a great deal of money.

She added, "I instruct my son Arik and my daughter Dita, along with their families, to live in mutual understanding, in friendship, love, fraternity, and peace for all of their days."

In October 1989, Vera's last will and testament was opened. It is not certain whether Dita accepted Vera's $25,000, although Weisglass, by way of an envoy, tried to influence her to take the bequest.

Sharon and his sister, despite multiple attempts by family friends, remained estranged. They met once, in 1999, when Sharon, serving as foreign minister in Netanyahu's government, visited her in her Fifth Avenue apartment in New York City. The NYPD closed off the street as he slipped into her two-room flat on the tenth floor. He emerged an hour later.

Senior members of Sharon's administration say that throughout his years as prime minister he never once returned to his sister's home, despite frequent visits to New York City. Dita even chose not to attend her mother's funeral. Longtime residents of Kfar Malal later saw her in the village. One resident says she waited until the last of the mourners left the Scheinermans' house and then slipped in alone, to grieve in private. She came out of the house distraught and never returned, he says.

Dita, alone and childless, boils in angry silence to this day. Since 2000, she has not left her apartment once, not even to attend the funeral of her husband, who died in 2004. She has excommunicated herself from the outside world. She orders groceries and other bare essentials over the phone. She refused to leave the apartment when one of her curtains caught fire and smoke could be seen spiraling out of her window. The fire department had a hard time persuading her to open the door.

As the last of the British troops prepared to leave Palestine, the battles between Arabs and Jews intensified. Scheinerman felt both the thrill of emerging from a firefight unscathed and the pain of losing brothers in arms. On May 14, 1948, though, he was jubilant. He was seeing Margalit for the first time in two months. He came to her school in his dust-covered battle fatigues and kissed her. Arik had to hurry back to his soldiers to command a strike on a bridge near Qalqilya. As he and his squad were setting off, they heard David Ben-Gurion's voice reverberate proudly from the school's PA system as he read Israel's Declaration of Independence.

The bridge-bombing mission went well. Ten days later, on May 23, he headed out to the Hulda Forest to take part in the Battle of Latrun. On the morning of the twenty-fifth he was shot in the stomach and saved from certain death by Ya'akov Bugin.

An armored personnel carrier driven by Yossef Levi wound its way around the cratered battlefield. Levi and combat medic Shoshana Cohen searched for wounded soldiers in need of evacuation. Suddenly Cohen saw a soldier limping toward them with a bleeding officer on his back. She jumped out of the armored vehicle and examined the officer's stomach wound. Scheinerman whispered for water, but Cohen, aware that drinking was dangerous in his condition, wet her collar and instructed him to suck the water from her shirt. Ram Oren describes in *Latrun* how Scheinerman and Bugin joined ten other wounded soldiers in the back of the armored personnel carrier as Levi sped through the burning fields.

Scheinerman was taken to the nearby village of Akron and from there to the Indian hospital near Rehovot that had once tended to the British troops. In a soft voice, a nurse asked Scheinerman for a urine sample. When the injured officer said he was unable to provide one, she called out for a catheter, a move that made him far more compliant. The nurse kissed him on the cheek, and he lost consciousness. Shortly thereafter his attending physician decided to move him to Hadassah Hospital in Tel Aviv for a lifesaving operation.

The drive to the hospital turned out to be more harrowing than the abdominal surgery. As soon as the ambulance reached Balfour Street in Tel Aviv, the driver slammed on the brakes and ran from the vehicle along with the nurses, leaving Scheinerman alone and immobile in the back. Seconds later, Egyptian warplanes bombed the city. The ambulance crew then returned to their abandoned patient.

Once the operation was over, Scheinerman was moved to a recovery room with other wounded soldiers. In the hospital for weeks, he was haunted by harsh memories from the burning battlefield in Latrun. Scheinerman fought depression by analyzing the flawed battle tactics that had led to the bitter defeat of his troops. He shared his conclusions with his soldiers when he got back to the base. In *Arik: The Commandos' Commander*, Maty Shavit quotes Scheinerman as saying:

I remember that then, in the hospital, the defeat ate away at me. I didn't think I'd serve in the IDF again at the time. Like many others, I felt I'd been drafted to do a job, to finish the war, and then go home. Personally, I had plans to study agriculture, like Father, and continue on in the farm. But that escape [from the valley in Latrun], that dreadful feeling of helplessness, that was awful.

In the hospital, I had time to analyze what had happened. I didn't have all of the details, but I'd figured out that a lack of faith among many of our troops in all matters concerning movement under fire, along with a lack of intra-force coordination between our different units, weakened the force as a whole, and in general we were weakened by the absence of a fighting spirit. . . . I believe that with a bit more fighting spirit we would have gotten to the top and taken Latrun.

Years later, as he climbed the military ladder, he institutionalized each lesson learned at the Battle of Latrun. Many were enshrined in what the IDF calls its Battle Torah. An ironclad rule is that an officer in the field must lead by example—if he calls for a charge under fire, he is first to his feet. After the disaster in Latrun, Scheinerman internalized the importance of meticulous planning and solid intelligence gathering as well. During his years as a commander, he exhibited an unsurpassed level of preparedness before every battle.

CHAPTER 7

Unit 101

IN EARLY JULY 1948, FIVE WEEKS AFTER THE BATTLE, SCHEINERMAN lost his patience with the recuperative process. Outside his rubber-soled hospital world, events were unfolding at a rapid pace: The Jewish Quarter of Jerusalem's Old City had fallen; the Jordanian Arab Legion had been halted at the border between Israel and Jordan; the Egyptian Army had been brought to a stop on the outskirts of Ashdod; the IDF waged a naval battle off Tel Aviv; and the Israeli Air Force bombed the capitals of Lebanon, Syria, and Jordan, swinging the momentum of the war in Israel's favor.

Scheinerman asked his doctors many times to release him, but they refused. His wounds had not yet healed and he needed medical supervision. A friend smuggled him some clothes. When the attending nurse stepped away, he threw them on and slipped out undetected. He made it to the road and hitched a ride back to his base.

Still too weak for combat, he was posted to the 32nd Battalion of the Alexandroni Brigade as an intelligence officer. He spent his first two days back in uniform searching for body parts around the city of Lod, where Jordanian troops had butchered twenty-eight Israeli soldiers. As he picked up parts of hands, feet, human faces, and detached organs, the images from Latrun came back in sickening waves. He saw himself once again lying bleeding in the wheat field as Arab villagers shot and robbed his downed soldiers.

Shortly after, he crashed his jeep and broke several ribs. Again he was hospitalized, and again he hurried back to his unit prematurely. Days later, on July 11, 1948, he led Company C of the 32nd Battalion of the Alexandroni Brigade to the Arab village of Ras al-Ain, which had been fortified by Iraqi troops. Ribs taped and in pain, Scheinerman hoisted battle gear onto his back and led his men to victory.

Toward the end of the year he was promoted to company commander. On February 24, 1949, a cease-fire with Egypt having been signed, he left the southern front and returned to Central Command's HQ. In the aftermath of Israel's fiercest war, he had to decide whether to return to the farm, study agriculture, and satisfy his father, or stay in the army, where he enjoyed his status as a bold and promising young officer.

He spoke openly with the brigade commander, Col. Ben Tzion Fridan-Ziv, airing all his grievances and his deliberations. The colonel grew convinced that Israel needed officers of Scheinerman's caliber. As an incentive to extend his service, Fridan-Ziv promoted him to commander of the brigade's reconnaissance platoon. A few months later, he was asked to command the elite Golani Brigade's reconnaissance unit in the northern part of the country.

Avraham Yaffe, commander of the Golani Brigade, saw vast potential in Scheinerman, raised his rank to major, and sent him, in the summer of 1950, to the battalion commanders' course in Tzrifin. Yitzhak Rabin, future IDF chief of staff and prime minister of Israel, was his commander. Scheinerman excelled above all others, and upon graduation, he was made chief intelligence officer for the Central Command.

Scheinerman served in Ramle, under the command of Zvi Ya'alon, an amiable officer. Yet his first year there was grueling, as he endlessly patrolled Israel's long, conflict-ridden eastern border. During his time there, the IDF was dealt a number of stinging blows—terrorist attacks—and was largely unable to respond to them.

Scheinerman gleaned intelligence from maps and dossiers. He had a keen ability to gather and analyze intelligence, and to plan— paying unwavering attention to detail. These qualities, as well as his habit of volunteering for every complex and high-risk combat mission that came his way, stayed with him throughout his time in uniform.

In 1950, the Central Command squared off in simulated battle against the Southern Command, led by the already legendary general Moshe Dayan. Scheinerman had never met Dayan before, and he was spellbound by his charisma. Dayan was the polar opposite of the easygoing Zvi Ya'alon—he was short-tempered, decisive, and cunning.

As soon as the drill began, Dayan sent his forces forward, violating the ground rules of the exercise. Scheinerman, for his part, came to the rescue of a lost officer from the Central Command and led him around the enemy troops to the southern city of Beersheba. Pleased with his all-night navigation, he was surprised to be called to Central Command headquarters and chastised for leaving his post. An intelligence officer needs to assist the brigade commander in analyzing the reports from the field, not navigate troops in enemy territory, he was told.

The dressing-down was enough to convince Scheinerman that the Intelligence Corps was not for him, a point hammered home when Dayan hastily proclaimed unilateral victory. Dayan sent a plane to drop leaflets on the defeated Central Command troops. They showed a fox, the Southern Command symbol, smiling victoriously over a toothless Central Command lion.

Throughout his two-year stint in Central Command headquarters, Scheinerman suffered from a persistent case of malaria. Once every two weeks, the disease would knock him out. In late 1951, after his doctor advised him to switch climates, he left the country for the first time. He had an aunt in New York, an uncle in Paris, and three friends in London: Yitzhak Moda'i, a future peer of Sharon's in parliament and former comrade at arms at Latrun; Dov Sion, future husband of Yael, Moshe Dayan's daughter; and Cyril Kern, a Jewish British volunteer during the War of Independence, who, fifty years later, would find himself at the center of police investigations against Prime Minister Sharon.

Scheinerman's first stop was Paris. Before leaving, he went shopping with his father in Tel Aviv for civilian clothes. Despite his best efforts, he elicited gasps from his French uncle when he deplaned. His offending blazer was immediately discarded. In Paris, Uncle Yossef bought him his first suit.

Scheinerman spent his first two weeks abroad eating, drinking till the late hours, and walking the percussive streets of the capital. He found the whole experience intoxicating. From Paris he took the ferry to London, spent some time with his friends, and continued on to New York. He decided to get a driver's license before setting out across North America. He failed the written section of the exam, but the driving instructor, impressed by his rank and experience in the IDF, passed him.

Scheinerman crisscrossed the United States. He was impressed with the vastness of the country, its eclectic nature, and the immense differences between America and his home. He returned from his first vacation malaria-free and energized. Arik Scheinerman's next post was in the Northern Command, again as an intelligence officer. To his delight, Moshe Dayan was now the region's supreme commander.

While Scheinerman learned the inner workings of the Lebanese, Syrian, and Jordanian armed forces, as his job demanded, he still secured permission from Dayan to participate in all missions conducted by the northern reconnaissance team. Before long, a routine had been established: Scheinerman led the team on all combat missions. His name was beginning to precede him.

In November 1952, Dayan summoned Scheinerman to his office in Nazareth. He wondered aloud whether it would be possible to kidnap two Jordanian soldiers. Perhaps, he thought, a pair of Legionnaires could be used as bargaining chips to secure the release of two Israeli soldiers who had been captured while training near the Jordanian city of Qalqilya.

Scheinerman answered with a knee-jerk affirmative, but said he'd have to look into the matter. As soon as he left the general's office, he rifled through maps in search of Jordanian positions within striking distance. The Sheikh Hussein Bridge, which crossed the meandering Jordan River, seemed a suitably vulnerable point. With nightfall, Major Scheinerman and Lieutenant Shlomo Grover of the northern reconnaissance team set off in a flatbed truck. They parked on the shore of the Sea of Galilee and made their way to the river on foot. On the opposite bank they saw two soldiers smoking cigarettes. The Israeli officers grabbed metal rods protruding from the bottom of the ruined bridge and made their way across the shallow river in silence. On the eastern bank, they crawled to the guards' hut and pulled out their pistols.

Scheinerman and Grover grabbed the two soldiers from behind, gagged them, and marched them back across the river, guns to their heads. Back on the Israeli bank, they cuffed their hands and threw them in the back of the truck. Grover hopped in after them, and Scheinerman drove like a wild man across the hills of lower Galilee toward Nazareth.

The truck pulled in to the city with first light. Scheinerman and Grover marched the Jordanians into the night officer's room and gave them tea and sandwiches. Two hours later, when Dayan entered his office, he found a note from Scheinerman on his desk. The Jordanians he had wondered about were waiting for the general in the holding cell, it said. Dayan called Scheinerman— by now shaved and spit-polished—to his office and asked for the whole story.

The one-eyed general was pleased with the major's chutzpah, daring, and initiative. Scheinerman did not need to have things spelled out. Dayan liked operating in this theater of the unsaid, where orders were given in silence and plans were set in motion with raised eyebrows and imperceptible nods. Officers were given vast leeway, and the question of ultimate responsibility was ambiguous. Eventually, this modus operandi would sour their relationship: Success has many proud parents, but failure is frequently an orphan.

The euphoria ebbed within weeks. IDF chief of staff Yigal Allon promoted Dayan to deputy chief of staff and commander of operations. That move, combined with orders for a policy of restraint, meant that Scheinerman had to focus on the nuts and bolts of his intelligence work: tracking enemy troop deployments, chasing infiltrators, and investigating the scene of terror attacks. After each attack he was sent to collect evidence and bring it to U.N. observers, who were supposed to continue the investigation on the other side of the border. It was an exercise in frustration.

Major Scheinerman had reached another crossroads, and again civilian life beckoned. After a long internal battle, the army offered him a third way: a break for studies with an option to return to a military career. While on leave he was made commander of a reserve battalion in the Jerusalem Brigade.

Scheinerman registered at Hebrew University's Mount Scopus campus for a degree in Middle Eastern history. He rented a small apartment with a friend and saw Gali often. As soon as she graduated from nursing school, she followed him to the capital and began a training period as a psychiatric nurse in a small Jerusalem hospital. In the spring semester, on March 29, 1953, they were married. An IDF rabbi wed them in private, with no guests in attendance. Only later did they send out celebratory cards to their parents and friends.

The young couple rented an apartment in the quiet Jerusalem neighborhood of Beit Ha'kerem. Gali had friends from work over for dinner often, and the two reveled in each other's company. Arik picked Gali up from work and marveled at her bedside manner. She, in turn, looked upon his in horror. Scheinerman could only stare at her patients, despite her encouragements to speak to them. On his first day of studies, Scheinerman rolled a notebook into his pocket and walked to the university. He came home deflated. Academic studies were boring.

The tension on Israel's borders and the persistent terror attacks kept Scheinerman in a military frame of mind. He spoke with his friends more about military tactics than about his studies, telling them that the army needed to retaliate after each attack.

Like all Israeli males between the ages of twenty-one and forty-five, Scheinerman was in the reserves. The Jerusalem Brigade, comprised mostly of Palmach veterans, was called up to execute specific missions as necessary. Once, Scheinerman initiated and executed an ambush without the blessing of the general staff. Uzi Benziman describes the mission in his book *Sharon: An Israeli Caesar*. The young battalion commander felt that the Palestinian villagers of Qatana were deliberately crossing the Jordanian border into Israel. Tired of their perceived intransigence, he laid several of his men in ambush with orders to fire on all trespassers. They shot two distant figures, both women on their way to draw water from a well. Although many accepted his leadership without question, criticism of his tactics began to spread through the ranks.

The same could not be said of his superior officers. Not long after that incident, the Jerusalem Brigade commander, Col. Mishael Shaham, summoned Scheinerman to his office in downtown Jerusalem. The two friends talked at length about the recent terror attacks, bemoaning Israel's policy of restraint. Scheinerman suggested that the army assemble a commando unit capable of striking behind enemy lines.

Scheinerman returned to school certain that nothing would come of the conversation, but Shaham took his idea to the chief of staff. Several weeks later, in July 1953, Margalit was leaving for work when she bumped into a harried soldier who had an urgent letter for her husband.

At Colonel Shaham's office, Scheinerman learned that the chief of staff had approved a mission on the Jordanian side of the border as a trial run for the commando concept. Their target was Palestinian terrorist Mustafa Samueli, a man allegedly responsible for several attacks in Jerusalem. The day before their meeting, a guard in Moshav Beit Nakofa had been killed. The murderer's tracks led back to Samueli's hometown of Nebe Samuel. Shaham proposed that Scheinerman cross the border with a small group of soldiers and kill Samueli in his home. The IDF, bureaucratic and clumsy, couldn't handle this type of mission, Shaham told him. Scheinerman could handpick his team.

He was stunned: On the one hand, Shaham's proposal matched his own feelings exactly; on the other hand, he couldn't shake the thought that he was a civilian who had a test on the history of Middle Eastern economics the following day. He thought of Margalit, their one-year-old marriage, and her undoubtedly negative reaction to this news. He blurted out the first thing that came to mind, something about a big test. "Listen carefully," Shaham said. "Some people study about others' historic acts. Others make the history that people study."

The next day, Scheinerman had seven men hunched over maps and battle plans on Margalit's living room floor. Shlomo Baum and Yehuda Dayan were from the Golani reconnaissance unit. Scheinerman had taken Baum from his cowshed in the middle of milking. Yoram Lavi was an old friend from Kfar Malal. Three others came on

Shaham's recommendation, and Yitzhak Ben-Menachem, known as Gulliver, an old friend of Scheinerman's from Latrun, had been pulled out of a Hebrew University law class.

They suited up in civilian clothes at Camp Schneller in Jerusalem and crossed the border at night. Nebe Samuel lay northeast of the capital in the pale desert high above the Dead Sea. The squad slipped into the village undetected and found Samueli's house. Gulliver and Baum put an explosive device at the foot of the door and waited. The explosion failed to dislodge the sturdy old iron door from its hinges. Worse, Samueli was not home—and the rest of the village was coming to life. When a burst of fire erupted from an alley, they knew it was time to depart. They threw a few grenades through the windows of the house and took off down the steep slope to the Sorek River and up the hill to Jerusalem. They arrived at Camp Schneller sweaty and dusty.

Scheinerman felt like a failure, but the colonel seemed pleased with the result. Eight men had left, all had returned, and a message had been sent to Samueli. He ordered them a hot meal and called Prime Minister Ben-Gurion's military attaché. As far as he was concerned, the IDF had begun a chain reaction of deterrence.

IDF chief of staff Mordechai Maklef issued orders to establish a top secret commando force. Two weeks later, he summoned Scheinerman to his office and asked him to take charge of the project. Again, the young soldier hesitated, worrying about his studies and his relationship with Margalit, which was finally blossoming after years of forced separation. He walked out of the office without committing, but the IDF brass knew he would never turn his back on the type of offer they had made. After all, as Shabbtai Teveth documents in his book *Moshe Dayan*, Scheinerman, during his first year of studies, once waited for Dayan outside the prime minister's office. When he emerged, the history student tucked a folded note into Dayan's hand: "I'm a student right now," it read, "but I'm still around. If things need to be done—I'm ready to do them."

In August 1953, Shaham asked Scheinerman for a detailed training plan, a wish list of weapons, and a list of names. During their next meeting they christened the new commando squad Unit

101. The unit existed for a total of five months, from August 1953 to January 1954, and it never numbered more than thirty soldiers; yet it left a lasting mark in the minds of citizens, soldiers, and IDF commanders.

None of the soldiers, some of whom are still household names in Israel today, had any idea what they were signing up for. They came because of Arik's name and the mystery surrounding the initiative.

Scheinerman designed a training regime that would take his soldiers beyond their physical limits. They would march for days on end, find their way through harsh terrain without a map, and learn to survive alone in the field. He did not place much weight on the necessity of a good night's sleep. He wanted to take each soldier and build him anew.

One of the early standouts was a sinewy nineteen-year-old from Kibbutz Ein Harod, Meir Har-Zion, whom Dayan later called "the greatest Jewish warrior since Bar Kochba." He described his first meeting with his new commander in his autobiography, *Pirkei Yoman* (*Memoir Chapters*):

> I met Arik on top of the police building in Abu Ghosh; I straightened and saluted, as the rules demanded. I had a giant wooden suitcase in my hand. . . . Arik sat with his deputy, Shlomo Baum, and ate canned beef. Waving my suitcase in my hand I announced: "Sir, I have arrived!" Arik said: "Sit down then and eat some canned beef." I sat down and ate. That was my first introduction to the unit and its commander.

Har-Zion, soon to be Scheinerman's closest friend in the unit, sees the canned beef episode as symbolic of the atmosphere in Unit 101. In the commando unit, each soldier was judged by his ability and not by the rank he wore on his shoulder. Within months, Har-Zion would lead soldiers—and officers—to battle behind enemy lines.

In the unit's training base, on a lonely hilltop outside Jerusalem, Scheinerman cultivated a spirit of informality, believing that only self-discipline, as a result of a true desire to excel, could bring out the best in his recruits. They hunted birds and wild animals for food, prepared gala feasts after missions, took target practice on glass bottles, avoided military pomp and discipline, and wore whatever their personal sense of style demanded—shorts, sandals, Arab headdresses, loud party shirts.

The first time they crossed the border, Scheinerman felt fear in the ranks. He stopped the squad in their tracks and began pointing out the area's landmarks, knowing that his familiarity with the surrounding darkness would calm them. They continued on toward the Jordanian village of Bateen Abu Lahiyeh in an effort to acquaint themselves with danger. A guard just twenty yards away sprayed automatic fire in their general direction. The squad huddled behind boulders and returned fire before retreating.

Shimon Kahaner, called Katcha, another of the unit's legendary fighters, arrived at the base in late August 1953. Meir Har-Zion took him out to the field and ran him ragged before allowing him to enter the unit. Once he was accepted, it didn't take him long to fall under Scheinerman's spell: "When I first came to the unit and met Arik I couldn't sense anything special about him. But after a week in his presence it was clear to me, and to anyone in the 101st, that he would change the course of history."

In September 1953 they were given their first mission: the expulsion of the Bedouin tribe that had settled on Israeli lands near the Sinai Peninsula. Scheinerman, along with sixteen of his men, drove to the southern prairie lands and stormed the tents where the al-Azzazmeh tribe had camped, scaring off the Bedouin families by firing in the air. Once they had gone, the soldiers collected the firearms that had been left behind and burned the tents to the ground.

Moshe Dayan came down south to personally express his gratitude for a job well done. But there were those in the unit, most prominently Har-Zion, who thought a commando unit should be fighting enemy soldiers rather than chasing harmless trespassers. Scheinerman disagreed, explaining that by evicting the Bedouins, the young state was asserting its sovereignty. Later in the month he was asked to execute a retaliatory mission in al-Bureij, a Palestinian refugee camp in what was then Egyptian Gaza, the source of numerous terror attacks.

Scheinerman planned a surprise attack, targeting both the central area of the refugee camp and an isolated house that served as the headquarters of the fedayeen, the infiltrators. In the evening, around the fire, he announced the plan to his men. Some of them were concerned that innocent civilians would be killed. Shmuel Nissim, known as Phalah, an Arabic term connoting a lowly field worker, got up and announced that he would not take part in the mission for humanitarian reasons.

"I told Arik," he says,

> that he's heading into a refugee camp full of innocent people. It's not a specific target lurking with terrorists. It's the same thing as going into an Israeli town and opening fire in hope of killing an Israeli soldier. Arik answered me, "If you don't want to, you don't have to! You'll go to a different mission."

Scheinerman removed Nissim from the al-Bureij force and inserted him into the force planning to bomb the fedayeen house, a mission he agreed to undertake.

According to Nissim, that wasn't the last time men under Scheinerman's command took issue with his orders: "Some of us were critical of him. We felt that Arik cared far more about the military results than the consequences of his actions and the number of dead civilians on the other side. There were bitter arguments before a number of retaliatory missions."

The 101st set out the following night. They walked, in three separate squads of four men each, from Kibbutz Kissufim to Gaza. At the entrance to al-Bureij they encountered two armed guards. Har-Zion incapacitated one of them, but the second fled and sought help. Soon Scheinerman's squad found themselves backed against a wall by an angry crowd. But Shlomo Baum's squad reached them from the opposite direction, shooting their way through the civilians.

The two squads ran out of the refugee camp, regrouped, and made their way back across the border. The third squad executed their mission smoothly, blowing up the fedayeen headquarters. One soldier was injured, the unit's only casualty in four months of combat missions. The following day's paper reported fifteen killed and twenty wounded in the refugee camp.

Har-Zion was audibly upset with his commander after the mission. He asked him, in front of everyone, whether he thought the crowd in al-Bureij was responsible for the recent terror attacks in Israel. Arik answered that without retaliatory attacks the entire camp would turn into one big fedayeen base. In the aftermath of the deadly operation, the Gaza Strip had quieted. As far as Scheinerman was concerned, Har-Zion's objection had been answered.

Chief of Staff Maklef demanded answers for the many casualties as well. Scheinerman explained that the alertness of the guards had thrown off his original plan. Despite the raised eyebrows and veiled criticism from IDF brass, it was clear that Arik Scheinerman's unit, bloody and bold, daring and cruel, effective and dangerous, was becoming Israel's weapon of choice.

CHAPTER 8

Qibiya

AFTER THE ATTACK IN AL-BUREIJ, EVERYONE HAD HEARD OF THE 101st. Some idolized the small band of fearless warriors; others found their methods despicable. Scheinerman, now twenty-five, noticing people's stares, enjoyed his first taste of fame.

Meanwhile, the security situation in Israel was deteriorating. Late at night on October 12, 1953, a group of fedayeen sneaked into the town of Yehud, east of Tel Aviv. They threw grenades into a randomly selected house, killing Susan Kanias and her two children. The murders sparked outrage in Israel. The following day, Prime Minister Ben-Gurion met with acting defense minister Pinchas Lavon, IDF chief of staff Mordechai Maklef, and IDF operations chief Moshe Dayan. They decided to raid Qibiya, Jordan, the town thought to have hosted the infiltrators, and destroy fifty homes. Unit 101 was selected to carry out the operation.

Major Scheinerman, called on for retribution, organized his twenty-five men, along with a hundred paratroopers, in the Ben Shemen forest. Hours before embarking on the mission, Scheinerman received word that Dayan urgently wanted to see him in his office.

The commander of operations was worried that should the 101st encounter overwhelming adversity, Scheinerman would persevere even in the face of grave losses. "If you see it's proving too difficult," Dayan said, "be satisfied with a few houses and come back." Scheinerman, confident and certain of the justice of his mission, said he would see the operation through.

Scheinerman returned to the forest and began delegating hundreds of pre-mission chores. Most of his soldiers would be "humping" dynamite that evening. Scheinerman, still bothered by the weak blast in Nebe Samuel, planned to carry more than half a ton of explosives to Qibiya. Nissim, who studied law during his service, had received a day pass from Scheinerman for a test. He thought the amount of dynamite excessive. "Arik loaded the truck with half a ton of dynamite, enough to level the whole village. I went up to him and asked: 'What's this? Why do you need so much explosive?' He answered me: 'You have a test in jurisprudence today? Go to your test.' "

At seven in the evening the force drove to Beit Nabbalah. They loaded up and set out on the five-mile march to Qibiya. Scheinerman, walking point, did not feel the invincible bounce in his step that typically comes with leading an elite force. Instead, the paratroopers irked him with their clumsiness and heavy feet. At the designated site the force split into three groups: The 101st attacked from the east, two platoons of paratroopers attacked from the west, and Scheinerman, along with the last platoon of paratroopers, stayed put with the dynamite.

Over the next four and a half hours, the soldiers under Scheinerman's command destroyed Qibiya. The Legionnaires that had fired on them on the way into the city had fled. The place seemed deserted, a lone radio echoing through empty streets. When they returned to Israel, the soldiers hugged one another. The operation seemed a grand success. Scheinerman reported to Dayan that twelve Jordanian soldiers had been killed and no civilians. An envoy of the general staff met the combined force at dawn and handed Scheinerman a handwritten note from Dayan: "You all are the best." Scheinerman got in his car, drove to Jerusalem to see Margalit, and fell asleep in midstory.

He awoke twenty-four hours later. By then, to his profound shock, Arab news stations were reporting sixty-nine dead in Qibiya: Many women, children, and elderly people had hidden in the attics and cellars of their homes; some had been buried alive. World news outlets reported from the devastated city at length, and the Israeli government, proud of its moral superiority in war, was thrown into upheaval.

Scheinerman drove to Central Command HQ. He reported that once the village had been captured, he personally had joined the central demolition squad. They went into each room with a flashlight, he said, and only once they were sure the house was empty did they blow it up. "I was in all of the houses and I didn't see any people," Sharon said, according to Uri Eban in *Arik Sharon: A Patch of a Fighting Man.* "We committed no acts of cruelty. On the contrary, one officer heard a young girl cry in a house that was about to be blown up. He went inside and escorted her out. We bumped into a wandering kid on the street and we showed him where to run to." Most of the residents of the city fled, he said, but some must have hidden in their homes in places where the soldiers couldn't see them.

The explanation did not suffice. His military career and the future of the 101st hung in the balance. Some claimed that the soldiers didn't find the civilians because they didn't care to look: They charged into a house, sprayed the ceiling with bullets, called out "Is anyone home?" in Arabic, and then commenced the detonation.

On October 19, 1953, four days after the attack in Qibiya, Prime Minister Ben-Gurion proclaimed to the country that "we've done a thorough investigation and found that no unit, not even the smallest of the IDF's forces, was AWOL from its base on the night of the attack." He theorized that the tragic retaliatory attack had been carried out by enraged citizens from the border regions, or still-seething Jewish refugees from Arab lands, or the long-preyed-upon survivors of the Nazi camps. "It's possible that a group of civilians, tired of the fedayeen's infiltrations, decided to avenge the blood of the fallen. The government of Israel had no part in the action, wishes to distance itself from such actions, and condemns the citizens who took the law into their own hands."

On October 25, the United Nations Security Council condemned Israel for the attack.

Scheinerman felt betrayed by Ben-Gurion's radio address to the nation. Shortly thereafter, Ben-Gurion called him to a meeting. They met privately for more than an hour. Later in life, Sharon described the meeting as exhilarating. Ben-Gurion questioned him about his childhood in Kfar Malal, where several of the prime minister's friends lived. He even inquired whether Arik was in fact the son of Scheinerman the agronomist, the first man to grow clementines in Israel.

Agricultural curiosity aside, Ben-Gurion wanted to know the ideological affiliation of Scheinerman's soldiers—to ascertain whether Scheinerman had handpicked them from within the ranks of the Etzel and the Lehi, thereby posing a real threat, or from the kibbutzim and moshavim affiliated with Ben-Gurion's own Mapai Party. Assured that the latter was the case, Ben-Gurion asked Scheinerman whether he could control the unit. Michael Bar-Zohar, in *Ben-Gurion,* provides Scheinerman's response as Ben-Gurion recorded it in his diary: "He promises that there's no threat of them becoming professionals. If we do not retaliate to an Arab attack—there'll be an uproar, but he is certain none of them would act on their own. They will maintain discipline. They were not in an uproar over the [radio] broadcast."

Ben-Gurion was pleased with the conversation. He told Scheinerman that it didn't matter how Qibiya was perceived in the eyes of the world; what mattered was the local, Middle Eastern interpretation of events, and in that regard the attack enabled the citizens of Israel to continue living in peace. "Scheinerman," Ben-Gurion said, a smile spreading across his face, "I think it's time to give you a Hebrew name."

"Scheinerman—handsome man," Ben-Gurion said excitedly. "You'll be Sharon. You were born in the Sharon, no? Sharon—like Scheinerman, only Hebrew." Ben-Gurion, thinking that "Arik" was a nickname for "Aharon," wrote, after a conversation with "Aharon Sharon," that the 101st would stand. Major Arik Scheinerman picked himself up out of the chair and left his first meeting with the prime minister trying to get used to his new name: *Arik Sharon. Ariel Sharon.*

CHAPTER 9

Commander of the
Paratroopers

CONTROVERSY CAME QUICKLY ON THE HEELS OF THE QIBIYA MISSION.
Behind his back, Sharon was called "the Uniformed Partisan" and
commander of the "Murderers Gang Ltd." His supporters continued to see him as brave, charismatic, and brilliant.

The soldiers' devotion never wavered, and in all military brief-
ings and public comments, Sharon never once tried to shift blame
to those under his command. If there was a problem—and he was
sure there was not—then it was his alone.

On December 6, 1953, IDF chief of staff Mordechai Maklef
stepped down after a bitter dispute with acting defense minister
Pinchas Lavon and acting director general of the Defense Department Shimon Peres. Ben-Gurion, serving as both prime minister
and defense minister, appointed Moshe Dayan IDF chief of staff.
The following day, Ben-Gurion stepped down and retired to his
kibbutz in the desert. Foreign Minister Moshe Sharett inherited
his position. Pinchas Lavon was appointed to the post of defense
minister.

The political turmoil did not bode well for Sharon. Moshe
Sharett, a political moderate, opposed the hard-line notion of retaliatory strikes after each Arab attack. Sharon feared that under
Sharett, the 101st would no longer be deemed necessary. Dayan,
in an effort to spread the fighting ethos of the unit, decided to
merge the 101st with the paratroopers.

Sharon and Dayan conspired to keep the merger secret.
Sharon invited the chief of staff to the unit's base under the guise
of a celebration. Dayan began by admiring their work at length,
but the soldiers soon realized that the general had come to bury

and not to praise. Dayan, in his eulogy, explained to them that the time had come to spread their winning tactics to the army at large. Tempers flared for hours after Dayan left the dining room. Sharon's oratory calmed the soldiers but didn't placate them, perhaps because they realized that their commander was the only person set to benefit from the merger.

Dayan, intent on tripling the size of the unit into a brigade, knew whom he had appointed to command the paratroopers. He knew Sharon was undisciplined and independent-minded, that he would always be his own man, but that in the field, commanding troops, on the tactical level and, more so, on the emotional plane, persuading men to follow him into battle, Sharon had no equal.

The merger did not go well. Not only did the soldiers of the two units disdain each other, but many of the paratroopers were unwilling to accept Sharon's leadership. Some cringed at joining what they perceived to be a guerrilla group, and many still revered their previous commander, Lt. Col. Yehuda Harari. Harari spoke first at the ceremony marking the change of command. He thanked the officers who had left their posts in protest, asking them to step forward out of formation. They obliged. Embarrassed, Sharon pocketed the speech he had prepared, eager for the ceremony to pass as quickly as possible.

Sharon parted with several soldiers from the 101st, redeployed platoon and company commanders still loyal to Harari, and promoted many of his old soldiers to command positions. He then began a flurry of field maneuvers meant to instill a sense of pride in the soldiers, band the new unit together, train those unskilled in the commando trade, and ensure that they would have little time—or strength—to gripe.

Sharon found that his touch with the common soldier was the same whether he had thirty men under him or three hundred. The paratroopers learned that their new commander demanded perfection. Sharon hammered home the message that the paratroopers could do more than anyone else. They were told many times a day that they were the best of the IDF. The rest of the time they were running—through thorns and sand, obstacle courses and hilltops, often with open stretchers and heavy packs on their shoulders.

After an especially arduous week, Sharon would arrange a feast followed by a campfire, giving the soldiers the feeling that they were members of a rarefied elite. He drafted attractive female recruits to serve in the battalion as parachute packers. The goal of every teenage boy in Israel was to join the red-bereted troops.

Margalit paid the price for her husband's fame and dedication. He hardly ever came home, and when he did, it was for only a few hours—during which time he subjected her to long-winded army stories. She asked him many times to be around more often, but Sharon was engrossed in his military life.

On March 17, 1954, a group of Jordanian fedayeen seized control of a public bus near Scorpion Hill in the Negev Desert and killed eleven passengers. Shortly thereafter, the IDF general staff summoned Sharon and assigned him a mission in Nahhalin, a town near Bethlehem. It was clear to Sharon that the brigade's success on their initial mission would determine their status with the general staff.

Dayan and Sharon were in the same boat. The government had agreed to the retaliatory strike on the basis of Dayan's conviction. Failure would look bad for both of them. It would also mean the end of retaliatory strikes as a weapon against terrorism. Neither of them could afford another Qibiya.

Again the soldiers were instructed to raze homes as a form of vengeful deterrence. Sharon handed out a small flashlight to each soldier. He instructed them to search each room carefully before blowing up a house. Moments before the force was set to cross the border, they received word that the Jordanians had sensed their movements and set up a roadblock on their planned route. After a quick consultation with deputy commander Aharon Davidi and Meir Har-Zion, Sharon decided to change the plan.

"We look at Arik," Har-Zion wrote in his memoir, "as he takes on this enormous responsibility. The hundreds of soldiers will march at his command. Is he not sending them to untold, unfathomable disaster? But he is the commander. He must decide—and he does."

Under the old plan, the paratroopers were supposed to take the town of Nahhalin by storm, blow up its houses, and block all access routes into the area. The new plan, crafted on the hood of Sharon's jeep, called for impromptu roadblocks on the road to Nahhalin and a sniper's ambush of the passing enemy troops. With Qibiya in mind, Sharon decided that an easily attained minor success was far better than a great risk.

Aharon Davidi, the deputy commander, led the charge on Nahhalin. Jordanian troops that came in response were picked off by the sharpshooters. In the morning, when the force returned, many of the soldiers celebrated. Sharon kept his emotions in check, remembering all too well the morning after his last mission. He spent many tense hours waiting for the Arabic news on the radio. Only when he heard that seven soldiers and three civilians had been killed in the attack did he know that the raid would be considered a success.

After that mission, the paratroopers were put to work. Over the next two and a half years they carried out more than seventy official raids and hundreds of reconnaissance missions in enemy territory, some authorized, some not. Sharon capitalized on the unit's success, drafting talented officers and soldiers and increasing the budget.

Ben-Gurion remembered the twenty-six-year-old Sharon fondly, and invited him to multiple meetings. At first they met in Kibbutz Sde Boker, but after 1955, when the old man returned to politics as defense minister, Sharon came to his office in Tel Aviv. Ben-Gurion wanted to hear about the paratroopers' methods and the details of their missions. He, in turn, told Sharon war stories from his days with Britain's Jewish Legion in World War I, and recommended Thucydides' *The Peloponnesian Wars*. Ben-Gurion made an enormous impression on Sharon. One time, he came home from a meeting and told Margalit that he had laid out his thoughts on politics and that the old man had been impressed.

Sharon's relationship with Ben-Gurion won him few friends among the IDF brass. At top level meetings the defense minister would frequently request the presence of the young major. The generals were enraged when they had to lean over Sharon, a fixture at Ben-Gurion's side, to introduce themselves to the defense minister. Sharon enjoyed it all.

The paratroopers were dominating all of the IDF's high-profile missions. Sharon, only twenty-six and not even a graduate of officers' candidate school, was hoarding fame with both hands, acting as though he had reinvented the military wheel as he hurdled over many links in the army's rigid chain of command, directly pushing the chief of staff and the defense minister to adopt his new techniques.

Gaza, at the time under Egyptian rule, was fast becoming a trouble spot for Israel. On numerous occasions, Egyptian forces opened fire on Israeli patrols. Again, the paratroopers were sent to retaliate. Sharon chose a forward Egyptian base overlooking Kibbutz Kissufim. Fifty soldiers, in dug-in positions, guarded the base. On a hot August night in 1954, Sharon set out on "Operation Eye-for-an-Eye" at the head of a column of one hundred paratroopers.

Sharon's attack force of forty-five soldiers burst into the base in three small teams. Sharon was shot in the leg while storming the Egyptian position. A medic dropped to his knees under fire and bandaged him. Although the Egyptians put up a good fight, the battle ended with their retreating from their own base. Sharon, lying on a stretcher in the middle of the base, called the three commanders of the attack teams to him, insisting on the usual post-mission debriefings—with a bullet in his leg.

While recuperating once again, Sharon had some time to think. He replayed the battle in his mind and recalled the moment of his injury. He had been shot as he entered the fortified canal around the perimeter of the base. That necessary hesitation at the mouth of the canal needed to be addressed.

Ben-Gurion came to the hospital to pay the major a visit. He praised him for a job well done, and soon thereafter Sharon was promoted to lieutenant colonel.

In late June, Max Reiner, a farmer from Ra'anana, had been killed by Jordanian infiltrators from the West Bank town of Azun. A squad of paratroopers, under the command of Major Aharon Davidi, was sent to retaliate for the murder. The seven-man squad, operating alone in enemy territory, had to walk thirty-six miles through rough country to exact their revenge. On the approach to the Jordanian camp, one of the soldiers stabbed a startled shepherd to death, ensuring that he could not raise the alarm. Proceeding in silence, the squad killed three Jordanian Arab Legionnaires as they slept in their tents. Yitzhak Jibli, though, was shot in the stomach. At 2:30 A.M. the squad stopped, still miles from the border. They had only two hours of darkness and way too much ground to cover. Meir Har-Zion and Aharon Davidi felt they had no choice but to leave their friend behind. Davidi kissed him on the forehead and sprinted the last few miles to the border. The Jordanians captured Jibli and threatened to try him for murder.

Sharon hounded Dayan for a series of raids aimed at liberating his imprisoned soldier. As far as he was concerned, Jibli's return to Israel was a test of his leadership. He had to show his soldiers that they would be rescued at all costs. Sharon was also racked by guilt. Not only had his soldiers turned their backs on their comrade, but Jibli's father had died not long after learning of his son's fate. In fact, Sharon had not wanted to include Jibli in the mission, saying he should stay in Jerusalem near his hospitalized father. Jibli had pleaded, though, and Sharon had relented.

The episode received extensive press coverage. The Foreign Ministry persuaded the United Nations and the Red Cross to pressure Jordan to surrender the soldier, but the Jordanians refused. The IDF general staff authorized the paratroopers to carry out a series of missions in search of Jordanian soldiers who could be captured and held as bargaining chips. The missions were codenamed "JYL," a Hebrew acronym for Free Yitzhak Jibli. Sharon spent the summer months cooking up kidnapping plans. One time, he and several of his soldiers painted their jeep United Nations white. Two other soldiers wore the garb of poor Arab day workers, while Meir Har-Zion masqueraded as an Israeli policeman. Their plan was to cross the border under the guise of a U.N. outfit returning two lost Jordanian workers to their homes; the most senior members of the welcoming party would be kidnapped and whisked back to Israel. A suspicious Jordanian officer saw through their cover and sent them back to Israel empty-handed.

For four straight months Sharon tried everything in his power, and more, to secure Jibli's release. His reckless attempts—few of which were sanctioned by the general staff—began to worry Dayan. At one point, Sharon sent two young women across the border to seduce Jordanian soldiers. His soldiers recall a man possessed. Each day he would tell them, "We don't leave wounded men in the field." Sharon was haunted by the memory of Latrun.

In early September, Dayan asked U.N. Truce Supervision Organization chief E.L.M. Burns what might happen if the Israelis "unconditionally" freed their prisoners. Burns passed the offer on, and Israel released prisoners the following day. Jordan, in order to save face, waited several weeks. They released Jibli on October 29. When Jibli returned home and heard how many missions, even including attempts to seize control of the Beitunyeh jail, had been made to secure his return, he hugged Sharon.

One wound from the harrowing episode endured: Sharon's unstoppable drive to secure the freedom of his soldier, with or without the approval of the general staff, angered Dayan and seeded distrust between the two. It was only a matter of time before the two men—individualistic, stubborn, independent-minded, and proud—would clash.

CHAPTER 10

The Tragedy in Qalqilya

On February 28, 1955, Sharon led the paratroopers on a three-pronged raid. Their targets included an Egyptian Army base in Gaza City, a nearby railroad station, and a water pumping station due east of the base. Yitzhak Rabin, commander of the IDF's training department, sent Lt. Col. David Elazar to observe the retaliation raids. He wanted to implement the paratroopers' successful tactics into all IDF units. In addition, Moshe Dayan asked Elazar to pay special attention to Sharon. He wanted to see what happened to his direct orders once Sharon took them into the field.

All told, Sharon's force killed thirty-six Egyptian soldiers and wounded twenty-eight; they lost eight of their own men, and thirteen were injured. Despite the losses, the soldiers returned to Israel in song. Dayan waited for them at the border. He hugged Sharon when he arrived and congratulated the paratroopers on their bravery and fortitude. Margalit Sharon, a registered nurse, had helped the medical crew organize before the mission. She saw her husband come back from the attack, the dead and the wounded splayed on stretchers.

Sharon's close friend Meir Har-Zion did not take part in the mission. His sister, Shoshana, and her boyfriend, Oded Weigmeister, had been killed by Bedouins while hiking across the border in Jordan's redrock desert near Ein Gedi, and he had vowed revenge.

Sharon arranged a meeting between his top commando and the chief of staff. They tried to persuade him not to set out for the mission, but Har-Zion was immovable. He would settle the score. Sharon gave his soldier a weapon and food and drove him to the border. Three paratroopers agreed to accompany him—Amiram Hirschfeld of Kibbutz Deggania Bet, Ze'ev Slutsky of Moshav Nahalal, and Yoram Nahari of Kibbutz Ein Harod. Sharon added Yitzhak Jibli to the squad.

They crossed the border into Jordan. Har-Zion, who, in the past, had trekked twenty-five miles inside enemy territory to the ancient Nabitean city of Petra, and as a fifteen-year-old had been taken hostage by Bedouins while hiking with his sister in Syria, earning three weeks in a Damascus prison, ambushed the men he believed were responsible for the murders. After a brief interrogation, he killed five of the men with his own hands and released a sixth—to bear witness.

Jordan protested the violation of its sovereignty; Har-Zion was arrested. Prime Minister Moshe Sharett wanted to bring Har-Zion to trial, reasoning that Israel could not rightfully demand the prosecution of Arab terrorists if it failed to bring its own murderers to trial.

Sharon came to his soldier's aid. He secured the services of Shmuel Tamir, a former Etzel man and a lawyer who would later serve as justice minister and specialized in cases against the government. Sharon's decision to hire the antiestablishment advocate angered Ben-Gurion, who demanded that Sharon sever all contact with Tamir. In the end, Dayan, working behind the scenes, had the case closed. Har-Zion was released after twenty days in jail. His punishment: six months' banishment from the army.

In April 1955, the Egyptian Intelligence Corps established a fedayeen unit tasked with carrying out terror attacks in Israel. They drafted Palestinian volunteers from among the 280,000 residents of the Gaza Strip, two-thirds of whom were refugees. In August 1955, the unit staged its first attack against civilians—seventy-five miles north of the border. Before long, the unit had become one of the main weapons against Israel. In 1955, 258 soldiers and civilians were injured in their attacks.

The IDF responded with their own wave of attacks. The paratroopers raided Gaza in a variety of formations, at times in small bands of mobile warriors and at times with full battalions. Most of their raids were aimed at military targets. Sharon seemed to thrive on the nonstop action. He presided over complex missions and continually sought new and unconventional modes of warfare.

On one occasion, when ordered to kidnap an Egyptian soldier, he instructed his men to leave a shiny black tire on the side of an Egyptian patrol road. Waiting in ambush, his soldiers watched the scene unfold exactly as their commander had predicted: The jeep slowed, the driver came out to inspect the booty, and the trap was easily sprung. Tactically, whether in small missions or on complex multitroop operations, Sharon was unrivaled.

Nonetheless, there were those who hated him, seeing him as bloodthirsty, impulsive, and undisciplined. One of his soldiers even brought him to trial, claiming that Sharon had handcuffed him and struck him in the face. The trial ended when the complainant was killed in a shooting accident. Others, such as Maj. Gen. Meir Amit, demanded an explanation for the fact that the paratroopers' reprisal raids always seemed to escalate beyond what the general staff had authorized. This sort of complaint would surface throughout Sharon's career: in 1956 at the Mitla Pass; in 1973 at the Suez Canal; and in 1982 on the way to Beirut. Each time, Sharon offered written proof that he had acted within the limits of his orders. His interpretation of those orders, though, was often imaginative.

Senior IDF officers accused Sharon of unbridled ambition during the years of the reprisal raids. He bullied junior officers and coddled politicians in order to get his way, they charged.

On November 2, 1955, the paratroopers attacked five Egyptian bases near Nitzana, an area that should have been demilitarized according to the armistice agreement. The Egyptians had stationed an infantry battalion there. The paratroopers took the bases, killing eighty-one Egyptian soldiers and losing five of their own.

The defeated Egyptians did not return to the area, and Sharon, eager to silence the wagging tongues that had criticized the paratroopers, celebrated their victory with a parade through Beersheba. Citizens heard the reports of the battle on the radio and poured out onto the streets to embrace his tired soldiers.

Sharon sent one of his officers to report the results of the battle to Ben-Gurion. He wanted the old man, serving as prime minister and defense minister again, to hear of his troops' success before he heard about the parade and the accusations of megalomania.

One soldier absent from the parade was Shimon Kahaner. He was in a hospital bed, thanking God for Ariel Sharon:

> Arik saved my life twice during the battle in Nitzana. I'd been shot in the neck and had taken shrapnel all over my body, and Arik demanded that I be evacuated to a hospital in the middle of the battle, without delay. In the morning, he suddenly saw me lying in a field hospital in critical condition. He called soldiers, after a night of battle, to come and personally take me to the hospital in Beersheba. That was the second time he saved my life in a twenty-four-hour span. I owe him my life and that ties us together, to this day."

On the night of December 11, 1955, Sharon led the paratroopers on their most complex raid: an all-out attack against the Syrian strongholds on the eastern shores of the Sea of Galilee. The plan called for an amphibious landing; a crossing of the Jordan River; a sweeping move up and around the cliffs of the Syrian Golan Heights; the use of air support; and a simultaneous 10:00 P.M. strike. Sharon boarded the rear command boat and set sail across the choppy water.

Although fifty-four Syrian soldiers were killed and thirty captured, as opposed to six Israeli dead and fourteen injured, the men in command positions paid a steep price. While leading the charge, Rafael Eitan, later the chief of staff during the Lebanon War, was critically injured, and Yitzhak Ben-Menachem—Gulliver—was killed during the first minutes of the battle. On board the command boat, Sharon spent long minutes leaning over his dead friend. After the initial mission in Nebe Samuel, Gulliver had left the army and gone to law school. After much cajoling from Sharon, he had rejoined Battalion 890. For Sharon, it was a sad end to a stormy year.

The breadth of the mission and the extent of Syrian casualties stirred an international uproar. Syria filed a complaint at the United Nations. The U.N. Security Council condemned Israel for the action. So, too, did the Israeli prime minister. Moshe Sharett was furious. While the raid was taking place, he had been in the middle of a meeting with American secretary of state John Foster Dulles. The two were discussing an Israeli request for fighter planes, which was subsequently denied.

Sharett was upset with his defense minister, Ben-Gurion, who claimed to have authorized a different type of mission, which had then been altered as it made its way down the ranks to Sharon.

Ben-Gurion called Sharon and Dayan to a meeting to try to establish how his orders had been skewed. He told them that the mission "had been too good." He was obviously upset, but during the following weeks, he showed that he still trusted Sharon, instructing Dayan to swell the ranks of Battalion 890 to a full brigade, under Sharon's command.

On September 10, 1956, a Jordanian National Guard unit attacked a group of IDF soldiers on a map-reading exercise. After an initial and deadly exchange of fire, the Jordanians dragged the Israeli soldiers across the border to Jordan and mutilated the bodies, severing their genitalia. The following day the paratroopers stormed the Jordanian police fort in Khirbat a-Rahwa, in South Mount Hebron. During the attack, Jordanian troops shot Meir Har-Zion—back from exile and serving as commander of the paratroopers' first reconnaissance unit—in the neck. Dr. Morris Ankelevitch pulled the downed commander to cover, cut open his trachea with a penknife, and inserted a rubber tube into his lungs, allowing him to draw breath. The chief of staff later awarded the doctor Israel's highest military honor.

Sharon came to inspect the wounded and saw his confidant, his right-hand man, the person he trusted above all others in battle, wavering between life and death. Har-Zion would never return to fight again with Sharon. The doctors saved his life, but his body was weakened by his injuries. He retired to a farm on a tall ridge above the Beit She'an Valley. Although he has refused media interviews for years, he came out of isolation in March 2005 to criticize Sharon's Disengagement Plan from Gaza. He told *Maariv*: "Sharon's gone crazy, he's dangerous."

The fedayeen attacks intensified. On October 4, four Jewish

workers were murdered in Sdom. On October 9, two more workers were killed in an orchard near Tel Mond. Their ears were cut off. In response, Ben-Gurion ordered an attack on the Qalqilya police fort in Jordan.

On October 10, 1956, two battalions of paratroopers, a reconnaissance company, an armored company from Brigade 7, an artillery battery of 155mm guns, and three tanks set out for the police fort under Sharon's command. Some one hundred policemen and Arab Legionnaires guarded the fort, and several regiments of Jordanian National Guardsmen also camped in the vicinity of Qalqilya.

Sharon planned to take both the police compound and the Legionnaire fort at Tzufin. Dayan found the plans overly ambitious. He ordered Sharon to capture the compound and merely lay an ambush a few kilometers west of the fort so that they could cut off any reinforcements. He saw no reason to risk soldiers' lives capturing an armed fort. Sharon felt it needed to be captured in order to protect the troops' flanks. In the aftermath of the mission, the two would accuse each other of dooming the mission to failure.

Sharon briefed the troops for the last time in a field near his parents' house in Kfar Malal. With darkness fully settled, the troops set out. At 10:00 P.M., Motta Gur's regiment stormed the police compound, defeating the hundred Jordanian troops with relative ease. The ambush team failed, however, to halt the reinforcements streaming in from the east, and the Jordanian troops eventually encircled the reconnaissance company that had laid the ambush. While the remaining troops fought to reach their surrounded comrades, the Jordanians sent snipers to the top of the fort at Tzufin. From there, they inflicted grave damage on the Israeli troops.

At 2:30 A.M., nine of deputy brigade commander Yitzhak Hoffi's half-tracks were able to break through a wall of enemy fire and reach the ensnared reconnaissance team. They loaded dead, wounded, and healthy onto the tracked vehicles and set off in a westerly direction, toward Israel. The Jordanian soldiers opened fire from Tzufin, killing six more soldiers and wounding twenty. In all, eighteen soldiers had been killed and sixty-eight wounded—the largest death toll since the 1948 War of Independence. The Jordanian casualty count, ninety dead, did little to soothe Sharon.

In an internal debriefing, Sharon criticized the chief of staff for changing his battle plans several times. A member of the general staff heard the criticism and relayed it to Dayan. Furious, Dayan convened a meeting of all the IDF's field commanders and berated Sharon for improper use of artillery and irresponsible placement of the reconnaissance team in Jordanian territory. With the debate unresolved, Dayan, Sharon, and Ben-Gurion (at this point acting as both prime minister and defense minister) all realized that the age of reprisal raids had come to a close.

The next day's leading articles all asked the same questions about the efficacy, and necessity, of such raids. "On the morning of October 11," Dayan wrote in his book *Sinai Campaign Diary*,

> once the units that took part in the mission returned to their bases, I went with the paratroop brigade commander, who had been responsible for the mission, to report to the defense minister. Like all of us, Ben-Gurion was saddened and troubled by the heavy losses. . . . Although Ben-Gurion did not criticize the mission itself, his questions all revolved around the same axis: Was it necessary to suffer so many losses among our troops? Neither the brigade commander nor myself could provide unreserved defense of the mission, since we, or at least I, were hardly at ease with what had happened. In the end it was a nerve-racking conversation between three people whose hearts were in mourning.

The press kept the issue of the heavy losses alive. Sharon was surprised to receive an invitation to sit with the country's top newspaper editors, and even more surprised to see how fast the IDF brass authorized the interviews. He suspected it was no coincidence that Dayan had sent him to the press after a failed mission. For Sharon, it was a painful end to a proud period. As he saw it, the paratroopers, over the course of seventy authorized cross-border raids, had instilled a new fighting spirit into the IDF and changed the way the Israeli Army did battle.

The nadir for Sharon came when his driver delivered a package to the chief of staff and overheard a roomful of senior officers laughing about the look that would be on Sharon's face when he found out he'd been stripped of his command position and placed behind a desk. The driver hurried to Be'er Ya'akov, where Sharon and his wife lived, and relayed the news.

First thing the next morning, Sharon went to Dayan's office, but the chief of staff wouldn't see him. Sharon marched out of his office and drove straight to Jerusalem to see Ben-Gurion. He pulled off the highway, calmed himself, and made a call, asking permission to meet with the prime minister. Ben-Gurion replied: Come at once. In *Warrior,* his autobiography, Sharon describes himself walking into the old man's office with tears of rage in his eyes. The prime minister listened patiently to the twenty-eight-year-old brigade commander. When Sharon was through venting, Ben-Gurion counseled patience. He told him a Chinese legend about a fisherman who found a body washed up on shore. The fisherman asked the dead man's family for money in return for the body. The distraught family asked advice of a wise man, who told them to wait and not pay. The fisherman saw the same wise man, who told him to wait as well. The moral: In the end, both sides will tire of waiting and they will reach a settlement. Ben-Gurion laughed at the end of the parable. Sharon, uplifted, understood that the prime minister would never allow him to be stripped of his command.

CHAPTER 11

The Mitla Trap

THE SUEZ WAR, WHICH BEGAN LESS THAN THREE WEEKS AFTER THE last of the reprisal raids, smothered the Qalqilya controversy in clouds of fine desert dust. On October 26, during a celebration for the paratroopers in Ramat Gan, Sharon received word to drop everything and prepare his brigade for battle. At Central Command HQ he learned that the paratroopers would have a critical role in the brewing war.

According to Israeli defense doctrine there were five developments that would each constitute a casus belli: a disruption of day-to-day life as a result of terrorism; the closure of shipping lanes and airspace in Eilat; a change in the balance of power between the Arab nations and Israel; the entry of an Iraqi expeditionary force into Jordan or Syria; or the signing of a three-way war pact between Egypt, Syria, and Jordan.

Over the course of the previous two years, each and every one of those criteria had been met. Egypt had been operating an infiltration unit since 1955, spreading terror from the southern deserts to the Jordan River. By April 1956, attacks were peaking. In September 1955, weeks after Sharon's deadly reprisal raid, Egypt signed a massive arms deal with Czechoslovakia. Weeks later, they closed the shipping lanes and the airspace surrounding Israel's southern port city of Eilat. In April 1956, Syria signed an arms deal with the Soviet Union, which promised them fighter planes, bombers, tanks, and artillery. In October 1955, Egypt and Syria signed a mutual nonaggression pact. One year later, in October 1956, Jordan joined Syria and Egypt in the pact. At the same time, an Iraqi division mobilized on the Jordanian border, at King Hussein's request, and an expeditionary force entered the Hashemite kingdom. The noose tightened around the young Jewish state. All arrows seemed to be pointing to war.

Israel spent months attempting to procure weapons that would narrow the gap between them and the Arab states, but the world's weapons producers were closed to them. Britain, the former colonialist power of much of the Arab world, refused to sell Israel tanks and planes; the United States cultivated neutrality. The only state willing to sell Israel state-of-the-art weaponry was France. In April 1956, France sold Israel hundreds of fighter planes and tanks, 105mm artillery, half-tracks, mortars, radio equipment, trucks, and ammunition.

The opportunity for cooperation between Israel, France, and Britain arose when Gamal Abdel Nasser nationalized the Suez Canal, threatening European business interests, none more so than those of Britain, which had owned the canal up until 1954 and whose economy was still based in sea trade. According to the signed arrangement, Britain reserved the right to safeguard its interests in the event of a war. In late fall of 1956, Britain wanted Israel to attack Egypt, allowing them to intervene.

Ben-Gurion refused. Israel would appear aggressive, while France and England, seemingly interested only in "quieting the rowdy natives," would emerge clean-handed. The Israeli prime minister also feared that the British would bail out at the last minute and leave Israel hanging. In the end, an agreement was reached whereby Israel would stage something less than an all-out war. Public opinion internationally and in Israel would favor a large-scale reprisal raid as a means of combating terrorism. As for the pretext of Britain and France's involvement, Chief of Staff Dayan suggested that Israel drop a regiment of paratroopers deep in Egyptian territory—enough of a provocation for Britain to intervene and, if they failed to mobilize, an initiative small enough to pack up in a hurry. On October 25, 1956, in a Parisian villa, Ben-Gurion covertly signed the Sèvres Agreement and prepared to return to Israel for war.

The following day the prime minister called Sharon and Dayan to his office and explained the goals of the mission. Israel would push the fedayeen from the border and open the Strait of Tiran, freeing the shipping lanes out of Eilat; Britain would reclaim Port Said and the Suez Canal. Ben-Gurion stressed that the IDF should proceed with caution, so that they could retreat if necessary.

The French, uncertain of the IDF's ability to carry out its part of the plan, sent a Colonel Simon to Israel. Simon, who had lost an eye in battle and whose body was covered with scars, visited the paratrooper base, where he met Sharon. The Israeli lieutenant colonel spun a web of stories and took the Frenchman on a tour of the booty the paratroopers had taken in cross-border raids. Most impressive to Simon were the confiscated Arabian horses, snorting gallantly in their stables.

Israel's invasion plans began with the paratroopers. One battalion, under the command of Rafael Eitan, would parachute into the Mitla Pass, just eighteen miles from the Suez Canal. The rest of the brigade would fight their way south, through 110 miles of desert, along the Kuntila-Themed-Nahal route until they joined Eitan's troops at the foot of the pass. Sharon drafted the battle plan with Col. Assaf Simhoni, the new OC Southern Command.

The two officers, aware that the area was well fortified, decided to drop the Israeli force on the eastern side of the mountain pass, near the Parker Memorial. They would dig in and hold tight for forty-eight hours, until Sharon and the rest of the brigade joined them. Sharon informed Eitan of the plan on Saturday, October 27, forty-eight hours before they took to the sky. On Monday, Chief of Staff Dayan and other senior officers came to the base to have breakfast with the paratroopers before battle.

At three in the afternoon, Eitan's battalion of close to four hundred soldiers filed onto rumbling Dakota planes. A jump instructor hooked the pensive soldiers to a static wire for the IDF's first jump over enemy territory. Meanwhile, Sharon, at the head of a ragtag convoy of civilian and military vehicles, began the 110-mile race to Eitan and the Parker Memorial. They had three Egyptian Army forts blocking their way. The Egyptian soldiers fled Kuntila before the paratroopers arrived; Themed succumbed at dawn, in half an hour; and by evening Nahal had fallen, leaving their path clear. On Tuesday, October 30, at midnight, thirty hours after they'd landed at the foot of the pass, Eitan spotted pinpoints of light in the distance. At once, the tense quiet of guard duty and reconnaissance was shattered by hoots of joy.

Early that morning, the 2nd Brigade of the Egyptian Army had planned to attack the paratrooper battalion. Forward scouts from Eitan's battalion, however, spotted the convoy and called in air strikes as they approached the western edge of the pass. Sharon received word that the Egyptian brigade had been thoroughly crippled. He assumed that the pass, like the desert that lay beyond, was devoid of enemy troops. In truth, Battalion 5 of the 2nd Brigade had made their way into the nooks and crags of the pass. Later in the day, another battalion joined them. Both had lodged themselves deep in the canyon walls; neither had a viable path of retreat.

On Wednesday morning, October 31, Sharon asked the general staff for authorization to move into the pass. He argued that the area near the Parker Memorial was flat and susceptible to armored attack. The negative response left him snorting mad. He had no idea that Dayan was keeping the paratroopers from charging toward the Strait of Tiran for diplomatic, rather than tactical, reasons: The British and the French had delayed the start of their offensive against Egypt by twenty-four hours, and he wanted to leave Israel the option of retreat under the guise of a mere reprisal raid. Sharon thought the delay was unwarranted, tactically unsound, and counter to paratrooper doctrine, which demanded a constant push toward the enemy. Personally, he thought the glory of opening the strait and taking the Sinai Desert should be his alone.

Sharon located an Egyptian armored force thirty miles northwest of the Parker Memorial. Again he asked for permission to take the high ground, and again he was denied. As the commander in the field, he applied relentless pressure on his superior officers to allow him to take the decision he deemed necessary. In response, Dayan flew the chief staff officer of the Southern Command, Lt. Col. Rechavam Ze'evi, to the Parker Memorial to soothe and dissuade Sharon.

He achieved neither. In fact, while updating Sharon on developments in the region, he enraged him even more. Other IDF units were streaking through the desert on their way to the glorious Red Sea port of Sharm al-Sheikh. Sharon demanded that Ze'evi allow him to send a reconnaissance patrol to the pass. Ze'evi agreed on condition that he send nothing more than a lookout patrol and that they refrain from seeking an encounter with Egyptian forces. Before boarding his light aircraft, Ze'evi saw Sharon assembling a battalion-sized force.

In the early afternoon, battalion commander Mordechai (better known as Motta) Gur, a future chief of staff and a longtime bitter foe of Sharon's, set out for the pass at the head of a column of armored personnel carriers, tanks, mortars, and a supply vehicle. Sharon ordered Gur to move cautiously toward the pass. If fired upon, he said, find cover; do not storm the pass. Yitzhak Hoffi, the deputy brigade commander, joined Gur, along with battalion commander Aharon Davidi.

The Egyptians allowed Gur's troops to saunter through their killing field. Only when his battalion had passed through the first ambush did they attack, firing with everything they had, from every side. Gur's half-tracks became death traps. Yitzhak Hoffi, certain that Gur was ahead of him, fought through the wall of fire to the western side of the pass. Later, he tried unsuccessfully to fight his way back toward the troops pinned down at the apex of a narrow turn at the top of the pass. With radio reports streaming back to the command center and Egyptian planes swooping down on the trapped troops, Sharon had no choice but to thrust the brigade, which was camped five miles down the valley, into battle.

The only possible way to extricate the troops from the pass was to engage the Egyptians in face-to-face firefights in the crags and weathered canyon corridors high above the pass. Sharon sent Battalion 890 under Eitan's command, along with the brigade reconnaissance company, to join Davidi's force at the entrance to the pass and launch a counterattack. Unable to locate the quiet Egyptian guns, Eitan and Davidi asked for a volunteer to race through the high pass in a jeep, drawing the enemy fire and revealing their positions. Davidi's driver, Yehuda Ken-Dror, volunteered. He drove around the first bend, drew a long burst of accurate fire, and continued west until his jeep exploded. His commanders were sure he had died, but Ken-Dror, mortally wounded, crawled back across the pass throughout the night. He spent three months in a hospital before expiring.

Sharon sent two additional companies to the pass with instructions to climb over the sheer walls and attack the flanks of the embedded enemy. The Egyptians, trapped, fought to the last. During seven hours of close-quarter battle, they lost 260 men. The paratroopers lost 38, with 120 injured. At eight in the evening, the battle died down. Sharon had spent the entire time at the foot of the pass, giving orders over the radio and directing the establishment of an airstrip, while Gur called in air strikes with a tank radio and fought for his life.

In the aftermath of the battle, Dayan accused Sharon of disobeying orders by sending an attack force rather than a reconnaissance patrol. The chief of staff felt the battle had been worthless and the soldiers had died in vain. Sharon, he said, used the inexact word "patrol" as a guise. In *Sinai Campaign Diary,* Dayan wrote: "Some discontent members of the general staff have alerted me to the fact that I treat the paratroopers with kid gloves—even though I know they attacked the Mitla Pass against my direct orders and that their actions had fatal consequences."

Dayan continued:

> There's no need to say how sorry we all are for the heavy death toll paid during the battle for the pass, but the outcry— the roaring outcry—I harbor for the paratroopers' command staff is that they hid behind the word "patrol." It saddens me that they did that and it pains me that I was unable to establish a trusting relationship between myself and the command of the paratroop brigade, so that, when they disobey orders, they would at least do so directly and in the open.

Eleven years later, after Sharon emerged victorious and triumphant from the Six Day War, he seized the opportunity to strike back at the former chief of staff turned defense minister. In *Arik: The Commandos' Commander,* Maty Shavit records Sharon's comments at a postwar press conference: "When we approached the Mitla Pass I wanted to cable the defense minister: 'We're at the Mitla again; this time with permission.' But yet again there was no communication between us."

Dayan appointed Maj. Gen. Chaim Laskov to look into the matter. Sharon told the investigating officer that once he had joined the 890th at the Parker Memorial, he felt susceptible to armored attack. He claimed that had the armored force he had seen thirty miles to their northwest not retreated to the canal, the paratroopers would have suffered far greater losses at their hands. He restated that Ze'evi had authorized a patrol and that as far as he knew the pass was unmanned. The nature of the mission, and not the size of the force, had been mentioned. Once his troops had been caught in the death trap, Gur and Hoffi were forced to fight for their lives, and he had been left with no choice but to throw the brigade into battle and take the pass.

Laskov's report was vague and inconclusive. Ben-Gurion read the document and summoned Sharon and Dayan to his office.

Ben-Gurion asked Sharon whether he felt the offensive action had been unnecessary. Sharon responded that now, as the three of them sat sipping tea, he was willing to concede the point, but that then, alone in enemy territory, he had acted correctly based on the available information. Dayan offered his perspective on events. In the end, Ben-Gurion, who, like Begin years later, found Sharon irresistibly heroic, said he was unable to rule on such tactical military matters, letting Sharon off the hook with no significant punishment.

Ben-Gurion could not, however, clear Sharon's name in the eyes of many of the paratroopers, some of whom spent the night after the battle stranded in the mountains, with comrades dying slowly around them while their fellow soldiers listened from afar. Motta Gur, liberator of Jerusalem in 1967, could not excuse Sharon, commander of the paratroopers, for remaining at the Parker Memorial, supervising the construction of the airstrip, while his troops died in battle. Gur wasn't alone. Many senior officers in the brigade demanded an explanation for Sharon's behavior; after all, he himself had instituted the cardinal rule that the commander must lead by example, always walking at the head of the formation. Uri Milstein, an Israeli military historian, asserts that Motta Gur and the other commanders voiced their grievances with the full backing of the chief of staff, who was keen to have Sharon relieved of his command.

On Thursday and Friday, November 1 and 2, Sharon patched up his battered brigade and regrouped for the final stages of the war. They joined up with airborne reinforcements at a-Tur and completed the occupation of the Sinai Desert together. Brigade 9 waited for them in Sharm al-Sheikh. The war's objective had been met: The strait was opened, the shipping lanes freed.

The paratroop brigade was changed by the Suez War. They were no longer willing to walk blindly behind Sharon. The territory they had fought for had to be surrendered at the behest of the United States, the Soviet Union, and the United Nations. Sharon understood that after three years of nonstop combat and 105 dead soldiers under his command, it was time to go.

CHAPTER 12

Death Comes Home

THE SHARONS MOVED TO TZAHALA, AN UPSCALE NEIGHBORHOOD IN Tel Aviv, home to many career officers. They bought their new house from Maj. Gen. Chaim Laskov, the officer charged with investigating Sharon's conduct during the Suez War. Sharon's parents were disappointed with the decision. They had already located a plot near them on the farm. When Samuel first visited them in the city, he dispensed with pleasantries and told his son that he had made a grave error. His place in life, he said, was in Kfar Malal, near the earth.

Samuel was infirm. He was in and out of the hospital with heart problems, both before and after the war. During one of his postwar visits to his father's bedside, Sharon, after years of frustration and fear, could at last tell him that a grandchild was on the way.

On December 27, 1956, during the long negotiations over the IDF's deployment in the Sinai Desert, Sharon learned that he was the father of a baby boy. He rushed to the maternity ward in Jaffa, just south of Tel Aviv, to see his son, Gur. Four days later, his father died. Sharon was at his side hours before he passed away. His father hugged him and whispered final words in his ear.

Despite his long acquaintance with death, Sharon was only twenty-eight years old. He had hardly known his father as an adult. Since Arik was seventeen, they had not shared the same roof. Vera Scheinerman cared for her husband during his sickness, tending to his every need. On his last day, Samuel asked Vera to go back to the farm to bring him his will. Once she had gone, he felt himself expiring. He called a nurse to his side and asked her to pass his last words to his wife.

Sharon's professional life was tumultuous as well. The Mitla

Pass haunted him. Senior IDF officers grew cold when he entered the room. At a victory party organized by Ben-Gurion, Sharon was comforted by the fact that the prime minister still insisted he sit by his side, but he was disturbed by the blatant hostility of the IDF brass.

In September 1957, Sharon flew to England with his family to attend Camberley Staff College, where he took a yearlong command and staff course. Sharon lived in an on-campus dormitory and rented an apartment in London for Gali and ten-month-old Gur. Formally, the posting in Great Britain was part of his career track, but Sharon, aware that he had been sent by Dayan, understood that there was an element of exile to his new assignment.

Sharon applied himself to his studies, but in private he derided his instructors as medal-laden and unimaginative. He based much of his criticism on recent history. In the Suez War, he felt, the British forces had been clumsy, hesitant, and robotic.

Nonetheless, the year in England was like a balm for the overworked officer. He had been driving himself hard ever since he left school to form Unit 101. For the first time in four years he could relax from the temple-pounding stress of constant readiness. He took a break from politics and current events, enjoying well-poured ales in the officers' club, seeing movies and plays with Margalit, and walking in the snow with Gur. He even met Queen Elizabeth.

His return to the IDF was disappointing. Sharon, the first commander of the paratroopers, was chained to a desk. Lt. Gen. Chaim Laskov, newly promoted to chief of staff, may not have been damning in his report about Sharon's actions at the Mitla Pass, but he was certainly of no mind to further his meteoric rise. Appointed chief instructor of the IDF Infantry School, Sharon was charged with instilling the skills he had developed in battle in the army's young infantry recruits. Although he chafed at the posting, he had to stick it out. Laskov had assured him it was his only path to promotion. Shortly after his thirtieth birthday, Sharon earned his third brass leaf. The colonel woke each day in his own bed, at home, to a job he despised.

Ben-Gurion had had a hand in Sharon's appointment. Although he was troubled by Sharon's lack of discipline and the erratic truthfulness of his reports from the field, the prime minister revered his bravery and unconventional mind. But his admiration was guarded. At one point, the prime minister, who tended to see modern Israel with biblical eyes, remarked that the young officer was a kind of Yoav Ben-Tzruya—King David's chief warrior, who eventually defied the king's wishes for a treaty and stabbed his brother's slayer-cum-peacemaker to death.

Toward the end of 1958, Sharon was called to Ben-Gurion's office. The prime minister asked him whether he had "weaned himself of the habit of speaking untruth." Ben-Gurion wrote down Sharon's response: "Arik admitted there were several times he hadn't told me the truth, but he is weaned of this characteristic." Ben-Gurion liked the forthright answer. On the spot he told Sharon that he had his backing. Ben-Gurion, aware of Laskov's aversion to Sharon, advised him to take the posting at the infantry school and not to worry about the future. After the conversation, Ben-Gurion spoke with Chief of Staff Laskov, telling him that Sharon had "negative characteristics and blessedly positive ones. I'd like for him to be given a chance to right himself, because he is an important soldier."

Over the following years, Ben-Gurion's support was all that kept the axe from falling on Sharon's neck. He went to visit the prime minister regularly, often explaining his military philosophies to him at length. Ben-Gurion wrote in his diary: "The man's an original thinker. If he could steer clear of gossip and kick the habit of speaking untruth, he'd be an extraordinary military leader." Another time, Ben-Gurion wrote of Sharon, "There's some of [Orde Charles] Wingate in him—Wingate's morality notwithstanding."

Sharon held on to his staff position for a year before the inevitable transpired. He quarreled with his direct commander, Maj. Gen. Yossi Geva, who dismissed him from his post after an unexplained absence from a meeting. Although the two disagreed, and clashed about most everything, Sharon felt that the root of the animosity lay in resentment—Geva had been commander of the Givati Brigade while Sharon had led the celebrated paratroopers.

Ben-Gurion came to Sharon's aid again, persuading the chief

of staff to appoint him commander of the IDF Infantry School. In essence, another desk position. Sharon considered his three years away from the field and battle command posts an unduly imposed exile.

The rank-and-file soldiers in the infantry school revered Sharon, trading stories of the 101st. Sharon, introverted and angry, was unsparing with the troops, lashing out at will at those under him as he raised their level of combat readiness. Much of this behavior can be attributed to his frustration at having been barred from the IDF's fighting units.

During what he termed his "wasted" years, Sharon enrolled in Tel Aviv University Law School. In 1962, Lt. Gen. Zvi Tzur inherited Chaim Laskov's position as chief of staff. Sharon, in the middle of his studies, viewed the development with despair, all too aware that Tzur was determined to sink his career.

On May 2, 1962, Sharon was dealt a terrible blow. He was at home with Gur after a day spent together at the infantry school. It was dark, and Margalit, who was now a psychiatric nurse at the Health Ministry in Jerusalem, was late getting home. Suddenly he heard hesitant knocks on the door. His neighbor, Motti Hod, the Israeli Air Force commander, asked Sharon to step into the yard and then told him about the car accident and his wife's death.

"Despite all the years that have passed," Hod says,

I remember that sad day as if it was yesterday. You don't forget those types of moments. It was awful. The IDF personnel director . . . tracked me down and told me that Margalit had been killed in a car accident. Since he knew that we were very close neighbors with Arik and Margalit, and that Arik had persuaded us to move into the house next to him, he asked me to go over to Arik and tell him about the death of his wife.

I dropped everything and drove to Tzahala. Arik opened the door, and I said: "Arik, let's go out to the yard." We walked around the yard for a bit till I mustered strength and told him that Margalit had been killed. He took it very harshly, very, very harshly. I waited a couple of minutes for

him to digest the terrible news and then signaled the soldiers from the IDF Manpower Division, who were waiting
out on the street, to come in.

Margalit Sharon had been killed in the morning, on her way to
work. Driving the family car, she veered out of her lane on the way
up the second of the three hills leading to Jerusalem. A truck coming in the opposite direction slammed into her Austin head-on.
She was pronounced dead in Sha'arei Tzedek Hospital in Jerusalem.

Sharon was emotionless at the funeral. He read a eulogy for
his childhood love from a folded piece of paper, sorrow spreading
across his face but never cracking the calm veneer.

CHAPTER 13

A Second Marriage

SHARON, A CAREER SOLDIER USED TO SLEEPING IN THE FIELD AND seeing his son on weekends, suddenly had a motherless child. Gur, now five and a half years old, would not believe his father when he told him that his mother was gone forever. "She would never leave me," he said. Margalit's younger sister, Lily, a fixture in the Sharon house and Gur's favorite aunt, filled the void left by her sister.

Lily Zimmerman was born in 1937 in Transylvania, Romania, four years after her older sister. She immigrated to Israel at age ten and enrolled at the Mosensohn School along with her older siblings. Her parents stayed in Europe with her younger sisters, Olga and Yaffa, for several more years.

Lily met Arik soon after he and her older sister fell in love. Arik, for his part, acted like an older brother. Yossef Margalit, Sharon's neighbor from Kfar Malal, recalls Sharon inviting both sisters over for family dinners and holidays. The two always seemed happy and giggly around Arik, he says.

At the age of eighteen, Lily was drafted into the IDF. Sharon, pulling a few strings, got her into the paratrooper battalion, in a noncombat role. Although he had brought his sister-in-law to the unit, he was very correct in his dealings with her, even short. Lily couldn't see why he had to be so strict. At the time, she wondered why her beautiful sister had chosen him. Gradually, however, they grew close. Lily became part of the family, dividing her time between the base and the Sharons' home.

Discharged from the army at twenty, Lily wanted to stay in Tel Aviv. Her parents, in the northern bayside city of Haifa, lived an Orthodox lifestyle. She enrolled at the Avni Institute of Fine Arts in Tel Aviv and helped her sister care for Gur. It was during this period that Margalit died.

There was a change in Sharon after Margalit's death. He no longer spent nights at the base, choosing instead to come home to his son and sister-in-law. The army no longer dominated his attention. For the first time in his adult life, he invested the majority of his energy in his family. After her death, he found himself doing all the things Margalit had begged him to do during the harrowing years of the reprisal raids, only now it was with Lily. They went out to upscale steakhouses, spent time listening to good music and playing with Gur. The hardened and unapproachable Arik Sharon, son of the notoriously turtle-shelled Scheinermans, opened up entirely to Lily, speaking to her in a soft voice and sharing all with her. The two fell deeply in love. Lily became a mother to Gur.

Lily left her studies and took a job with the police. It was a far cry from the career she had dreamed of, but at least she utilized her skills, sketching the likenesses of wanted criminals. A year after Margalit's death, Arik and Lily married. Lily left her police job immediately, feeling it was only right that she devote her time to Gur.

Rumors swirled around Sharon after Margalit's sudden death. Lily explained the circumstances of her marriage to the *Hadashot* daily in September 1988:

> I married him because it was good for Gur. Today, I can say that I probably loved him already then. But love didn't decide it. The situation was such that we were two adults with a noble cause—to tend to a child that had lost his mother. Arik was a great father to Gur and to my two sons, may they live long lives. He was involved, kind, and good. He, already twenty-five years ago when it wasn't the norm, would wake up in the middle of the night to change and feed the babies. Most of the time he was in the army, but when he was at home, he took care of the kids. We really shared.

Lily was very different from her sister. Margalit had tended to blend into her surroundings. She waited long hours for Arik at home and suffered from spells of loneliness. Lily, a firebrand, was involved in, if not in control of, all aspects of her husband's military and political career. She dazzled at social events and served as

Sharon's adviser, waiting for him to emerge from meetings so that they could analyze the proceedings together.

The harmony he found at home became a source of strength for Sharon. During the tough times in his career, he would always return to the farm and to his family. Lily devoted her life to her husband. When asked by Sarit Yishai-Levy of *Hadashot* if she hadn't forsaken her own talents for the sake of Sharon's career, she said:

> I chose, and if the decision is by choice, then it's okay. I want to be available for Arik whenever he wants. If you're going to be in someone's shadow, then only Arik's. Besides, I don't see myself as part of his shadow. I see myself as completing him. That's my joy, my fun. Should I go try to find myself? I found myself a long time ago, at Arik's side. I'm his wife, full-time.

Lily tended to Arik. She chose his clothes and prepared his food. Over the years, her influence became dominant. She hand-picked his confidants and weighed in on all major decisions.

Sharon seemed to thrive on her devotion. "I love sitting with Lily, talking with Lily, eating with Lily," he told *Hadashot*.

> I place a lot of value on what she says. She has the unique capacity to grasp the slightest nuance. Same goes for people. She reads the papers before me and then guides my attention to things. She's much quicker than I am. It's ridiculous that people say she's my shadow. She has so much to offer in her own right. If I had to summarize our relationship in one sentence, I would say we have a real friendship.

As his new relationship flourished, his days in the IDF Infantry School dragged. He'd been there for three years, and with Zvi Tzur as chief of staff, there was no light at the end of the tunnel. At last, Ben-Gurion, now both prime minister and defense minister, pressed Tzur into promoting Sharon to a command position, in the Armored Corps—a traditional rung in the IDF ladder that led to the rank of general.

The shift from infantry to armor is complex. A commander needs to learn how the single unit works, its strengths and shortcomings, how combined units operate as a whole, and the intricacies of combat against other tanks, helicopters, specialized antitank troops, and Soviet-supplied armor. Sharon learned about tank warfare in theory and in practice. As opposed to the limited firepower of an infantry brigade, he now commanded a far more devastating force. After an acclimation period, Sharon was appointed commander of a reserve tank brigade.

Sharon's career took another turn for the better in late 1963 when the new prime minister, Levi Eshkol, appointed Yitzhak Rabin chief of staff. Ben-Gurion had grown particularly close to Rabin during his last term in office and had promised him the appointment. When he left office four months later, he passed the vow on to Eshkol. Not long after the nomination, Rabin went down to Kibbutz Sde Boker to visit Ben-Gurion on his birthday and thank him for the posting. Ben-Gurion asked a personal favor of Rabin. In his autobiography, *A Service Notebook*, Rabin explained that on a personal level he felt obliged to promote Sharon. In Rabin's final conversation with the defense minister, Ben-Gurion urged him to treat Sharon differently from his predecessors. The seven lean years had come to an end: In 1964, Rabin appointed Sharon Northern Command chief of staff.

"During my first week as IDF Chief of Staff," Rabin wrote,

> I called Arik to my office and said: "Everyone knows you're a great army man. Your problem is that there are those who claim you lack humanity. I don't know you well enough in a general perspective. I want you to advance, but I need to make sure that your accusers are not right. I'll appoint you to Chief of Staff of the Northern Command. If after a year of service, your direct commander, the OC Northern Command, says you acted like a man—you'll be promoted to general. Your test, then, is your ability to get along with your commanding officers."

OC Northern Command Avraham Yaffe accepted Sharon, aware of the cost—and the benefit—the man would bring. Arik and Lily moved north, into the vacant moshav home of "Zevele" Slutsky, who had served with Sharon in the 101st and the para- troopers, and who was abroad at the time in the service of the Mossad. That summer, on August 19, 1964, Lily gave birth to a baby boy, Omri.

Arik and Lily Sharon worried about Gur—how he would adjust to the new surroundings and to his new baby brother. But he set- tled in well, making new friends and excelling in school. His love of horseback riding, a necessary skill on the moshav, ensured his acceptance in his new rural surroundings, and for his ninth birth- day, his parents bought him a mare, which he rode every free minute he had. Sharon was ebullient. His military career was fi- nally back on track, and his personal life had never been better.

As the second in command in the tense northern sector, Sharon was given enormous responsibility by his friend and commander Avraham Yaffe. Syria, in an effort to erode the Jewish state's re- solve, used many of their fifteen thousand soldiers along the high plain of the Golan Heights to attack the residents of the Galilee below. Fishermen in the northeast part of the Kinneret (as the Sea of Galilee is locally known) were harassed by sniper fire, and farm- ers were prevented from getting to their fields. Artillery rounds were part of daily life. In a whirlwind of released energy, Sharon set to work safeguarding the roiling northern sector.

Sharon had his hands full. In early January 1965, Yasser Arafat's Fatah organization carried out its first terror attack in Israel, tar- geting Israel's national water carrier. Several months earlier, Syria had begun efforts to divert the Hatzbani, Wazani, and Banias rivers into Jordan. Israel made clear that the continuation of the project was an act of aggression that would be met with force. Sharon encouraged his troops to assert sovereignty over the agricultural lands near the border, and he responded with unprecedented force to Syrian attacks, hammering their bases with artillery rounds and tank fire. He enjoyed every moment of command under Yaffe, but in late 1964, Yaffe retired from the army. In his place, Rabin ap- pointed Maj. Gen. David Elazar, who immediately began restrain- ing Sharon and limiting his sphere of influence.

Sharon, helpless in the face of his new commander's hostility, decided to accompany his former commander, now in charge of Israel's Nature and Parks Authority, on an educational trip through eastern Africa. The two flew to Ethiopia, where they were supposed to learn about nature conservation. During their trip they tore through the deserts under the type of big sky seldom seen in Israel. At one point they grew disoriented and nearly died of thirst before circling around and finding the correct track back to civilization. When he returned to Israel, Sharon found that the Northern Command remained a hostile place. In a conversation with Rabin, Sharon asked for a new post. Rabin refused his request.

Sharon went back to his job under Elazar and waited for word from Rabin. Frustrated, he returned to his old pattern of unpredictable behavior, one minute lashing out at, the next laughing with, his soldiers and superior officers. His uncertain tenure under Elazar, marked by a lack of trust and conflicting security ideologies, finally came to a head in October 1965. Sharon retired to his home for three full months, drawing a salary and maintaining a colonel's rank but doing nothing more than seething in silence. During the day, he waited for a call from the general staff. Only when Gur came home from school was he able to put aside his bitterness as the two rode their horses through the Jezreel Valley's rolling hills of mustard grass and small oaks.

In January 1965, Chief of Staff Rabin released Sharon from his virtual house arrest. He called him to his Tel Aviv office and demanded an accounting for his ruined relationship with Elazar. Placing all of the blame on Sharon, Rabin chastised him for improper behavior and explained that yet again he would not receive a command position. To Sharon's surprise, at the close of the talk, Rabin informed him that he was appointing him chief of the General Staff Training Department and commander of a reserve battalion in case of war.

In his book, Rabin wrote that as far as he was concerned, Sharon had passed the test he had set for him during his service under Yaffe. Arik and Lily celebrated the promotion, inviting neighbors and friends over to their flower-filled house in Nahalal for a goodbye party before moving to the vicinity of IDF headquarters in Tel Aviv.

In February 1966, Colonel Sharon took command of the training department. Toward the end of the year, in November, another
son, Gilad, was born. Sharon's position as head of IDF training allowed him to emerge from the cloak of obscurity that had covered
him since the Suez War. The challenges he faced were tremendous. He was now in charge of drafting the army's codes of battle.
After a year in the new post, he had the general's crossed olive
branch and sword pinned to his shoulder. He was still not yet forty,
and his future looked promising.

CHAPTER 14

Fame at Abu Ageila

ON MAY 14, 1967, TWO MONTHS AFTER BECOMING A GENERAL, ARIEL Sharon attended Israel's nineteenth Independence Day celebrations. As army bands marched down a Jerusalem street, Sharon, in the grandstands, learned that Egyptian forces had begun moving toward the Suez Canal, a demilitarized area since Israel's withdrawal after the Suez War. By the following day it was clear that the entire Egyptian Army had been placed on war-level alert and that two full infantry divisions were rolling through the Sinai. Jordan and Syria had mobilized their militaries. Thus began the three-week wait that ended with the outbreak of war.

Sharon was relieved of his duty as chief of the General Staff Training Department and sent south to command the 38th Division, charged with stopping the Egyptians in the central Sinai sector in the event of war. Sharon drove to Camp Shivta in the sandy desert near Nitzana and began readying his troops. Many were reservists. They arrived in their own cars, dressed in civilian clothes, and began transforming themselves into soldiers.

On May 18, Egyptian chief of staff Muhammad Fawzi ordered U.N. observers out of the Sinai Peninsula and the Suez Canal area. On the twenty-second, Egyptian president Abdel Gamal Nasser closed the Strait of Tiran, sealing Eilat, which, as far as Israel was concerned, was a cause for war. By the end of May, Egypt had seven divisions in the Sinai. The radio was booming with the bombast of Jordanian, Syrian, and Egyptian leaders predicting victory in the coming conflict.

In Israel, wedged as it is between these three nations and the Mediterranean Sea, public opinion turned against Prime Minister and Defense Minister Levi Eshkol, who was seen as weak and hesitant. On May 26, he transmitted a radio address known as "the

Stuttering Speech." Sharon, near the Egyptian border, listened to the broadcast and found Eshkol disappointingly indecisive. In 2004, Col. Ami Gluska published a research paper for *Ma'arachot*, an IDF Department of History and Defense Ministry publication, that showed that while Prime Minister Eshkol clung defiantly to his reluctance to declare a preemptive strike, Sharon advised Chief of Staff Yitzhak Rabin to detain the Cabinet, announce a coup, and declare war in their stead.

Fear spread throughout the country. But among Sharon's men, many of whom had left home just days before, there was little time for worry. Sharon had them in the field, allowing breaks only for inspections and motivational chats. He kept discipline—not usually a word found in the reservist's lexicon—rock solid.

On May 23, Chief of Staff Rabin collapsed from the stress. On the twenty-fifth, after thirty-six hours in bed, he and Eshkol drove south to inspect the troops along the southern border. Eshkol was led to one of the divisions' war rooms, where Rabin and OC Southern Command Yeshayahu Gavish presented the IDF war plan.

The plan, dubbed "Atzmon," called for the IDF to take the Gaza Strip and small parts of the northern Sinai, as far as El Arish. The advance would force Egypt's hand, and they would withdraw their troops from the desert and open the strait. A second option presented to the prime minister was "Atzmon 2," which called for the IDF to continue west from El Arish, capturing a swath of territory that led to the entrance to the canal. At this point, no one even considered "Kardum," a shelved plan outlining the capture of the entire peninsula.

Sharon was stunned by the presentation made to the prime minister. He thought the plans cowardly and defeatist, betraying a lack of self-confidence among the IDF general staff and the country's leaders. When the chief of staff finished his presentation, Sharon asked Rabin for permission to speak. He directed his remarks at Eshkol. The incremental advance was a grave error, he said. No matter how much land they took, the international pressure to retreat would be the same. What Israel needed, what he was sure they could accomplish, was to crush the Egyptian Army and take the entire Sinai Peninsula.

The war room went silent. Eshkol and Rabin fumed, but said nothing. Only Sharon's old friend Yaffe spoke up in agreement. When the meeting ended, Eshkol asked Rabin and Sharon to stay behind. The prime minister castigated Sharon for his irresponsible plan.

Three weeks later, Sharon offered a replay in front of Eshkol and the rest of the general staff. This time he wasn't in such a minority. The legendary pilot Ezer Weizman, now heading the IDF operations branch, backed Sharon, as did several other generals. Eshkol, under immense pressure from the United States, Great Britain, and the Soviet Union not to initiate all-out war, made it clear that the international powers wanted peace in the region, and that Israel could not exist without outside support. After the meeting, Eshkol called Sharon impulsive and irresponsible.

Later in the day, Major General Sharon returned to Shivta and secluded himself in his command trailer. The boxy caravan was simply furnished: There was a rectangular table, a tall tin cabinet filled with canned food and stashed paperwork, a faucet, a water tank, a bar of soap, a small mirror, and a towel. Three carefully folded blankets covered two adjacent benches to form a makeshift bed where Sharon slept and left a windbreaker. The rest of his personal gear was stuffed into a backpack inappropriately small for a man his size. Sharon spent all of that night hunched over crowded topographical code maps rehearsing the parry and thrust of battle in his mind. By early morning he had drafted an independent, complex, and far-reaching plan for his division in the looming war.

Sharon's battle plan aimed to crush the Egyptian Army's primary fortification in the central sector: the Abu Ageila–Um-Katef complex and the smaller Kusseima fort twelve miles to the south. The main forts, Um-Shikhan and Abu Ageila, located fifteen miles west of the Israeli border, dominated the route to the Suez Canal. The fortified positions were built in the Soviet style. The southern side of the seven-mile-long position was secured by the steep sandstone cliffs of Mount Dalfa; the northern front was rendered impenetrable by three rolling sand dunes. In each of the folds in the earth, the Egyptians had dug trenches with concrete bunkers and machine-gun nests. The eastern flank was fenced with four miles of barbed wire, land mines, and trenches. The western Um-Shikhan region contained artillery batteries, which could strike at all attackers. The Egyptians guarded the complex with an infantry brigade, 83 tanks, 78 artillery guns, and a number of antiaircraft batteries.

Later in the day, an unexpected visitor stopped by Sharon's trailer—Member of the Knesset Moshe Dayan. Sharon pulled out his maps and detailed the plan he intended to pitch to Eshkol and Rabin. His division would circle north, on foot, through twelve miles of seemingly impassable sand dunes. Paratroopers on loan to his division would approach in helicopters and attack the artillery in the rear. Most of the division's tanks would pinch in from the east and northwest. His troops would attack at night, putting the ill-equipped Egyptians at a disadvantage. Ambushes would isolate the area.

MK Dayan did a lot of nodding during Sharon's presentation. At the end, Dayan asked whether, during the battle, he could ride with Sharon, clearing the air between them after ten years of tension and animosity. Sharon was happy to comply. On May 27, though, he welcomed a different Dayan to the division: The general's daughter, Yael, serving in the IDF's spokesman's office, had asked to accompany Sharon. He put her in staff officer Dov Sion's jeep. Only later, when the two got married, did Sharon reveal that he had been playing wartime matchmaker.

On June 1, 1967, Sharon learned along with the rest of the country that Israel had formed a broad unity government and Eshkol had surrendered his second post, as defense minister, to Dayan. The move lifted the spirits of the agitated IDF brass. On Friday, June 2, the Knesset's Foreign Affairs and Defense Committee convened a meeting with the IDF general staff. At the meeting, Sharon again presented his plan to take the Sinai in one fell swoop. This time, the defense minister accepted the plan immediately.

Dayan ordered all three Israeli divisions into attack mode, just as Sharon had advised, changing the Southern Command's war plans entirely. Moreover, it was decided that Israel had waited long enough: On June 5, 1967, at 0745 hours, Israel would launch air strikes against the air forces of Iraq, Syria, Jordan, and Egypt. Half an hour after the strikes, the armored divisions commanded by Sharon, Avraham Yaffe, and Yisrael Tal would cross into Sinai and break the back of the Egyptian defenses. Their goal: to destroy the majority of the Egyptian Army's forces and race to Sharm al-Sheikh to open the strait. By Saturday morning the Southern Command staff officers had drafted new war plans in accordance with Dayan's orders.

Sharon returned to Shivta to prepare. He sent Yoram, his driver, to Beersheba to buy three hundred flashlights with red, green, and blue lenses. He handed them out to the three infantry battalions that were slated to storm the trenches in Abu Ageila, explaining that the lights would mark the troops so the tank gunners could avoid hitting them as they made their way to the trenches.

On Friday, June 2, Yael Dayan returned to Tel Aviv. Since her father lived in the same neighborhood as the Sharon family, she knocked on their door and delivered Arik's regards to Lily. She saw the three Sharon boys in the yard and went to the middle son, Omri, and made small talk. When she told him she'd be going to see his father soon, in Shivta, Omri picked two flowers and handed them to the uniformed Dayan. He asked her to give them to his father. Throughout the war, Sharon kept them pressed in his personal papers as a lucky charm. Dayan also handed Lily a letter from Arik. He told her how much he loved her and that he would stay safe since he knew what a fantastic family he had waiting at home. Woven in between the lines of optimism, though, he also asked Lily to watch over the boys, come what may.

On June 4, the 38th Division was told that war would commence in the morning. Sharon called home and then prepared himself in his trailer, shaving, washing, and donning a fresh pair of fatigues. He got into his civilian car and led the division's staff officers to an intersection near Nitzana. Then he threw his pack into a jeep and met with the division's senior officers. The briefing ended late at night. Sharon, aware he would not be sleeping for the next few days, spread his blankets on the ground between two half-tracks, wrapped himself up in his windbreaker, and went straight to sleep.

Sharon was accompanied by an old friend, Maj. (Res.) Ze'ev Slutsky, who had served with Sharon in the 101st. Slutsky had left his covert Mossad posting abroad and returned to Israel when it was clear that war was imminent.

Yael Dayan woke Sharon, as instructed, at six-thirty in the morning. She asked him if he wanted a final taste of fresh food before moving on to C rations for the foreseeable future. Before setting off to fix eggs and tea, she noted that Sharon, after a night on the ground between greasy half-tracks, with battle looming, looked as fresh as though he'd spent the night resting between satin sheets.

At 7:14 in the morning, 183 Israeli warplanes took to the sky and attacked the unprepared Egyptian Air Force. Nearly two hundred of their planes, 70 percent of their air force, were destroyed on the ground. At 7:30, Sharon gave the order to mount up. Forty-five minutes later, they pushed the ignition buttons and headed west. His command half-track crossed the border at 10:37 A.M.

Sharon proceeded as planned. Two infantry battalions, a tank company, and the division's reconnaissance teams laid ambushes along all routes leading to Abu Ageila. As the 63rd Armored Battalion swept far to the north, toward the rear of the fortified area, a brigade of tanks stormed two east-facing frontal posts, taking them with relative ease by noon. The brigade, under the command of Mordechai Zipori, drew much of the Egyptians' attention.

At one in the afternoon, Sharon ordered Col. Kuti Adam to begin the wide sweep north, toward the rear of the fort, with his infantry brigade. His force was tasked with marching through the deep sand and then attacking, at dark, from the rear. The soldiers boarded civilian buses put at the disposal of the IDF to take them to the drop-off point. Sharon, not wanting them to forget where they were going, had the buses covered in mud, figuring it would get them in the right frame of mind. Before they left, he had gathered them together in a three-sided formation and explained that the fate of the war on the southern front rested on their shoulders: If they took Abu Ageila, the rest of the Sinai, all the way to the canal, would fall as one.

They rode until the sand threatened to trap the vehicles. They would cover the last twelve miles on foot, wading through the dunes, but skirting the front line of trenches. At ten at night, Colonel Adam reported that the troops were in place, waiting in silence.

Hours earlier, once dark had settled, Col. Danny Mat had been flown with the paratroop brigade to the Um-Shikhan area, where the Egyptian artillery batteries were placed. Sharon, internalizing Motta Gur's criticism of his conduct at the battle in Mitla Pass, where he had remained in the rear, ordered his half-track forward. At 9:52 P.M. he received radio confirmation that each of the forces was in place and ready to go. From the front he could see the Egyptian trenches and imagine Adam's forces lying in silence just beyond them. On the division-wide frequency he told all commanders that in a matter of minutes they would begin the most complex battle the IDF had ever fought.

At ten minutes to eleven he told the commander of the artillery battery, Ya'akov Aknin, to open fire. "Make it shake!" he said. Aknin, who would fight by Sharon's side in the Yom Kippur War as well, had the last word. "Oh, it'll shake," he said. Over the next twenty minutes, Abu Ageila–Um-Katef was pounded by six thousand shells. Flares lit the sky an eerie white. Sharon moved his half-track next to Aknin so the two could communicate by yelling over the deafening decibels of the guns. Mostly they just watched in awe. "What fire," Aknin said. "I've never seen hell like this before."

After fifteen minutes of shelling, Sharon ordered Colonel Mat and the paratroopers, who had taken cover behind a sand dune near Um-Shikhan, to charge the Egyptian artillery forces. That first step in the multipronged attack would allow the infantry brigade under Colonel Adam the luxury of charging fortified trenches without having to contend with the steel rain of artillery. Adam's forces shone the colored flashlights as a sign to the tanks behind them and the troops to either side of them.

Obstacles arose. Zipori's armored brigade, charged with driving a wedge between the two halves of Um-Katef, was stuck in a minefield. Sharon felt the fog of war swirling through the radio as the commanders tried locating the mine-clearing vehicles, which had last been seen several miles to the rear and were currently nowhere to be found.

The setback was potentially devastating. The Egyptians had seventy tanks inside the fortified area. If Zipori didn't move his tanks through the minefield quickly, his brigade would be trapped and the entire raid would crumble. The predicament rattled Sharon. He urged Zipori—a bitter rival during the Lebanon War— to solve the problem as quickly as possible.

Sharon ordered his combat engineer battalion to the area to painstakingly clear a lane for the Sherman tanks. Within half an hour the tanks were storming ahead in a coordinated pincer strike with the 63rd Armored Battalion. Together, they wiped out the Egyptian tanks.

In the middle of the battle, OC Southern Command Gavish radioed Sharon to ask whether Avraham Yaffe's division could pass them by as they engaged the Egyptians and freed the path to the central Sinai. Sharon agreed, immediately clearing all supply trucks from the road and sending a jeep ahead to lead the armored division safely past the fighting and onto the correct route. Sharon stood on his half-track and watched the thousands of lights rumble through the desert.

Sharon declared victory at three in the morning, but, in fact, the battles raged until ten. By noon, the soldiers under his command were asleep in their tanks, half-tracks, and trucks. The spine of the Egyptian defense of the Sinai had been broken; the battle had been brilliantly executed, the route to the strait opened to Israeli armor. The division had accomplished their task, but the price had been dear: 32 Israeli soldiers were killed and 140 wounded.

The Egyptians suffered far worse, losing nearly a thousand men. Once word traveled to the nearby fort at Kusseima, the soldiers there detonated their supplies and fled. Sharon walked through the ranks, shook soldiers' hands in appreciation, and organized the evacuation of the wounded. There was no time to waste. Sharon called Gavish and asked for his next assignment, eager to continue west before the enemy had a chance to regroup. Gavish ordered him to corral the troops and have them sleep, eat, replenish gear and gas, and wait.

Sharon woke early in the morning on Wednesday, June 7, the third day of what Israelis call the Six Day War. After breakfast he received orders to chase and destroy the fleeing 6th Division of the Egyptian Army, due south of his position.

A small force under the command of deputy brigade commander Mordechai Ben-Porat tailed the fleeing column of hundreds of tanks, trucks, and armored personnel carriers. Sharon ordered Ben-Porat to stay on the Egyptians, pestering them with fire, while he laid an ambush south of Nahal. Sharon's division began a 120-mile sprint through the desert.

According to the plan, Sharon's troops would beat the 6th Division to Nahal and ambush them as they emerged from the narrow mountain pass leading out of the city. At the same time, the 38th Division's infantry troops, in half-tracks and jeeps, would attack from the rear. Sharon ordered his troops to hold their fire until the Egyptian tanks were within two hundred yards of them. At two in the afternoon Sharon rode south, sweating in his half-track as the division raced toward Nahal, their treads kicking up a giant dust cloud.

Shortly after midnight, the division's reconnaissance company, charged with leading the half-blind tanks and half-tracks, got stuck in a minefield. While waiting for the route to open, Sharon heard over the radio that the paratroopers had taken Jerusalem's Old City, home to the Western Wall, Judaism's holiest site. Since they were stuck in place anyway, Sharon celebrated with an impromptu feast of canned beef, vegetables, chocolate, and a bottle of whiskey one of his officers had taken from the Egyptian base.

The other officers sharing the feast, sitting on the floor and passing the chocolate and whiskey, had no idea that Sharon was suffering inside. During all his years as commander of the paratroopers, he had always dreamed of liberating the holy places. Now, as he listened to the familiar sandpaper voices of the paratroopers over the radio, picking out friends and acquaintances by call names, listening to them describe in emotion-choked voices how they raised the flag over the Temple Mount, jealousy curdled his heart. The commander of the paratroopers was Motta Gur, his sworn foe ever since the battle at Mitla Pass.

Sharon spread a few blankets on the ground and, with both elation and envy coursing through him, fell asleep. The next morning, June 8, he ate breakfast off a topographical map, rehearsing the day's battle plans. (Even under the pressing demands of battle, Sharon did not skip meals, and it was starting to show. Once full-bodied, he was now obese.)

In the afternoon Sharon sprang his trap. As the Egyptian division approached the pass, four Israeli warplanes dropped napalm on them, turning parts of the convoy into burning steel death traps. The rest of the fleeing division fell straight into Sharon's ambush, strategically positioned beyond a decline on either side of the route.

Sharon's division turned the flatland south of Nahal into a killing field of fire, twisted steel, and charred bodies. Hundreds of Egyptian soldiers abandoned their vehicles and were gunned down with ease. Sharon watched the battle unfold from the top of a mountain pass. The fighter pilots dropped their fourth and final load. As they prepared to head back to Israel, they spotted Sharon, dipped low over his head, and greeted him with a waggle of their wings.

The pilots were not the only ones who had spotted Sharon. Minutes later, six Egyptian tanks opened fire on the Israeli commander's position. Sharon leaped out of his jeep and jumped to safety in a crippled tank.

The battle was over in five hours, the Egyptian division demolished. The remaining Egyptian troops either fled through the desert or surrendered. Sharon drove down to the killing field and felt the inferno of burning steel in the desert. Now and again the heat set off an explosive round.

Suddenly, a long burst of fire came his way. A group of Egyptian soldiers had been hiding in the bushes. But the thick black smoke made him an elusive target. Sharon returned fire along with his staff officers, silencing the Egyptian guns.

Sharon turned back toward the Egyptian base in Nahal. The path revealed postbattle sights of fleeing soldiers and scattered bodies. Sharon nonetheless decided to stop at the base, remembering how, during the Suez War, he had found homemade beef jerky at an Egyptian base. This time, he was greeted by dozens of dead bodies. He left the base in a hurry and continued to the open country beyond the base, where he established the division command headquarters before crashing on a foldable field bed. A flapping canvas tent, tied to two half-tracks, shaded him.

Anguish made its way through the Israeli rank and file. What they had seen in the killing field beneath Nahal preyed on the soldiers' minds. Even Sharon, who had drafted the deadly ambush plan, felt dejected. The next day, he flew to Tel Aviv for a general staff meeting, where he met Lily. She asked what was wrong; his eyes lacked their usual confidence. Sharon told his wife that he had seen many dead people, and that it had been his worst day as a soldier.

Sharon moved the divisional HQ farther into the desert, fleeing the smell of ripening death. Sharon's trailer was brought down from Nitzana, and the division, having moved to the Bir Gafgafa area, began to adjust to the usual drone of military rhythms in a new and barren place. Yael Dayan returned to Tel Aviv for a few days' leave. She asked Sharon if he wanted her to bring something back. "A helicopter-length sausage and a chunk of Camembert" was the reply.

Several days later Defense Minister Dayan, operations chief Ezer Weizman, air force commander Motti Hod, OC Southern Command Yeshayahu Gavish, and deputy operations chief Rechavam Ze'evi visited central Sinai. Over maps at the division's HQ, it was clear to all that the battle Sharon had commanded at Abu Ageila would go down in IDF history as one of the most complex and brilliant battles fought by the young state.

A fleet of foreign reporters arrived in the generals' wake. Sharon escorted them to a large military tent and answered questions patiently. An American journalist asked Sharon how it was that the IDF was able to defeat seven Arab armies in six days of war. Sharon responded with a story from an Israeli jail. Captive Syrian officers, he said, had asked Egyptian peers they met behind bars how the mighty Egyptian Army could have lost to the Jews. "The Israelis don't play by the rules," the Egyptian officer had replied. "There's your answer," Sharon said to the journalist.

Chief of Staff Rabin called Sharon to Tel Aviv and put him in charge of IDF deployment in the Sinai, the Egyptian POW situation, and the governance of the occupied areas. On June 18, Sharon was at last granted leave to see his family in Tel Aviv. He folded his blankets, packed his little knapsack and put it in his car, and boarded a helicopter, along with Yael Dayan and Omri's pressed flowers.

Sharon asked the pilot to fly toward El Arish and then to drop down low over the coast. Dayan sat next to him. "We sat together and looked at the view beneath us as it appeared from the open helicopter door," she wrote.

> On the way—Mount Libni, El Arish, the palm trees on the beach, the white sands of Rafah, the camps near Gaza, the beauty of the empty beach and the dunes—Arik tried to yell over the noise of the helicopter, making sweeping motions with his hands, pointing out the view, but he had to write his sentiments in a note: "All of this is ours," he said, smiling like a child. I wanted so badly to tell him that now I know what the words "true leader" and "glorious commander" mean, and I understand that special magic that instills confidence and drives people to risk all at his command.

In Tel Aviv, the two drove in silence toward the neighborhood they shared. At the entrance to the Tzahala neighborhood, Arik spotted Lily. He jumped out of his car and hopped into hers. She put her head on his shoulder. At that moment, as far as they were concerned, the war had ended.

ISRAEL AFTER THE SIX DAY WAR

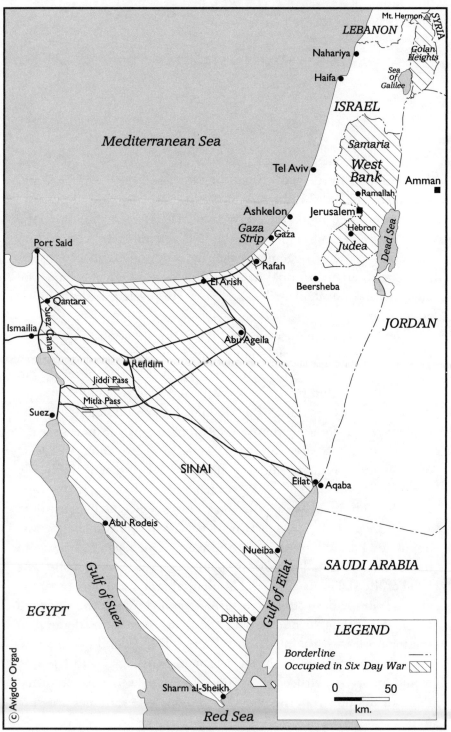

LEBANON

Mt. Hermon

SYRIA

Nahariya

Golan Heights

Haifa

Sea of Galilee

ISRAEL

Mediterranean Sea

Samaria

West Bank

Tel Aviv

Amman

Ramallah

Ashkelon

Jerusalem

Gaza Strip

Gaza

Hebron

Dead Sea

Judea

Rafah

El Arish

Beersheba

Port Said

Qantara

JORDAN

Ismailia

Suez Canal

Abu Ageila

Refidim

Jiddi Pass

Mitla Pass

Suez

SINAI

Eilat

Aqaba

Abu Rodeis

Nueiba

SAUDI ARABIA

Gulf of Suez

Gulf of Eilat

EGYPT

Dahab

LEGEND

Borderline

Occupied in Six Day War

0   50

km.

Sharm al-Sheikh

Red Sea

© Avigdor Orgad

CHAPTER 15

Gur

ARIK SHARON RETURNED A HERO OF THE SIX DAY WAR. HIS NAME, previously relegated to late-night war stories, was now all over the papers and mentioned on every street. He was the darling of the press corps. His adversaries on the IDF general staff accused him of using the war to become a celebrity, purposely failing to distinguish between operational necessities and personal ambition. The criticism did not dent Arik's euphoria. He reveled in the public's admiration.

The first three months after the war was a period of unbridled national optimism. Israel had taken the Sinai Peninsula from Egypt, the Golan Heights from Syria, and the Old City of Jerusalem from Jordan, including the Western Wall, Judaism's holiest spot. In six days of war the country had doubled and redoubled its size. Israel's two-year-long economic recession snapped. Some saw the return of the holy sites to Jewish hands, after two thousand years of occupation, as divine authorization of Herzl's fantastical scheme.

At work, Sharon sneaked away from his desk often, taking long trips through the newly captured territories. Once he had acquired a firm grasp of the area, a two-stage plan to control the heavily populated Palestinian region of the West Bank began to emerge in his mind. The initial part of the plan was easily accomplished. As head of the IDF's instructional branch, Sharon moved many of the army's training bases to the eastern, occupied side of the so-called Green Line. The second part of the plan—civilian settlement in the territories—was already on his mind, but beyond his reach so long as he wore a uniform. He reasoned that facts on the ground would fortify Israeli leaders in their hours of weakness, allowing them to stand firm in the face of inevitable international pressure to cede the territories.

His home life was bliss. He spent quality time with Lily, played with Omri, now three, and Gilad, nearly a year old, and went horseback riding often with his eldest son, eleven-year-old Gur. He rode behind him, watching his straight back and proudly observing his skills as a rider. In his autobiography, *Warrior*, Arik writes that Gur, a strikingly good-looking boy, had become a leader among his peers. He loved watching as other children instinctively circled around his son.

On October 4, 1967, the day before Rosh Hashanah, the Jewish New Year, Arik was sitting alone in his bedroom, talking on the phone, wishing his friends a happy new year, while Gur played with a neighbor boy in an adjacent room. At nine in the morning, Gur popped into the bedroom to tell his father that he and his friend were heading out to the yard. He snapped a playful salute and scurried out the door. Two minutes later, the crack of a rifle shot shattered the suburban quiet. Sharon heard a thud, followed by a shrill cry.

He dropped the phone and ran to the yard. A horrific scene awaited him: Gur was lying on the ground, bleeding from a bullet hole in his face, near his eye. An antique ornamental rifle that the Sharon family displayed on the wall was lying next to the child. The smell of gunfire hung in the air. Gur's friend stood nearby, pale and shocked. Omri and Gilad looked on from a few feet away.

Sharon picked Gur up in his arms and ran to the car. It was not in its usual spot. Lily had taken it for a pre-holiday shopping trip. He ran to his neighbor's house, but Motti Hod, the commander of the Israeli Air Force, wasn't there. He ran out into the street. Screaming, he flagged down a passing car. He asked to be taken to the nearby medical clinic. There, the doctor told them not to waste another moment, but to drive straight to the hospital emergency room.

In *Warrior*, Arik wrote that as someone who had seen many fatal wounds, he was all too aware of the hopeless nature of his son's injury. As soon as he saw his limp body on the backyard grass, he knew he had lost him. But like any father, he wanted to believe in a miracle. He ran back to the car, climbed into the backseat, and held Gur in his lap, his shirt soaking up his son's blood. The ride seemed interminable. By the time they reached the hospital, Gur had died in his arms.

Lily Sharon spoke publicly about the matter once:

I went to town to buy presents for my mother-in-law and
the children. The only thing I had time to buy was a track
suit for Gur. Nowadays, all kids have track suits, but back
then it was a dream come true. I realized I was running
late, so I called home to tell Arik, because I knew he had to
go to the base for a New Year's toast. The telephone was
constantly busy. I called one of the neighbors and asked
them to get hold of Arik. She asked me: "Lily, where are
you?" I said: "In town." She said: "You don't know?" I said:
"Know what?" She said: "Gur's hurt. Lily, they took him to
Tel Hashomer hospital." I drove like a madwoman. The
whole time I prayed he had hurt his finger. That it was
something inconsequential. I made it to the hospital and
asked to see Gur Sharon. They said: "That's not possible."
They asked me who I was and I said: "His mother." It just
came out spontaneously. They said: "You can't see him." I
asked why not and then they took me to a room with a doctor and told me.

It happened one minute after I left the house. I
promised him I'd be right back and then I'd take him to get
a haircut. I was sure that I'd come home and he would
jump into my arms as soon as he saw the track suit. He really wanted that suit. All of a sudden, you fully understand
what people mean when they say their world went black. I
couldn't stand the sunlight, couldn't stand the fact that I
was enjoying the light and he wasn't. I lost half a year of my
life. Gilad was eleven months old and I have no recollec-
tion of his development during that period. And Arik, he
never got over it. He just learned to live with it.

In response to the journalist's question about whether Gur had
been shot with one of Sharon's guns, Lily said:

In addition to the pain and the tragedy, there was the vi-
cious gossip. He wasn't killed by one of Arik's weapons.
This was just after the Six Day War. Arik had gotten a few

150-year-old rifles from one of his soldiers as a present. They were rusty old muzzle-loaders, but Gur liked them. He asked us to hang them up in his room as decorations. On the day of the tragedy, one of the neighbors' kids came over. He was a known troublemaker. He took the rifle off the wall. He brought the gunpowder over. It took just moments for Gur to die. It happened when all of my children were within three square feet. Gilad was in his crib and Omri was standing next to Gur. It was a miracle all three of them weren't killed.

On October 8, 1967, the morning after the holiday, the daily newspaper *Yedioth Ahronoth* published an article about the tragedy. It made no mention of the other boy, placing all responsibility on Gur. Sharon, unable to abide that depiction, demanded an in-depth police investigation. He hired Shmuel Tamir, the lawyer who had represented Meir Har-Zion. Sharon asked Tamir to ensure that the police conducted a thorough investigation. The police found that the children had put metal bits and gunpowder in the weapon.

Shmuel Tamir, in his autobiography, *Son of This Land,* recounts his role in the investigation:

> In his anguish and pain, Arik came to me with a request: "Gur was taught from the dawn of his days about guns. He knew he wasn't allowed to touch them and he never played with them. I'm sure he didn't shoot himself by accident. I'm certain it was the older kid who shot him by accident. I don't want to sue anyone. But I do want the police report to be made public and for the police to be convinced that Gur did not fire the gun . . ." I agreed to his request. I spent a month going over the details of the case, even studying the ballistic reports. According to the facts I presented, the police accepted Arik's version of events.

Gur's friend's family has a very different account of those tragic moments. They agree that the boy (today married with children) was the first to take hold of the gun, but they contend that

Gur grabbed the rifle seconds before it was fired to see what was wrong, and that while he peered down the barrel, he mistakenly pulled the trigger. The boy's family says, "There were all kinds of weapons in the Sharon house after the Six Day War," and "It was easy for Arik and Lily to blame the other kid who was there at the time of the accident." Longtime residents of the neighborhood attest to a bitter relationship between the two families ever since the accident. Sharon never forgave the boy and confronted his mother and stepfather, blaming their son for Gur's death. At one point, the boy's stepfather (his biological father was killed in the War of Independence) sent a letter of complaint to the IDF's chief of staff regarding Sharon's behavior.

The loss left Sharon broken. He wanted to bury Gur next to his mother, Margalit, in the Kiryat Shaul cemetery, just several hundred yards from his home, but the *hevra kadisha,* the religious authorities charged with burial ceremonies for Jews in Israel, could not grant him the space on such short notice. Distraught, Sharon called his close friend Shlomo Goren, the IDF's chief rabbi. His connections with the religious authorities straightened the matter out. Rabbi Goren, at the cemetery to make sure that his request had been followed in full, stood over Margalit's grave and told Sharon that she had taken Gur back to her.

The funeral was arranged in a hurry. Under Jewish law, the body had to be buried prior to the beginning of the holiday that evening. Before the funeral procession began, Sharon asked to look at his son one last time, alone. He remembered how he'd seen Gur last, smiling playfully as he saluted him in his bedroom. He asked for a military car to carry his son to his grave.

The radio announcement drew a crowd of thousands, come to console the general in his hour of need. One specific image stands out in Sharon's memory: As the procession began its mournful pass through the hospital's gate, a man Sharon recognized, but did not yet know, appeared. Menachem Begin, the bespectacled, square-jawed leader of the Gahal Party, stood at the side of the road. Arik watched him through the window and never forgot the look of pain on his face.

Half an hour later, as he stood over his son's open grave, Sharon recalled a terrible moment from five and a half years before. He remembered how, just a few feet away, he had promised his wife, as they laid her in the ground, that he would watch over their son.

Sharon had been dealt a crippling blow. Desperate thoughts chased him twenty-four hours a day. His mind replayed the chain of events in loops. The seven days of mourning were unbearable. Ze'ev Slutsky and the other men from the 101st and the paratroopers did not leave his side for the entire shivah.

Afterward, he slipped into a deep melancholy. His friends could not bring him comfort. "We were very worried about Arik in those days," one of them says, "because after Gur's death he simply could not be consoled. Luckily, Lily was by his side. She gave him the strength to survive and to carry on." Sharon tried to drown his grief in work. But as soon as he came home to the house in the Tzahala neighborhood of Tel Aviv, he was hit by waves of sorrow, emitted by every object and wall. He would regain his calm during those hours by talking to Lily, at length and about anything. When they talked about Gur, both of them would weep.

Sharon organized horse races in Gur's memory for years, but he never spoke publicly about his fallen son until January 2003, thirty-six years after that dreadful morning. He had just secured his second term as prime minister when he agreed to speak with Rafi Reshef, the host of a popular news program on Israeli TV's Channel 2.

At the start of the interview, Reshef showed the seventy-five-year-old prime minister a photo album. There were shots of his father, Samuel, his mother, Vera, his sister, Dita, and his three sons, Gur, Omri, and Gilad. The pictures were shown on the screen before the camera settled back on Sharon's stormy features. "With your permission, I'd like to talk about a specific picture that touched me deeply," Reshef said. "The one of your firstborn, Gur. He looks like a charming child."

"Yes," Sharon answered, "he was charming and he was uniquely charismatic, a real leader, very talented, a great horseback rider. He participated in many riding contests. He was eleven when he was killed. It wasn't from an accidental discharge; he was shot by another child."

RESHEF: From a bullet accidentally fired by another child?

SHARON: Yes. He lost his mother, my first wife, Margalit, whom we called Gali. She was killed at a very young age in a car accident on the way to Jerusalem.

RESHEF: She was twenty-nine.

SHARON: She was very talented. She achieved a lot in her field as a psychiatric nurse. Before she died, at a very young age, she already served as chief supervisor.

Quiet. The camera rests on Sharon's face. It looks as though his mind is drifting back in time. The interviewer does not intervene, waiting for Sharon to break the silence. "That boy really was very special," he said at last. "Maybe the most terrible aspect of this whole thing was, ah, the morning he was killed. I was at home and suddenly I heard a shot. I went outside and saw him lying there next to his two brothers, Omri and Gilad. I held him in my arms and waited for someone to take me to the hospital. He died like that, in my arms. He was shot in the head. He really had no chance."

Another silence, and again the prime minister speaks first. "Of course," he said, "I have many memories of hiking and traveling with him. He really was a special child. It's very interesting how so many years have passed since he was killed on the eve of Rosh Hashanah and still, even though we never announce any memorial, his friends come. Still, his school friends come. He was such an accomplished child."

RESHEF: Is it a cliché to say that time heals the pain?

SHARON: Look, this type of pain has no cure. At first you are struck thousands of times a minute. You, ah, you say to yourself, What would have happened had I done this? What would have happened had I done that?

RESHEF: Is there a feeling of guilt?

SHARON: No, not guilt. You know, you debate yourself. Afterward it continues to strike at you all of the time. If you ask me, there isn't one day that I don't remember it. But when you are busy doing things—and I don't know what it is like for those who aren't busy and who wallow in their bereavement—but when you are busy creating things, it helps you overcome.

RESHEF: There are people who never overcome their loss, certainly not such a sudden loss. In your case is it a personality issue or a decision you made?

SHARON: To a great extent it has to do with personality. It's not that it doesn't hurt—you see that it hurts—but I have the ability to overcome very hard things.

CHAPTER 16

Tacit Agreement

SHARON REMAINED IMMERSED IN MILITARY AFFAIRS, BUT MELANCHOLY came calling often and unannounced. Those who knew him witnessed a more contemplative, introspective, and levelheaded man. He kept a hoe and a watering can in the trunk of his car. Each time he happened past the Jerusalem cemetery where his wife and firstborn were buried, he would water the graveside flowers and turn the earth.

A war of attrition sparked and simmered along Israel's borders with Egypt and Jordan and, in a more limited way, from the postwar period until August 1970, near the shared borders with Syria, in the Golan Heights, and Lebanon, in the Galilee. In the Sinai, the war of attrition took the form of sporadic small arms and artillery fire on Israeli patrols, as well as Egyptian Army raids on Israeli positions along the Suez Canal. The eastern front, along the border with Jordan, was plagued by frequent infiltrations and terror attacks. All told, 721 Israelis lost their lives during the war of attrition, and thousands were injured. Over the course of the eighteen-month war, the IDF retaliated with 5,270 operations, killing 10,000 Egyptian, 500 Syrian, and 300 Jordanian soldiers and 1,800 Palestinian terrorists and militiamen.

In January 1968, Chief of Staff Yitzhak Rabin retired and accepted the post of Israeli ambassador to the United States. Haim Bar-Lev, Rabin's deputy, was promoted over Chief of Operations Ezer Weizman, a personal friend of Sharon's. Rabin consulted with Sharon about the appointment and learned that despite his friendship with Weizman, Sharon thought Bar-Lev the better man for the position. As chief of staff, Bar-Lev's first mission was to secure the territory Israel had taken in the war—more than four times the country's initial size.

In early 1968 the general staff considered a number of options for deployment in the Sinai. As chief of the General Staff Training Department, Sharon favored securing the southern sector with light patrols and surveillance along the canal, and armored brigades set five to fifteen miles in the rear. In that way, he argued, Israel had a mobile force that could respond to infiltrations in a hurry, but was situated beyond the reach of Egyptian artillery. The Israeli force could adapt itself to a variety of Egyptian attack modes.

Bar-Lev disagreed. He decided to entrench Israel's forces on the banks of the canal, arguing that only a massive force along the water could guarantee Israeli dominance over the canal's eastern bank. Politics played a part in his decision. A massive Israeli force sent a clear message: Israel rules the peninsula in its entirety and, like the Egyptian forces sitting opposite them, has control over the canal. The Israeli chain of forts along the canal was known as the Bar-Lev Line.

Sharon accepted Bar-Lev's decision, but incessantly hounded the chief of staff to change his mind, calling Bar-Lev's concept of defense stupid and dangerous. During meetings, most of the general staff sided with Bar-Lev. Although only he and Maj. Gen. Yisrael Tal openly disagreed with the chief of staff, Sharon believed that many of the other generals simply favored promotion over open dissent. Sharon told his friends he pitied the IDF generals who labored in the service of other people's opinions.

Bar-Lev, aware of Sharon's support in the days leading up to his nomination, tried to avoid a confrontation, but Sharon was relentless, bringing up the issue at every general staff meeting. Sharon labeled the difference of opinion a "battle between originality and stagnancy"; Bar-Lev called it a "battle between recklessness and deliberation." Soon their feud was carried in the papers and debated over the airwaves. As far as Bar-Lev was concerned, taking the matter public was a violation of trust. Senior officers fingered Sharon as the culprit.

Their dispute came to a head in April 1969. After Maj. Gen. Avraham Adan had built the first few forts, Bar-Lev convened the general staff to discuss the escalating violence along the southern border. Bar-Lev, with Defense Minister Dayan in attendance, called Sharon out, accusing him of leaking the disagreement to the press and intentionally spreading panic among the public. He had no loyalty to his peers, Bar-Lev said. Sharon responded venomously, saying that the Bar-Lev Line was the reason so many soldiers had lost their lives near the canal, and that terrible mistakes of judgment had never been answered for. As far as leaks were concerned, he said, "The one who's running around talking about generals in the press and with ministers is first and foremost the chief of staff and no one else."

Carmit Gai documented the chief of staff's response in *Bar-Lev*:

Ever since I've known the IDF there have been mistakes, blunders, and glaring errors. Since Arik raises the issue [of mistakes], I recall two of his that I wouldn't exactly take pride in: the seventeen dead [soldiers] in Qalqilya and the battle at the Mitla Pass. And still, as far as I know, no personal conclusions about Sharon have been drawn. I don't remember IDF officers using mistakes to attain personal gain. In this forum there's no need for me to waste verbiage and explain. Arik, except for you, no one else is smiling, and that's good enough for me.

At this point Dayan interjected and put the discussion back on course.

Two days later the forum convened again. Bar-Lev announced that "the topic of our discussion is how officers, particularly of the upper echelon, should comport themselves when discussing decisions that they think are mistaken." As soon as he opened the forum to comments, OC Southern Command Yeshayahu Gavish and OC Northern Command David Elazar lashed out at Sharon. They accused him of dereliction of his duties as chief of the General Staff Training Department. Instead of concentrating on the tasks at hand, they charged, he spent all of his time tinkering with internal IDF politics, undermining the authority of the chief of staff, and manipulating the press to serve his own purposes.

Sharon pushed his chair back and got up in the middle of Gavish's comments, saying he had been under the impression that the point of the meeting was to debate the pros and cons of the Bar-Lev Line, not to sit for a trial by his peers. Moshe Dayan interjected. "This is not a courtroom . . . this is a meeting of the general staff, a body charged with discussing many different matters."

SHARON: I have no intention in taking part in this type of discussion.

DAYAN: You're not obligated; you can just shut up.

SHARON: I need to leave the meeting.

DAYAN: I'm asking you to sit down. As far as I and the chief of staff are concerned, a discussion on how to voice criticism is completely warranted. You see no reason to take part in the discussion and voice an opinion? Don't say a thing. This is a general staff meeting, and you cannot just get up and leave.

Sharon sat back down, saying that if the staff meeting continued to deal with these matters, they'd have to do so without him. Silence lingered for several seconds before Gavish started up exactly where he'd left off. By the time Gavish finished his first sentence, Sharon was out of his chair again.

As he reached the door, Dayan called out, ordering him back to his seat. Sharon stormed out, slamming the door. Major General Elazar said, "I see no reason, other than the 'Sharon Legend,' which I denounce, that he should sit in judgment over us."

Sharon did not show up for the following week's staff meeting. Two days later he received a call from the IDF's personnel department. The secretary wanted to clarify some procedural issues concerning his retirement. Sharon, not yet aware that Bar-Lev had fired him and appointed his former deputy in his place, said he had no intention of leaving the army.

Once again, Sharon, for hardly the last time, felt he was being singled out. He went to Dayan hoping he could change Bar-Lev's mind. Dayan tried coaxing Bar-Lev, but the chief of staff was resolute. Sharon appealed to Prime Minister Golda Meir. She made it clear that she had no intention of intervening.

After the meeting with Meir, Sharon understood that with Rabin and Ben-Gurion out of the picture, he was likely to find himself thrown out of the army in disgrace, unless he could find a way to make a graceful leap from uniform to the Knesset. With a general election looming, he hastened to meet with childhood friend Yosef Sapir, a farmer from Petah Tikva who had been friendly with Samuel Scheinerman and was one of the heads of the right-wing Liberal Party. As a child, Sharon used to visit Sapir in his orange orchards. Formally, Major General Sharon, like all Israeli generals at the time, was a Mapai Party member. Although there was no policy dictating that all of the IDF top brass align themselves with Mapai, it was virtually impossible to ascend to the top ranks without joining the country's dominant political party.

Sharon asked Sapir whether Gahal, a unification of the Liberal and Herut parties, the primary opposition to Mapai, would consider placing him in a top position on their Knesset list. Sapir arranged a meeting with Herut leader Menachem Begin. In July 1969, just before the hundred-day deadline for adding candidates' names to Knesset lists, Sharon met Begin in Jerusalem's King David Hotel.

There was no chemistry between the urbane gentleman with the European manners and the country general from Kfar Malal. Begin spoke at length about the chances of the Opposition in the coming election without ever promising Sharon so much as a seat in the Knesset. Sharon, a political rookie, proposed the obvious—that Begin use his status as a war hero. At the end of the meeting, the two agreed to cooperate in the future, and Begin ordered cognac to toast their partnership.

The next day's headlines carried the news: MAJ. GEN. SHARON JOINS GAHAL. In the left-wing camp, which had held the majority and formed each government since Israel's inception, the talk of the day revolved around Sharon and the broken taboo. Before Sharon, the path from the upper echelons of the IDF to the top government offices was well trodden, but it always led straight to the socialist, left-leaning parties.

The Labor bloc's fears were compounded by the fact that Prime Minister Meir was most vulnerable on her lack of military knowledge—so much so that Finance Minister Pinchas Sapir, in Washington at the time of the announcement, called Chief of Staff Bar-Lev and implored him to find a spot for Sharon in the army. He then called Meir and asked her to twist the arm of the defense minister. From Washington, Sapir created a lobby in Jerusalem. Their campaign to keep Sharon safely ensconced in uniform went public, and Sharon became the most courted man in the country.

The media frenzy stopped one week later, when Bar-Lev relented. Sharon was given a compromise position: international IDF lecturer. Aside from fulfilling the traveling post, he was also promised "a fitting post" after the elections. The IDF's first and only full-time traveling lecturer was given a position that would keep him in the army, away from politics, and out of Bar-Lev's hair. In September 1969, two months before the elections, Sharon accepted his new position and flew to the United States to begin his tour.

Sharon kept his end of the deal. On July 9, 1969, he sent a letter to the heads of Gahal, Menachem Begin and Yosef Sapir:

> Over the past two months I've been deliberating how best to contribute to the State of Israel. After careful consideration I've reached the conclusion that in these tough times, as the IDF is at war on all borders, as our soldiers' blood is spilled defending the freedom and independence of Israel, I must be shoulder to shoulder with them, on the front line. In friendship and with deep admiration, Maj. Gen. A. Sharon.

Sharon also sent a personal letter to Sapir. Arieh Avnery published both letters in *The Liberal Connection:*

> Dear Mr. Sapir:
>   . . . Initially I planned to speak with you before sending this letter, but I understand . . . that it is somewhat uncomfortable for you to meet me, alone and in public, during these times. In conversation I wanted to make clear to you, and to you alone, out of a sense of closeness and personal admiration, how Sunday's meeting with Mr. Begin affected me, and how, as a result of that meeting, I reached the conclusion that I will in no way enter politics dependent on the aforementioned. I would like to stay in contact

with you and would be very pleased if you would invite me to your house next week for a heart-to-heart. I'm sorry for causing you discomfort and difficulty, and I thank you again for your warm and friendly relationship. I hope and believe that our relationship will continue into the future.

With great friendship, yours, Arik Sharon.

After that, he got on the first plane to New York. For the next two months, Sharon plowed through the lecture circuit. He spoke at college campuses in the United States and met senior diplomats and army officials in Washington, D.C., Mexico City, Tokyo, Beijing, and Seoul. During his time abroad he returned to Israel only once, on the eve of the Jewish New Year, to visit the grave of his son. Immediately following the ceremony, he flew back to continue lecturing. "I got the fattest ticket El Al can print," Sharon recalled in an interview in 2000, "and I could go wherever I wanted. I made a fascinating trip around the world, to America, Japan, Korea. They let me go wherever I wanted, so long as I didn't land before the elections."

Sharon finished the lecture tour after the elections and waited for word of his new posting. On December 15, 1969, after the new government had been sworn in—Golda Meir as prime minister, Moshe Dayan as defense minister, and Pinchas Sapir as finance minister—Ariel Sharon, much to the chief of staff's chagrin, was appointed to one of the IDF's top positions: supreme commander of the southern sector.

CHAPTER 17

Isolating Gaza

BEFORE RECEIVING HIS NEW APPOINTMENT AS OC SOUTHERN COM-
mand, Sharon had to apologize to Bar-Lev. In a private meeting, he
assured the chief of staff that he would restrain himself in the future. His new command, several times larger than the rest of Israel, stretched from the Dead Sea to Eilat, across the Negev Desert
to the Gaza Strip, and down into the Sinai Peninsula. Sharon left
his house in Tel Aviv and moved to Beersheba, the drab southern
city that hosted the Southern Command HQ.

In late December 1969, the war of attrition was in full swing:
On December 13, two Israeli soldiers were killed and one taken
hostage when their jeep was ambushed along the canal; four days
later the IDF lost another soldier to Egyptian fire near al-Balah.
Shots were fired every day. In February two more soldiers were
taken hostage.

Although Sharon opposed the concept, and the dreadful reality, of the Bar-Lev Line, he now kept his thoughts to himself and
labored to fill the chief of staff's orders, fortifying the front line
along the canal and the second line six miles east of the water. In
June 1970, Sharon, Dayan, and Bar-Lev were caught in heavy artillery fire as they toured the front lines. They slipped into a bunker
with a few soldiers. When it was over, they posed for pictures with
the men, their smiles hiding deep disagreements—chief among
them that Dayan and Bar-Lev, along with most of the general staff,
accepted the heavy human toll along the canal as a necessary evil.

The chief of staff and the defense minister backed Sharon on
the other pressing issue in his sector: the war on terrorism along
the wide open southern border and the densely populated Gaza
Strip. In early 1970, terrorists began infiltrating Israel from Jordan

along the shared border that runs for hundreds of kilometers through the desert to the Red Sea. Sharon turned the acacia-spotted riverbeds and razor ridges into a land of pursuits. He kept surveillance planes in the air, motorized reconnaissance patrols at the ready, and intervention forces on their stomachs, lying in ambush along the infiltration channels. The terrorist bands, habituated to unchecked entry via the desert, suspended much of their activity.

The surprising success of the new OC Southern Command in curtailing infiltrations made waves through the general staff and the pool of public opinion. Sharon, enacting one of the IDF's holy tenets—strive toward the enemy—immediately began badgering Dayan for authorization to operate in the Southern Command's most sensitive and complex area—the Gaza Strip.

In the three years since the Gaza Strip, population 400,000, was taken by Israel, it had emerged as the center of terrorist activity. By 1970, armed members of the Popular Front for the Liberation of Palestine (PFLP), a terrorist organization with a Communist bent, were parading through the streets of the Jibalya and Shati refugee camps. During that year alone, 445 terror attacks were perpetrated in the Gaza region, claiming 16 Israeli lives and wounding 114 civilians.

On January 2, 1971, two Israeli children were killed and their mother badly wounded while driving through Gaza. The public raged, and Dayan, touring the scene of the crime along with Sharon, agreed that a massive antiterrorism operation was necessary. Sharon argued that Israeli restraint, in Arabic, translated as "weakness." Over coffee, Dayan gave the go-ahead to Sharon's plan to obliterate terrorism in the region.

Stage one began in early 1971. Southern Command troops fenced the Gaza Strip, isolating the target area. Troops were put on the ground. Roads were widened and paved to accommodate armored vehicles. Troops were split into small groups and assigned a neighborhood, which they were to learn inside and out. Each night a five-man reconnaissance team patrolled the area, stopping fearful civilians at random to gather information.

Five months later, Sharon moved to stage two. During the next seven months, Sharon's troops conducted relentless raids through-out the area, forcing the terrorists into hiding. After months of intel-ligence work, Sharon split the area into dozens of small plots and coded each one. Special Forces units led troops from door to door, arresting wanted men and confiscating illegal arms. Israeli comman-dos were given free rein. They burst into houses at night, conduct-ing long and intrusive house and body searches. They sifted through each shack, orchard, factory, and home; when an area was deemed "clean," Sharon checked it off on his master code map.

The troops, aided by coerced informants, found hundreds of stashes of explosives and weapons. In order to aid their exhaustive searches, Sharon cut down trees and orchards that served as cover for armed resistance. He had the entrances to caves and wells sealed with concrete. Houses that stood in the way of his road-widening project were destroyed. Sharon, involved in all details of the operation, joined the commandos on patrols.

The pressure reaped certain rewards. By the close of 1971, 104 potential terrorists had been killed and 700 captured. The fol-lowing year, 1972, 60 terror attacks originated from the Gaza Strip, compared to 445 in the year before the offensive. The down-turn continued for years, but the military action drew criticism.

The international press reported that Sharon's commandos ex-ecuted captives at will. Sharon vehemently denied those allega-tions; he did, however, admit that his troops had no special orders to take prisoners. Some reports have Sharon patrolling the area with a list of names, crossing them off as they fell. Years later, as prime minister, Sharon would duplicate the Gaza offensive on a grander scale, implementing widespread assassinations across the West Bank and the Gaza Strip, killing, among others, the heads of Hamas, Sheikh Ahmed Yassin and Dr. Abde Aziz Rantisi, in succession.

The brutal offensive avoided negotiation with local Palestinian leadership, preferring martial might over diplomacy. Sharon's main detractor was the commander of the Gaza Strip and northern Sinai, Brig. Gen. Yitzhak Pundak. Pundak felt the best way to com-bat terror was to invest in the citizens. He wanted to develop the area financially and reach long-term agreements with the Palestinians. Sharon felt that the terrorist infrastructure needed to be obliterated and only then could they reach an agreement with the leadership, which, he emphasized, aided and abetted the terrorists.

On several occasions, Dayan patrolled with Sharon and Pundak. He tried to bridge the gap between the two. Pundak argued that uprooting trees and orchards was unnecessary and that it denied Palestinian civilians the most basic of rights. Moreover, he said, Sharon's troops terrorized the public, walking around with batons and denying residents the right to pick fruit on their own land. Sharon contended that the only way to fight terrorism effectively was to ensure that the local public did not support terrorism, and that, he argued, could be accomplished only by intimidation and force.

The Israeli press spilled a great deal of ink on the Gaza offensive. Reports of nighttime curfews and house searches were printed next to statistics showing a significant reduction in terrorist activity. Sharon considered the offensive a gleaming success. He even invented a slogan for the campaign he'd been waging in the tight alleys of Gaza: "Guerrilla vs. Terror."

One night in early February 1972, Sharon sat at home in Beersheba watching the news and heard Dayan announce the end of the antiterror campaign in Gaza. Shocked, Sharon listened as Dayan praised him lavishly—never a good sign. The following day he learned that the authority over Gaza had changed hands, to the Central Command.

In the months before Dayan's dramatic move, Sharon had laid the groundwork for a policy that still reverberates throughout the region. As the son of farmers, Sharon felt that boots on the ground were an insufficient claim to territory; only civilians working the land could make it their own. Poring over his beloved maps, Sharon fingered an area south of Gaza City. There, at the Rafah Salient, along the dunes that divided Gaza from the Sinai, Sharon decided to build a chain of Israeli settlements. They would sever the territorial continuity, serve as a barrier to infiltrations of men and weapons, and stake Israel's claim to the land.

The only impediment was the local inhabitants. Bedouin tribes lived in the area. Although they were no longer nomadic, the tribes still lived in tents, fishing and farming for sustenance. If Israeli settlements were to be established, the Bedouin tribes would have to be banished.

During a flight over the area, Sharon laid out his argument to Dayan, stressing the need for a barrier between the hostile urbanity of Gaza and the open, unruly desert of the Sinai. Early the next morning, Israeli soldiers raided the Bedouin encampments, destroying their tents and their tin-roofed shacks, chasing away the inhabitants, and fencing off the area.

Four leaders of the Bedouin tribes petitioned the Israeli High Court of Justice to return the ten thousand inhabitants to the fifty square kilometers that had been taken from them. They argued that the defendants, OC Southern Command Ariel Sharon and the Government of Israel, had, on January 14, 1972, forcibly and illegally evicted them from the lands they had been born on. The expulsion, they said, was not born of military necessity.

The IDF argued that, on the contrary, the area was a staging ground for terror attacks and an open channel for drug and arms smuggling. The High Court of Justice rejected the Bedouins' petition. The Israeli left labeled the expulsion of the tribes from the Rafah Salient as an illegal population "transfer." The press debated whether Israel had the right to move civilians from the lands taken in the 1967 war.

Human rights organizations took up the Bedouins' cause and pointed the finger at Sharon, labeling him a cruel and unbridled general, the kind of man who wouldn't think twice about chasing women and children from their homes. The leaders of the kibbutz movement, especially those in the Negev, protested the brutal expulsion of their Bedouin neighbors.

Sharon spoke at several kibbutzim and defended his actions. He told the members of Kibbutz Nir Oz that the Bedouins had settled in the Rafah Salient only after the 1967 war; their claims to the lands were moot. Several kibbutzniks present answered that they remembered that the Bedouins were in the area well before the country was established. Sharon described the landscape as a hotbed for terrorism and smuggling, listing the numbers of bombs, explosives, and hand grenades recently seized. Sharon told them it was all well and good to defend Arabs, but they might also consider the safety of Jews.

In his conversations with the kibbutz members and the press, Sharon accentuated the need for security while cloaking the settlement plans. Years later, as a politician, he spoke proudly of his actions to settle the Sinai and the Gaza Strip.

"Settlement is an entirely political act," he is quoted as saying in Uri Eban's *Arik: The Way of the Warrior*:

> Under the cover of the war on terror—I moved the border. As a soldier I would dictate diplomacy. I initiated, I contacted the prime minister. . . . In the end the legislative branch authorized my actions. . . . There's not a minister [in the Knesset] I didn't speak with about the borders. I handled the settlement of the Gaza Strip. I raised it, I evacuated the [Bedouin] residents from there, I pushed for it. [The settlements] Sadot, Dikla, Nahal Sinai, Nahal Yam: With incessant pressure, I made them into civilian settlements.

Nonetheless, in the Sinai, and again twenty-five years later in the Gaza Strip, Sharon willfully destroyed what he had built, his policies apparently no more rooted than the desert sand.

CHAPTER 18

A Not-So-Honorable Discharge

In January 1972, Lt. Gen. Haim Bar-Lev retired and was replaced by an even greater foe of Sharon's. One of Lt. Gen. David Elazar's first moves as chief of staff was to ask Maj. Gen. Aharon Yariv, director of military intelligence, to ascertain whether Sharon had been given orders to build a fence around the Bedouin lands near Rafah. Sharon freely admitted that he had not, that he had acted of his own volition and was proud of it. Elazar summoned Sharon to his office for an oral reprimand.

A few months later, Elazar informed Sharon that he should prepare for civilian life. Sharon, forty-five, felt that he had served as an exemplary commander of the southern sector. As far as he was concerned, there was no professional reason to oust him from the army.

Beyond the acrimony between the two, Elazar was intent on ushering in a new generation of generals. In June 1972 he slipped general's rank onto Shmuel Gonen's shoulders, and in September he appointed Eli Zeira as director of military intelligence in place of Aharon Yariv, who had held the post for the previous nine years. The commanders of the navy, the infantry, and the personnel department were also replaced. Sharon would later claim that the housecleaning hindered the IDF when it was called to arms in October 1973.

By the end of 1972, only four generals from the pre-Elazar period remained on the IDF general staff: Air Force commander Motti Hod, OC Central Command Rechavam Ze'evi, Tank Corps commander Avraham Adan, and OC Southern Command Ariel

Sharon. The first three were all slated to retire; the fourth was being ushered out the door. Sharon, seeing himself as the natural successor to Elazar, refused to leave without a struggle. In May 1973, Dayan informed him that his army career would be officially terminated in January 1974 with the completion of his term as OC Southern Command.

The meeting ended in a crescendo of bad will. Sharon refused to accept his fate. As usual, he appealed to the prime minister, but Golda Meir declined to play Ben-Gurion's role. Sharon realized he had come to the end of the line in uniform. The long-coveted top spot was beyond his reach.

After consulting with Lily about his future, it was clear to him that he would not place himself in a position where his advancement hinged on the will of superiors. Politics was the natural choice. He lacked the funds to start his own business, he wanted to have an impact on the future of the country, and he loved power and publicity. More than anything, he was convinced that the majority of the people running the country were small, nearsighted bureaucrats, without the means and the know-how to move the country forward.

The next general elections were scheduled for October 31, 1973. As a career officer, Sharon was required by law to wait at least three months before entering the political arena, meaning that he would have to be out of uniform by the end of July. Aware that with retirement he would also lose his house in Beersheba, Sharon began looking for a new place to live. Tel Aviv and the bourgeois neighborhood of Tzahala were out of the question. What he really wanted was to return to his roots and work the land.

After her husband's twenty-five years in uniform, Lily Sharon worried about the family's financial future. She pushed Sharon to find a farm, arguing that politics is a fickle beast, whereas farming is something you can lean on. Recalling those days, she told the *Hadashot* daily in September 1993, "Arik won't sit at home and wait for someone to offer him a job. I want to have to say to whoever calls: 'He's riding his horse, call back in the evening.' Or: 'He's working in the field, call back in the afternoon.' "

The freedom of civilian life can be bewildering after more than two decades of military service. Sharon knew plenty of war heroes who whiled away their days in Tel Aviv's coffeeshops, chewing the fat, their stories enhanced by time.

Determined not to settle on a moshav like his parents, Sharon scoured the country for a piece of land where he could start his own farm. Finally, he found a stretch of land in the northwestern corner of the Negev, near the town of Sderot. There was nothing on the thousand-acre plot of bare desert but a few sycamore trees and a dilapidated building. The sparseness appealed to him. In 1950, the land had been leased by the Israel Lands Authority to Rafi Eitan, the spymaster who ran Jonathan Pollard. Eitan, later one of Sharon's closest advisers and a member of the Knesset today, sold the land several years later to an Australian Jew.

The Australian bought the land hoping it would induce his son to move to Israel and start a sheep ranch. In the fifties the man immigrated, but the frequent terror attacks from Gaza and the overall economic hardship turned him and his Israeli wife back to Australia. Although the farm continued to operate after the couple left, the property had been on the market for years.

The desolation of the place enticed Sharon. He took Lily to see it, suppressing thoughts about the cost of the land—their worldly assets wouldn't amount to one-tenth of the price.

Sharon tried securing a loan from several banks. To his dismay, not one bank in the country was willing to issue a loan to a general with ambiguous future plans.

Sharon needed two million liroth, or six hundred thousand dollars, to acquire the land. Help came in the form of Avraham Krinitzi. The first mayor of Ramat Gan and a personal friend of Sharon's from the days when he commanded the paratroopers, Krinitzi listened to Sharon's woes and said he knew someone who might help. Meshulam Riklis, an Israeli tycoon and former owner of the Riviera Hotel and Casino in Las Vegas, held right-wing views on Israeli politics and remained in touch with high-profile political figures. Krinitzi knew Riklis was concerned by the recent ousters of Ezer Weizman and Sharon. When Krinitzi approached him about funding Sharon's ranch, he got an affirmative answer

on the spot. Riklis told him that in his opinion, men like Arik
Sharon should not have to concern themselves with earning a living. His attention should be on the future of the state. Riklis met
Sharon and offered him a $200,000 loan, open and without inter-
est, so long as he promised that he would involve himself with
more than sheep and seek a pivotal role in government.

Riklis's cash covered one-third of the cost of the ranch. The
Exchange National Bank of Chicago, an American bank that had
just opened its first branch in Israel, lent him the rest of the
money. The bank manager, Samuel Zacks, a U.S. Army veteran,
knew Sharon well. In total, Sharon promised to pay fifty thousand
dollars a year to the bank.

Sharon was excited on the day they signed the contract. To
mark the celebration, he asked a security guard to get him a falafel
sandwich, a custom that followed him through his years as prime
minister—only by then he preferred to mark joyous occasions with
two sandwiches, eaten in quick succession.

Arik and Lily Sharon changed the name of the farm to
Sycamore Ranch. By 2006, the developed property—three large
homes, an office building, greenhouses, a goat shed, a dairy farm, a
herd of cows and sheep, roads, lighting, a lookout tower, nine hundred acres of agricultural fields, and orchards filled with lemons,
oranges, grapefruits, cantaloupes, watermelons, and vegetables—
was worth more than ten million dollars. The Israeli taxpayers provided Sharon with the roads, lighting, and security patrols on his
private ranch.

Sharon now felt he was wasting his time in uniform. His post-
army path was clear, and he wanted to get cracking. He sent a letter to the chief of staff informing him of his imminent retirement,
and he set up a meeting with Defense Minister Dayan. In July
1973, Dayan let Sharon know that Shmuel Gonen was to replace
him as commander of the southern sector. Sharon made it clear
that in his opinion, Gonen, known as Gorodish, was unfit for the
task.

The parting ceremony for the outgoing OC Southern Command was held on the morning of July 15. Omri, Gilad, and Lily attended. An honor guard presented the flags of each of the IDF's fighting units, and Sharon, looking dejected, saluted. Back at the house in Beersheba he signed the last of his military forms, took off his uniform, and put sandals on his feet long accustomed to confinement in boots. He got in his car and headed out to the ranch to see the flock of grazing sheep that had arrived that day.

A few days after the formal farewell, Sharon invited staff officers and commanders from the southern sector, along with Bedouin tribal leaders and journalists, to a party at his house in Beersheba. Arik Lavie, a popular singer, performed, and all the guests were in high spirits—until Sharon delivered his farewell speech.

Sharon attacked the chief of staff and other army brass, saying he had been forced out of the service and that he wanted to say so publicly, since so many supporters had been urging him to remain in the army. He was proud, he said, to have acted alone, instructed by his own conscience, and not as part of a lobby or clique. He ended by saying it was only natural that after thirty years of service to his country, he would continue to be active in the same vein.

His speech claimed the following day's headlines, embarrassing the chief of staff and the defense minister. Later on, Sharon further shamed Elazar by refusing his invitation to a goodbye dinner. Instead, Sharon suggested that Elazar send him the watch—the traditional present given by the chief of staff to all retiring generals—in the mail.

Sharon asked to say a few words at his last general staff meeting. When he arrived, he saw that the defense minister had shown up, too—perhaps to part with him formally and perhaps to supervise the unpredictable general. Dayan started the meeting by complimenting Sharon at length, elegantly diffusing the tension in the air. Sharon, pleased, thanked Dayan for the kind words and stuck to a conciliatory script.

After the meeting, Sharon asked a favor of Dayan: to be appointed an armored division commander in the reserves, and to be called up only in the case of all-out war. He was rather certain Dayan would refuse, considering the tension between them, and the even greater rift between Sharon, the new commander of the southern sector, and the chief of staff. Dayan surprised him by approving his request on the spot—doubtless realizing that the yardstick by which you measure a general in time of peace is different from the one used in time of war.

CHAPTER 19

Founding the Likud

Sharon declined the IDF spokesman's offer to hold a press conference to mark his retirement. If he wanted to inform the public of his views on issues of national importance, he said, he would do so on his own time. To journalists he turned an equally cold shoulder. Sharon played his cards close to his chest in July of 1973.

Sharon had his pick of political parties. Both Labor and Liberal had guaranteed him a spot on their lists of candidates for the Knesset. This would have been the standard route into politics: Leave the army, obtain a junior diplomatic post, and fight your way up the ranks. Sharon wanted more. He had witnessed the nation's growing disappointment with the Mapai Party, which had dominated Israeli politics from its inception, and saw a unique opportunity for change.

Meshulam Riklis, in from the United States to assist Sharon during his first days as a civilian, spent hours at Sycamore Ranch discussing political plans with Arik, Lily, and Samuel Zacks. All agreed that the two Opposition parties, known collectively as Gahal, had no chance of disrupting Labor's hegemony. In 1965, Gahal had won 26 seats, to Labor's 65; four years later, Gahal earned only the same number of mandates in Israel's 120-member house.

Sharon, along with Zacks and Riklis, decided that only a unification of the varied and fractious right and center parties could dislodge Labor from power. In that endeavor, his greatest weakness was also his greatest asset. As a political newcomer, he was not yet entangled in the sticky web of personal grudges and debts that dominated the seemingly endless opposition parties of Israeli politics. The rancor ran so deep that unification was widely seen as the pipe dream of a political freshman. Nonetheless, Sharon, always eager to approach from an unexpected angle, set to the task.

The sticking point on the path to unification lay in the open and personal animosity between Opposition leader Menachem Begin and the leader of the Free Center Party, a group that splintered off from Begin's Herut in 1966 and was headed by Shmuel Tamir, the lawyer who had represented Sharon in the police investigation of his son's death. Sharon decided to reveal his plan to the public and the politicians simultaneously. That way, he reasoned, an inalterable momentum would be set in motion before it could be killed in the backrooms of the Knesset.

On July 17, 1973, two days after his official discharge from the army, Sharon sold two tons of grain and produce. Cash in hand, he rented the main room of Beit Sokolov, the headquarters of the Israeli journalists' union. In a blue shirt and khakis, his face tanned by the sun, Sharon looked around the room and realized that at the very least, the first stage had been a success. His decision to avoid the standard IDF-organized press conference—where generals ordinarily make headlines for a day with long-winded sermons about the existential threats facing the country—and call one on his own time and his own dime had generated considerable curiosity. The place was packed.

"Don't let the Labor government do with us, all of us, as it pleases," he urged.

> I believe in the necessity of creating alternatives in government. Israel is considered a democracy and yet, in one realm, we are lacking: the realistic chance of voting out the government. It is absolutely forbidden to allow [the perpetuation of] a system where the same government holds power for decades, since the establishment of the state, with no risk of eviction. We cannot make do with a loyal Opposition [party].
>
> Against the Labor bloc we must establish a wide opposing bloc that will be able to transcend the disputes and hatreds of the past in favor of the national interest. It is only natural that Gahal will stand at the center of this bloc. It's

not important how many MKs join. What's important is the concept: to show the public a readiness for change, a widening of the system, to allow new people to act . . . to pit bloc against bloc—that is my primary goal.

Not everyone was pleased by the next day's headlines. Some found Sharon's bombast unfounded and naïve; few, though, were indifferent. As the talk raged, Sharon contacted his old friend Ezer Weizman—the jocular, fly-by-the-seat-of-your-pants fighter pilot who would later serve as Israel's president and was already a member of Herut—and suggested that the two of them bond together and issue an ultimatum to the powers that be: We'll join Gahal only if a right-center bloc is formed. The press got wind of the idea.

On the morning after the press conference, Sharon piled his family into the car and drove to palm-lined Haruba Beach in northern Sinai. In 2000, he told *Yedioth Ahronoth* about the experience:

I remember one of my most embarrassing moments was when I went with Lily and the kids to one of the beaches in Sinai. Aside from us, there was one other family there. They had a radio on full blast, and one of the weekend political shows had an analyst talking about my proposition. He dismissed it and called me a "political newborn." I wanted to bury myself in the sand, but with my proportions, it isn't that easy.

Sitting in the sand, the sun beating down hard, Sharon thought the matter through and decided he needed to meet with Begin. Begin alone held the keys to unification. If he decided to invite the smaller parties to form a larger coalition, they'd have a hard time resisting; if he refused, the plan would never get off the ground.

Sharon's relations with Begin did not have the warmth of his ties to Ben-Gurion, but there was a deep-seated trust between the two. As head of the Opposition in the Knesset, Begin would come down to the southern sector for firsthand inspections of the Sinai border with the OC Southern Command, and Sharon would often visit Begin in his Tel Aviv home.

His frequent visits to Menachem and Aliza Begin's house made a deep impression on Sharon. The former commander of the underground during the British Mandate, head of the Opposition since the inception of the state, and world-renowned figure lived in jarring simplicity. Sharon couldn't find one chair he could trust with his weight. They all wobbled, or had no back or no armrest. Begin's minimalist austerity charmed Sharon, and Sharon's long record of valor made a similar impression on Begin. Nonetheless, their first meeting ended badly. Begin demanded that Sharon join either the Liberal or the Herut party before he would discuss the idea of a right-center bloc. Sharon interpreted the demand as an attempt to absorb him into a political machine controlled by Begin, thereby dooming the chance of any of the splinter parties' joining the Gahal monolith. Moreover, Sharon felt Begin was far off the mark in his asking price: A retired war hero like himself should have been courted more aggressively; merely incorporating him into the ranks as a first stage on the path to further negotiation was insufficient.

Sharon was a political novice, and it showed. Instead of trying to reach an agreement with the Opposition leader, Sharon categorically refused to join Gahal. He engaged in a harsh exchange of words with Begin, telling him he would continue to work toward a right-center bloc regardless. Begin was left with the impression of a forceful man who would not accept authority.

Hours later, aware that his idea was taking on water fast, Sharon called Begin and asked to meet with him again that same night. This time, in the Knesset, with Sharon turning on his considerable charm, he detailed his plan again, only now it was delivered in a soothing voice, as a request. Moreover, he declared his willingness to join the Liberal Party of Israel on the spot. Pacified, Begin responded that he would take the unification idea to Gahal Party leaders, even if he was skeptical of its chances for success. He doubted it was possible to bridge the animosity between himself and Shmuel Tamir, who had attempted an intra-party coup after Gahal's stinging loss in the 1965 elections. Begin and his tight group of supporters from Etzel days tamped down the rebellion, driving Tamir and Ehud Olmert, along with four other Gahal members, to start the Free Center Party. In 1969 the splinter group got two seats to Gahal's twenty-six in the Knesset.

Sharon kept his part of the bargain with Begin. In early August 1973, Dr. Elimelech Rimalt, chairman of the Liberal Party of Israel, announced that Sharon had joined their ranks, even handing out copies of his membership card. Sharon had good reason to choose the Liberal Party. That party—as opposed to Herut, which was dominated by the towering rhetorical prowess of its leader, Begin—was virtually his for the taking.

Sharon began the grueling negotiations with potential partners of the right-center bloc, which he and Begin had tentatively decided to call the Likud (the Bond). The two of them put their mutual goal of overthrowing the Labor Party and the common sense of a right-center coalition ahead of affection and friendliness. Before long all four parties—Herut, Liberal, Free Center, and National List—had sent negotiating teams to the headquarters Sharon had established at the Zionists of America House.

Sharon concentrated on pulling in Shmuel Tamir's Free Center and the National List of Yigal Hurevitz and Zalman Shoval. Both parties, closer to the center than the right, were essential to Sharon's plan. Without them, the right-wing parties lacked legitimacy. The vast majority of the Israeli public saw Herut and the Liberal Party of Israel as extensions of the fanatical underground; in very few circles were they considered viable contenders to Mapai's throne.

The divide between the different right-center parties was mostly personal and prestige-driven. In the Israeli electoral system, each party presents the public with a ranked list of candidates. The public, voting for a party rather than a person, decides how many slots each party receives. The leader of the party with the most votes is charged with forming a government from the different parties. Each, depending on its weight and ideological leaning, has a different asking price. Sharon's negotiations faltered early, with all four parties bickering over the placement of their respective members on the numbered party list.

August was spent in daily negotiations. Sharon worked in the fields during the day, then got in his car and drove two hours north to Tel Aviv for talks with Tamir, Begin, Shoval, and Liberal Party of Israel leaders. The thorny relationship between Begin and Tamir had Sharon feeling like Sisyphus.

The first move in the direction of compromise came from Tamir. The Free Center Party had voted overwhelmingly in favor of unification. Based on sunny prediction polls, Tamir asked for four seats in the top thirty-two spots of the Likud list. Begin agreed to three. Sharon persuaded Tamir to settle for slots 6, 16, 29, and 35, but Begin refused.

Distressed, Sharon drafted Weizman to help him soften the Herut leader. They agreed to serve Gahal an ultimatum: Either accept Free Center's offer, or lose the two of us—the only generals in your midst, the sole representatives of the IDF, the organization Israelis trust over all others. The challenge roiled the meeting; Sharon and Begin exchanged harsh words. Sharon spoke first:

> Tamir's proposal is difficult, but it isn't spiteful. I'm new here. I don't belong to the Free Center, National List, or Herut . . . in the meanwhile I belong to the Likud. I harbor no grudges. I'm willing to put myself in the thirty-eighth position. Let's accept the offer and win the excitement of the public. . . . The Likud is a matter of principle; placement is not. The opposition to the proposal speaks of an unpreparedness for the Likud. I'll put the responsibility on everyone. Since I've placed the Likud as a condition, I'm sorry, but I won't be [with you] in the Likud. I could have contributed in the political sphere and I'm sorry if it won't work. My feeling is that those that could be bonded [*l'laked* in Hebrew, a verb form of *likud*] are not ready for the Likud, since they can't overcome difficulties that are not based on principle. I say this with deep heartache.

Begin responded:

> I feel great affection for you, Arik. I was one of the ones who waited for you. I didn't advise you to leave the army, just as I didn't advise Ezer [to leave], as the army needs military men of your kind. But I did say that if you left, I would embrace you. Ezer I hugged physically, and you,

Arik, in my heart. My decision to found the Likud came after long deliberation, the likes of which I haven't had since I left the underground. The dispute here is not over one mandate. The whole building will collapse if we accept the proposal. . . . Tilt your ear toward what your old friend Menachem is saying. Dear friends, you say: "Accept Tamir's offer or else we're not with you. We'll leave you alone in the campaign if you do not surrender." Don't act this way. Do you truly believe that you can influence friends with threats of retirement? Let Gahal decide its path along with you. A minority does not enforce its will on the majority in a democracy. . . . I call on you, Ezer and Arik, to abandon these tactics.

Gahal voted to reject Tamir's proposal. Sharon was removed from the negotiating team, and the idea of unification seemed out of reach. Simha Erlich and Elimelech Rimalt spoke to Begin in a more conciliatory tone, though, while Sharon continued to work on Tamir. Within forty-eight hours, Begin and Tamir agreed that spots 8, 16, 29, and 36 would go to Tamir's party. At that moment the Likud was formed.

Three days later, on September 14, 1973, they put their agreement on paper. Within seven weeks of shedding his uniform, the political novice had changed the reality of politics in Israel. Arieh Avnery described the transformation in *The Liberal Connection:*

> Until Arik Sharon entered politics, the bulldozer was considered an excellent machine for clearing dirt and ruins and fortifying positions. But ever since Sharon stormed onto the targets he'd chosen with the full force of his 265 pounds, he's proven that politics is not shaped with the surgeon's scalpel. What works for a rebellious refugee camp and a charging division also works for attaining political goals.

Sharon summed up his feelings by saying, "I thought I was a political newborn, but soon enough I was nursing."

The future seemed promising. One month shy of the general elections, opinion polls showed that the majority of the public approved of the establishment of a right-center bloc. Sharon, as the architect of the unification, was appointed Likud campaign manager. His future seemed bright and certain.

CHAPTER 20

Shock on Yom Kippur

SHARON, NOW FORTY-FIVE, PREPARED FOR THE UPCOMING ELECTION by going on a diet. As campaign manager, he'd have to appear on TV often, and he knew he was ballooning to an unsightly size. It was the first of a series of diets, none of which worked. Sharon liked sausage, cheese, mutton, and falafel, but mostly his emphasis was on quantity. His weight didn't bother him, but, wary of the gluttonous image he portrayed, he dieted hard before elections and rewarded himself with food after they were over.

In late September 1973, Sharon delivered the Likud's opening campaign speech. He noted that the nation seemed poised to enjoy several years of quiet, allowing the Likud, if the citizens of Israel would give it the chance, to close some of the social gaps then existing. One week later, the tables turned.

On October 5, 1973, Sharon received a call in his office. Brig. Gen. Uri Ben-Ari, chief of the OC Southern Command's staff, told the sandal-shod Sharon that Egypt seemed to be deploying an alarming number of troops. Sharon put the phone down and walked straight out of the office.

Two hours later he was back in a very familiar place. Although he hadn't been on the base of OC Command in Beersheba in three months, it had been his home for years. He looked at several long scrolls of aerial photos, working his way down the black-and-white strips, growing ever more troubled. The Egyptians had amassed an invasion-sized force. They had heavy portable bridges near the canal. War was imminent.

The IDF's war plans were predicated on a minimum of two

days' warning before attack, allowing time to call up the reserves, the meat of Israel's army. As the Egyptians amassed troops, Military Intelligence, charged with assessing the national security risk, remained firm in their opinion that the chances of war were low. After the bruising defeat in 1967, and without a major upgrade to their air force, they believed the Egyptians didn't want war. According to Eli Zeira and his men in Military Intelligence, the forces assembling near the canal were taking part in Tahrir 41, a large interdisciplinary army maneuver.

On Yom Kippur itself—a day marked by empty roads, solemn prayer, and fasting—Military Intelligence finally changed their assessment. War would commence at 6:00 P.M., they said. That, too, was incorrect. Egypt and Syria had set their coordinated attack from south and north for 2:00 P.M. The timing was ideal for Egypt, enabling their armor to cross the water at night, but inopportune for Syria, which wanted an early morning attack, which would force the Israelis to look east across the Golan Heights into the rising sun.

Sharon, worried by what he saw in the aerial photos, grew surly when he learned that the reserves had not yet taken their positions as called for in "Dovecote," the emergency plan he had drafted as OC Southern Command. He called the command room of the division he was to lead in the event of war, the 143rd, and instructed them to assume the highest level of alert. Then he went back to Beersheba, where Lily, Omri, and Gilad waited to be taken back to the ranch for Yom Kippur.

At the farm, as the open sky began to brighten, Arik put the children to sleep in their beds and went out for a walk with Lily in the cotton fields. Sharon put on his ironed uniform, working the buttons with familiarity, and drove the whole family to division headquarters. As they drove to the base, Israeli reserves were called up. The Egyptians wrongly assumed that Israel would struggle to contact its reserves on Yom Kippur, since the call-up system relied heavily on radio. Sharon's division, though, like many others, was easily reachable. Every family in the country was in one of two places: home or synagogue.

At headquarters, under taut camouflage netting, Sharon and his family watched the mechanics scurry from tank to tank as

Sharon issued directives and advice. Satisfied that the division was in good hands, he ferried his family back home, telling Lily he'd be back for a final dinner before the war. From there he continued to Southern Command headquarters to receive an update on enemy troops and IDF readiness.

On Yom Kippur, at 1:55 P.M. on Saturday, October 6, 1973, the war began, with the Syrian Army attacking in the north and the Egyptian forces in the south. The Syrians stormed across the Golan Heights with 1,650 tanks in five divisions (twenty brigades), heavy air force cover, and 1,250 artillery guns. Israel had one division, with 177 tanks and 44 artillery guns. In the south, the Egyptians attacked with 2,200 tanks, 2,000 artillery guns, two field armies consisting of ten divisions, and multiple commando battalions flown deep into Israeli territory. On the other side of the water, behind sand embankments and gas lines that were supposed to set the canal on fire in the event of an invasion, Israel had one division, 290 tanks, and 70 artillery guns. The surprise was absolute, the preparedness next to nil.

Sharon knew his reserve unit would need forty-eight hours to mobilize. The Egyptian onslaught and the IDF state of unreadiness knotted his stomach, but left no mark on his face. At night he came home accompanied by staff officers. Lily apologized for the meager meal, saying she hadn't been able to make all she had planned on owing to a case of the flu. Sharon seemed pleased, though. He ate until it was hard for him to inhale, putting an end to his pre-election diet.

Toward the end of the meal there was a knock on the door. As in the Six Day War, Zevele Slutsky had come in from the cold to fight. Sharon hugged his old friend. Lacking a full uniform, Slutsky asked Sharon for a pair of army boots. As Lily ducked into the closet to pull out her husband's reserve boots, Arik went into his children's room. He kissed them good night as they slept, hugged Lily, and then jumped onto a flatbed truck with Slutsky.

At three in the morning on October 7, the truck, a civilian vehicle taken for use in an emergency (a common practice in a civilian army), left Beersheba, heading toward the central sector of the Sinai. Brig. Gen. Avraham Tamir, an old friend of Sharon's who had ditched his desk job in Tel Aviv, sat next to the major general.

The division's intelligence officer shared the back seat with Slutsky, the Mossad man, and Uri Dan, a journalist friend of Sharon's.

Their mood was grim. Sharon, still wearing his red paratrooper's beret, gripped the wheel in silence. Every once in a while he'd ask Tamir to find the news on the radio, but the reception was scratchy and incomprehensible. As they passed Um-Katef, Sharon complained that in 1967 they had surprised the Egyptians and not the other way around.

The 143rd Division, called up just five hours before the coordinated attacks began, needed forty-eight hours to mobilize. When the reservists arrived, they found that the emergency stores had been plundered by time and overconfidence. Sharon, distressed by the lack of binoculars, flashlights, fire-retardant jumpsuits, and rifles, and not wanting to waste any more precious time, ordered his division south immediately. They were told to forget about waiting for the giant, slow-moving flatbeds and to board their tanks as soon as they were ready, company by company, rumbling the 120 miles to the front on their metal treads.

The Dovecote plan, completed in May 1973, was intended to defang a surprise attack by containment. According to the plan, the reserve armored division had to hold the attacking Egyptian forces in the corridor between the canal and Lateral Road, eighteen miles east, until the reserves joined the fray.

Owing to a general level of laxity on Yom Kippur and the fact that the IDF expected war to commence at six in the evening, Maj. Gen. Albert Mandler's division was not in position at 1:55 P.M. when the Egyptian onslaught began. In some of the fortified embankments the soldiers hadn't even put on helmets and battle jackets until just before the attack. Tanks had not been properly positioned or concealed. On orders issued by OC Southern Command Shmuel Gonen and approved by Chief of Staff Elazar, only one armored brigade had been deployed to the front line. All told, 450 soldiers in sixteen forts were asked to hold the line along the canal; of the division's 290 tanks, only 3 were on the front line and 88 were spread across the corridor between the water and the Lateral Road. They were backed by only 28 artillery guns.

Sharon arrived early on Sunday morning, October 7, the second day of war, at the command post in Refidim, fifty miles east of the canal. Although his troops had yet to turn up, he called Maj. Gen. Yisrael Tal, IDF commander of operations, and demanded that the IDF strike back in the Qantara region and cross the canal. According to Sharon, this would psychologically wound the Egyptian Army, crippling its will to fight.

In Refidim, Sharon met Ya'akov Aknin, the artillery commander he had served with during the Abu Ageila battle, and the rest of the divisional staff officers. Over the radio, Major General Mandler detailed the crushing losses his men were suffering on the front lines. As Sharon listened, female soldiers brought out heaping plates of army issue salami, half-burned omelets, and a loaf of bread, which he ate ravenously.

After the meal Sharon left the command bunker and drove to a more forward base in Tasa. The soldiers greeted him with a round of applause. Sharon filed through the ranks of soldiers and shook their hands. From there he went down into the division's bunker, his war room. It had the feel of a submarine. The air was thick and throbbed with the hum of a generator, the lights gave off a yellow glow, the passages were narrow, and the radio systems were bumper to bumper with verbal traffic.

Sharon settled into a ten-foot-wide cell, along with twenty other people. Col. Amnon Reshef, an armored brigade commander in Sharon's division, updated the commanders on the situation in his sector. He told them how on the previous night, twenty of his men had been killed when they had gone out to rescue soldiers trapped in one of the forts. Only one man had returned. He had seen the rest of them die. Sharon, aware how those serving under him would watch his every move, asked questions regarding life and death in a completely calm and steady voice. At 4:00 P.M. he assumed command of the central sector.

The army radios carried the frontline soldiers' anguish in short bursts. In each of the forts, somewhere between ten and forty soldiers, deafened and terrified by Egyptian artillery, were being asked to keep multitudes of commandos and armored troops at bay. Sharon, hearing the panic spreading through the ranks, called each of the forts, asked them how many losses they had sustained and what their precise situation was, and made sure to provide tasks that would keep their feet moving and their minds quiet.

Max Maman, an enlisted soldier, broke through the radio traffic with a plea. "Tachachan asking for assistance," he said, using his call name. "We can't hold on, if anyone can hear me . . . we don't have the strength."

His voice took Sharon back to Latrun. "We read you, Tachachan," Sharon said. "You'll get help. Don't go outside." The constant buzz of the radio went silent. Finally Maman responded. "I know you. You're the former commander of the southern sector. I thank you very much. Please don't leave me . . . please talk to me the whole time." Sharon stayed on the line with Maman as long as he could, calming his nerves and bolstering his spirits. After the war, their conversation became legendary.

Sharon was already critical of the way the war was being handled in the southern sector. Had the forces been deployed according to his plans, he said, the one standing Israeli armored division in Sinai could have prevented the Egyptian tanks from crossing the canal, or at the very least destroyed them immediately after crossing. Chief of Staff Elazar and OC Southern Command Gonen charged that it was the plan and not the deployment that was faulty. Moreover, the number of reserve units in the Sinai was far too small, they said. Sharon raged at them for not arranging an evacuation of the soldiers manning the Bar-Lev Line. He called their behavior scandalous.

On October 6, two-thirds of the tanks on the eastern side of the canal were positioned far from the front line. They did not take part in the first wave of battle. Sharon complained that that strategy had rendered the front line of forts a no-man's-land. By October 7, nine hundred Egyptian tanks, two mechanized divisions, and five infantry divisions had crossed the canal virtually unopposed by Israeli fire. Elazar and Gonen argued that they had protected the tanks with good reason: They were, at the time, the only thing standing between the canal and Tel Aviv.

Sharon directed most of his rancor at Gonen. Having commanded the southern sector for years, Sharon felt that his own grasp of the battle, as it unfolded, was better than Gonen's. Sharon had never held Gonen in high esteem. When he heard him issuing orders over the radio, he frequently voiced his disagreement with the man who was now his commander.

By noon on October 7, the second day of the war, more than a hundred of Sharon's tanks had reached Tasa. Gonen ordered them to defend the Lateral Road. The IDF general staff assigned Sharon's division the central sector, Avraham Adan's division the northern sector, and what was left of Albert Mandler's division the southern sector.

By nightfall on October 7, the three divisions had set up a defensive line five to ten miles east of the canal. Sharon pressured the general staff to authorize a rescue mission. He called for a hundred tanks to move west, toward the canal, where they could evacuate the dead, wounded, and trapped soldiers. Elazar feared it was too early for a counterattack. He preferred to amass troops along the second line of defense in preparation for the following day's offensive.

Sharon, as always, persisted. He called Defense Minister Dayan directly and made his case for an immediate counterstrike. Dayan told him that he was going to a meeting with the chief of staff at the Southern Command war room and would bring up Sharon's plan there. But Dayan, along with Elazar and Prime Minister Meir, had no intention of heeding Sharon's plan. Dayan called it "Arik's patent."

The meeting was set for seven in the evening. At five, Sharon waited for a helicopter to pick him up in Tasa and fly him to the meeting. After receiving a message that the area was too dangerous for flight, he drove to a distant and well-protected landing zone, where he waited for two hours. Sharon was certain that an invisible hand had directed the pilots to skip his pickup, thereby ensuring that no one would hear his opinion of the faulty battlefield decisions reigning over the southern sector.

Arriving well before Sharon were Gonen, Adan, Mandler, Elazar, Rabin (who was accompanying the chief of staff), and Dayan. The subject of the meeting was the next day's offensive. Elazar ordered a measured strike against the forces that had already crossed into the Sinai. Adan's division would attack the following morning from the north, near Qantara, and move south toward Bitter Lake. The other two divisions, Sharon's and Mandel's, would stay put, in a defensive position. If Adan's division faltered, they'd be on call; if Adan's attack succeeded, then they too would go on the offensive. Rabin thought the plan "was the best possible option."

As the group left the bunker, they bumped into Sharon. Elazar explained the plan, and Sharon pressured him again to authorize an attack that night, to rescue those on the front line. Elazar refused. As the two argued, Rabin came up to Sharon, put his hand on his shoulder, and in his smoky bass voice said, "Arik, we're counting on you." The discussion ended with handshakes all around. Rabin and Bar-Lev boarded a helicopter and lifted off into the darkness, Tel Aviv–bound.

Sharon turned to Gonen and explained that the plan was a mistake. He and Adan had to attack together. He could tell Gonen wasn't listening. He, Adan, and Gonen were on the worst of terms. In Adan's account of the war, *On the Banks of the Suez,* he writes that he and Sharon sat in silence on the dark helicopter as they flew back to their divisions in the desert. Sharon returned to Tasa at one in the morning. He called his officers together for a briefing. The headlights of two jeeps and a command car illuminated a wooden blackboard full of topographical code maps and aerial photos. The officers, sitting in the sand, listened as Sharon explained the next day's mission. Satisfied that everyone had understood what was needed of him, Sharon lay down on a blanket in the bunker and grabbed an hour of sleep. He woke up at 4:30 A.M. and called Gonen, asking permission to join Adan's offensive and to rescue the trapped soldiers. Gonen refused.

From this point on, the commanders' recollections take divergent and contradictory paths. To this day, historians have been unable to provide a definitive record of events during the counterstrike of October 8, 1973. The rest of this chapter will not lift the fog of war; rather, owing to the labyrinthine nature of the arguments, it will be based on Sharon's subjective view of the battle.

After receiving his orders from Gonen, Sharon and his staff officers drove to a forward position just five miles from the canal.

Sharon lay flat on a sand dune and watched for Adan's tanks, eager to follow Israel's first offensive move of the war in the Sinai. Major General Tamir lay down next to him, while Slutsky, smoking a cigarette, watched their backs. Suddenly their waiting was pierced by the shrill sound of incoming rounds. The first two landed two hundred yards away.

Sharon remained prone. But a moment later another few rounds whistled closer to them. The Egyptians had forward artillery scouts in the nearby bushes leading the Egyptian guns closer to Sharon's seven half-tracks. Sharon, Tamir, and Slutsky scurried back into their armored vehicles and retreated to a more distant vantage point.

At 9:45 in the morning Sharon saw Adan's tanks through his field glasses. They were moving west, as expected, but rather than charging as one clenched fist, they moved forward in small bands of armor. Sharon, shocked, said he knew then the counterstrike would fail.

The first two hours of battle were filled with optimistic radio reports. Based on the information from the Southern Command, Chief of Staff Elazar announced in a Tel Aviv press conference, "We'll continue to attack and we'll break their bones."

Gonen called the chief of staff and received immediate clearance to change the previous night's war plans. Based on Adan's progress, Gonen activated Sharon's division. At 10:45 A.M. he gave Sharon new orders: They were to leave the Tasa area immediately and roll sixty miles south on the Lateral Road, skirting the Egyptian Third Army without drawing fire. From there they would turn west, toward the city of Suez, where they were to seize control of the three Egyptian bridges across the canal. The plan, working off Adan's success against the Egyptian Second Army, would give Israel control of the southern sector of the Sinai.

Sharon demurred. It was a mistake to leave the high ground west of Tasa. He called Gonen and warned him of failure, imploring him to come to the field to see the erroneous nature of his orders with his own eyes. Gonen said Sharon would obey the order to the letter, or he would be relieved of his command.

Sharon obeyed the order, sending his three brigade commanders—Col. Haim Erez of the 421st Brigade, Col. Amnon Reshef of the 14th Brigade, and Col. Tuvia Raviv of the 600th Brigade— south as fast as possible. Within an hour, thousands of Sharon's tanks and other military vehicles were on the way to Suez. They made the first forty-five miles in three hours, undisturbed by enemy fire.

The general staff allowed itself a few moments of optimism. De- fense Minister Dayan, visiting the war room at IDF headquarters in Tel Aviv, joked about Sharon's aspirations, saying he knew he wanted to cross the canal and that from there he'd be off and running—to Suez, to Cairo, and of course to the head of the Likud Party.

Reality set in at two in the afternoon. Egyptian Sagger antitank missiles wiped out seventy of Adan's 170 tanks. As Sharon's divi- sion made its way south through the Jiddi Pass, an Israeli Air Force helicopter appeared. A senior officer from the Southern Command jumped out, told Sharon of the failed counterstrike, and handed him written orders: He was to turn around.

Sharon was enraged. Not only had an entire day been wasted, but his troops had given up the high ground without a fight. The division turned around. All told, they had spent the day driving hot tanks through ninety miles of desert. From that point on, Sharon's officers heard him complain loudly and without restraint about Elazar, Adan, and Gonen.

When they returned to the Tasa region, they found that Egyp- tian armor had taken their place. Just hours after they'd left the area, Sharon's division fought into the night to retake the hills. As opposed to the previous war, when many Egyptian soldiers fled for their lives through the desert, they now fought valiantly, and Sharon's troops suffered heavy losses. Sharon was furious throughout the battle, fuming at the thickheadedness of his peers.

Sharon and Adan were at odds. One point of contention was the abandonment of the hills. Sharon claimed he had received or- ders to leave as soon as possible; Adan felt his flanks had been left unguarded and that Sharon should have waited for him to take the high ground before leaving.

Sharon left his half-track at four-thirty in the afternoon, tired and upset. He went into his old war trailer and called Dayan. The chief of staff and the commander of the southern sector never come to the front, he said, so they have no idea what's happening in the field. Their orders are divorced from reality. He hung up and called Lily, asking how she and the boys were holding up. She asked him for some good news. The country, always fraught with existential concern, truly seemed on the edge of a precipice, as Syrian troops bore down on the Sea of Galilee. Sharon responded that he couldn't lift her spirits at that point.

Near midnight, Dayan, Elazar, and Gonen met with the southern sector division commanders. Elazar listened to reports of the failed counterstrike. Sharon suggested they reconsider his initial suggestion to attack with two divisions, his and Adan's, and cross the canal. Elazar categorically refused. He ordered the divisions to sit in defense and wait for further reserve troops to arrive and for the war on the northern front to be settled.

Elazar's orders meant that Sharon's troops would stay put for a week. He also ordered the troops in the forts to retreat on their own. At three in the morning a helicopter shuttled Dayan and Elazar back to Tel Aviv. They would have to tell the government that the previous day's briefing about the successful strike had been mistaken. The mood on the helicopter was grave.

On the night of October 8, the Egyptian forces completed their crossing of the canal. Sharon returned to Tasa frustrated. He spent the rest of the night running missions to save the soldiers still trapped on the front lines. Although his division was able to rescue the thirty-three soldiers in Fort Purkan, the vast majority of forts fell to the Egyptians, and the soldiers defending them were killed or captured. During the darkest hours of the night, he heard Max Maman's fort fall.

CHAPTER 21

Crossing the Canal

ON TUESDAY MORNING, OCTOBER 9, THE TANKS OF SHARON'S 143RD Division still prowled the sandy front lines, looking for a way toward the outposts. At 9:30, an Egyptian brigade attacked one of the division battalions, which remained unscathed as it destroyed thirty-five tanks. Sharon ordered the battalion to chase the fleeing Egyptian forces and attack two enemy strongholds. Their attack was rebuffed, the death toll high. Sharon sent Colonel Reshef's brigade to join the battle. Although they were able to capture one of the strongholds, the death toll continued to climb. That morning Sharon's division lost fifty tanks, eighteen of which were abandoned in enemy territory.

As far as Gonen was concerned, Sharon had ignored a direct order from the chief of staff to stay in a defensive position and wait for the rest of the reservists and a favorable turn of the tide on the northern front. Sharon claimed he had not disobeyed an order: The Egyptians had simply been fleeing, and it would have violated the basic rules of combat to allow them to escape. After several hours of fighting, Gonen flew into the battle zone and personally ordered Sharon to sever all contact with the enemy and retreat.

Gonen landed in Tasa. At the time, though, Sharon was commanding the tank battle from his armored personnel carrier. The armored vehicle, covered with swaying antennas and mounted machine guns, looked surreal as Sharon, giving orders through his headset, stood next to Shlomo Goren, the IDF's chief rabbi. As the white-shirted, gray-bearded rabbi prayed, the armored vehicle charged, lurching and tipping through an artillery bombardment. With dust clouds everywhere from the incoming fire, Sharon dropped the rabbi off at the foot of one of the dunes, behind cover.

Gonen grabbed a jeep and set off to find Sharon. After the war, he remarked that even after speaking to Sharon face-to-face, he remained wholly unconvinced that Sharon would follow orders and quit the offensive. Be that as it may, on October 9, the 143rd Division destroyed eighty Egyptian tanks and stopped the advance of the 2nd and 16th Egyptian divisions. When they were through, they had established a defensive line five miles east of the canal.

In the afternoon, Sharon had his first moment of satisfaction since looking at the aerial photos on Friday. In search of paths to the front line, his divisional reconnaissance unit had stumbled on a route that led straight to Fort Matzmed. The outpost, along the northern edge of the canal, near the Great Bitter Lake, in an area code-named "the Yard," had always been designated the canal crossing point in all of Sharon's war plans as OC Southern Command.

Sharon pored over the code maps, trying to discern why the route was clear of Egyptian forces. He soon saw that the path to Matzmed wound through a no-man's-land between the Egyptian Second and Third armies. After three days of frustration and despair, he felt he had at last found a weak point in the overwhelming Egyptian force, the kind that could change the tide of war. If Sharon's division crossed the canal it would rob Egypt of offensive momentum, potentially trap their forces on the Israeli side of the water, and pose a direct threat to the not-too-distant Egyptian capital.

At six-thirty in the evening, Sharon got Gonen on the radio and told him that he was at the water's edge. Gonen was not pleased. Sharon explained that his troops had happened on the area in the course of a long day of battle, during which they had stopped an Egyptian advance in its tracks. Gonen accused Sharon of disobeying orders. Sharon, unperturbed by the accusation, asked for clearance to cross the canal before the Egyptians got wind of the hole in their lines. Gonen said he would check and get back to him. "Get him out of there!" Elazar shouted at Gonen over the phone. "I'm not crossing!"

Sharon was ordered back to Tasa, ten miles east of the canal. He obeyed, but felt that the opposition to his plans was personal rather than professional. Perhaps, he thought, they were even political. After all, the entire general staff were Laborites, and Sharon would be returning to the Likud after the war. That night, Gonen asked Elazar to relieve Sharon of his command. Elazar called Dayan and scheduled a meeting at IDF headquarters.

Elazar explained the events of the day as they pertained to Sharon. He had willfully disobeyed several orders from the commander of the southern region and the chief of staff. In his book, *Daddo: 48 Years and 20 More Days*, Hanoch Bar-Tov quotes from the meeting between the defense minister and the chief of staff:

> Dayan: "It's no surprise that Arik's lying." Elazar: "But it is driving me out of my mind." Dayan: . . . "When I looked at Arik yesterday I thought to myself: He's asking himself . . . what will I get out of this? I'll stay here, in place, stagnant . . . or I'll come down to the canal and make order. So, please . . . if it works—great. If it doesn't work—the people of Israel lose two hundred tanks."

Nonetheless Dayan refused to fire Sharon. Instead, he suggested switching the hierarchy between the two men, giving Sharon back his old command and putting Gonen in charge of the 143rd Division. The chief of staff refused. In the end the two agreed that the current minister of industry and trade and former IDF chief of staff, Haim Bar-Lev, would be brought in to command the southern sector.

On Wednesday morning, October 10, Haim Bar-Lev took control of the region. Sharon greeted the appointment with mixed emotions. Bar-Lev had tried to oust him from the army, and the two had clashed over the Bar-Lev Line concept, but they had also cooperated well when Sharon was the southern sector's supreme commander. Mutual respect was certainly lacking at that point in time on the Sinai's battlefield. Bar-Lev soon learned that the Southern Command had been taping radio transmissions to and from Sharon, verifying whether he followed orders.

In the evening, Bar-Lev convened the sector's divisional commanders and staff officers for an assessment meeting. Suddenly, calm and quiet reigned. Sharon advocated crossing the canal. Mandler supported him, Adan opposed him. Bar-Lev decided to leave the divisions in place, forgoing the offensive.

Bar-Lev had known in advance there would be no offensive action in the near future in the Sinai region. Elazar, Dayan, and Meir had decided to attack deep into Syria the following day, threatening the capital. The air force would throw its full weight into the attack to the north and merely ensure clear skies in the southern sector. For the next five days, until October 15, the southern sector's ground troops were instructed simply to keep the Egyptians at bay.

The days of waiting frayed Sharon's nerves. Each passing day without an offensive, he felt, allowed the Egyptians time to dig in on the eastern side of the canal before the inevitable cease-fire. As that reality set in, rumors floated his way about the possible termination of his command. Sharon complained to the people around him that the motivation behind those rumors should be traced back to the Knesset, where elections waited in the wings of war.

At one point, people close to Sharon complained that a busload of foreign journalists was detained on the way to meet Sharon in Tasa, and they were taken instead to see other generals in the region who were ideologically in sync with Bar-Lev and Elazar. The truth, however, is that Sharon was surrounded by journalists for the majority of the war. During the first seven days of the war, a long list of top-level Israeli reporters interviewed him, including his friend, *Maariv* military correspondent Uri Dan, who spent the entire time at his side. The longer the IDF remained passive in the Sinai, the greater Sharon's frustration and the more he sniped at his military superiors in the press.

On the night of October 12, Dayan visited Sharon and heard his plans to cross the canal. Dayan described the atmosphere in his book *Milestones*:

Adan and Arik sat there, their eyes feverish, looking tired, hoarse, unshaven, and drained . . . they were under prolonged physical strain, jostling around in tanks, without rest, shouldering a burden of unsolvable and infinite prob-

lems in a hastily drafted division. Arik was steaming mad.
He studied, analyzed, and understood what was happening in the region. His solution was correct—to cross the
canal, destroy the missiles, and circle the Second and Third
Armies. But he emphasized that we couldn't bank on a miracle. We couldn't plan on capturing an Egyptian bridge in
working order. We needed bridges and Unifloats of our
own—and those were not yet in the vicinity of the canal.

Sharon awoke at four in the morning. His forces had spotted
four Egyptian helicopters loaded with commandos. Although they
had destroyed the force on the scene, Sharon knew immediately
that the commandos presaged an Egyptian offensive. At 6:10 A.M.
the Egyptians unleashed an onslaught of artillery fire followed by
tanks and infantry, focusing on the 143rd Division.

At seven in the morning Sharon's half-track was on the battlefield; at nine he reported to his deputy, Brig. Gen. Ya'akov Even,
that there was a heavy concentration of Egyptian tanks to his west,
from the 21st Division, which he "could nail and have a party with."

Over the following hours, one of the biggest armored battles of
all time raged in the desert, as 1,000 Egyptian tanks fought 750 Israeli ones. Israeli tankists, previously plagued by the joystick-
guided Sagger missiles of the Egyptian infantrymen, were now able
to wage the type of battle they had trained for. By afternoon, 270
Egyptian tanks had been taken out of commission, 120 of them destroyed by Sharon's division, while only 6 Israeli tanks had been
destroyed. Sharon saw hundreds of Egyptian soldiers running
through the smoke, seeking help. It was the Egyptian Army's first
defeat of the war.

Once victory seemed firmly in hand, Sharon again asked Bar-
Lev for authorization to cross the canal. Momentum was on their
side, he said, and the Egyptian soldiers were on the run. Bar-Lev
was hardly able to restrain Sharon, since his soldiers, in hot pursuit of the fleeing Egyptians, were fast approaching the water.

Sharon met Dayan later in the day in Sharon's bunker, the
"submarine." He detailed the morning's victory, explaining how
they had stopped the Egyptian offensive cold, and he pressed as

vehemently as ever for the commencement of an Israeli offensive aimed at crossing the canal. From there he accompanied Dayan to his helicopter, got into his half-track, and raced back to the battle.

Although Dayan restricted himself to no more than a few words of encouragement and refrained from authorizing the crossing, Sharon knew that once the Egyptians had been stopped, the Israeli offensive was only a matter of time. Certain of the inevitability, and not wanting to plan on paper alone, he left his headquarters in Tasa on October 14 and streaked down to the proposed crossing point along with several tanks and armored personnel carriers. The formation made it through the sand dunes on either side of the Second and Third armies without any hitches. They looked out at the 180-yard-wide swath of blue water near the northern edge of Bitter Lake and then returned to base unnoticed.

Shortly before midnight on October 14, the government, with the backing of Defense Minister Dayan and Chief of Staff Elazar, authorized the crossing of the canal. Haim Bar-Lev proposed to Prime Minister Meir that Sharon's division, bolstered by a brigade of paratroopers, secure a bridgehead on the east bank north of Bitter Lake, ferry the brigade of paratroopers to the western side of the canal during the night, and then lay the bridges for the rest of the division. Once the bridgehead had been secured, Adan's division would charge through and attack deep into Egypt.

Bar-Lev assigned Sharon another mission: widening the gap between the two Egyptian armies so that the heavy engineering bridges could approach the canal unhindered. To ensure their safe passage, Sharon's division had to take two areas still dominated by the Egyptians. The fortified positions code-named "the Chinese Farm" and "Missouri," both held by entrenched Egyptian armor, had to be cleared if vulnerable troops were to pass on the routes code-named "Tirtur" and "Akavish." This additional mission would stand at the heart of the postwar dispute between Elazar and Bar-Lev on the one side and Sharon on the other.

At six o'clock in the morning on October 15, Sharon's staff officers sat on a sand dune and listened as their commander tapped out a battle plan on the plastic-covered maps behind him. The tip of his pointer guided them through the arrows on the map. At last, he said, they were going to cross the canal and attack.

Sharon directed Amnon Reshef's force (the 14th Brigade) to open Akavish and Tirtur, the routes to the water, and to secure the Chinese Farm and Missouri, thereby providing cover for the bridgehead. Once Reshef's brigade had completed its mission, Col. Danny Mat, commander of a reserve brigade of paratroopers (the 247th Brigade), would seize control of the Yard and establish a bridgehead on the far side of the canal. The 421st Brigade, under the command of Haim Erez, would be ferried across the canal while the 600th Brigade, under the command of Tuvia Raviv, attacked in the central sector, drawing the Egyptians' attention away from the crossing.

Crossing the water barrier under enemy fire was a tall order. Sharon, having practiced the maneuver many times as commander of the southern region, knew he would need precision timing, the kind readily attainable in pinpoint raids but often beyond reach in all-out war. The tanks, artillery, and infantry of both his and Adan's divisions would have to work in absolute unison with the Engineering Corps' three battalions as they attempted to deliver a two-hundred-yard-long, four-hundred-ton roller bridge through enemy-controlled territory to the water, along with a pontoon bridge known as a Unifloat and a slew of older French amphibious vehicles called Gilowas that, latched together, could ferry a tank or create a flimsy bridge.

The mission, code-named "Stouthearted Men," was to start at eight-thirty in the evening and last for twelve hours. Sharon ended his briefing to his officers by saying that he would see them on the other side of the canal with first light. As he made his way to the front for a final surveillance of the staging area, he saw improvised huts, made with armaments boxes and topped with palm fronds, reminding him that the Jewish holiday of Sukkoth had begun.

During the afternoon of October 15, moments before giving Raviv's brigade the order to move out and begin the diversionary attack, Sharon faced a difficult decision. The heavy equipment for crossing the canal was stuck behind endless lines of traffic on the way to the front. Bar-Lev offered Sharon a twenty-four-hour extension, until the equipment arrived at Tasa. Just before four in the afternoon, Sharon called Bar-Lev and told him he had decided to go ahead as planned. The paratroopers, also held up, would set out across the water at midnight rather than 8:30 P.M. as originally planned.

Sharon would later say that the decision to push ahead with the plan without knowing whether the bridges would show up was one of the hardest of his life. After two weeks of pressing for the move, he felt bound to proceed, for two reasons: The government's will to act offensively, and the Egyptian ignorance of the seam in their troop deployment, might not last through the waiting period.

At 4:00 P.M. Raviv's brigade, its ranks thinned and tired from battle, moved west in the direction of Ismailia, commencing the diversionary attack. The attack surprised the Egyptians, who had yet to recover from the previous day's battle. As far as Sharon was concerned, the goal of their mission was to draw as many enemy tanks as possible into battle far from the route to the Yard. Amnon Reshef's brigade waited in the dark for the Egyptian tanks to be drawn away before setting out in a northwesterly direction, toward the water.

One hour later, Raviv's brigade came under heavy artillery fire. With last light, Reshef's brigade began moving in the direction of the canal. On their way, at the Chinese Farm, they met 140 enemy tanks. They engaged in an armored battle at point-blank range. Despite reports of heavy casualties, Sharon gave Mat's paratroopers the order to move in the direction of the Yard and prepare for the crossing.

At this point the Egyptian forces were certain that the Israelis were attacking the Chinese Farm. They battled valiantly, claiming 60 tanks and 120 Israeli soldiers during what was one of the most bitterly fought battles of the war. Even after Sharon sent two backup armored battalions to the area, the routes to the water were still not safe for the heavy equipment.

Under fire and slightly tardy, Mat's troops reached the canal at half past midnight with the paratroopers' rafts and the Gilowas. By one-thirty in the morning the fully loaded rafts were in the water. The Egyptians didn't notice them as they crossed the 180-yard-wide canal. On arrival the paratroopers detonated pipe bombs, clearing the area of barbed wire, and dug in on the western side of the water. By dawn, the paratroopers had set up a 3.5-mile-wide bridgehead.

On the other side of the canal, Sharon was bedeviled by the delays. Any element of surprise would be lost with first light. Egyptian artillery would rip apart the bridges and any heavy armor on them, stranding his forces on the far side. He arrived at the Yard at five in the morning along with ten tanks from Haim Erez's brigade. Anxious to get things rolling, he hopped out of his halftrack and began directing a bulldozer to the red bricks that marked a soft spot in the berm that had been thrown up to provide cover from artillery. The driver rammed the supposed soft spot a number of times with no success. Tired of the incessant delays, Sharon climbed onto the bulldozer, threw it into gear, and began charging into the wall. "Like that," he said. Within a few moments the barrier crumbled into the water.

Danny Mat, wearing his red beret, strode through the gap and shook Sharon's hand. A former soldier of Sharon's from as far back as the Mitla battle, Mat was joined by Shimon Kahaner, an even older veteran. Sharon ordered the Gilowas into the water and, along with the bulldozer driver, headed over to punch another hole in the earthen barrier. At 6:00 A.M. the soldiers pushed the first of the old French Gilowas into the water, prompting a relieved Sharon to call out for some breakfast.

An hour later the first of the Israeli tanks lumbered onto African soil to an ovation from the dug-in paratroopers. By 10:00 A.M., twenty-seven tanks and seven APCs from Haim Erez's brigade had crossed the canal. Although the force was sufficient to protect the paratroopers, Sharon's mission was far from complete: The primary crossing gear—the rolling bridge and the Unifloat pontoons—had yet to arrive; the routes to the water had not been cleared of enemy troops; Missouri and the Chinese Farm were still in Egyptian hands.

The top commanders met on the morning of October 16 to decide the fate of the crossing. Dayan, afraid that Mat's men were stranded on the west side of the water and susceptible to an attack that could end in slaughter, wanted to return the troops to safety. Bar-Lev and Chief of Staff Elazar disagreed with Dayan and decided to leave the troops in place. Sharon wanted to shift as many troops as possible to the west side before the Egyptians got wind of the maneuver, but all present deemed the plan too risky.

Quiet reigned over the Yard well into the afternoon. The Egyptians had not yet noticed the crossing. Sharon left the area and drove in his armored personnel carrier to the Chinese Farm. There he saw 50 crippled Israeli tanks beside 150 Egyptian ones. Amid the charred vehicles and the splayed treads he saw dead Israeli and Egyptian troops side by side, all having jumped out of flaming tanks.

The other side of the canal looked pastoral. Fruit trees and palms dotted the Egyptian shore. Sharon asked his communications officer to get Lily on the line. Owing to a faulty wireless connection, Sharon announced the exciting news of having crossed the canal to some woman named Lily who was not his wife.

CHAPTER 22

King of Israel

THE TRAVAILS OF CROSSING THE CANAL AND ESTABLISHING THE bridgehead position changed the face of the war: For the first time since the initial Egyptian onslaught, Israel had taken the upper hand. With most of its tanks engaged on the Israeli side of the canal, Egypt had only 225 tanks standing between Sharon and Cairo.

An eager Sharon waited until the quiet morning hours before getting on one of the tanks that was crossing the canal. He hurried to the Yard to oversee the pandemonium in the staging area. Racing against time, engineers, technicians, and heavy equipment operators struggled to load as many tanks as possible onto the Gilowa rafts before Egyptian intelligence spotted the crossing. Sharon knew that from the moment the crossing was noticed, they would be under a constant barrage of artillery fire.

While working at a feverish pace, Sharon received an order to cease and desist from all crossing activity at the canal. The general staff and the Southern Command headquarters were worried that the bridgehead was too weak and narrow and that the forces on the far bank could be cut off and caught in a death trap. Sharon, furious, felt the order was outrageous. He admitted that he had been unable to clear the routes leading to the Yard during the night, but his forces on the Egyptian side of the canal, he told them, were proceeding west with impunity. Haim Erez's tanks were already positioned eighteen miles beyond the canal.

The battlefield on the Israeli side of the water spoke of a far harsher night. Despite their grueling efforts, Amnon Reshef's brigade had not managed to clear the Tirtur access route, which was lined with entrenched Egyptian antitank forces and needed for the transport of the mobile bridges. The route remained narrow and to a large extent in Egyptian hands. The Chinese Farm, a fortified Egyptian stronghold lined with deep irrigation ditches, had not yet been taken, leaving the bridgeheads on either side of the water in a precarious position. Although the Akavish route had been opened, it was unlikely that Sharon's force, at that point, could have weathered an Egyptian assault.

Nonetheless, Sharon pushed in favor of continuing the offensive, eager to capitalize on the confusion on the Egyptian side. Chief of Staff Elazar, long worried that Sharon, unleashed on the western side of the canal, would storm toward Cairo no matter what was happening behind him, had little trust in the division commander's reports from the field. In 48 Years and 20 More Days, Hanoch Bar-Tov quotes from a conversation Elazar had in the IDF's Tel Aviv headquarters on the morning of the sixteenth: "His reports were arrogant, not informative. At one point I said, 'Tell me, what's happening?' He said: 'Don't worry. You have nothing to fear. Everything will be fine.' Who said anything about fear? Just tell me what's happening."

Defense Minister Dayan's impression of Sharon, as recorded in his autobiography Milestones, was markedly different: "I don't know a better field officer than Sharon. I don't mean to say I've never found fault with his ways . . . we fought more than once, but even when I want to 'kill' him—at least I know there is someone to kill."

At eleven in the morning on October 16, Sharon received a direct order from Bar-Lev and Gonen, with the authorization of the chief of staff, not to send another tank across the canal. Repeatedly, Sharon called for the senior command to come to the field and read the situation in real time, but no one would arrive until October 19.

Lt. Col. Dr. Elchanan Oren published an official IDF history of the war in December 2004. In The History of the Yom Kippur War, he writes:

As a result of hitches in the schedule and the timetable, the morning of October 16 was laced with tension between Major General Sharon and Southern Command staff. When Sharon demanded that Division 162 (Adan's division) be tasked with opening the routes, the OC Southern Command demanded that he first send Brigade 421 [Haim Erez's brigade] to fulfill its mission [opening the routes on the eastern bank]. Major General Sharon would prefer to cross the canal and drive deep into Egypt, but Lieutenant General Bar-Lev and Major General Gonen demanded that he first clear all of the routes and secure the lane [to the canal].

Sharon felt that the sixteenth, instead of marking the beginning of victory, was wasted by the order to stop the crossing. During the course of the day, the Egyptians located the bridgehead and attacked Danny Mat's paratroopers and Erez's twenty-seven tanks. Despite the attack and the endless stream of complaints from the brass, Sharon's troops were able to widen the bridgehead on the western side of the canal, capture an Egyptian air base, and destroy five SAM missile batteries.

On the night of October 16, Sharon went to sleep on the warm hood of a tank, his mind ill at ease. He awoke early the next morning to the sound of heavy engineering equipment. More Gilowas had at last arrived. At seven in the morning an Egyptian barrage began. By four-thirty in the afternoon, despite the hail of artillery, the amphibious vehicles, susceptible to artillery but able to bear the weight of a tank, had been linked together to span the canal.

At nine in the morning on the seventeenth, Slutsky, once again watching Sharon's back, noticed an incoming round heading in their direction. He yelled out to Sharon, who instinctively jumped headfirst into an armored personnel carrier. The quick reflex saved his life, as the ground behind the vehicle was now a crater.

A few seconds later a second round rocked the area. In the scramble, Sharon hit his head on the vehicle's mounted machine gun. Blood poured down his face and he slipped out of consciousness. He heard one of the officers say he'd taken a direct hit and that the divisional commander had been killed. He opened his eyes. The wound had hurt, and his head was covered in blood, but he was in no danger.

Crowned with a white bandage, Sharon got back on his feet and saw Egyptian tanks fast approaching the Yard. He radioed Amnon Reshef and asked for immediate backup. At that point most of the tanks defending the Yard had left to try to help the paratroopers in their bloody battle in the Chinese Farm (forty dead, sixty wounded). Reshef came with alacrity. His tank and two others stormed the Egyptian tanks and wiped them out.

As the threat subsided, Sharon realized Slutsky was no longer by his side. He asked the people around him what had happened and received evasive replies. Finally he was told that Slutsky had been hit by a round near the bridgehead and that he had been evacuated in critical condition. The truth was less ambiguous. Slutsky had been killed by an artillery round, his feet still laced into Sharon's boots. Sharon took the news of the grave injury badly. He knew his close friend and battlefield companion had been lost.

In a foul mood, Sharon complained bitterly for the rest of the day, arguing vociferously with his commanders about the manner in which the crossing had been handled. On the far side of the canal, Mat had lost twelve men, and twenty-two had been injured. At 1:00 P.M. Sharon was summoned to an urgent meeting with Dayan, Elazar, Bar-Lev, and Adan. The meeting was held at Adan's headquarters, twelve miles northeast of the Yard.

Sharon changed his blood-soaked bandage before the meeting. On the way to Adan's headquarters he encountered throngs of admiring soldiers and officers. Sharon's detractors say he already had his mind set on the coming elections, which explains why he rode around without a helmet, eager to exhibit his bandage and his heroism. Sharon responded that the ones who needed to wear a helmet were his commanding officers, with whom he'd settle the score after the war.

On arrival, only Dayan greeted him, and even he was cold. The rest of the generals stared in silence. Sharon hadn't seen them since the crossing commenced. Although he thought his actions spoke for themselves, Bar-Lev began by charging him with what he saw as a vast and troubling disparity between what he had promised to do and what had happened in the field. Bar-Lev said he had not fulfilled his mission on the eastern side of the canal—clearing the routes to the bridgehead. Even now, Bar-Lev complained, Tirtur was not fully in Israeli hands. After the war, Sharon revealed that at that moment it took a superhuman effort to quell the urge to slap Bar-Lev in the face.

The generals sat down on the hot desert sand for what Dayan termed in *Milestones* a war council. "Arik's reading of the situation," Dayan writes,

> and his opinion of what steps should be taken, were almost always at odds with those of his superiors. Worse, there was no mutual faith. Arik felt he was being discriminated against and that his reports from the field [were] not accepted at face value. His superiors contended that Arik was not carrying out their orders and that he was motivated by personal ambition—exhibiting himself and the accomplishments of his unit—and that he was breaking the most basic rules of discipline, calling friends from the front and illicitly involving them in military matters.
>
> Arik arrived with a bandage wrapped around his head. His forehead had been scratched by shrapnel, his silvering hair wild, his face carrying the signs of several days and nights of warfare. His division fought valiantly, suffering very heavy losses but never shirking their responsibilities. All of them, from Arik on down to the last of his soldiers, had been under constant fire.

During the battle for the bridgehead alone, two hundred soldiers had fallen. In Reshef's brigade, each of the company commanders had been killed—first the original officers, and then their replacements. By this stage of the war, the companies were commanded by the third wave of officers.

The hour-and-a-half war council revolved around the question of which full division would cross the canal first. Sharon demanded to be allowed to run forward and release his division west and crush the enemy. Bar-Lev answered acerbically that he had been hearing about this "crushing" for a week, but that he had seen little result. Sharon replied, "Soon you'll say I didn't fight at all."

Chief of Staff Elazar ruled against Sharon: No more tanks would cross the water until the bridge was put in place. Once it had been erected, Sharon's division would stay on the eastern side, ensuring and asserting control of Akavish, Tirtur, and Missouri. Adan's entire division would cross the canal over the bridge Sharon's men had laid. At the close of the meeting, Elazar turned to Sharon and said he understood that he wanted to be in Africa, but first he had to complete his duties in Asia.

Sharon was offended. He had come to the war council after long battles and treacherous work along the canal. He felt that Bar-Lev and the other top officers were denying him the glory of crossing the water en masse so that he could not announce before the elections that he had won the war by crossing the canal at the head of triumphant troops.

The meeting ended at 2:00 P.M. As Elazar and Bar-Lev climbed into a helicopter, Dayan asked them to tell Prime Minister Meir that he would miss that evening's government meeting. He was staying with Sharon. He sat down in Sharon's half-track and headed off to the crossing point in a cloud of dust. Dayan asked him about his injury, and Sharon, aware that Slutsky and Dayan were from the same moshav, told him about his friend's mortal wound. Sharon felt Dayan's burning desire to get to the other side of the canal.

As though on command, the artillery fire stopped as soon as Dayan approached the Yard. Sharon walked the defense minister over to one of the openings in the dirt berm and sat down, looking out at the water. Dayan wrote in *Milestones,* "Arik and I crossed the water in an amphibious vehicle. . . . In Africa Arik wanted to get on an armored vehicle. I preferred to walk a bit . . . when I returned to the Yard, the bridge was complete, the rafts linked to one another and stretching from shore to shore. It was four in the afternoon."

Dayan flew back to Tel Aviv, and Sharon, burning for action, began complaining about the long wait for Adan's tanks. He issued a number of radio calls over the next several hours complaining

about the waste of the unused bridge. Adan's division, backed up
on the Akavish route for logistical reasons, began crossing at midnight. By the morning of October 18, two of Adan's armored
brigades had crossed the canal.

From early evening until midnight, the troops fitted the Unifloat bridge together. Twenty-four hours later the roller bridge,
which was pulled by a dozen tanks over treacherously uneven
ground and through a number of combat zones, was laid across the
water. Once it was in place, Sharon asked for authorization to prepare his troops to cross the canal and head for Ismailia. Bar-Lev
and Elazar denied his request, insisting he take Missouri, still held
by entrenched Egyptian forces.

Sharon was up in arms. He argued that Missouri no longer
threatened the bridgehead; the routes were open; and the battle
to dislodge the Egyptians would just result in useless loss of life.
Instead of shedding blood on the eastern bank of the canal, they
should send more forces across the water and attack Ismailia and
Cairo, Egypt's underbelly. Sharon fought the decree in all possible ways, but in the end, with what he termed "no choice," he
complied.

On October 21, at 3:00 P.M., forty of Tuvia Raviv's tanks attacked Missouri. They disabled twenty Egyptian tanks but, suffering many losses on their own side from the dreaded Sagger missiles,
were unable to take control of the position. Bar-Lev and Gonen demanded that Sharon ready his troops for another attack the next
day. Their arguments over the plan developed into a shouting
match.

Sharon would not relent. After midnight, he called Dayan to
complain about the mission, citing the senselessness of losing life
in an immaterial battle. Dayan called Deputy Chief of Staff Yisrael
Tal and asked him to investigate Sharon's claims, saying that he
could not ignore this type of request from Sharon. Tal, one of
Sharon's few supporters on the IDF general staff, woke Chief of
Staff Elazar and asked whether he could absolve Sharon of the
mission. Elazar said later that when he was woken up that night,
he thought to himself, "This is it—you can't force a senior commander in the field to attack if he doesn't want to."

The next day, October 22, the U.N. Security Council issued

Resolution 338, stating that a cease-fire would go into effect that evening at 6:52. Once Adan's division had encircled the Egyptian Third Army, Meir's government hastened to accept the cease-fire. At the time, Sharon was in the midst of a race with his forces toward Ismailia, on the western side of the canal. His goal, to trap the Second Army, was thwarted by the U.N. proclamation. Sharon called Menachem Begin and asked him to pressure Prime Minister Meir to delay accepting the cease-fire. But by the time Sharon's forces reached the outskirts of the city, Israel had accepted.

The IDF halted at an advantageous position militarily. They had taken five hundred square kilometers of territory in the Golan Heights, including the pivotal Mount Hermon; Damascus lay at their feet. On the southern front, the Egyptian Third Army, forty thousand men strong, was surrounded, the city of Suez was cut off, and the Israelis had stopped at the edge of Ismailia, a hundred kilometers short of Cairo. The surprise attack and the death toll, however, had snapped Israel's six-year euphoria. The vaunted Military Intelligence Service had been caught unaware, and the Arab armies, long considered laughable, had fought with frightening valor. In the face of the shock of the surprise attack and the offensives from north and south, Sharon stood firm. His head bandaged, he never lost his poise. As the Bar-Lev Line fell, he alone called for a counterstrike, eventually changing the tide of war.

After sixteen days of war—quiet. Sharon called Ze'ev Slutsky's wife, Dalya, from outside the city. He wanted to tell her personally what he had known for several days—that Zevele had died. After he hung up the phone, Sharon cried, tears flowing uncontrollably.

After the cease-fire, Sharon's popularity soared. Signs on the division's vehicles read "Arik, King of Israel." The sentiment spread across the Sinai Desert. Intersections were crowded with reservists holding the same signs. At home, people saw Sharon as the hero of the war, the man who had crossed the canal and reversed the tide. Against a backdrop of arrogant and complacent intelligence officers and IDF commanders, Sharon was perceived as the country's savior.

Sharon did not bury his wartime grudges. He played a major

CEASE-FIRE LINES AFTER YOM KIPPUR WAR, 1973

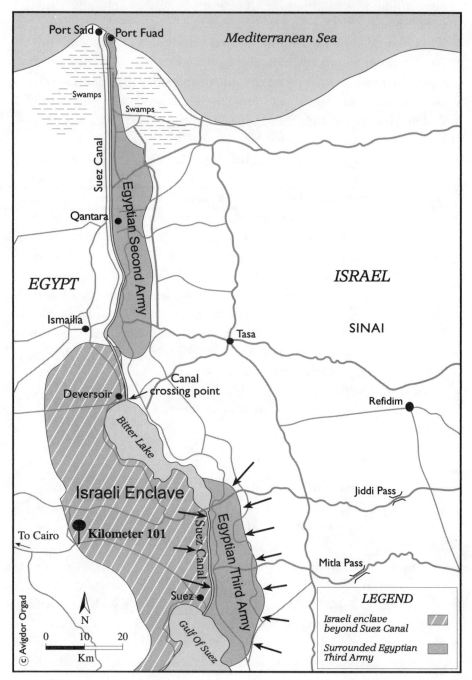

role in the battle of the generals that came on the heels of the war. Speaking to *The New York Times* after the war, he attacked both Elazar and Gonen. The article ignited a bitter war of words. Elazar published a critical response to the article and did everything in his power to oust Sharon from his position as a reserve division commander.

Major General Gonen filed a formal complaint against Sharon, charging that he had disobeyed an order on the night he refused to thrust his troops back into battle at Missouri. Sharon was vindicated when the Agranat Commission, a national committee of inquiry tasked with examining the many failures leading up to and during the Yom Kippur War, found that Sharon's behavior had not strayed beyond IDF norms and that it corresponded to the disciplinary needs of the army.

On January 20, 1974, after twenty-five years of service, three months of intense bickering, and a sense of stability at last in the Sinai, Ariel Sharon announced his final retirement from the army. As usual, he felt it unnecessary to coordinate the decision with the chief of staff. In his public announcement, he made it clear who the great winner of the war was:

"Warriors," he wrote to his soldiers,

> three and a half months ago we went out to war. It was a difficult and bloody war. We were called up on Yom Kippur and we, the reservists, together went to the crumbling front. Our division faced the heart of the enemy's attack. Each and every one of you, fighting with valor and expending supreme effort, was able to stop the Egyptian forces. Our division took initiative and responsibility for the hardest, most difficult, and most brutal task of the war—the crossing of the canal. The crossing of the canal is what brought the change in the war. The crossing of the canal is what won the war. It is incumbent upon us to remember that our victory in the Yom Kippur War is the greatest of our victories. If—despite the snafus and the mistakes, the failures and the trip wires, the loss of calm and of control—we were still able to attain victory, then we should all know that this was the IDF's greatest victory.

Hundreds of the best of our warriors fell in battle and far more were wounded over the course of the war—but we won! You, despite it all, won, and you did it with dedication, self-sacrifice, stubbornness, and bravery. . . . With the close of the war I announced I would stay with you for as long as the reserves were needed. I promised I would stay with you, but today I must go. To you, the soldiers, the true heroes of this war, I owe an explanation. The war is over, the negotiations with Egypt are over, and I feel I need to fight on a different front. We must struggle, with all our might, to ensure that there will be no more war. That's why I am leaving. I want you to know I have never served in the company of warriors of your kind. You were the greatest of them all! I have never felt closer to brothers in arms and had a deeper sense of comradeship than with this division. The warm welcome home you provided instilled in me the certitude of our strength and abilities. Today I leave you with sorrow. My wishes are that each one of you is hastened home, but if we ever need to return and fight—I promise to fight alongside you.

Many viewed Sharon's last statement as political, especially since that afternoon he called a press conference at Beit Sokolov in Tel Aviv. International news crews waited for his first utterance. In a black turtleneck and a black leather vest, Sharon spoke in Hebrew and then in English. He ridiculed the manner in which the heads of the Labor Party had conducted the negotiations with the Egyptians. From the press conference he continued on to a protest rally in Tel Aviv called "The Withdrawal from Both Banks of the Suez in Exchange for Nothing."

The steady rain that day did not keep thousands of people off the street. Umbrellas packed the square as people listened to the speakers, Menachem Begin, Yitzhak Shamir, and Ariel Sharon. Sharon labeled the Israeli withdrawal "the withdrawal of a victorious army led by a beaten leadership." The protesters took up the chant "Arik, King of Israel."

When the speakers finished, Sharon tried to plow a path to his car, but the crowd surged toward him, trying to hug him, shake his hand, kiss him. He found himself swept up by the human wave and pushed to the far side of the street. Only an hour later, after the police arrived, could he reach his car. Physically drained, he marveled at the potency of public affection, a feeling he had not previously known.

CHAPTER 23

Political Rookie

On December 31, 1973, Israelis cast their votes for the eighth Knesset. Although the Likud managed to increase their representation from twenty-six to thirty-nine seats, they failed to seize control of the house. Sharon was deeply disappointed. Despite all, Israeli citizens seemed to prefer those responsible for the Yom Kippur disaster to the Likud. In December 1973, the Labor government, led again by Prime Minister Golda Meir, received just five fewer seats than in the previous elections.

On March 10, 1974, Meir assembled a coalition led by Labor and including the National Religious Party (for years a centrist party that now sits on the far right of the political map), Ratz, and the Independent Liberals. The new member of the Opposition, MK Ariel Sharon, had not met with his parliamentary benchmates since his summons to the front lines on the eve of Yom Kippur. The leaders of the Likud found the former general conceited and arrogant.

In early 1974 he set about the task of learning his parliamentary role and fulfilling his duties. Although he enjoyed the status of membership in the Knesset's Foreign Affairs and Defense Committee and the prestige of chairing the Subcommittee for the Defense Budget, the daily routine of a parliamentarian left him bored. He hated the plastic smiles, the double-talk, and the minor feuds that are the bread and butter of the Knesset. He found his chores numbing. Often he sat in the Knesset lounge holding lengthy conversations with Avraham Yaffe and Muhammad Abu Rabi'a, an Israeli Bedouin leader.

In early April 1974, the Agranat Commission published its interim report. To the shock of most citizens, the five-person panel, led by Supreme Court chief justice Shimon Agranat and including Supreme Court justice Moshe Landau, State Comptroller Yitzhak Nebenzahl, and former IDF chiefs of staff Yigael Yadin and Haim Laskov, decided that IDF chief of staff Lt. Gen. David Elazar and Director of Military Intelligence Maj. Gen. Eli Zeira both bore heavy responsibility for the intelligence failures that led to the surprise attack. They had, the commission members wrote, been blinded by the mistaken concept that Egypt would not wage war without a stronger air force, unattainable at the time. In dismissing Zeira, they wrote: "In light of his grave failure, Major General Zeira cannot continue to serve as Head of Military Intelligence." As for Chief of Staff Elazar, "We see it as our duty to recommend the termination of his tenure."

The committee found fault with Gonen, too. They termed the manner in which he deployed his troops in Sinai, once the onslaught began, "a woeful order" and "a dreadful mistake." In the summation of the forty-page interim report, the commission members wrote: "At this point we will not issue a recommendation as pertains to Major General Gonen's ability to continue to serve in the IDF; however, we do recommend that he not fill any active position until the committee finishes its inquiry into all matters pertaining to the battle to stop the advancing enemy."

It was music to Sharon's ears. Eight months later, in late 1974, the committee published its second interim report. This time they repealed their earlier recommendation regarding Gonen and his suitability to serve in the IDF. Sharon, though, felt vindicated yet again. The committee dismissed the insubordination charges Gonen had leveled at Sharon. They found that Sharon's behavior as commander of the 143rd Division was perfectly compatible with IDF norms:

> We wish to linger for a moment on the unique issue of discipline, which has created public discourse in the wake of an interview . . . in which Maj. Gen. Ariel Sharon implied that, in his opinion, in certain circumstances it is proper for an officer not to fulfill orders. When Major General Sharon appeared before us as a witness we questioned him

on that subject in order to clarify the matter. Major General Sharon testified that a certain action, taken during one of the last days of the war, ate away at his conscience. On that day he had been given an order to attack a certain area with his division. He was of the opinion that fulfilling the order would translate into a great loss of life, and that the officer issuing the order, were he on the field of battle and were he knowledgeable of the conditions thereon—information he did not have, according to Sharon—then he would not have issued the order. Therefore, he, Major General Sharon, opposed the order for hours, but, in the end, with the order still standing, he obeyed and carried out the attack. Afterward, he found he had attained nothing that would have made him change his mind earlier. He submits that case as an example of an order that should not have been carried out, but answered for after the fact. In his testimony he stressed that such examples are very rare.

In his own words, Sharon told the committee: "I admit that it's possible I shouldn't have said it, because ever since then there's been a trail of things I didn't say following me, no matter how many times I argue and deny and explain and reissue my denial. I've already become a figure ostensibly opposed to fulfilling orders. I don't think I don't obey orders. . . . I think one needs to obey orders to the letter . . . and I explained that numerous times." The commission ruled that "Major General Sharon's views, as expressed to us, are in harmony with the demands of military discipline."

The Agranat Commission dealt harshly with Zeira and Elazar, but absolved the national leaders of responsibility. Neither Dayan nor Meir was taken to task for their roles in the surprise attack. The Israeli public was sharply critical of that approach. There was immense pressure on Meir to step down, and on June 3, 1974, she bowed to public demand.

Yitzhak Rabin, glorious victor of the Six Day War, was chosen as head of the Labor Party and prime minister. The former ambassador to Washington and minister of labor assembled a coalition government in July 1974. He named Shimon Peres defense minister.

Sharon tried to harness the tailwinds of the Agranat Commission's report. Immediately following Elazar's premature retirement, Sharon, stultified by parliamentary work and long covetous of the IDF's top spot, let it be known that he wished to be appointed IDF chief of staff. The botched rescue at a school attacked by terrorists in Ma'alot, in northern Israel, and the difficulties of the negotiations with Egypt, only aided his campaign.

Menachem Begin pushed for Sharon, but the Labor government preferred his old rival, Motta Gur. In June 1974, Yechiel Leket, chairman of the Young Guard of the Labor Party, charged in the party paper that "Sharon is capable of conducting a military coup just to be in government." Sharon responded with one word— "heresy"—but Leket's fears were widespread in the party.

Sharon, bitterly disappointed by the choice of a rival as chief of staff, was consoled by the fact that Rabin had inherited the premiership. In his quest to find Sharon a suitable position in the IDF, Rabin encountered great resistance. Both Gur and Peres contended that the army needed to rid itself of the in-house fighting that had plagued it, and that Sharon represented exactly the opposite. The battle over Sharon's worth signaled the beginning of a twenty-year struggle between Rabin and Peres for control of the Labor Party.

Sharon, still in the opposition Likud Party, held his tongue throughout the summer of 1974 in anticipation of good news from Rabin. At last Rabbi Shlomo Goren joined the fray and persuaded Peres to relent. The defense minister met with Sharon and Shmuel Gonen in Beersheba. Over lunch, Sharon and Gonen agreed to retract the charges they had filed against each other. In December 1974, Sharon was appointed to the ambiguous post of senior reserves field commander in the southern sector.

The appointment riled many anti-Sharon Labor members. They contended it was unethical to serve in the military and the Knesset at the same time. Eventually they passed a bill in parliament barring any active army officers with a rank higher than colonel from serving in the Knesset. Sharon labeled the law the "Anti-Sharon Bill."

Sharon continued to surprise political pundits and party mates. On December 16, 1974, he resigned from the Knesset with no prior warning. "I am truly sorry," Sharon wrote in his resignation letter, "about the arbitrary and antidemocratic law passed in the Knesset—a bill known as the Sharon Decree, which forces me out of the Knesset just so that I can fulfill my basic right as a citizen and serve in the reserves. This decision is, in my opinion, anticonstitutional. With the danger of looming war, I must, however, ignore the bill and concentrate on my contribution to state security."

Sharon's retirement was greeted with surprise and without sorrow. He'd made a poor impression in his first year as an MK. He seemed bored and had raised the ire of Likud members with his dogged courting of Rabin, constantly trying to please him, promoting little more than his own ambitions. Shmuel Tamir, his former lawyer and Opposition partner in the Knesset, called Sharon "a man with no restraints." To Likud members he explained that the outrageous anti-Sharon law had left him with no choice. Quietly he hoped that the new posting, although only in the reserves, left him a chance of promotion to chief of staff once Gur vacated the post.

But Sharon clashed immediately with Gur over IDF deployment in the Sinai after the Separation of Forces Agreement with Egypt. Sharon drafted plans, but Gur dismissed them out of hand and replaced them with plans drawn up by the general staff. Once Sharon took the liberty of sharing his ideas with soldiers along the front, Gur resolved to avoid contact with Sharon and render his appointment moot. Left with no alternatives, Sharon returned to the farm.

Israel was in the midst of a drought. The Sharon family's agricultural endeavors were sinking, along with much of the postwar economy in Israel. Small business owners and farmers, often subsisting through loans, suffered greatly from the recession and the rising rate of inflation. Sharon was horrified to learn that during his time in the Knesset, the farm had been brought to the brink of bankruptcy.

Sharon decided to restructure the business and sell to the foreign market. His crew of workers—including many Arabs—worked day and night. Sharon went out to the watermelon fields early, came back at nine in the morning for breakfast, and then went back out until it was time for lunch, which Lily always prepared.

After several months of intensive work and a total shift to export, the farm climbed out of debt.

The transition took half a year, a period of time Sharon would later call the happiest of his life. It was the first, and not the last, time the farm would serve as a refuge.

During those days Sharon maintained moderate to light contact with the heads of the Likud and devoted most of his time to his family, riding with Omri, now ten, and Gilad, eight, through the desert. In the summer of 1975, after a year-and-a-half hiatus from politics, Sharon received an unexpected offer from Prime Minister Rabin. Rabin offered him the position of Security Adviser to the Prime Minister. Peres and Gur were dumbfounded.

Peres and Gur pushed hard to limit Sharon's sphere of influence. They were unwilling to have him attend the general staff meetings. Under pressure, Rabin relented and barred him from the meetings and changed his title to General Adviser to the Prime Minister. Attorney General Meir Shamgar ruled that Sharon could serve as both prime ministerial adviser and a reserves general in the southern sector.

Sharon approached his new task with vigor, but soon found his influence reduced to nil. Each of his political security moves was rejected out of hand. It soon became clear to him that Rabin had him on retainer not because he saw him as future chief of staff, but as a way of silencing criticisms from the right about an interim agreement with the Egyptians.

Since March 1975, American secretary of state Henry Kissinger had been making the rounds between Cairo and Jerusalem in an attempt to push the sides closer together on an agreement that would officially end the war. Kissinger and President Gerald Ford brought massive pressure to bear on Israel to retreat from all areas between the canal and the Jiddi and Mitla passes. On August 31, 1975, the two sides reached an agreement.

Up until his appointment as an adviser to Prime Minister Rabin in July 1975, Sharon had vehemently opposed the interim agreement proposed by Kissinger. As a member of the Foreign Affairs and Defense Committee, Sharon had dismissed the idea of relinquishing control of the Jiddi and Mitla passes as a clear threat to the security of the State of Israel. After taking the position in the prime minister's office, he learned that the proposed withdrawal was far greater than he had known, leaving him with a dilemma: Should he remain loyal to his original ideas and speak out against the brewing settlement between Rabin and Ford, or should he remain loyal to his boss and stay mum? Sharon decided to silence his misgivings, which only heightened his frustration.

In August 1975, Kissinger toured the Middle East. The right-wing religious settler movement Gush Emunim (Bloc of the Faithful) organized mass rallies decrying his policies each time the Jewish secretary of state came to Jerusalem. Rabin assembled a team of specialists to pore over the fine points of the agreement and determine the precise extent of the withdrawal. The team included Defense Minister Shimon Peres, Foreign Minister Yigal Allon, Chief of Staff Motta Gur, Attorney General Meir Shamgar, General Adviser to the Prime Minister Ariel Sharon, and Adviser to the Defense Minister Yuval Ne'eman.

Toward the end of the month the group toured the Mitla Pass, trying to determine the exact line of withdrawal. Peres and Gur, the two most senior members of the group, opposed the idea that Sharon would accompany them. Rabin relented and allowed Sharon to accompany them to the pass, but not to the meeting afterward. Gur and Peres recommended that Israel placate the American administration and retreat to the Jiddi and Mitla passes, settling for a demilitarized zone between the Egyptian and Israeli forces and a warning station.

On August 31, the Israeli-Egyptian agreement was finalized. Rabin wrote in *A Service Notebook:*

> It was my adviser, Arik Sharon, who, as opposed to others, recommended that the warning station be situated as close to our troops as possible. In general, I drew much encouragement from Sharon's behavior. He told me: "I disagree with your conception and am firmly opposed to the interim agreement, but so long as I am your adviser I will give you the best advice I can within [the confines of] your policy." In that, Sharon displayed loyalty and fairness, as op-

posed to Yuval Ne'eman, adviser to the defense minister, who, while filling a diplomatic post, turned his office into a base for Gush Emunim's attacks on the prime minister. . . . The comparison between Sharon and Ne'eman reveals fairness versus hypocrisy. It was no coincidence that Ne'eman worked with Shimon Peres and Arik Sharon with me.

As adviser to the prime minister, Sharon was responsible for facilitating negotiations between the government and the members of Gush Emunim who had settled in Sebastia, the mythological city built by Herod on the grounds of the biblical town of Shomron. The settlement in Sebastia, initiated shortly after the November 10, 1974, U.N. resolution that declared Zionism to be a racist ideology, became the symbol of the Gush Emunim movement's struggle against the Rabin government.

The settlement movement in the West Bank had begun in earnest. Sharon had first come to Sebastia under different circumstances: On December 1, two days after the first settlers arrived, Sharon and Begin led a convoy of four hundred supporters to the area. It was Hanukkah, and Arik was happy to observe the holiday by blithely eating doughnuts handed out by Israeli poet Naomi Shemer.

Five days later, Sharon returned as Rabin's mediator. Rabin, distrustful of Peres because he felt that his defense minister shied away from conflict with the settlers, asked Sharon to keep an eye on Peres during the negotiations. Peres and Sharon met the Gush Emunim leaders in an abandoned railway station in Sebastia, and there, for the first time, the government capitulated to the settlers: The protesters who had holed up in Sebastia would move to a nearby IDF army base until the government decided on the matter of Jewish settlement in the West Bank and the Gaza Strip. According to Peres, Arik Sharon came up with the compromise.

Sharon and Peres helped thirty families move into the nearby army base in Kadum. On May 9, 1976, half a year after the settlers moved into the army base, their victory was sealed. Rabin's government decided not to build a permanent village inside the Kadum base, but to move the settlers to "a permanent settlement that shall

be granted them as per the authorized plan of the government."
On April 17, 1977, Rabin's government authorized the building of
Kedumim, a settlement just next to the base at Kadum. The set-
tlers from Sebastia moved in.

Sharon was proud of his role in Sebastia, knowing that it was a
landmark case in the issue of Jewish settlement in the occupied
territories. Other than that, though, he felt he was wasting his
time. He asked many times to resign, but Rabin insisted he stay.

In December 1975, after half a year on the job, Sharon surprised everyone with a plan of his own devising. The Five-Point
Plan called for the government to announce a state of national
emergency; the establishment of a ten-minister unity government;
a freeze in talks with Secretary of State Kissinger, who, in Sharon's
opinion, had slighted Israel in the negotiations with Egypt; the
preparation of the people for war; and the immediate and massive
settlement of Judea, Samaria, and the Gaza Strip.

Rabin, of course, was opposed to his adviser's plan. In March
1976, nine months after he started working for Rabin, Sharon
quit. But his short stint in the prime minister's office was worth its
weight in gold. During those nine months, an internship of sorts,
Sharon learned how Israel was run. He saw Rabin make decisions
under pressure, and he developed ties with world leaders. At one
point, during a meeting with Kissinger, the secretary of state told
Sharon he had heard that he was the most dangerous man in the
Middle East. "The most dangerous man in the Middle East,"
Sharon told the American secretary of state, "is you."

CHAPTER 24

The Shlomtzion Debacle

IN MARCH 1976, FOURTEEN MONTHS BEFORE THE GENERAL ELECTION in May 1977, Sharon returned to the ranch and readied himself for another assault on the legislature. The changing of the guard in the Labor Party, from Meir and Dayan to Rabin and Peres, did little to quell the public's anger and disdain toward the ruling party in the wake of the Yom Kippur War fiasco. Talk of corruption among the Labor elite contributed to the general atmosphere.

Sharon recognized that the mood was ripe for the first great political change in the country's history. But the Likud, the party he had founded in the summer of 1973, was reluctant to embrace him, a rogue MK who had served as Rabin's adviser. His relations with Begin were chilly. Simha Erlich, chairman of the Liberal contingent and the second most powerful member of the Likud, vehemently opposed Sharon's return to the party he had founded.

On April 22, 1977, with the campaign in full swing, Erlich, ordinarily a cautious politician, told *Yedioth Ahronoth* that "Sharon is an impulsive prima donna, is incapable of teamwork, and is utterly unfit for politics. Ezer Weizman pressured me to accept him, but I repeatedly said that he is irresponsible, unserious, and unstable. I feared that Arik would accrue power through us and cross the lines to Labor." In the lobby of the Waldorf-Astoria Hotel in New York City, where both were attending the Zionists of America Conference, Erlich told Sharon that the Yom Kippur War had taken a toll on both the lira and the general's prestige.

In early 1976, Sharon met with a number of well-liked apolitical personalities in an attempt to draft them into a new political party, which he would lead. Most prominent among them were former air force commander Ezer Weizman, former directors of military intelligence Meir Amit and Aharon Yariv, former IDF chief of staff Haim Laskov, Professor Yuval Ne'eman, and industrialist Steph Wertheimer. They all refused his offer. Undeterred, Sharon gathered a group of unknowns and in 1977 formed a new party, Shlomtzion.

At first, supporters flocked to the party's small office space in Tel Aviv. In the dramatic press conference he called to announce the inauguration of the new party, Sharon proclaimed that the Likud was no better than Labor; he wouldn't return to its ranks even if it won the coming elections. Initially, in early 1977, the polls were promising Shlomtzion eight seats in the Knesset, and Sharon's path to the center of the political map seemed assured.

Aiming at the undecided voters in the middle, Sharon softened his political message. Less than a month later, Yigael Yadin, an archaeologist and general, launched the Democratic Movement for Change (DMC) Party along with a select group of army men, professors, and economists. The party took the public by storm and eclipsed the relatively anonymous Shlomtzion.

As the DMC rose and Shlomtzion floundered, it became increasingly hard for Sharon to secure funding for the party. The polls were now predicting just two seats, the mood at party headquarters was dismal, and Sharon, for perhaps the first time in his life, told Lily he wanted to quit. His short and unsuccessful political career seemed on the verge of collapse.

But Lily, although opposed to his decision to run at the head of his own party from the outset, supported him, encouraging him to finish the campaign at all costs. She loaded the kids into the car along with a few buckets, rags, and mops and went to the office to clean. The few party supporters who saw her there lent a hand, and for a few hours at least, the staff seemed inspired. Only Sharon continued to walk around the office with his head down and his spirits low.

In March 1977, two months before the elections, Shlomtzion's campaign funds had virtually run dry. Only a last-minute fundraising drive in the United States kept the party afloat until election time.

The Likud, smelling an upset, urged all right and center voters to stick to the main party and not throw votes away to parties like Shlomtzion that might not even make the cut for the Knesset. Desperate, Sharon sought to rejoin the Likud. He approached Begin, but on March 22, 1977, the prime ministerial candidate had a heart attack. Sharon visited him in a hotel on the Herzliya shore, where he was recuperating, and proposed a merger. Begin told Sharon he'd have to consult with senior Likud members Yitzhak Shamir and Ezer Weizman.

Sharon's attempts to rejoin the ranks of the Likud disappointed Shlomtzion members. Many of them wanted to stay in the race till the bitter end, but Sharon steadfastly courted high-level Likud members. As the deadline to submit a list of party members neared, Sharon met with Yitzhak Shamir in a Tel Aviv café to finalize the terms of the merger. At the end of the meeting, Shamir told him he'd have to check with Simha Erlich. The two made themselves scarce. After hours of frustrating phone calls, Sharon submitted his party list for the Knesset. Behind him, in second place on the party list, was Yitzhak Yitzhaki, an anonymous schoolteacher.

Simha Erlich put the notion to rest. On April 17, 1977, he penned a letter to a friend. Arieh Avnery published it in his book *The Liberal Connection:*

> No man has done more than I to bring Arik into our midst, and no man has done more than I to make sure he does not return. I did not push him away. He chose to serve Rabin as an adviser, in essence an obedient clerk. In 1973 I said: "I admire those that barred him from the post of IDF chief of staff because Arik as chief of staff would have been a disaster for the nation." I see him as a danger to democracy and free society because he, were he to gain control of government, is capable of establishing prison camps for political dissidents. My firm stance prevented the crumbling of the Likud and much national woe—which he would have caused. That man has no principles, no human feelings, and no moral standards, making him a menace to society. Go ask anyone who admired him up until two months ago

and they'll tell you of his cruel ways. I feel that barring him from the Likud is a mission of national importance, and I say that without the slightest exaggeration.

On May 15, 1977, two days before the elections, the Likud campaign staff announced that Begin, as prime minister, would pick either Ezer Weizman or Ariel Sharon as defense minister, furthering the message that a vote for Shlomtzion was superfluous. Sharon's camp interpreted the announcement as yet another blow to their chances of making the Knesset. Their standing in the polls continued to plummet.

On May 17, 1977, Election Day, Arik and Lily went to vote in Rehovot, their temporary home while they renovated their ranch house in the desert. That evening's news did broadcast word of a revolutionary development: For the first time in the history of the state, after twenty-nine consecutive years of Mapai Party rule, Menachem Begin's opposition would form the next government. The Likud won 43 out of 120 seats.

Shlomtzion garnered 33,947 total votes, barely enough to squeeze into the Knesset with the minimum of two seats. Despite the meager support, Sharon felt a sense of relief. He knew full well that the disgrace of being barred from the Knesset would have ended his political career. As a member of the Ninth Knesset, he called Begin to congratulate him. Begin invited him to join the Likud on the spot, and advised him to send a conciliatory letter to Erlich. In short order, Shlomtzion merged into the Herut faction of the Likud. The disappointed Shlomtzion members watched in dismay as Sharon left them leaderless while he endeared himself to those he had witheringly criticized only days before.

Begin assigned Sharon to the coalition negotiating team. On June 20, the former underground leader presented his coalition government of 45 Likud seats, 15 DMC seats, 12 National Religious Party seats, and 4 ultra-orthodox Agudat Yisrael Party seats. Begin picked Dayan, who had turned his back on Labor, as his foreign minister, and Ezer Weizman as defense minister. He offered Sharon the post of minister of security services. Sharon turned him down, feeling that he would have little influence in that post.

Instead he requested a post closer to his heart: minister of agriculture.

Begin acquiesced and, no less significantly, appointed him chairman of the Ministerial Committee for Settlement Affairs. These two posts put him in a position to change the political landscape of the Middle East.

The entire Sharon family attended the inauguration of the new government. Swearing allegiance from the speaker's podium of the Knesset, Sharon looked at his eighty-year-old mother, Vera. As tears welled in her eyes, the identical thought passed through both of their minds: How unfortunate that the ostracized agronomist from Kfar Malal, Samuel Scheinerman, had not lived to see his son sworn in as Israel's minister of agriculture.

CHAPTER 25

Minister of
Agriculture

As a child of Kfar Malal and the owner of a vast private ranch, Sharon was a natural for the post of minister of agriculture. Yet for the first term of Begin's premiership he concentrated, rather, on Jewish settlement of the West Bank and the Gaza Strip, lands captured by Israel in the Six Day War.

Sharon focused on settling strategically located hilltops along the ridges of the West Bank, intersecting the contiguity of Palestinian towns and villages. The committee he headed determined the size and location of the settlements, dealt with the construction companies, and helped the new settlers find jobs and funding.

As chairman of the Ministerial Committee for Settlement Affairs—the official title for the individual charged with crafting the country's settlement policy—Sharon sought to capture the biblical lands of Israel by settlement. As he saw it, military conquest was temporary; the permanent contours of the country would be determined by the plow, and by demographics. For Sharon, this was a natural extension of Ben-Gurion's and Mapai's pre-state settlement policy.

Already on July 26, 1977, over the course of a twenty-minute meeting of a committee consisting of seven ministers and seven members of the Histadrut (the Israeli trade union), the settlements of Eilon Moreh, Ma'ale Adumim, and Ofra were given legal recognition. As official towns, the settlements were eligible for government funds, and Sharon made sure they received a steady flow.

The American administration opposed the decision. Secretary of State Cyrus Vance said the settlements violated international law and constituted an obstacle on the path to peace. That position had no effect on Sharon's decision to settle the Gaza Strip and the West Bank with Jews.

Sharon's decision to focus on settlements, rather than the pricing of water for agriculture or the limits on egg distribution for henhouse owners, elevated him above most ministers. Rather than appearing as a pale shadow of Defense Minister Ezer Weizman, Sharon emerged as the man most involved in shaping the country's future. Sharon's personal agenda for the territories taken in 1967, and the facts he laid on the ground, would become critically important in the Israeli-Palestinian conflict that unfolded over the following three decades. The fact that Begin made him a member of the Ministerial Committee for Defense further empowered the man who had barely made the cut for the Knesset just weeks earlier.

For the business of running the settlement enterprise, Sharon drafted a small team of confidants, some formerly of Shlomtzion, and placed his friend Uri Bar-On in charge. Sharon rarely involved members of the Ministry of Agriculture in the settlement matters that dominated his day. It took two months to research the details and draft a settlement map. Over the course of that period, Sharon's envoys climbed hills and identified crucial road junctions. In mid-September 1977, Israel's defense cabinet convened to discuss the future of the West Bank. Sharon came armed with a detailed plan. He brought a giant map to the meeting, spread it out for the ministers attending, and related at great length the details of the plan he unsurprisingly called "the Sharon Plan."

The Sharon Plan for Settlement in Judea and Samaria—the biblical name for the region—proposed to address Israel's problems on the eastern front, with the Palestinian populations bordering Jordan, Syria, and Iraq. The first issue the plan addressed was the disparity in birthrate between the quickly growing Palestinian population and the slower, nearly Western rate of increase in the Jewish areas. His second fear was that the Palestinian population beyond the Green Line—the borders of the armistice agreement with Egypt, Syria, Jordan, and Lebanon signed in 1949—would spill into Israel's pre-1967 lands. The third problem related to topography and the way the ridges of the West Bank loomed over Israel's narrow waist along the coastal plain, where most of the population lived, huddled by the sea in large population centers. It was a gravely vulnerable position militarily.

Sharon proposed solving these problems with a chain of dozens of settlements along the ridgelines. On September 26, Sharon spoke passionately before the ministerial committee about a new dawn in which the critical mass of settlement activity would be moved beyond the Green Line to the West Bank. Sharon's settlement plan relied heavily on "The Double Spine," a position paper written by architecture professor Avraham Wachman. The paper, submitted to Rabin in January 1976 and summarily dismissed, had crossed Sharon's desk during his tenure as an adviser to the former prime minister. In 1977, Sharon reintroduced many of Wachman's proposals.

The plan had three central elements: the foundation of civilian and industrial settlements along the West Bank ridgeline; the establishment of settlements in the Jordan Valley, from Beit She'an to the Dead Sea, safeguarding Israel's eastern border and blocking territorial contiguity from the Palestinian West Bank population centers to Jordan and Iraq; and, primarily, a ring of Jewish settlement around the Arab neighborhoods of Jerusalem. The buffer zone around Jerusalem began south of Bethlehem in the Gush Etzion area, stretched east to Ma'ale Adumim at the edge of the desert that slopes to the Dead Sea, and ran north of Ramallah to Beit El. The Sharon Plan called for numerous east-west roads with settlement blocs alongside them, dissecting the Palestinian population centers.

Sharon sketched an exact outline of the roads he planned to pave in the West Bank, which would enable both settlers and the IDF to move more freely throughout the area. He then elaborated on the ideological goal of the plan: strengthening the Jewish grip on Jerusalem as the eternal capital of Israel and the Jewish people. Sharon emphasized the need for an increase in settlement around Jerusalem and provided details of his plan to stimulate Jewish growth in the area. He ended his presentation by saying, "I am not speaking here so that my words will go down in the protocol. Weigh this carefully. As soon as [this plan] is authorized, I will carry it out."

On October 2, 1977, the government authorized Sharon's settlement plan. On November 9, Sharon presented the plan to the Knesset. He enjoyed the full backing of Prime Minister Menachem Begin and the fervent support of Gush Emunim, a settlement arm of the religious-nationalist camp, which now saw Sharon as their patron and ally.

In order to realize his plan, Sharon had to persuade young Jewish men and women to leave the comforts of Israel proper and move to isolated settlements on the terraced desolation of West Bank hilltops, surrounded by an occupied and hostile Palestinian population. He partnered with Gush Emunim and their spiritual leader, Rabbi Zvi Yehuda Kook, who called for the settlement of the land of Israel as documented in the Bible. The one was motivated by maps and strategy, the other by the Bible and the word of God. But both shared a common goal: putting facts on the ground, fast.

The government's position on settlement did not correlate with the pace of expansion. As Begin's administration negotiated with the United States and the centrist elements of its coalition, Gush Emunim continued to build as quickly as possible. Sharon, positioned between the government and the settlers, was frequently accused of aligning himself with the latter at the expense of the former. At times the settlers admitted that Sharon encouraged them to build settlements before receiving legal permission, in order to multiply the faits accomplis.

Sharon paid special mind to the foundation of two settlement blocs, one ringing Jerusalem and the other on the eastern side of the Green Line, dividing the Arab population in Israel proper from that in the post-1967 lands. In 1977, Sharon presided over the establishment of the settlements Beit El, Elkana, Sal'it, Rimonim, Halamish, Migdal Oz, Shavei Shomron, Tekoa, and Kedumim. In the next two years, Mevo Dotan, Ariel, Karnei Shomron, Shilo, Tapuah, Kochav Ha'shahar, and Eilon Moreh were built.

During Begin's second term, with Sharon serving as defense minister, he pushed the settlers to continue their expansion efforts. During those years they built dozens more settlements, including Alfei Menasheh, Emanuel, Nokdim, Efrata, Psagot, Vered Yericho, Hermesh, Giv'on Ha'hadasha, Na'ami, Alei Zahav, Ateret, Ganim, Dolev, Yitzhar, Ma'ale Levona, Sha'arei Tikva, Kiryat Netafim,

Karmei Tzur, Ma'ale Amos, Ma'ale Michmash, Neve Daniel, Telem, Barkan, and Otniel.

A steady torrent of money was diverted from the Ministry of Agriculture to the settlement enterprise. The heads of Gush Emunim knew that they could spend private funds without worry— sooner or later Sharon would bring pressure to bear on Begin and the government would reimburse them for the money spent prior to legal recognition of a new settlement. That was certainly the case in October 1977, when Sharon paid Gush Emunim nine million shekels for their expenditures in building Ofra and Kadum, established well before they were deemed legal. Sharon asked the Knesset Finance Committee to allot funds for access roads, an electricity grid, a waste management system, a dining hall, houses, a synagogue, a library, and salaries for the resident laborers. Left-wing Opposition members protested in vain. The facts were on the ground.

In September 1977, Sharon suggested allowing settlers to move into IDF bases across Judea and Samaria and incrementally expanding the area to include civilian settlements. Sharon suggested that at first the Gush Emunim loyalists settle on the IDF base in Beit El and then on six other bases, where they would work in security posts. The proposal enraged Ezer Weizman and sparked an open conflict between the two.

Later, Sharon encouraged the country's trade union to recognize Gush Emunim as an official state body charged with the settlement of the country. MK Yossi Sarid, a member of the left-wing opposition to Gush Emunim, said what everyone already knew: "The coming recognition of Gush Emunim as an official settlement movement comes in part to facilitate the swift flow of government funds and resources to the Gush's cash till."

Sharon's forceful, oppressive behavior during the decision-making process regarding settlement expansion, coupled with his phenomenal ability to establish a settlement enterprise the likes of which had not been seen since the early days of Zionism, earned him the nickname "Bulldozer." By the end of Begin's first term, Sharon had presided over the establishment of sixty-four new Jewish settlements on the West Bank.

On November 9, 1977, the Egyptian media reported that President Sadat planned to make an important speech that evening. The leader of the strongest and most important Arab country in the Middle East dropped a bombshell: He announced his willingness to travel to Israel and speak before the Knesset, making him the first Arab leader to recognize the Jewish state. Ten days later, on November 19, Sadat's plane touched down at Ben-Gurion International Airport in Israel.

This development stunned Sharon. In fact, every government minister except Foreign Minister Dayan, who had negotiated the visit behind the scenes, was taken by surprise. Sadat emerged from the Egyptian plane and made his way down the red carpet, shaking hands as he progressed. He lingered for a moment opposite Minister of Agriculture Ariel Sharon. "Aha, it's you," he said. "I had hoped to capture you on Egyptian soil in October 1973." Sharon smiled, and said, "I'm glad I managed to avoid you."

When Sadat left the country, the two met again. "Sharon," Sadat said to him at the airport, "so good to see you." Sharon responded: "I hope next time I'll see you as minister of agriculture, in Egypt." "We'll be happy to receive you there," Sadat said, shaking his hand warmly.

Sharon concealed growing concern behind his smile. The talk of peace came with demands. Cairo's conditions—Israel's complete cessation of settlement building on occupied lands, recognition of the Palestinian people's right to self-determination, and withdrawal from all lands taken in 1967, including east Jerusalem—made Sharon's fleet of bulldozers a burden in the eyes of several government ministers, none more so than Defense Minister Ezer Weizman.

In December 1977, Begin, Weizman, and Dayan reciprocated with a visit to Egypt. The Ismailia Conference, as the meeting was known, failed to reap any breakthroughs in negotiations. On the contrary, the gaps between the two sides seemed impossibly vast. Sadat demanded that Israel return the Sinai Peninsula in full to Egypt and relinquish control of the Gaza Strip and the West Bank. Begin agreed to return the majority of the Sinai Peninsula but none of the Gaza Strip or the West Bank. Sharon understood it was time to put the bulldozer in neutral. He asked the leaders of Gush Emunim to slow the building process and wait for a more opportune time.

In early January 1978, a group of ministers convened to discuss the future of Jewish settlements in the Rafah Salient, the area in the northeast corner of the Sinai Desert known in Israel as the Yamit settlements. In the wake of the failure at the Ismailia Conference, Sharon suggested strengthening the settlement bloc in the area as a means of signaling to Egypt and the world that Israel had no intention of withdrawing from the Rafah Salient of the Gaza Strip or from the West Bank.

In his book *The Battle for Peace,* Ezer Weizman describes the meeting. Sharon arrived, as always, with his maps. To Weizman it was clear that Sharon intended to establish further settlements in the Sinai, an action he interpreted as a direct obstacle on the path to peace:

> Sharon always knew how to present his ideas so that they would appeal to the majority of the ministers, if not all of them. His fingers fluttered across the maps, which remained largely illegible to most of the members of the government. At times it seemed to me that the markings on the map were not exactly precise. None of the people around admitted to a lack of understanding. Sharon intended to set hard facts, and fast . . . members of government were quick to comply.
>
> In essence, Sharon presented nothing more than a few symbolic settlements—several trailers, water towers, and trenches. To my chagrin, I couldn't stop myself from comparing Sadat's and Sharon's offers. The Egyptian president spoke of big business while we were dealing with petty matters, and how: building pseudo-settlements that might serve as sticks in the wheels of peace.

On the matter of the Palestinian population, Begin offered autonomy, but not independence, to the Arabs of the West Bank and the Gaza Strip. He promised Sharon that the Jewish settlers in those areas would remain full-fledged citizens of Israel. Finally, he satisfied Sharon by assuring him that Israel alone would be responsible for security in the territories.

Nonetheless, in a closed meeting held a short time later, Sharon warned that autonomy for the Arab population in the territories might turn into "a death trap" in the long run. His sentiment was leaked to the press, eliciting an outcry from his peers in government. Part of Sharon's rancor can be attributed to the fact that since Sadat's visit, Dayan and Weizman had dominated center stage, while the settlement-building minister of agriculture had been pushed far from the limelight. Sharon was forced to watch from the wings as Begin, Dayan, and Weizman began shaping a historic peace deal with Egypt. Despairingly he watched as his greatest rival, Ezer Weizman, became the Israeli closest to Sadat.

In January 1978, the government convened to discuss the future of the settlement movement, which had been frozen since November 1977 in order not to crack the fragile relations with Egypt. Sharon accused Weizman of joining hands with Sadat. Despite Weizman's and the DMC Party members' opposition to continued settlement, Sharon, with the help of Begin and Dayan, pushed the government to authorize the building of three new settlements in the West Bank and the strengthening of the settlement bloc in the Rafah Salient.

Sharon sought to build up the settlements in northern Sinai in order to signal to the Egyptians that Israel was unwilling to recede from the entire peninsula in return for peace. Sharon suggested expanding the settlements' territory by claiming nearby land, plowing it, and dotting it with water towers, buses, and trailers. The idea appealed to Dayan and Begin. They could test the Egyptian reaction this way without endangering the negotiations. Dayan invited Weizman and Sharon to his house. Over maps, they marked twenty-three settlements where land could be annexed, plowed, and dotted with the trappings of ownership.

The plan backfired. One week after the meeting, the Israeli press published a sketch of the government's intentions. The United States and Europe viewed the plan as an Israeli provocation, issued only days before the Israeli-Egyptian bilateral security committee was to meet for the first time in Jerusalem to discuss the security issues of the coming peace deal. The government's stance, that the move was merely to strengthen already existing settlements, did little to quell the criticism. A furious President Jimmy Carter sent a strongly worded letter to Begin, who found himself pinned. In relenting, he placed most of the blame on Sharon.

Amos Keinan, a journalist, wrote in *Yedioth Ahronoth:*

> I couldn't believe it when I read the news in the paper. The article said the minister of agriculture had established 25 fake units. Representatives of the settler movement were asked to amass grain near the fake units, to give the impression of a farming community. In some places they even put up water drilling towers. The goal of the deception was to set new political facts on the ground. The intent of those political facts was to ensure that Israel forgo its claim to the pseudo-settlements during negotiations in return for Egypt forgoing their claims to the real settlements in the Rafah Salient. American planes, charged with overseeing the Israeli-Egyptian separation agreement in Sinai, filmed the deception, and that was the end of that. . . . As such the Sharon Plan for Plastic Zionism was born.

Sharon felt betrayed by the government's capitulation. He pressed Begin to announce that the minister of agriculture had acted in accordance with a governmental decision and not of his own volition. Begin soon dealt Sharon another blow. In the spring of 1978 he moved the matter of settlement policy from the committee Sharon headed to the Ministerial Committee for Defense. In the field, Gush Emunim continued to build, but at a greatly reduced rate. At the same time, the public began to hold Sharon responsible for blocking progress toward peace. Peace Now, a nongovernmental organization (NGO) formed in March 1978 in response to the Egyptian peace plan and continued Israeli settlement expansion, accused Sharon of confiscating the private lands of Palestinians and trampling their basic rights in the name of ghost towns for settlers.

In fact, many of the outposts built during those days consisted of nothing more than a water tank, a generator, and two trailers. But Sharon, despite attacks from the papers, the Knesset, and the government, remained firm in his belief that the ghost towns would turn into thriving Jewish towns and cities that would irrevocably alter the lay of the land. The public criticism did not bend his will. On August 8, 1978, he posed for a press photo at an outpost under construction. He was quoted as saying that "hundreds of families are waiting for authorization to settle in Judea and Samaria. We are currently at the peak of the settlement wave." He initiated a tour of the area with Knesset reporters in September 1978 and announced: "Today, in the territories, Israel is building the security skeleton it needs in order to solve its security problems."

Early that same month, American president Jimmy Carter invited Egyptian president Anwar Sadat and Israeli prime minister Menachem Begin to Camp David, the presidential retreat in Maryland, to try to bridge the gaps between the two nations. Weizman and Dayan accompanied Begin to America. Sharon stayed home.

Two major issues remained unresolved: the Palestinian situation and the future of the Israeli settlements in northern Sinai. Sadat categorically refused to leave the Jewish settlements on Egyptian land in place. He insisted they be evacuated in any peace deal. Weizman and Dayan pressured Begin to relent, but the prime minister felt Israel had to hold on to the airfields in the Rafah Salient and the settlements in the Yamit area.

On the morning of September 14, the last day of negotiations, the talks seemed slated for failure. The Israeli and Egyptian leaders would not so much as talk to one another. Dayan, Weizman, and Begin had already packed their bags, prepared to fly back to Israel.

At that point, out of sheer desperation, Weizman decided to call Sharon, the man most vehemently opposed to a total withdrawal from Sinai, and ask him to persuade Begin to dismantle the settlements in the Rafah Salient. "I wasn't sure he'd do it," Weizman wrote. "He was seen as a champion of the settlement movement and had, as commander of the southern sector, been the one who pushed for the settlements in the Rafah Salient. They were the apple of his eye." Weizman turned to his adviser, Maj. Gen. Avraham Tamir, and said, "We've got nothing to lose. Call Arik."

Tamir called Sharon and explained that Weizman and Dayan

wanted to yield to Sadat's demands but that Begin wouldn't budge. Sharon surprised him. He said he would be willing to call Begin and let him know that in his opinion a historic peace with Egypt was worth sacrificing the settlements of the Yamit bloc. As Sharon was talking to Begin from his home, Gershom Sheft, a Gush Emunim leader, stopped by unannounced. Sharon put down the phone and informed Sheft that he had just told Begin he agreed that settlements should be dismantled for the sake of peace with Egypt. Sheft was stunned. He reported back to Gush Emunim, which began a public campaign against the withdrawal.

Sharon's double-edged attitude toward the settlement enterprise had been revealed. He backed the idea and the expansion of settlements across Greater Israel, but he was also prepared to destroy what he had built at a moment's notice.

Opinions differ over Sharon's capacity to reverse his stance on settlement. Critics say his equivocation pointed to a desire to use the settlement enterprise merely as a springboard for personal career gain. Supporters contend that he was motivated by practical necessity, and that his goals were national, never personal. According to this theory, Sharon championed the settlement enterprise in order to establish a critical mass of Jews that could one day be used as bargaining chips in the high-stakes game of final borders. Either way, what is clear is that he was above all a pragmatist rather than an ideologue.

On September 17, 1978, Israel and Egypt signed two agreements at Camp David. The first promised normalization and peace in return for an incremental Israeli withdrawal from all of Sinai. The second agreement promised the Palestinians of Gaza and the West Bank autonomy for a transitional period of five years. These two agreements were ratified by a wide margin in the Israeli Knesset. On March 26, 1979, the Camp David Peace Accords between Israel and Egypt were signed at the White House. Menachem Begin later revealed that the phone call from Sharon had helped him make one of the toughest decisions of his life: to uproot Jewish settlements.

CHAPTER 26

Defense Minister

SHARON'S APPOINTMENT AS MINISTER OF AGRICULTURE IN 1977 CRE-
ated a conflict of interest: The owner of one of the largest farms in
Israel now controlled water distribution and agricultural produce
levels. Moreover, one of the main crops on Sharon's ranch was cotton; the director general of the Ministry of Agriculture, Sharon's
subordinate, was chairman of the Israeli Cotton Council. Melons
posed a problem, too, as the ranch exported them through Agrexco,
a government company under the auspices of the ministry.

On August 15, 1977, the Asher Commission, charged with examining conflicts of interest in politics, published its findings. The
committee recommended that government ministers with property
or interests under the control of their offices should transfer the
properties to an independent, nonsubordinate source. The government accepted the committee's findings, which put Sharon's tenure
at the Ministry of Agriculture in peril, since he refused to relinquish control of Sycamore Ranch.

In July, Sharon transferred half the property to Lily and announced that he no longer ran the ranch. Aharon Barak, attorney
general and future Supreme Court chief justice, found the measures insufficient. Lily responded by saying, "The committee can't
force someone to abandon his way of life." In February 1978,
Sharon leased his property to four Israeli farmers for the duration
of his term in office. The four signed a non-durable power of attorney, enabling them to act in Sharon's place until further notice.
Barak found that measure wanting as well.

The back-and-forth between Sharon and the attorney general
was covered in depth. Dozens of newspaper articles stirred public
debate. Sharon asserted that the ranch was his home and not

merely an occupation. The government appointed another committee of inquiry, headed by former judge Max Kennet, but it too
found the situation untenable.

Only in 1980 was an agreement reached. Sharon's driver during the Yom Kippur War, Motti Levy, created a company that leased
the farm. Later that year the Israel Land Administration sold 123
additional acres to Levy and the Sycamore Ranch. The agreement
between Levy and Sharon lasted for ten years, until 1989, when
the property was transferred to Sharon's two sons, Omri and Gilad.

Over the years, Sharon would star in numerous investigative
articles and state comptroller reports for supposed conflict of interest, nepotism, and even criminal behavior. Although he never faced
criminal charges, suspicion swirled around him for many of his
years as prime minister, resulting in several police investigations,
one of which, the Annex Research affair, implicated his son Omri,
Sharon's campaign manager for the Likud primaries in 1999, and
resulted in a plea bargain and a sentence of nine months' time
served.

On October 23, 1979, after Begin appointed Dr. Yosef Burg of
the National Religious Party to head the negotiating team for
Palestinian autonomy, Moshe Dayan, feeling stripped of authority,
quit the post of foreign minister. At the same time, Begin found
himself stuck between Sharon and Weizman, one pulling right and
the other left. The most divisive issue of that period was the settlement of Eilon Moreh, which dominated cabinet meetings and
eventually came before the Supreme Court.

The settlers of Eilon Moreh, veterans of the settlement within
the army camp at Kadum and the civilian settlement of Kedumim,
tried to establish themselves, without legal permits, on a bare
hilltop near Nablus. The IDF evacuated them eleven times. International news crews came and filmed them being carried away.
On January 7, 1979, the government recognized the Eilon Moreh
group as official candidates for eventual settlement, without determining the precise location of the future village. Sharon rented
a helicopter, circled the Nablus area, and located what he deemed
the perfect spot: private Palestinian land next to the village of
Rujayeb.

Four separate times Sharon pushed to have the area recognized by the government, but each time Dayan, Weizman, and Yadin led a majority opposed to his designated site. They contended that there was no justification for building a settlement on private Palestinian land, in the midst of a densely populated area, when there was so much unclaimed land in the West Bank. "That man and that group," Weizman complained to Begin, "are dragging the government into positions that risk its very existence." "Who is 'that man'?" Begin asked somberly. "Arik Sharon, of course," said the defense minister. Weizman argued that Sharon's settlements threatened the fragile peace with Egypt and damaged Israel's standing in the court of international opinion. "Our next visit to Cairo," Weizman said, "will be made on the turrets of Arik's tanks."

In June 1979, the government, with the backing of Begin, approved the settlers' request to settle on 198 acres of private land southeast of Nablus. The appropriation order was signed on June 4, and the settlers, Gush Emunim loyalists, hurried onto the land that day, eager to establish ownership before the Palestinian owners could file suit at the Israeli High Court of Justice, which, as opposed to the state court system, heard Palestinian claims. Deputy Minister of Agriculture Uri Bar-On led the operation and even settled on the hilltop with the faithful. The timing of the move, on the eve of the Palestinian autonomy talks with Egypt, deepened the rift between Weizman and Sharon.

To Sharon's dismay, Weizman canceled his emergency posting in the reserves. Sharon's relation with his fellow ministers was at an all-time low. He spoke crudely around the government table, lashing out at ministers who dared to disagree with him. At one point, he told Gideon Patt of the Liberal Party of Israel, "You are not worthy of having me even reflect upon your statements. I don't reflect on the words of an IDF deserter." Patt responded: "You infant!" Sharon directed similar outbursts at Foreign Minister Yitzhak Shamir and Deputy Prime Minister Yigael Yadin, and, according to press reports, he frequently showed disrespect toward Prime Minister Begin himself.

On May 26, 1980, Ezer Weizman quit the government. The official rationale for his departure was a drastic cut in defense department spending, but the true reason lay in the ruined relationship between him, Begin, and Sharon, and his opposition to the government's decision two weeks earlier to bomb the Iraqi nuclear reactor in Osirak.

With the departure of Weizman, the competition for the post of defense minister began. With Dayan out of the picture, Sharon gave himself even more leeway at cabinet meetings, becoming ever more unruly. At one point, the deputy prime minister, Professor Yigael Yadin, accused Sharon of expanding seven settlements beyond what the government had authorized. Sharon responded: "I'll strip you naked and bare on the government table." Later he explained: "For seven straight days Yadin accused me of deception and cheating. . . . I had no intention of physically stripping him, but to strip the subject of his accusations politically."

At one cabinet meeting, Sharon criticized Begin for his far-reaching concessions to the Egyptians and the Americans on the issue of Palestinian autonomy. Begin turned the other cheek and maintained his forgiving, even paternal attitude toward Sharon. Political analysts attributed Begin's demeanor to his blind admiration for the military and for Sharon's long record of valor, but in truth, Begin, a firm believer in Greater Israel, also sided with Sharon on the issue of settlements.

On one issue Begin stood firm. He withstood Sharon's withering campaign to be appointed defense minister. At one point Sharon even threatened to step down if he was not nominated. Begin fumed, "If Arik steps down, I won't stop him," and appointed himself to the position, manning the two most important ministerial positions in the government, just as Ben-Gurion had done during Mapai's reign.

In August 1980, the Sharon-Begin relationship nearly came to an end. According to press reports, Begin called Sharon "a danger to democracy." In response, Sharon issued an unprecedented attack on the prime minister, saying he made decisions in "an irresponsible and offhanded way." All present at the next cabinet meeting condemned Sharon. Begin denied uttering the comment attributed to him and said to Sharon: "You surely know that I gave you a place in the government in spite of Shlomtzion's propaganda . . . so how could you do this kind of thing to me?" Sharon apologized.

The next general elections loomed on June 30, 1981. Begin and the Likud were slipping in the polls. Sharon, fearful of a Labor resurgence, began building settlements at a feverish pace. With Labor in power, the settlement enterprise would be dealt a severe blow. Days before the elections, many settlements, with the aggressive assistance of Sharon, were hooked up to the national electricity and water companies.

Sharon featured in the Labor election campaign. He was portrayed as the appropriator of private Arab land and a voracious spender of public funds on empty settlements. His assistant at the time, Eli Landau, suggested that he defend the enterprise with an initiative called "We're on the Map." Dubbed "the Sharon Tours" by the press, the program took three hundred thousand potential voters on guided tours of the West Bank, highlighting the security importance of the settlements.

But the elections may well have been decided in the afternoon hours of June 7, 1981, three weeks before the country went to the polls. A low-flying pack of Israeli F-16s flew hundreds of miles over enemy territory and attacked Iraq's nuclear reactor. At 5:30 P.M. the pilots reported that the mission had been accomplished, the reactor destroyed. Most states condemned Israel for the violation of Iraqi sovereignty. Even the United States, a firm ally, backed the United Nations' condemnation of Israel and froze all sales of American planes to the country. But nothing shook the conviction of the Israeli public. All felt relieved that Saddam Hussein had been stripped of his budding nuclear capacity.

Sharon was seen as one of the fathers of the plan, urging Begin to execute it. Sharon's stock soared among right-wing voters. Many realized that within one term he had radically altered the map in biblical Israel. Sixty-four settlements, some of them outposts and others bustling towns, had been built in the West Bank and the Gaza Strip during his four years in office, changing the territories, in their eyes, from a military zone where Palestinians lived under IDF rule to an area teeming with Jewish life.

The minister of agriculture made his presence felt within the

Green Line as well. On his watch, fifty-six new Jewish towns and villages had been built in the Galilee, an area populated largely by Arab citizens of Israel. By the time he left office in 1981, Sharon had overseen the building of twenty new kibbutzim and moshavim and thirty-four communal villages, which he termed "lookouts." In furthering his objective to "Judaize" the Galilee, Sharon claimed more than seventy-five thousand acres of land for the state.

Sharon could point to a long list of professional successes. During his term as minister of agriculture, the national agricultural output rose by 15 percent and wheat by 21 percent. Export was up 16.5 percent, from $379 million in 1977 to $576 million in 1981. Sharon prioritized government aid to farmers in the kibbutzim, moshavim, and border towns of the Galilee.

On Election Day, June 30, 1981, Sharon braced himself for a loss. Election polls had been predicting a Labor victory since the beginning of the year. After a stunning campaign by Begin, Israel's greatest orator, and the attack on the Iraqi nuclear reactor, the race seemed deadlocked on the twenty-ninth. But momentum pushed the Likud over the top. Their forty-eight mandates, one more than were won by the Peres-led Labor Party, allowed them to join hands with the religious parties and form a right-wing government with a slim majority.

Over the course of the campaign, Sharon, second on the Likud list, came to realize that he had replaced Begin in the minds of many Israelis as the most feared politician in Israel. The long-demonized Begin, an individual Ben-Gurion called "the man seated next to MK Bader" during his decades-long tenure as head of the Opposition, had changed his standing in the public eye after his first term as prime minister. Sharon now wore Begin's old mantle. But his forceful, antidemocratic image, derived from his days in the army and reinforced by his tough stances, would come back to haunt him.

On August 5, 1981, five weeks after the elections, the new government was sworn in. Sharon, realizing his dream, was appointed defense minister. Begin struggled with the idea for a long time, even voicing his concern to *Yedioth Ahronoth* on July 17, 1981: "If Sharon acts in a manner contradictory to government decisions—

I'll fire him." One year later, Sharon and IDF chief of staff Rafael "Raful" Eitan would lead Israel into the Lebanon War.

Eitan reflected on Sharon's nomination in his autobiography:

> Sharon treats the soldiers and officers under him roughly. He is domineering, conceited, and aloof toward them. He'll never pass up an opportunity to demonstrate his superiority. He had a problem with me, though. We're roughly the same age. We'd accrued similar experiences since the War of Independence . . . he knew he couldn't look down on me and reduce my worth. He scolded, chastised, and yelled at others without remorse. Our relationship was correct. He never yelled at me, never scolded me. [Therefore] I reached a firm conviction within myself: I wouldn't tell the prime minister that I would quit if he appointed Arik . . . but if Arik's behavior as defense minister eroded my authority or the army's structure, or if he held fast to opinions diametrically opposed to mine on matters of critical importance—I'd get up and go home, simply, quietly, and without causing a stir.

Sharon kept himself in check during his first weeks in office. He promised Begin that he would report to him daily and would include him in all decisions. His door was always open to advice, he said. Sharon, fifty-three, seemed to be on an unalterable rise. Political analysts pointed to him as Begin's heir apparent.

His most pressing issue upon taking office was the withdrawal from the Sinai and the evacuation of the Yamit bloc of settlements, as mandated by the peace deal with Egypt. Begin followed the rise of the movement against the Sinai withdrawal with dread. Some say that his fear at having to carry out the forced withdrawal of Jews from their homes was what tipped the balance in favor of Sharon, the Bulldozer, as defense minister.

Sharon, the great settler of occupied lands, suddenly found himself in charge of the first forced evacuation of Jews since the founding of the state. Seven thousand Jews had to be removed. Some of those evicted from Yamit moved north, to the Gaza Strip, only to be evicted from their homes again by the same man twenty-five years later.

The peace accords gave Israel eight more months to carry out the withdrawal. The date was set: April 21, 1982. Sharon's Gush Emunim partners were bewildered. Sharon continued to ardently support settlement in Gaza and the West Bank, yet he seemed poised and ready to expel entire communities from the Sinai. Moreover, the warm relations between Sharon and Egyptian president Hosni Mubarak, who had inherited the position after a Muslim dissident killed Anwar Sadat on October 6, 1981, puzzled them.

In November 1981, Sharon flew to Washington, D.C., to sign an Israeli-American strategic agreement. The pact gave the Americans a foothold in the Middle East at a time when Iraq and Iran were in upheaval and the Soviet Union's influence was on the rise.

The achievement didn't last long. In December 1981, Prime Minister Begin made a dramatic announcement regarding the future of the Golan Heights: The territory taken from Syria in the Six Day War would be formally annexed to Israel. In response, the American administration announced it would cancel the strategic agreement. Sharon, a staunch supporter of annexation, came out strongly against the Americans' verdict. "The decision to annex the Golan Heights," he explained, "was necessary in order to prove to the Americans and the entire world Israel's conviction never to return to the 1967 borders."

Sharon kept his word to Begin. During the first months of his tenure as defense minister he called him several times a day, updating him on even minor affairs. Affection between the two grew. Sharon even tried to comport himself with grace around the government table. On November 17, 1981, the left-wing daily *Al Ha'mishmar,* never a great fan of Sharon's, expressed awe at his new manner: "Ever since his appointment as defense minister, Arik Sharon has had center stage, and he is incrementally approaching the status of unchallenged heir to Begin, if he should decide to retire as prime minister."

The paper argued that Sharon's approach as defense minister was

> well thought out: reorganization of the military rule in the territories, increased dialogue with moderate West Bank

leaders, a hard-line approach to PLO supporters, the continuation of autonomy negotiations, and the slashing of the defense budget. With those measures under way, he flew to the United States and signed the strategic pact. Foreign Minister Yitzhak Shamir, Interior Minister Dr. Yosef Burg, and even Prime Minister Menachem Begin are almost invisible. Sharon is running the show by himself.

Begin did not regret his decision to choose Sharon as the man to evacuate Yamit. In early December 1981, the residents of Yamit locked their gates. Sharon arrived to negotiate the ground rules for the evacuation and the compensation each resident would receive. After the gates had been opened and the talks concluded, the chairman of the residents' board said, "Sharon didn't promise us anything beyond that he would look into the issue. We trust Arik; he's the only one who can get us out of this mud."

Two months before the evacuation, in late February 1982, many members of the movement to stop the withdrawal understood that Sharon had been playing a political game, sending reassuring messages in order to buy time. Sharon encircled Yamit with military roadblocks in order to cut the city off from nonresident supporters. In response, many residents tried physically removing the roadblocks. They planned to bring twenty thousand supporters to Yamit to complicate the evacuation.

Sharon learned of their plans. Without any warning, he deployed additional troops to five key points in the Sinai. Overnight, he established checkpoints manned by officers, and only longtime residents were allowed access to their homes. The outside supporters were sent home.

Within two days he delivered fifteen companies of soldiers to guard the routes between northern Sinai and Israel, along with ambulances, fire trucks, police riot gear, barbed wire fences, and tire-puncturing roadblocks—sending a clear message that force would be answered in kind. The movement protested the siege, but Sharon issued a statement: "The roadblocks will not be removed."

Two days later he gave the order to evacuate the residents of Hatzar Adar in the Yamit bloc. The eviction took one hour. Before the residents were loaded into police cars, they set rubber tires on fire and signaled that the big confrontation was yet to come, in Yamit.

The Israeli press reported that far-right elements were storing guns and grenades. Several supporters of Rabbi Meir Kahane, the Jewish Defense League founder, locked themselves in a basement as the evacuation began and announced their willingness "to fight and be killed." Hundreds more chained themselves together and huddled on the rooftops. Troops climbed ladders and herded them into crane-held cages with high-pressure foam spray.

Sharon then gave the order to destroy Yamit. At first he wanted to leave the city intact, saying, "We shouldn't start the peace with burnt earth," but three weeks later he told the government, "Left with no choice, we will wreck every building in Yamit to ensure that those opposed to the evacuation will not return to the city."

The Israeli public, virtually across the board, supported the evacuation of Yamit. Sharon was at the height of his power.

CHAPTER 27

The Road to Lebanon

JUST BEFORE MIDNIGHT ON JUNE 3, 1982, TERRORISTS FROM ABU Nidal's radical Palestinian organization shot Shlomo Argov, Israel's ambassador to the United Kingdom, in the head from close range. The assassin ambushed Argov outside London's Dorchester Hotel after a festive diplomatic dinner. Defense Minister Ariel Sharon heard the news of the assassination while visiting Romania with his family.

Begin had sent Sharon to Bucharest after Communist Romania contacted Israel through its secret service, asking to establish technology and science ties. Since a sudden visit by the Israeli defense minister was bound to raise a few eyebrows, it was decided that Sharon would go with his wife and children, pretending to visit Lily's hometown of Brasov, three hours outside Bucharest. Sharon kept his appointment schedule, meeting with several ministers, including head of state Nicolae Ceausescu, before flying back to Israel the following day.

The Cabinet met on the morning of June 4, without Sharon, for an emergency session regarding the intensifying terror attacks against Israel and international Jewish targets. Begin was in a stormy mood as Argov fought for his life in a London hospital. He asked the IDF chief of staff to present several attack options in Lebanon, the country that hosted many of the Palestinian terrorists and their organizations. At the time, Lebanon, a country whose borders had been artificially carved out by the French at San Remo in 1920, was in the midst of a civil war, threatening to tear apart along its religious lines: Muslim, Christian, and Druze.

Lieutenant General Eitan suggested attacking eleven targets, including PLO ammunition depots just outside Beirut. Begin accepted the chief of staff's recommendation and asked him, in case of a strong Palestinian response, to prepare for a ground assault on Lebanon.

Ever since January, the IDF, on orders from Sharon, had had such plans ready. "Oranim" (Pines), as the plan was known, called for the IDF to destroy terrorist bases and infrastructure in Lebanon; join hands with Christian forces in northern Lebanon; capture Beirut; and be prepared to destroy the Syrian forces in the Bekaa Valley all the way to the Beirut–Damascus highway. In May 1981 the IDF issued a new plan, "Oranim Katan" (Small Pines), which had "essentially similar goals to the regular Oranim," according to the plan itself. A third variation of the plan, "Oranim Mitgalgal" (Pines in Stages), described the IDF executing the goals of Oranim incrementally. It is unclear how well the government ministers understood the differences between these plans.

Oranim was intended to solve the various problems between Israel and Lebanon: pushing the terrorists' artillery, which plagued Israeli border towns, out of reach of Israeli population centers in the Galilee and along the border; annihilating the Palestinian terrorists' political and military infrastructure in southern Lebanon, in the Bekaa Valley, and in the vicinity of Beirut; neutralizing the influence of the terror organizations' primary sponsor, Syria, while attempting to avoid a direct conflict with Syrian armed forces in Lebanon; and delivering assistance to the Christian forces in northern Lebanon as they attempted to put together a stable, peace-seeking government. The Christian groups in Lebanon had been cooperating with the Israelis on the political and military level since 1976, during Rabin's term as prime minister.

Already, in 1976, Sharon had argued that the unchallenged Syrian advance into Lebanese territory weakened Israel. Sharon criticized Rabin's decision to mark a strip of territory across the map of Lebanon with a red line, with any Syrian deployment beyond it considered a casus belli. The "Mistake of '76," as Sharon called it, was inherited by the Begin administration. From that point on, any attempt to attack "Fatah-land," as Israelis derisively termed the terrorist-controlled areas of Lebanon, also meant a possible conflict with Syria. In 1978, Israel created a "Security Zone" in Lebanon. The area, a five-mile swath of territory along the border that was designed to stifle infiltration attempts and artillery fire, was controlled by Maj. Sa'ad Haddad, the commander of a Christian Lebanese militia. Ever since March 19, 1978, the United Nations Interim Force in Lebanon (UNIFIL) had been stationed north of the zone, as per U.N. Security Council Resolution 425.

In July 1981, the border battles between Lebanon and Israel intensified. The PLO launched a series of terror attacks, Israel bombed targets from the air, and in response the PLO launched thousands of Katyusha rockets into Israel. Philip Habib, President Reagan's special envoy to the region, began shuttling between Beirut and Jerusalem. Three weeks prior to Sharon's appointment as defense minister, Habib managed to hammer out a cease-fire agreement between Israel and the PLO. On August 5, 1981, the day Sharon stepped into office, quiet reigned over the country's northern border.

Although the Yamit withdrawal dominated the first months of his term, Sharon kept a close eye on the PLO's rising military and political power in Lebanon. Fifteen thousand armed Palestinian fighters were spread through Beirut and the areas south of the capital city known as Fatah-land. The different terrorist organizations broke the terms of the cease-fire repeatedly, sending terror groups to attack Israeli and Jewish targets. This was the context in which the Oranim plan was developed. Begin and Eitan were informed of the secret plan from the beginning; the government ministers learned of it at the December 20, 1981, cabinet meeting.

On January 12, 1982, Sharon paid a secret visit to Beirut. Sharon's entourage included the deputy chief of staff, Maj. Gen. Moshe Levy; the director of military intelligence, Maj. Gen. Yehoshua Saguy; the assistant to the defense minister, Maj. Gen. Avraham Tamir; the head of the operations division for the general staff, Uri Saguy; chief of paratroopers and infantry officer Amos Yaron; Sharon's assistant, Oded Shamir; several bodyguards; and one civilian, Dr. Boleslav (Bolek) Goldman, Sharon's personal friend and family doctor.

The group boarded an air force transport helicopter and flew to the Christian city of Jounieh. Bashir Gemayel, the leader of the

Christian Lebanese Phalangist Party, greeted him with a hug and said, "I knew you'd come! It's good you came, we've been waiting for you!" They continued from the landing strip to the harbor, where Sharon dined on some of the cuisine Lebanon is famous for: Mediterranean salads, hummus, tahini, kebab and other grilled meats, baklava, French and Dutch cheeses, and Lebanese halvah. The hosts showered Sharon with praise and admiration and kept the mood festive. They had every reason to court the minister in charge of the Israel Defense Forces: An IDF invasion would serve their purposes, crushing the terrorist organizations, chasing the Syrian troops from Beirut and the Bekaa Valley, and ushering in an era of Christian rule in Lebanon.

The dinner ended around midnight. The convoy set off from Jounieh to Beirut for a visit to the Phalangist headquarters in the capital. Gemayel explained the fine points of the Christian defense in the split city, where the east belonged to the Christians and the west to the Muslims and the terror groups. From there they visited the port of Beirut. Sharon slept for a few hours in a guarded villa in Jounieh before heading out to a seventeen-story building for a bird's-eye view of the city and the presidential palace in Ba'abdeh, the symbol of Lebanon's sovereignty. Several minutes passed as Sharon looked out at the city in silence. From there the entourage continued on to the ski resort on Mount Snen. While the others threw snowballs, Sharon stared out at the strategic Beirut–Damascus highway.

Gemayel urged Sharon to invade his country. Shimon Schiffer, a journalist, writes in his book *Snowball: The Story Behind the Lebanon War* that Sharon told Gemayel that Israel would uproot the terror infrastructure in Lebanon but would not operate against the Syrians. According to Shiffer, Sharon hardly spoke during the tour, but when the entourage stopped at a lookout point above Beirut's international airport, he turned to Gemayel and said, "I don't want to get into the particulars of our plan, because they have yet to be finalized. It would be premature to discuss the details. But one thing is clear, and it will be the bedrock of the IDF's ability to operate in Lebanon: When the time comes . . . we'll get close to Beirut on the coastal route."

To a spectator, Sharon's visit to Lebanon might have signaled what was to come. Sharon's lack of fear as he walked and rode around the streets of Beirut for two days, crossing roadblocks manned by Phalange troops and regular Lebanese Army personnel in the midst of a city torn by civil war, bordered on recklessness. Once he had visited the Phalange's headquarters on the night of the twelfth and spent the night on Lebanese soil, rumors of the Israeli defense minister's presence began to spread. By the following day, hundreds of people knew he was in town. It is hard to imagine the damage to Israel that would have been done had a terror group succeeded in taking the defense minister, the head of military intelligence, the operations chief on the general staff, and several more IDF generals hostage.

Sharon's ties to the Christian leaders in Lebanon would become one of the main points of contention during and after the war. Many Israeli politicians and journalists would charge that Sharon conducted himself in a manner that strayed from the IDF doctrine, which called for the armed forces to be used solely in the defense of the country. They asserted that Sharon led Israel into Lebanon not only to push the terrorists' guns out of range of Israeli villages, but also in order to chase the Syrians from the country and appoint the Israel-friendly Bashir Gemayel to the presidency. How symbolic, then, that on January 12, during the seaside feast in Jounieh, Elie Hobeika was in attendance. Several months later, Hobeika, head of the Phalangists' intelligence division, would command the troops that committed the massacre in the refugee camps of Sabra and Shatilla, an atrocity that nearly ended Sharon's political career.

On May 9, 1982, Begin and Sharon ordered the IDF to bomb terrorist bases in Lebanon in response to PLO mines laid in Israeli territory. The PLO countered by firing artillery rounds and primitive Katyusha rockets into open country in Israel. The PLO's decision to avoid firing into populated areas was a warning: Next time they'd rain rockets on the northern towns and villages. The government, to Sharon's consternation, decided to turn the other cheek.

But on May 16, 1982, the PLO announced that the cease-fire had come to an end. The northern border heated up again.

With this ongoing conflict in mind, the government did not need the physical presence of the defense minister to approve an IDF action on Friday, June 4. At 3:15 P.M. the IDF attacked eleven targets, two of which were in Beirut, causing severe loss of life among the Palestinians. Two hours later, at 5:20 P.M., Palestinian forces began firing at Israeli civilian centers.

On June 5, Sharon returned to Israel. He went straight to the Kirya, the IDF's downtown Tel Aviv headquarters, for a briefing by the general staff. At the meeting, Eitan informed Sharon that the IDF had sneaked tanks into the security zone in preparation for an attack. Eitan had ordered a partial call-up of the reserves and reinforced the front lines on the Golan Heights to avoid what he called "a surprise attack from the Syrians." The general staff informed Sharon that the air force would continue to attack in Lebanon, since bad weather had prevented them from hitting all eleven targets the day before.

Sharon went from the general staff meeting to the prime minister's residence in the Talbiyeh neighborhood of Jerusalem to attend an emergency cabinet meeting on Saturday night, June 5. The atmosphere was very tense. The exchange of fire along the northern border and the reports from London about Ambassador Argov's critical condition blackened the ministers' mood. Since the cabinet meeting a day and a half before, the Palestinian terrorist groups in Lebanon had fired on twenty-nine Israeli villages and towns, including the northern cities of Nahariya and Kiryat Shmonah. Since the beginning of the sabbath (sundown on Friday), Israeli citizens near the northern border had been living under a constant barrage.

Begin enumerated the Palestinians' violations of the July 1981 cease-fire and asserted Israel's right to respond with force. The ministers were told that the PLO had made a conscious decision to target Israeli civilians. "I am going to propose that we decide this evening to embark on Operation 'Peace for Galilee,' " Begin announced, using the Israeli term for the Lebanon War.

The prime minister turned to Sharon: "Would you be so kind as to explain the plan as though we are hearing it for the first time?

Although we have heard it in the past, we need to execute it and therefore need to know every detail." Sharon unfurled his maps, illuminated several slides, and explained the plan, which was based on Oranim. "The goal of Operation Peace for Galilee," he said, "is to push back the terrorists' artillery and mortars beyond the range of Israel's northern towns. We are talking about an operation forty kilometers [twenty-four miles] in."

Sharon presented the IDF's intention of flanking the Syrian forces north of Mount Hermon, intimidating them into withdrawing without a battle and thereby ridding the Bekaa Valley of both the terrorist organizations' artillery and the Syrian forces. Most ministers accepted these goals at face value. Only Minister of Communications Mordechai Zipori feared an inevitable entanglement with the Syrian troops. "I have a number of questions," said Zipori, a brigadier general in the reserves and a former armored brigade commander under Sharon in the Six Day War. "First of all, regarding the phrase 'pushing the terrorists forty kilometers back' . . . it seems to be an oversimplified phrase. I want to know the exact line the forces need to reach."

In his book, *In a Straight Line*, Zipori writes that the room went still with a weighty silence. "According to the way the issue of the terrorists in the Syrian region was portrayed, we will, in simple Hebrew, attack the Syrians," Zipori said. "I think that is not okay."

"Your attention, please, Mr. Zipori," Begin responded. "I said we would not attack the Syrians."

"It doesn't matter what type of decisions we make, Mr. Prime Minister," Zipori said. "The maneuvers described here will lead us to a combat engagement with the Syrians."

Begin replied, "The question is who initiates. If they attack our troops—we will have to respond."

Begin gave way to IDF chief of staff Rafael Eitan, who explained the matter of the forty-kilometer mark. "It's forty kilometers from Metulla," Eitan said; "That's almost up to Lake Karoun." Sharon said: "Along the coast it's forty-two kilometers to Sidon. On the eastern side it's all the way to Lake Karoun."

"Where does Beirut fit into this plan?" Deputy Prime Minister Simha Erlich asked.

"Beirut is out of the picture," Sharon responded. "There are foreign embassies there, and we need to stay away. According to what was authorized in the cabinet meeting, Operation Peace for Galilee is not intended to capture Beirut but to push back the terrorists. Right now we're talking about a range of forty kilometers." Sharon emphasized that "the goal of the mission is not to attack the Syrians. In that regard, an attack on the Syrians will be carried out only if the Syrians interfere." Sharon was asked how long the mission would take. He responded, "Up to the stage I'm talking about, around twelve hours. I don't know how things will develop, so I suggest we look at this in a twenty-four-hour frame. But as far as the forty-kilometer stage is concerned, it will be over sooner."

Begin put Operation Peace for Galilee to a vote. Fourteen ministers voted in favor, two abstained, and none were opposed. In *Israel's Lebanon War,* Ze'ev Schiff and Ehud Ya'ari assert that the ministers left the prime minister's house that night certain they had authorized a short military strike, limited in duration to one or two days.

The IDF received orders that spoke specifically of the need to be prepared to join forces with the Lebanese Christians and destroy the Syrian Army in Lebanon. Government ministers would later claim that at the June 5 cabinet meeting, there was no mention of the possibility of joining up with the Phalange in northern Lebanon or of reaching Beirut. After the war, they would blame Sharon for failing to present the full extent of his plans in Lebanon. Sharon and Eitan categorically denied those charges, asserting that each phase of Peace for Galilee came before the Cabinet and received authorization.

Late on Saturday night, Sharon returned to Sycamore Ranch to get some sleep before the next morning's invasion. The onset of Operation Peace for Galilee was scheduled for the following day, Sunday, June 6, at 11:00 A.M. In the future, some would label it "Arik Sharon's War."

CHAPTER 28

Ensnared in Beirut

AT 4 A.M. ON SUNDAY MORNING, JUNE 6, 1982, SHARON CLIMBED INTO a helicopter and flew to the northern sector's forward command center. There the chief of staff and the divisional commanders presented their final battle plans.

From the first, Sharon was involved in all of the details of the military planning in Lebanon. Some say he acted as a supreme commander, above Chief of Staff Rafael Eitan. Sharon never broke the military chain of command; Eitan always issued the orders to the IDF, but everyone knew who dictated the paces of war. This model was a sharp departure from that of Moshe Dayan and David Ben-Gurion. Sharon's total involvement in the minutiae of the war, perhaps born of his unfulfilled desire to serve as chief of staff, created an absolute sense of affiliation between Sharon and the war—for better or for worse.

Sharon left the forward command center and flew to Jerusalem for both the final cabinet meeting and the final Knesset Foreign Affairs and Defense Committee meeting before Operation Peace for Galilee began. At eleven in the morning, just as the IDF forces were setting out, Sharon and Begin met with the heads of the Opposition—Yitzhak Rabin, Shimon Peres, and Haim Bar-Lev. Begin informed them of the Cabinet's decision to initiate a ground assault against the Palestinian terrorists in Lebanon. Bar-Lev thought the government had acted injudiciously, saying, "This operation will get us into trouble with the Syrians." Begin replied, "There are special orders not to open fire on the Syrians." Sharon added that IDF forces had been given clear orders to keep a four-kilometer distance between themselves and Syrian forces.

After the fact, in an interview with Voice of Israel Radio, Peres gave his version of events at the June 6 meeting with Begin. "We were explicitly told," he recalled, "that this would be a three- or four-day war, forty kilometers, just to distance the artillery and nothing more. In response to their questions, Rabin and Bar-Lev were told that the IDF would not get to Beirut or close to it. It was also said we would not mess with the Syrians. All of us were shocked by what happened afterward."

After the meeting in the prime minister's office, Sharon flew north in time to see Israeli tanks enter Lebanon. On the first day of the war, the IDF force was split into four parts, each containing armor, artillery, infantry, and combat engineering troops. Three separate sectors were invaded: the western and central sectors of southern Lebanon, where the terrorists reigned and had established Fatah-land, and the eastern sector, in the Bekaa Valley, along the Syria-Lebanon border, where the Syrian Army was deployed.

The division-sized force in the western sector, under the command of Brig. Gen. Yitzhak Mordechai, was tasked with taking Tyre, crossing the Litani River, and charging north to Sidon. The second divisional force, under the command of Brig. Gen. Amos Yaron, was to execute an amphibious landing north of Sidon. The third divisional force, under the command of Brig. Gen. Avigdor Kahalani, was to head north from Metulla, up through the central sector, across the Litani, and toward Sidon. In the eastern sector, the fourth division, under the command of Maj. Gen. Yanush Ben-Gal, would advance north in the Bekaa Valley toward the Syrian forces. Ben-Gal's forces were ordered to stop several kilometers short of the Syrians, before the town of Hasbaiyeh, and wait.

At that evening's cabinet meeting, Sharon was authorized to open a fifth line of attack. A division commanded by Brig. Gen. Menachem Einan was given the job of advancing north along the central sector's seam between the Syrian and Palestinian forces, toward the Shouf Mountains, hemming the Syrians in. The initial intent of this plan was to drive the Syrians east, back to their own soil, thereby avoiding a military engagement. Ainan's force would prevent the terrorists from fleeing to Syria. Left with no choice, they would flee in one direction: north, toward Beirut.

THE LEBANON WAR, 1982
(OPERATION PEACE FOR GALILEE)

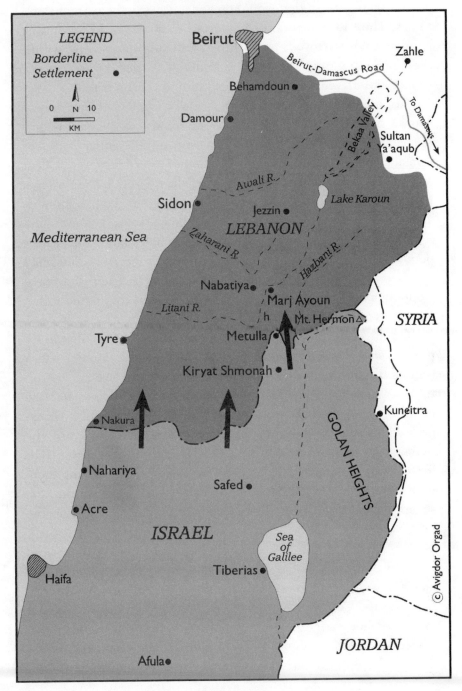

LEGEND

Borderline —·—·—
Settlement ●

0   N   10
KM

Beirut

Zahle

Beirut-Damascus Road

Behamdoun

To Damascus

Bekaa Valley

Damour

Sultan Ya'aqub

Awali R.

Lake Karoun

Sidon

Jezzin

LEBANON

Mediterranean Sea

Zaharani R.

Hazbani R.

Nabatiya

Litani R.

Marj Ayoun

h

Mt. Hermon △

SYRIA

Tyre

Metulla

Kiryat Shmonah

Kuneitra

Nakura

GOLAN HEIGHTS

Nahariya

Safed

Acre

ISRAEL

Sea of Galilee

© Avigdor Orgad

Haifa

Tiberias

JORDAN

Afula

As the land forces carried out their missions, the Israeli Air Force attacked the PLO's arms depots and dropped bombs with delayed-action fuses that would prevent access to the weapons and mines. The PLO's central headquarters in southern Lebanon was bombed and destroyed, unleashing confusion and shame within their ranks. During the first few hours of battle, IDF forces advanced unfettered through the western and central fronts.

Armored brigade commander Col. Eli Geva was at the front of Mordechai's division. Before noon one of his battalions was ambushed by a squad of RPG-armed Palestinian militiamen at a junction adjacent to the el-Batz refugee camp. Five soldiers were killed, and the battalion commander and two soldiers were taken hostage. Later, two of the three hostages were murdered by the Palestinians. This incident taught Sharon what he would be facing: Unable to defeat the Israeli Army, the Palestinians would hide among the civilian populations in the refugee camps and along the roads, in small bands, armed with shoulder-fired antitank rockets. Their chances of stopping a column of Israeli armor were nil, but they could inflict casualties and show they were undaunted by the might of the IDF.

On the evening of the first day of war, June 6, 1982, Sharon reported to the Cabinet that the fighting in the central and western sectors was proceeding as planned. In the eastern sector, Sharon told the ministers, the Syrians had augmented their forces and had begun shelling the IDF units in the area. The defense minister expressed his own opinion that the IDF pressure would not cause the Syrians to retreat from the Bekaa Valley and suggested that IDF forces continue north, flanking the Syrians and threatening them with total isolation and encirclement. He said, "I believe that the second stage, until forty kilometers, will be complete within the next twenty-four hours."

After the war, the idea of encircling and isolating the Syrian forces was strongly criticized. It was obvious that an Israeli move like that would lead to an armed conflict, critics said. Minister of Housing and Construction David Levy asked Sharon at the cabinet meeting whether the encircling maneuver changed the plan presented the previous night and whether that development placed the IDF beyond the forty-kilometer mark. Sharon answered, "Yes, we will pass the forty-kilometer [mark]." At the close of the meeting, the ministers decided that the IDF should go ahead with the flanking maneuver and that U.S. special ambassador Philip Habib should inform the Syrians that Israel planned to clear the area under their control of terrorists up to the forty-kilometer mark.

On the night of June 6, Sharon flew back to the forward command center in order to report the Cabinet's decisions to the chief of staff. While leaning over the maps and planning the next day's moves, neither of them knew that the Golani Brigade's reconnaissance unit, the sayeret, had just taken the Beaufort, a Crusader fort situated on a razor-edged ridge high above the Litani River, which afforded the PLO artillery access to Kiryat Shmonah and Metulla. The Beaufort, having withstood hundreds of Israeli Air Force attacks over the years, had become a symbol of the Palestinian resistance. Six Israeli warriors were killed in the battle, including the commander of the sayeret, Guni Harnik.

The following morning brought embarrassment as Sharon landed on the summit of the Beaufort with Prime Minister Begin and throngs of reporters and news crews. Sharon, unaware of the loss of life, happily told Begin and the news crews that the IDF had suffered no losses in the battle. At this point a young officer, a second lieutenant from the sayeret, interrupted them and said to the defense minister, "What's wrong with you? Six of my friends were killed here tonight, six warriors from the sayeret!" Sharon was shocked and shamed; the news media feasted on the affair. Looking back, this was the opening volley of what would become a massive public outcry against Sharon.

Battling hard over the next few days, the IDF took the refugee camps around the cities of Tyre and Sidon. Each camp was independently fortified to withstand an attack. The Palestinian fighters fought valiantly in the alleyways, firing antitank rockets from close range, throwing grenades from windows, and sniping from rooftops. In that sector alone, the IDF lost twenty-one soldiers, and ninety-five were wounded.

Einan's division, on the way to the Beirut–Damascus highway in the central sector, received orders to crush all PLO forces but to refrain from initiating contact with the Syrians if possible. At the same time, Yaron's amphibious force made its way from Damour to Aley. They too had the Beirut–Damascus highway as their goal.

On June 8 the government decided to open a diplomatic channel to Syria and send a letter via Philip Habib to Syrian president Hafez Assad, announcing that the IDF did not want war with Syria. The letter, written by Begin, carried assurances that so long as the Syrians did not fire on the Israelis, they would not be fired upon; it further demanded that the Syrians return their forces to the June 5 positions, and that Syria command the terrorists based in their region to retreat twenty-five kilometers to the north. If Assad abided by these Israeli demands, Begin wrote, the military stage of the battle would be over and diplomacy would begin. The prime minister's decision angered Sharon, who was opposed to any agreement that allowed the Syrians to remain on Lebanese soil.

That day, June 8, Begin spoke before the Knesset and announced that Israel did not want war with Syria. But in the field, near the city of Jezzin, IDF and Syrian forces had already engaged each other. The forces of Brig. Gen. Menachem Einan and Maj. Gen. Yanush Ben-Gal took the city by evening. In response, the Syrians reinforced their surface-to-air missile batteries and sent more troops into Lebanon.

On Wednesday morning, June 9, the Cabinet met to discuss a pivotal issue: Should they see their goals as accomplished once they had pushed the terrorists back in the western and central sectors, or should they try to drive the Syrians from Lebanon with a frontal assault? Sharon brought Amos Amir, the deputy commander of the air force, with him. Begin informed the ministers of a message to President Assad, transmitted via the Americans, stating that Israel would attack the Syrian missile batteries if the Syrian president did not withdraw them to Syria.

As they plotted, new intelligence reports arrived: More Syrian missile batteries were on their way to Lebanon. Sharon urged the ministers to attack. "We're eight kilometers south of the Beirut–Damascus highway," he said. "The Syrians won't sit with their hands in their laps. The worst situation as far as we are concerned is the arrival of six more SAM-6 surface-to-air missiles. . . . If we don't get an affirmative answer [from the Syrian president], then in my opinion it is critical to authorize this operation."

Minister of Communications Mordechai Zipori showed up at the meeting with maps and a ruler, illustrating to the ministers that the IDF had long ago crossed the forty-kilometer mark. As Zipori measured out the kilometers on the map with his ruler, Sharon snidely suggested to Zipori that from now on perhaps every minister should come to cabinet meetings equipped with a ruler.

Zipori, Sharon's main detractor in the government, penned severe accusations against Sharon in his book, *In a Straight Line.* "Sharon's great deception," he wrote,

> began to be revealed already on the first day of war . . . as the entire Cabinet—and in my opinion including its leader, Begin—assumed the IDF was penetrating 40 kilometers in the eastern and western sectors, [whereas] already on the first night of battle it was made clear without any doubt that the situation in the field far exceeded what had been planned, promised, and agreed upon. In the western sector, IDF forces reached Damour, some 80 kilometers from Israel's border. In other words, two times what was promised.

Zipori writes that none of the members of the Cabinet knew that the IDF had been given orders already on Saturday night to operate in the central sector and that in essence the IDF was prepared "to destroy the Syrian army in Lebanon." According to Zipori, the defense minister would repeatedly ask the Cabinet to authorize a "better tactical position" or "broadening of a route" or a "widening of a gap in a route," all in the name of the "proper," "efficient" progression, while carefully safeguarding the principle of avoiding a "real conflict with the Syrians."

In the end, the government decided that the IDF would attack the Syrian missile batteries but that Begin would concurrently send an additional letter to Assad, clarifying that Israel did not want war with Syria and that the previous letter still stood. Just before noon, Sharon left the cabinet meeting and called the chief of staff, ordering air strikes on the Syrian missile batteries in the Bekaa Valley.

That day, the IAF destroyed seventeen of the nineteen Syrian missile batteries in Lebanon. The small airspace over the valley filled with two hundred dueling fighter planes. The battle ended with twenty-nine downed Syrian MiGs and zero losses for the IAF. The events in the sky created a new reality on the ground: war between Israel and Syria. From that point on, Israel would be fighting two battles in Lebanon.

That night, President Reagan sent Prime Minister Begin an unequivocal message asking for a cease-fire by six o'clock the following morning, Thursday, June 10. Begin convened the Cabinet at four in the morning. Sharon, fearing the cease-fire would stop the IDF in its tracks before it reached the Beirut–Damascus highway, wanted to delay. He explained to the ministers that it was crucial that the IDF reach the road before the cease-fire went into effect because its possession would strengthen their hand during the post-battle negotiations and would afford territorial contiguity with the Christian forces. His campaign was successful. The government authorized the IDF to advance on both the Palestinian and the Syrian fronts.

On Friday morning, June 11, Begin announced that he, along with Foreign Minister Yitzhak Shamir and Defense Minister Ariel Sharon, had reached the conclusion that a cease-fire was in Israel's best interest. The cease-fire took effect at noon. In the western sector, the IDF was three kilometers south of Beirut's international airport and had taken the cities of Tyre, Sidon, Damour, and Khaldeh; in the eastern sector the IDF was but a few kilometers from the Beirut–Damascus highway in the Ein Zehalta area.

The ministers left their offices; negotiations regarding the terms of the cease-fire would begin after the weekend. Sharon convened the IDF general staff and told the chief of staff and the generals that the IDF had attained the goals of Operation Peace for Galilee in their entirety. However, while the cease-fire had terminated the battles with the Syrians in the eastern sector, the western sector, where the IDF was engaging the Palestinians, remained hot. On Friday, Saturday, and Sunday, the IDF and terrorist groups continued to exchange fire between Sidon and Beirut. The war was entering a new stage—the siege of Beirut.

After a week of fighting, the terrorist organizations were in dire straits. Arafat and his Palestine Liberation Organization were isolated. The IDF had encircled all of Fatah-land in southern Lebanon. Their only path of retreat led north, to Beirut. Sharon, hoping the Lebanese Phalange would do Israel's work and chase the terrorists from Beirut, flew to Jounieh on Friday to meet secretly with Bashir Gemayel. Disappointment awaited him. The Phalange's leader, a relatively young, American-trained lawyer, refused to take an active role in the fighting.

Sharon learned that the Israeli-Phalange relationship, carefully cultivated since the mid-seventies, would not bear the fruits Israel had hoped for. Gemayel preferred to sit on the sidelines. He and his Phalange followers would not be active allies during the remainder of the war.

In *Israel's Lebanon War*, Schiff and Ya'ari contend that Sharon tried to persuade the Phalange leader to meet the IDF southeast of Beirut, totally ringing the PLO forces in the city. Gemayel slithered around the request, and in the end, with little choice, they agreed that the IDF would move toward the Phalange forces and not vice versa. Sharon determined the meeting point and demanded that the agreement be committed to on paper; Sharon and Gemayel signed the paper and the map itself. In *Warrior*, Sharon's autobiography, he asserts that at that stage of the war he did not want the Phalange to undertake any military operations for fear of ensnaring the IDF in Beirut.

The following day, Saturday, June 12, Sharon flew to meet Brig. Gen. Amos Yaron's troops southeast of Beirut, near the presidential palace in Ba'abdeh. Although Sharon was unable to locate Yaron, he did happen on a Phalange soldier who said he could lead the defense minister to Yaron. The route they took went straight past a Syrian Army post in Beirut. Suddenly, one of the soldiers accompanying Sharon fired an unintentional round. The people in the car waited nervously to see whether the Syrians had heard anything. Had the Syrians sent a patrol to investigate the gunfire, they would have taken the Israeli defense minister hostage. Several minutes later the car arrived in Ba'abdeh and stopped opposite the municipal building. Brigadier General Yaron was shocked to see the defense minister, arms paddling at his sides, striding toward him.

Bashir Gemayel, aware of Sharon's presence in Ba'abdeh, sent an escort to bring the defense minister to him in the heart of the Christian section of Beirut. As in 1982, Sharon was taken with the city's beauty. He was also shocked by the cafés, with their coffee-sipping crowds oblivious to the war around them. Sharon indicated as much to Gemayel, expecting the Christian leader to take to heart the need to spur his people into action. Gemayel remained silent. Sharon boarded a helicopter in Ba'abdeh and flew to Jerusalem for the first cabinet meeting since the cease-fire.

After the war, Sharon recalled the night of the twelfth:

> The paratroopers continued . . . moving north to carry out their mission—linking up with the Christian section. In accordance with orders, they proceeded without fire. . . . By the afternoon of the thirteenth [the paratroopers] crossed the border into the Christian area and the linkage and contiguity were attained, allowing [our forces] to continue their noncombat advance north, to blockade the Beirut–Damascus highway near Beirut, cutting Beirut from Syria and the Syrian army. . . . On that day I reported to the government that we had linked up with the Christians and made it to the Beirut–Damascus highway. The briefing, as usual, was accompanied by detailed explanation on a map. I emphasized that the focus of the effort was on reaching the [Beirut–Damascus] road and not capturing Beirut, which had not been decided on.

Schiff and Ya'ari discredit this claim. In *Israel's Lebanon War* they assert that the IDF entered an Arab capital city not only without the government's authorization but in direct opposition to what the defense minister had promised the Israeli government. "It was one of the gravest moments of the Lebanon War," they wrote. "The facts were dictated from the field and the government was forced to bless already-done deeds."

Minister of Communications Mordechai Zipori relates a different version of events. According to Zipori, the continuing battles elicited a wave of rage and protest among the people. More and more soldiers in the field were exposed to deceit and denial, a feeling that only intensified with the airing of official statements from the offices of the prime minister and minister of defense.

"Throughout, Sharon spurred the troops toward Beirut as IDF armor came and went to the presidential palace in Ba'abdeh," Zipori writes in *In a Straight Line*. "On June 13 the palace was encircled and the fire, temporarily, ceased. The Israeli government was faced, for neither the first nor last time, with facts on the ground: As opposed to Sharon's declarations that the IDF has a tradition of not invading Arab capitals, there were forces now facing the eastern part of Beirut."

Chief of Staff Eitan sides with Sharon. In his book, *A Soldier's Story*, he recorded the events of Sunday, June 13. According to Eitan's account, the terrorist organizations paid no attention to the cease-fire, and the fighting against them continued full force. The IDF advanced through the Lebanese capital toward the Christians on the eastern side of Beirut. Once they linked up, control of the Beirut–Damascus highway was theirs. "Beirut is closed and shut," he wrote. "We have no intention of entering Beirut."

The truth is that at 1:00 P.M. on Sunday, June 13, 1982, a paratrooper force met Phalange representatives outside the Christian village of Saba, east of Beirut. Fadi Frem, Gemayel's deputy, met the paratroopers at a roadblock on the outskirts of the city. One hour later they were joined by Bashir Gemayel and, from the Israeli side, by Chief of Staff Rafael Eitan and OC Northern Command Amir Drori. Eitan and Drori were taken to Jounieh and the paratroopers continued on to Ba'abdeh, near the Lebanese Department of Defense headquarters—and there the Beirut–Damascus highway was first severed.

The ministers at the June 13 cabinet meeting all understood that while the cease-fire terminated all fighting with the Syrian forces, the fight with the fifteen thousand PLO loyalists and other Palestinian militia holed up in Beirut was far from over. The following day, the fourteenth, the IDF tightened its grip around Beirut. "Sharon emphasizes," Chief of Staff Eitan wrote, "that he places great political importance on the complete closure of Beirut and the tightening of the siege around the city," especially since the prime minister was set to leave for talks with the administration in Washington. The next day, the fifteenth, Begin flew to the United States.

The encircling of Beirut was a turning point in the media's and the public's relationship with Ariel Sharon. A particularly embarrassing episode occurred on June 13 when Prime Minister Begin was quoted on the radio as saying that the IDF was not in Beirut, which was followed by a live report from the outskirts of the city showing army vehicles streaming past. One day earlier, on June 12, the military censor banned a television piece reporting that IDF troops had reached the Christian part of Beirut and had seized control of the airport. The unaired report asserted that once the Israeli troops met their Christian allies, friendly territory would stretch from Jounieh to the Israeli border.

The enormous human toll also shocked the Israeli public. On June 14, nine days after the war started, the chief of staff announced the statistics of human loss—170 soldiers dead, 700 wounded. Several days later the public learned that the toll was even higher—214 dead, 1,114 wounded. The Israeli media began asking tough questions: To what extent had Prime Minister Begin been briefed by Defense Minister Sharon as to what was happening on the front lines? Had Begin known, and if so when, about the intention to go all the way to Beirut? For the first time in the country's short history, politicians, reporters, and wide swaths of the Jewish Israeli public dared to question the motives behind an ongoing war.

Sharon, deeply troubled by the escalating public opposition, labeled it "the fear campaign of the Opposition party." The polarization of the Israeli public while combat still raged, Sharon claimed, served the interests of the terrorists and made it more difficult for the IDF and the government to achieve their goals. "Internally," Sharon said in a guest lecture at Tel Aviv University in 1987, "we witnessed deplorable behavior by the Opposition and parts of the media, who were revealed in all of their irresponsibility during the siege of Beirut. In both of those groups there were those who in essence agreed with the terrorists who said that the terrorist attacks did not constitute a breach of the cease-fire agreement." Sharon remained convinced for the rest of his days that had the internal opposition not split the Israeli public, the IDF could quickly have chased the terrorists from Lebanon, returned the Syrians to their country, and installed a Christian regime in Lebanon, which would have signed a peace agreement with Israel.

On Tuesday morning, June 15, the Cabinet convened without Begin. The Cabinet decided to give the defense minister authorization to allow Phalange troops to enter Beirut and fight the Palestinian terrorists in the city. The government also allowed Sharon to promise the Phalange troops Israeli assistance so long as they and not the IDF shouldered the brunt of the burden. Sharon left for another meeting with Bashir Gemayel, but the Phalange leader was still unwilling to commit his troops, disappointing Sharon yet again. Sharon waited for the June 21 meeting between Begin and Reagan to know whether the American president would condone the continued IDF presence.

During the six days of waiting before the meeting, Sharon ordered the IDF to crawl forward and take additional positions along the Beirut–Damascus highway, strengthening their chokehold on the Lebanese capital, where six thousand Syrian troops were cordoned off along with the Palestinians. The IDF and the PLO exchanged artillery fire. On the June 20, one day before Begin's meeting with Reagan, the PLO and the Syrian troops retreated from Beirut's international airport, allowing Israeli troops to roll in uncontested.

Begin was smiling when he left the president's office the following day. Reagan accepted the Israeli demand that all foreign forces withdraw from Lebanon—meaning Syria as well as the IDF. He also recognized the need for a stable government in Lebanon. The Begin-Reagan meeting raised Sharon's spirits. He had begun to feel threatened by the media, the Opposition, and his own government. On June 24, after Begin returned from the United States, the government directed Sharon to finalize the capture of the Beirut–Damascus highway in the Aley–Dahar al-Bader–Behamdoun sector, pushing the Syrian troops from the area. The attack began that night and was over by the following day, June 25. The battle completed the siege of the Lebanese capital.

The following day, June 26, was historic: For the first time in the history of the State of Israel, a crowd of a hundred thousand gathered in Tel Aviv's central square, Kikar Malchei Yisrael, and protested against the government during an ongoing war, demanding the IDF's withdrawal from Lebanon. Several days later, Arik Sharon himself took part in a counterprotest supporting the government's actions. Bereaved families that had lost their sons in action were actively engaged in the debate. The rift in national opinion was glaring.

PLO chairman Yasser Arafat, pinned down in the densely populated western part of the city along with fifteen thousand of his men, refused to leave Lebanon. Under siege, he was able to alter his image, morphing from predatory terrorist to freedom fighter, battling an occupying army in the name of his people.

As the siege continued, Arafat, in his trademark black-and-white kaffiyeh, grew increasingly popular in the West. Arafat appeared on television every day, exhibiting wounded Palestinian children and smoldering Palestinian homes. The siege of Beirut transformed him, in the eyes of millions of viewers worldwide, into the heroic leader of the Palestinian people.

If up until that point the war in Lebanon had been seen as a legitimate Israeli action in the name of its citizens in the north, the tables were now turning. Israel's image was badly tarnished, while Arafat, ostensibly trapped and battered, thrived at Sharon's expense. For the next three weeks Arafat dragged his feet, wasting time while negotiating and drawing inspiration from the protest rallies in Jerusalem and Tel Aviv and the deepening divide in Israeli society that they represented.

Col. Eli Geva, a commander of one of the armored brigades laying siege to Beirut, announced that he intended to relinquish his command in the face of possible orders to invade Beirut. "It's not our battle," Geva told Sharon. The defense minister sent the colonel to speak with Begin. Forty-eight hours later he was released from the IDF and barred from returning to Beirut to bid farewell to his soldiers. The Geva affair, which captured the headlines and ignited social upheaval in Israel, fractured the last stronghold still fiercely loyal to Sharon: the IDF chain of command.

The siege of Beirut lasted through the first half of August 1982. PLO positions were bombarded from the air, land, and sea. The IDF moved forward incrementally toward the western part of the city. By the fifth of August, the Israeli Army had taken the Hai-a-Salum neighborhood in southwest Beirut, the Uza'i neighborhood along the shore, and the museum area all the way to the

Hippodrome, and had the Bureij al-Barajne refugee camp encircled. Arafat and his men were trapped in a fourteen-square-kilometer area. Many Israeli soldiers died in the urban war. The Americans were outraged by the invasion and demanded that Israel return to its previous line. Begin rejected the demand to withdraw, but ordered Sharon to halt the IDF's advance.

On August 9, the IAF bombed the refugee camps in southwest Beirut, increasing the pressure on Arafat. By the twelfth, a day known as "Black Thursday" by the trapped terrorists, the IAF had flown a hundred sorties. The bombings crushed many of the terrorists' bunkers, but they also killed civilians, fueling the fires of international condemnation. At the cabinet meeting on the twelfth—after Begin had fielded an irate call from Reagan, who demanded an immediate stop to all bombings of civilian areas—Sharon found himself alone. Ministers David Levy, Simha Erlich, Yosef Burg, Zevulon Hammer, Mordechai Zipori, and even Yitzhak Shamir castigated him for deciding to attack West Beirut so fiercely without first checking with Begin.

By the end of the meeting, Sharon had been stripped of his authority to order air strikes—an unprecedented decision. It seemed that Begin's attitude toward Sharon had changed, too. Up until that point he had given him almost complete backing. Five days earlier, though, on August 7, Begin had suddenly remarked, "I am informed about all of the operations, sometimes before the operation and sometimes afterward." During the stormy August 12 meeting, Begin scolded Sharon as he argued with the ministers around him: "Don't raise your voice. Let it be clear who's running this meeting." David Levy, minister of housing and construction, admonished Sharon, saying, "We'll yet leave Beirut without accomplishing anything . . . it's not only the people that are confused, but the government." Minister of Welfare Dr. Yosef Burg said, "What is happening is in opposition to the government's decision." Deputy Prime Minister Simha Erlich shouted at Sharon: "Demagogue!"

Minister of Communication Mordechai Zipori writes in his book that Begin reminded Sharon at that meeting that he represented the government to the army, not the other way around. According to Zipori, Begin said, "You don't enjoy any special privileges in this government, you're an equal among equals. . . . How is it that you allow yourself this kind of behavior!" Zipori writes that the ministers, "strained to their limits, uplifted by the sudden firmness of the prime minister, which had been absent throughout the months of war, were even sharper in their criticism. Some of them rebuked [Sharon] even more stridently. They accused him of issuing orders to the army that strayed from the government's decisions and even in certain situations of acting behind the back of the prime minister."

Sharon gave his version of events at a lecture in Tel Aviv five years later:

> I ordered air strikes on the terrorists' neighborhoods in south Beirut during one of our strongest attacks. That attack angered the Americans and triggered a harsh conversation between President Reagan and the Prime Minister [Begin]. The government was sharply critical as well. It was at a special cabinet meeting, which I asked Begin to convene, for authorization to occupy a cluster of abandoned houses that the terrorists used in order to snipe at our troops. I asked for permission to advance one hundred meters in the area of Beirut Grove, in order to take control of the orchard, which was used by the . . . terrorists.
>
> I informed the government that during the night we were forced to take action that strayed from the government's decisions: We took two houses near the Hippodrome that were used by the terrorists to fire on our troops. It was impossible to convene the government in the middle of the night to decide whether those two houses should be taken. It's unfeasible that the government will decide about each house. It's true that our government—and I am pleased by this—is involved in even the smallest military details . . . but we had reached the point, in my opinion, that approached unnecessary risk. The government did not authorize my plans, and reached the following decisions: A) Not to carry out the plans submitted by the defense minister. B) Not to employ the IAF without the express

consent of the prime minister or by his direct order. C) Not to alter the situation in the field without the government's decision.

Those decisions constituted a vote of no confidence in Sharon. Just as he was moving into position as heir apparent to Begin, the unbridled aspect of his personality had come to the surface. The same qualities that had hindered him in the past—an overabundance of self-confidence, a need for control, a disregard for the opinion of other politicians on all security matters—were once again in evidence.

The massive air strikes on the terrorists' neighborhood in Beirut were effective. On the night of August 12 and 13, Arafat agreed to leave Beirut with all of his followers. Between August 21 and September 1, 1982, nine thousand of his men left Beirut under the protection of a multinational force, along with the six thousand Syrian troops. On August 30, 1982, Yasser Arafat himself set sail for Tunisia.

It seemed that things were finally settling down. On August 23, 1982, one week before Arafat left Beirut, Bashir Gemayel was chosen to be president by the Lebanese parliament. Sharon hoped that soon his dream would be fulfilled: A Lebanese president friendly to Israel would sign a peace deal between the two nations.

On September 14, however, as Sharon made his way to a meeting in Tel Aviv, he received word by radio to come to the base as soon as possible. There he learned that a powerful explosive device had killed Bashir Gemayel while he was delivering a speech. He died just one week before his inauguration as president of Lebanon. Sharon's ally had been slain, and with him the possibility of peace between their two nations.

CHAPTER 29

Sabra and Shatilla

THE MORNING AFTER GEMAYEL'S MURDER THE IDF MOVED INTO West Beirut. Sharon and Begin, fearing that chaos would engulf the city, decided to enter the capital on the night of the murder. During the night of September 16 and 17, the IDF allowed Phalange forces to enter the Palestinian refugee camps of Sabra and Shatilla. Despite previous pledges to respect the laws of battle and fight only armed combatants, the Phalangists, eager to avenge their leader's murder, butchered hundreds of the civilians in the camps, including women and children.

The chilling pictures of the massacre shocked the world. The Israeli public reacted sharply. On September 28, 1982, under pressure from the media and the public, the Israeli government established a National Committee of Inquiry to investigate how the massacre had been perpetrated under the very nose of the IDF. Chief Justice of the Supreme Court Yitzhak Kahan headed the commission. Beside him on the bench sat former attorney general and future chief justice of the supreme court Aharon Barak and Maj. Gen. (Res.) Yonah Efrat.

The commission heard dozens of witnesses. Toward the end of its inquiry, in late November 1982, in accordance with Section 15(A) of the Commissions of Inquiry Law, the commission sent notices to nine individuals. The nine were Prime Minister Menachem Begin, Defense Minister Ariel Sharon, Sharon's aide in the Defense Department, Avi Dudai, Foreign Minister Yitzhak Shamir, IDF chief of staff Rafael Eitan, Director of Military Intelligence Maj. Gen. Yehoshua Saguy, OC Northern Command Amir Drori, Brig. Gen. Amos Yaron, and the Mossad chief, whose identity was not made public.

Sharon's notice read:

Defense Minister Ariel Sharon may be harmed if the Commission determines: A) That he ignored or disregarded the danger of acts of revenge or bloodshed perpetrated by Lebanese forces against the population of the refugee camps in Beirut without ordering appropriate steps to avoid those dangers. B) That the defense minister did not order the withdrawal of the Lebanese forces from the refugee camps as quickly as possible or adopt measures to protect the population in the camps when information reached him about the acts of killing or excesses that were perpetrated by the Lebanese forces. C) That in such abstention the defense minister failed to fulfill his duties.

The country awaited the commission's report with bated breath. Sharon, seen as the engine behind the entire war effort, was deeply worried. During the early stages of the hearings, an unknown young lawyer provided by the Defense Department, Dov Weisglass, had represented him. Weisglass, a reservist serving in the department's legal division, was asked to defend the defense minister during one of his most difficult hours.

Once the Kahan Commission sent out its cautionary letters, however, the civil service commissioner ruled that Sharon could no longer be represented by a state-provided lawyer. Sharon turned to Shmuel Tamir, even visiting him at home in an attempt to persuade Tamir to represent him, but he declined. With few other options, Sharon turned back to Weisglass, by now released from the reserves, and asked for his counsel as a private lawyer. Weisglass took the case. From that moment, the two of them were bound in friendship for life.

On February 7, 1983, the day before the publication of the commission's report, Menachem Begin received an advance copy. Sharon tried contacting Begin to learn the contents of the report, but for the first time in his life, he was unable to reach the prime minister by phone. When he finally got through to Begin, the prime minister told him he could not reveal the content of the report before its official release the following morning. Sharon felt as if the sky was about to come crashing down on him.

With the publication of the report on February 8, 1983, the Israeli public learned the exact chain of events that led to the Phalange's massacre of the Palestinians in the refugee camps of Sabra and Shatilla. On Tuesday, September 14, before it was clear whether or not Bashir Gemayel had been killed, Sharon had spoken with Begin, Chief of Staff Eitan, and Director of Military Intelligence Saguy in order to reassess the situation in Lebanon. At around eleven P.M. Gemayel's death was confirmed, and Sharon and Begin decided to send the IDF into West Beirut to preempt anarchy. Later, Sharon and Eitan spoke of including the Phalange in that move. "The matter of including the Phalangists in the entry into West Beirut," the commission reported, "was not mentioned at this point to the prime minister."

That night the chief of staff flew to Beirut, briefed the IDF commanders about the coming advance, and continued on to the Phalange headquarters. Eitan instructed the Phalange leaders to mobilize their forces, impose a closure on the areas under their control, and ready themselves to take part in the coming battle. The commission reported that the IDF chief of staff told the Phalange leaders that the Israeli Army would not enter the Palestinian refugee camps in the western part of the city, Sabra and Shatilla, and that the responsibility for fighting in those camps would fall to them. In his testimony, Eitan told the commission that the decision to send the Phalange forces into Sabra and Shatilla was made during a conversation with Ariel Sharon at 8:30 P.M. on September 14.

Eitan left the Phalange's headquarters and continued on to IDF headquarters in Beirut, located on the roof of a five-story building some 220 yards southwest of Shatilla. The two refugee camps were in essence one contiguous urban settlement of narrow alleys and squat houses. Sabra's dimensions were three hundred by two hundred yards; Shatilla was larger, five hundred and fifty yards square. It is unknown how many residents were in Sabra and Shatilla when the Phalange forces entered the camps, since many fled during the artillery shelling of the area, but it is estimated that six thousand people remained in the two Palestinian refugee camps.

At six in the morning on Wednesday, September 15, the IDF advanced into West Beirut. Eitan, situated on the roof, looked down into the camps with binoculars but could not see what was happening in the narrow, congested alleys of the camps. At first there was no resistance to the IDF invasion of West Beirut, but later in the day, perhaps as the surprise wore off, the PLO gunmen in the camps opened fire. Two hours after the IDF entered West Beirut, at between eight and nine in the morning, Sharon arrived at the rooftop command center. Eitan informed him of the agreements with the Phalange—the mobilization, the curfew, and the entry of the Phalange's troops into the camps. The commission reported that "the defense minister authorized that summary of events. Sharon called Prime Minister Begin from the rooftop command center and reported that there was no resistance in Beirut and that the operation was progressing smoothly."

The protocol of Sharon's visit to Beirut on September 15 contains an order Sharon gave to the chief of staff and the director of military intelligence: "Only one element, and that is the IDF, shall command the forces in the area. For the operation in the camps the Phalangists should be sent in."

Sharon went, along with the director of military intelligence, the commander of the Shabak (Israel's security service), and several Mossad representatives, to meet with the Phalange leaders. "At that meeting," the commission reported, "the Minister of Defense stated, inter alia, that the IDF would take over focal points and junctions in West Beirut, but that the Phalangist army would also have to enter West Beirut after the IDF and that the Phalangist commanders should maintain contact with Major General Drori, OC Northern Command, regarding the operation." From there the minister of defense went to Bikfayeh, to the Gemayel family home, to pay a condolence call.

Sharon returned to Israel on Wednesday, September 15. He got home exhausted at 6:00 P.M. Several hours earlier, Begin had met with the American ambassador to Israel and informed him that Israel had entered West Beirut in order to prevent bloodshed and that the Phalange forces were conducting themselves properly. Sharon spoke with Begin over the phone from Sycamore Ranch and said that by evening the IDF would be positioned in West Beirut, and that all was in order.

On Thursday morning, September 16, Sharon called the chief of staff, the director of military intelligence, and other senior officers to a consultation in his office. The chief of staff began the meeting by saying, "The whole city is in our hands, complete quiet prevails now, the camps are closed and surrounded; the Phalangists are to go in at eleven or noon. Yesterday we spoke to them." Sharon reiterated that the Phalangists should be sent into the camps, and then called the prime minister and reported to him, "The fighting has ended. The refugee camps are surrounded. The firing has stopped. We have not suffered any more casualties. Everything is calm and quiet." Once again, Sharon did not inform the prime minister of the decision to send the Phalange forces into the camps.

At approximately 11:00 A.M. on Thursday morning, September 16, the Phalange commanders arrived at the headquarters of one of the IDF divisions for their first coordinating session with OC Northern Command Amir Drori regarding their invasion of Sabra and Shatilla. Drori concluded with them that they would coordinate their entry into the camp with Brig. Gen. Amos Yaron, the IDF division commander in that sector. Their coordination session took place in the afternoon. They agreed that one company of Phalange troops, consisting of no more than 150 men, would enter Sabra and Shatilla.

During the briefing, Brigadier General Yaron told the Phalange commanders where the PLO gunmen's hideouts were located in the camp and warned them about harming the civilian population. Yaron testified that he stressed the point because he knew that the Phalange's norms of conduct were not in sync with accepted IDF protocol. Yaron placed observation points on the rooftop command post and on another nearby roof, but still the alleyways remained obscured from view.

The commander of the invasion force, Elie Hobeika, did not enter the camp, but spent the night at the IDF forward command post. As agreed upon with Yaron, a Phalange liaison officer with a radio communications set was stationed on the rooftop command post. At roughly six in the evening, Hobeika's men entered the camps.

At 7:30 P.M. the Israeli government convened along with the chief of staff, the Mossad chief, and the director of military intelligence to discuss the situation in Lebanon in the wake of Gemayel's murder. Begin and Sharon spoke, followed by Chief of Staff Eitan, who informed all present that the Phalange had entered Sabra and Shatilla and had begun fighting that evening.

Deputy Prime Minister and Minister of Housing and Construction David Levy said he accepted the IDF's contention that entering Beirut was necessary to avert anarchy, but he added a caveat: "That argument could be undercut and we could come out with no credibility when I hear that the Phalangists are already entering a certain neighborhood—and I know what the meaning of revenge is for them, what kind of slaughter. Then no one will believe we went in to create order there, and we will bear the blame. Therefore, I think that we are liable here to get into a situation in which we will be blamed, and our explanations will not stand up." No one responded.

While the ministers convened in Jerusalem, the Phalange fighters approached Shatilla from the south and west. From the moment they passed over the embankment surrounding the camp, their movements were no longer visible from the rooftop or other observation points. The PLO fighters swiveled their fire away from the IDF locations and directed it at the invading force. With darkness, the Phalange liaison officer requested and received illumination flares from the IDF. Mortars and plane-dropped phosphorus flares descended slowly over the camps.

During the night of September 16–17, reports reached certain IDF officials—though not the defense minister or the chief of staff—that the Phalange force was straying from its mission and operating against unarmed civilians in the camps. According to one report, on the evening of the sixteenth, the liaison officer, in the vicinity of Israeli officers in the mess hall, remarked that three hundred people, some of whom were civilians, had been killed thus far. Later in the evening he revised the number to 120.

OC Northern Command Amir Drori testified that he had not heard the liaison officer's comments in the mess hall. Drori had heard that the Phalange force was executing an "unclean mopping-up"—that is, that they did not call for civilians to exit homes, but simply charged in, firing. Based on that information, Major General Drori ordered Brigadier General Yaron "to halt the operations of the Phalangists, meaning that the Phalangists should stop where they were in the camps and advance no further." Yaron verified that the order had been passed down to the Phalange commanders. Drori spoke with the chief of staff on the phone and indicated to him that the Phalange had perhaps "gone too far." He informed Eitan that he had ordered them to cease their activity, and the chief of staff told him he would be in Beirut by the afternoon.

The chief of staff reached Beirut on Friday afternoon, September 17, and went with Drori to meet the Phalange commanders. According to a Mossad representative present at the meeting, Eitan "expressed his positive impression received from the statement by the Phalangist forces and their behavior in the field." Eitan testified that the Phalange commanders reported to him that the operation had ended and all was in order, and that since the Americans had been pressuring them to leave, they would be gone by five in the morning. The IDF chief of staff responded: "Okay, all right, you did the job."

The commission found that insofar as the meeting between Eitan and the Phalange commanders was concerned,

> It is clear from all the testimony that no explicit question was posed to the Phalangist commanders concerning the rumors or reports which had arrived until then regarding treatment of the civilian population in the camps. The Phalangist commanders, for their part, did not "volunteer" any reports of this type, and this matter was therefore not discussed at all at that meeting. The subject of the Phalangists' conduct toward those present in the camps did not come up at all at that meeting, nor was there any criticism or warning on this matter.

Eitan returned to Israel on Friday evening, September 17. Sometime between eight and nine in the evening he spoke with the defense minister. According to Sharon's testimony,

> the Chief of Staff told him in that conversation that he had just returned from Beirut and that "in the course of

the Phalangists' actions in the camps, the Christians had harmed the civilian population more than was expected." According to the Defense Minister, the Chief of Staff used the expression that the Lebanese Forces had "gone too far," and that therefore their activity had been stopped in the afternoon, the entry of additional forces had been prevented, and an order had been given to the Phalangists to remove their forces from the camps by 5:00 A.M. the following morning. The Defense Minister added that the Chief of Staff also mentioned that civilians had been killed. According to the Defense Minister's statements, this was the first report that reached him of irregular activity by the Phalangists in the refugee camps.

The conversation was not recorded or documented in any way, and Eitan denied having said that there had been killing beyond what was expected. The Kahan Commission published its finding regarding the discrepancy:

It is our opinion that the Defense Minister's version of that same conversation is more accurate than the Chief of Staff's version. It is our determination that the Chief of Staff did tell the Defense Minister about the Phalangists' conduct, and that from his words the Defense Minister could have understood, and did understand, that the Phalangists had carried out killings of civilians in the camps. Our opinion finds confirmation in that, according to all the material which has been brought before us in evidence, the Defense Minister had not received any report of killings in the camps until that same telephone conversation; but after that conversation, the Defense Minister knew that killings had been carried out in the camps—as is clear from a later conversation between him and Mr. Ron Ben-Yishai.

At 10:30 on Friday night, television military correspondent Ron Ben-Yishai had called Arik Sharon and told him he had learned from several IDF officers that they had heard that the Phalange force was killing civilians in the camps. "According to the Defense Minister," the report reads, "what he heard from Mr. Ron

Ben-Yishai was nothing new to him, since he had already heard earlier about killings from the Chief of Staff—and he also knew that as a result of the report, entry by additional forces had been halted and an order had been given to the Phalangists to leave the camps." No word was passed to Begin.

By five o'clock on Saturday morning, September 18, the Phalange force had yet to leave Sabra and Shatilla as promised. Brig. Gen. Amos Yaron ordered them out without delay, and by 8:00 A.M. they were gone. The IDF supplied food and water to the refugees of both camps, who were escorted into a nearby stadium. In the meantime, reporters and photographers rushed to the scene, following word of a massacre.

On Saturday, Sharon learned the extent of the killing. At one in the morning he heard from Dave Kimche, the director general of the Israeli Foreign Ministry, that the American ambassador had called and informed him that Palestinian refugees had been massacred. Sharon told Kimche that the Phalange's operation had been stopped and all Christian forces had been expelled from the camps. At this point, Red Cross crews discovered hundreds of slaughtered civilians, mostly women and children. The positions of the dead spoke of murder rather than combat.

There is great disparity in the estimated number of dead. Palestinian spokespeople contended that thousands had been murdered, but those reports seem tendentious and are not based on a reliable body count. Red Cross personnel counted 328 bodies, but the commission found the IDF's estimate of seven hundred to eight hundred (mostly in Shatilla) to be the most reliable.

The devastating images ricocheted around the world. Most of the reports attributed the massacre to the Phalange force, but the IDF and the State of Israel, seen as their controllers, were widely blamed. The IDF refrained from entering the camps out of fear that their presence there would be interpreted as a sign that they had participated in the massacre.

Prime Minister Begin first heard about the massacre on BBC radio on Saturday evening. He immediately called Eitan and Sharon and learned from them that everything had been stopped and that the Phalange force had been removed from the camps.

On Sunday night, September 19, with the end of Rosh Hashanah, Begin called a cabinet meeting at his house. The title of that evening's discussion was "The events in West Beirut—the murder of civilians in the Shatilla camp."

At the meeting, Sharon said that the IDF had not entered the camps, "which were terrorist bastions, because it was our interest not to endanger even one soldier in the camps." He added, "When we learned what had taken place there, the IDF intervened immediately and removed those forces." Sharon claimed that no one had imagined that the Phalange force would commit atrocities. The meeting concluded with a resolution expressing deep pain and anguish about the injuries to the civilian population perpetrated by a Lebanese unit that had entered the camps. The government rejected accusations that the IDF was responsible for the tragedy.

The commission carefully weighed the question of who bore direct responsibility for the massacre and who bore indirect responsibility. The commission found that the Phalange commanders and soldiers alone bore direct responsibility, since all evidence pointed to the fact that they had perpetrated the massacre and that no Israeli forces had been in the camps at the time:

> We have no doubt that no conspiracy or plot was entered into between anyone from the Israeli political echelon or from the military echelon in the IDF and the Phalangists with the aim of perpetrating atrocities in the camps. The decision to have the Phalangists enter the camps was taken with the aim of preventing further losses in the war in Lebanon [and] to accede to the pressure of public opinion in Israel, which was angry that the Phalangists, who were reaping the fruits of the war, were taking no part in it. . . . No intention existed on the part of any Israeli element to harm the noncombatant population in the camps.

With regard to indirect responsibility, the commission found that the decision to send the Phalange force into the camps after the murder of Bashir Gemayel was made by Defense Minister Sharon and the chief of staff. "The decision on the entry of the Phalangists into the refugee camps," they wrote, was taken without consideration of the danger—which the makers and executors of the decision were obligated to foresee as probable—that the Phalangists would commit massacres and pogroms against the inhabitants of the camps, and without an examination of the means for preventing this danger. Similarly, it is clear from the course of events that when the reports began to arrive about the actions of the Phalangists in the camps, no proper heed was taken of these reports, the correct conclusions were not drawn from them, and no energetic and immediate actions were taken to restrain the Phalangists and put a stop to their actions. This both reflects and exhausts Israel's indirect responsibility for what occurred in the refugee camps.

The commission accepted Begin's testimony—that he learned of the Phalange forces' invasion of the camps on Thursday evening, September 16—as wholly credible. "We may certainly wonder," they wrote, "that the participation of the Phalangists in the entry to West Beirut and their being given the task of 'mopping up' the camps seemed so unimportant that the Defense Minister did not inform the Prime Minister of it and did not get his assent for the decision; however, that question does not bear on the responsibility of the Prime Minister."

Regarding Sharon's responsibility, the commission found that the defense minister

> adopted the position that no one had imagined the Phalangists would carry out a massacre in the camps and that it was a tragedy that could not [have been] foreseen. It was stressed by the Minister of Defense in his testimony, and argued in his behalf, that the director of Military Intelligence, who spent time with him and maintained contact with him on the days prior to the Phalangists' entry into the camps and at the time of their entry into the camps, did not indicate the danger of a massacre, and that no warning was received from the Mossad, which was responsible for the liaison with the Phalangists and also had special knowledge of the character of this force.

It is true that no clear warning was provided by Military Intelligence or the Mossad about what might happen if the Phalangist forces entered the camps. . . . But in our view, even without such warning, it is impossible to justify the Defense Minister's disregard of the danger of a massacre. We will not repeat here what we have already said above about the widespread knowledge regarding the Phalangists' combat ethics, their feelings of hatred toward the Palestinians, and their leaders' plans for the future of the Palestinians when said leaders would assume power. Besides this general knowledge, the Defense Minister also had special reports from his not inconsiderable [number of] meetings with the Phalangist heads before Bashir's assassination.

In the circumstances that prevailed after Bashir's assassination, no prophetic powers were required to know that concrete danger of acts of slaughter existed when the Phalangists were moved into the camps without the IDF's being with them in that operation and without the IDF's being able to maintain effective and ongoing supervision of their actions there. The sense of such a danger should have been in the consciousness of every knowledgeable person who was close to this subject, and certainly in the consciousness of the Defense Minister, who took an active part in everything relating to the war. His involvement in the war was deep, and the connection with the Phalangists was under his constant care. If in fact the Defense Minister, when he decided that the Phalangists would enter the camps without the IDF's taking part in the operation, did not think that that decision could bring about the very disaster that in fact occurred, the only possible explanation for this is that he disregarded any apprehensions about what was to be expected because the advantages—which we have already noted—to be gained from the Phalangists' entry into the camps distracted him from the proper consideration in this instance.

As a politician responsible for Israel's security affairs, and as a Minister who took an active part in directing the

political and military moves in the war in Lebanon, it was
the duty of the Defense Minister to take into account all
the reasonable considerations for and against having the
Phalangists enter the camps, and not to disregard entirely
the serious consideration mitigating against such an action, namely, that the Phalangists were liable to commit
atrocities and that it was necessary to forestall this possibility as a humanitarian obligation and also to prevent the
political damage it would entail. From the Defense Minister himself we know that this consideration did not concern him in the least, and that this matter, with all its
ramifications, was neither discussed nor examined in the
meetings and discussions held by the Defense Minister. In
our view, the Defense Minister made a grave mistake when
he ignored the danger of acts of revenge and bloodshed by
the Phalangists against the population in the refugee
camps.

. . . Regarding the responsibility of the Defense Minister, it is sufficient to assert that he issued no order to the
IDF to adopt suitable measures. Similarly, in his meetings
with the Phalangist commanders, the Defense Minister
made no attempt to point out to them the gravity of the
danger that their men would commit acts of slaughter. Although it is not certain that remarks to this effect by the
Defense Minister would have prevented the acts of massacre, they might have had an effect on the Phalangist commanders who, out of concern for their political interests,
would have imposed appropriate supervision over their
people and seen to it that they did not exceed regular combat operations.

It is our view that responsibility is to be imputed to the
Defense Minister for having disregarded the danger of acts
of vengeance and bloodshed by the Phalangists against the
population of the refugee camps, and having failed to take
this danger into account when he decided to have the Phalangists enter the camps. In addition, responsibility is to be
imputed to the Minister of Defense for not ordering appro-

priate measures for preventing or reducing the danger of massacre as a condition for the Phalangists' entry into the camps. These blunders constitute the nonfulfillment of a duty with which the Defense Minister was charged.

Chief of Staff Eitan also received a sharp rebuke from the commission:

We find that the Chief of Staff did not consider the danger of acts of vengeance and bloodshed being perpetrated against the population of the refugee camps in Beirut; he did not order the adoption of the appropriate steps to avoid this danger; and his failure to do so is tantamount to a breach of duty that was incumbent upon the Chief of Staff.

The commission established the facts and reached conclusions regarding the responsibility of Prime Minister Begin, Foreign Minister Shamir, and the head of the Mossad, but felt that "it is sufficient to determine responsibility and there is no need for any further recommendations." They found similarly in the matter of OC Northern Command Amir Drori. The commission "arrived at grave conclusions with regard to the acts and omissions of the Chief of Staff, Lt. Gen. Rafael Eitan," but determined that there was no "practical significance" to a recommendation regarding the termination of his service, since he was set to retire from the IDF in any case. The commission members recommended that Maj. Gen. Yehoshua Saguy, director of military intelligence, not continue serving in his post. The commission recommended that Brig. Gen. Amos Yaron "not serve in the capacity of a field commander in the Israel Defense Forces, and that this recommendation not be reconsidered before three years have passed."

The commission's decision regarding Ariel Sharon was the gravest of all:

We have found, as has been detailed in this report, that the Minister of Defense bears personal responsibility. In our opinion, it is fitting that the Minister of Defense draw the appropriate personal conclusions arising out of the defects revealed with regard to the manner in which he discharged the duties of his office—and if necessary, that the Prime Minister consider whether he should exercise his authority under Section 21(A)(a) of the Basic Law: The Government, according to which "the Prime Minister may, after informing the Cabinet of his intention to do so, remove a minister from office."

CHAPTER 30

Alone on the Farm

On February 10, 1983, the Cabinet convened to discuss the implications of the newly released Kahan Report. Sharon was late. Peace Now activists and demonstrators demanding his resignation jammed the road leading to the ranch. A police escort had to clear a lane into Jerusalem. At the entrance to the government complex a large group of supporters waited for him outside the building. Their chants of "A-rik, A-rik" mingled with the jeers of the left-wing activists—"A-rik is a mur-der-er."

Sharon suggested that his fellow cabinet members announce new elections rather than accept the commission's recommendations. That idea was trounced in a 16–1 vote. Instead, he reached an agreement with Begin: He would step down as defense minister but remain in the government as a minister without portfolio. On Friday, Sharon told Begin he would clear out by the following Monday. Begin asked him why it would take so long.

That Friday, Sharon arrived at the Israel Bar Association in Tel Aviv to speak before an audience of lawyers. Again the police were forced to clear a path through the protesters. He and Lily, who escorted him everywhere during those harrowing days, passed through the taunts of left-wing protesters without so much as a flicker of expression.

"When a crowd stands outside the Israel Bar Association and calls me a murderer—that is a grave phenomenon," he said at the forum. "That does not create a positive atmosphere, that's verbal violence. I've never been indicted or stood trial for murder and suddenly I'm labeled a murderer. I don't take personal offense, but to my dismay, verbal violence has become a part of our society, and it's time that it too was uprooted."

Israel was in the midst of a roiling political storm. The night before, a right-wing supporter had lobbed a fragmentation grenade into a crowd of left-wing protesters as they marched to the prime minister's office, killing Emil Grunzweig, a Peace Now activist. The murder heightened the tension between the two political camps. "I want to express my grief and sorrow," Sharon said at the Israel Bar Association, "over the criminal assassination in Jerusalem of people who are the blood of our blood, who wanted nothing more than to express a political opinion. The hand of malice needs to be amputated. We will fight this type of phenomenon with all our might."

On Monday, February 14, 1983, the calm and restrained Professor Moshe Arens replaced Sharon, his predecessor and opposite. On his final day in the defense ministry, Sharon held multiple conversations with the ministry's workers. In his bleak farewell address, Sharon emphasized that no soldiers, officers, or politicians in Israel had been convicted of participation in the massacre in Sabra and Shatilla. Lily stood next to him at the ceremony. Throughout the day, members of his staff came into his office. Some cried, others brought flowers.

Arik and Lily Sharon went straight back to the ranch where, as before, he could lick his wounds with his family, away from politicians and cameras. Sharon was angry—at his governmental allies who had abandoned him, and at the Kahan Commission's conclusions.

He had become the pariah of the nation. People stared at him with hatred and disgust. The enthusiasm which had surrounded him since his days in the paratroopers evaporated. Once one of the most influential people in the Middle East, he was suddenly unacceptable to society. He was flooded by feelings of helplessness, emptiness, loss, and disappointment. He complained to Lily that it was absurd that a Jewish defense minister was paying the price for what Christian Arabs had done to Muslim Arabs.

A February 15, 1983, editorial in the liberal *Haaretz* daily captures the prevailing public sentiment toward Sharon. The day he left office, Yoel Marcus, a regular columnist, wrote:

> Mr. Sharon can thank God fate didn't have him serving in Stalin's Cabinet in 1953. Back then, when the leadership

wanted to get rid of a minister that everyone feared and no one trusted, they physically disarmed him of his two sidearms at a Cabinet meeting and sent him to a place no one came back from. Despite all, Mr. Sharon can admit to certain advantages in the democratic system.

In the beginning of his term as defense minister, Lily had miscarried. Now, they tried again to conceive, but they were unable to have any more children. People who visited Sharon recall a depressed, brooding man prone to fits of rage, though also eager to dispel his loneliness with conversation. He ranted on about cabinet members, reporters, and Prime Minister Begin. Many of those who had beaten a regular path to his door now stayed away. Alone and confused, he had no idea how to proceed. Politically, he seemed dead and buried.

Sharon was subject to even graver accusations abroad. *Time* magazine reported that the Kahan Commission had written in its classified appendix that Sharon had held talks with Bashir's brother, Amin, and Pierre Gemayel on the necessity of revenge. The magazine claimed that Sharon had spoken with Bashir's grieving relatives during his condolence call before the funeral. Sharon categorically denied the assertion.

On February 22, 1983, Razi Barkai, Voice of Israel's New York correspondent, announced that *Time* magazine was set to publish a damning article. Sharon called his lawyer, Dov Weisglass, and asked, "What's in the classified appendix?" Weisglass said he didn't know. He called Dan Meridor, the government secretary at the time, who informed him that the appendix contained technical facts about intelligence sources; there was no mention of a revenge meeting. Sharon decided to sue the magazine. The exhausting, heavily covered trial would go on for three years.

Sharon left the palatial offices and corridors of power for a small office in an unused building in Tel Aviv, which he called "an empty office in an empty building." Downcast, he decided to leave the Cabinet and escape the barely contained grins. Sharon told Uri Dan of his decision. Like a preacher in full throttle, Dan rattled off numerous reasons why it would be a mistake to leave public office.

Years later, Sharon admitted that without Dan's support, he would have backed out of public service.

Over the course of his deliberations about the future, Sharon formed what was to become the cornerstone of his political understanding: Politics is an ever-revolving wheel; sometimes you're on top and sometimes you hit rock bottom, but the wheel keeps on rolling. Sharon concluded that he couldn't go any lower and that his fortunes would soon turn. He simply had to stay the course.

In late April, Sharon broke his silence, delivering a speech at a Likud activists' convention in Tiberias that justified the IDF's actions in Lebanon, dismissed the Kahan Commission's conclusions, and enumerated the achievements of the war. The crowd cheered, loudly and without pause.

The successful speech raised his spirits, which were further buoyed by a gesture from Begin, who appointed him to the Ministerial Committee for Defense. In May 1983, several weeks before his speech in Tiberias, Sharon had flown to New York to speak before a crowd of fifteen hundred people at the Sutton Place Synagogue. The American Jews and Israeli émigrés in the audience cheered wildly as well.

Not all of his public appearances were in front of an adoring crowd. Both in Israel and abroad, his speeches often incited massive protests. In Montreal in early June 1983, a throng of left-wing Jewish and pro-Palestinian groups protested outside the Ritz-Carlton Hotel, opposite a group of Sharon-supporting Herut youth.

Two weeks after returning from Canada, Sharon met with Raya Hurnik, the bereaved mother of Gurni Hurnik, the fallen commander of the Golani Brigade's reconnaissance unit. One year earlier, after her son died taking the Beaufort stronghold, Raya Hurnik had said she would shoot the defense minister if she met him face to face. Over the year she sent him several letters, detailing the anguish of bereavement and the way it was magnified in her case— since the defense minister failed to apologize for having claimed that no one had been killed in the battle for the Beaufort. Sharon hadn't responded to her previous letters, but this time he asked to meet with her.

Sharon told Hurnik that as a father who had lost his son, he

knew how she felt. The two talked about the battle for the Beaufort and the Lebanon War before parting with a silent handshake.
"I didn't convince him," Raya Hurnik said, "and he didn't convince
me." But the meeting was significant for both.

On July 26, 1983, five months after the publication of the
commission's report, Sharon left the ranch and went to Metzudat
Ze'ev, the Likud national headquarters in Tel Aviv. The forum he
attended, encouraging the next generation to run in the municipal
elections, was of secondary importance. It was his first trip back to
party headquarters, and he wanted to gauge the insiders' sentiments.

Sharon, in an open-collared white shirt, complained that his
current government duties took up only about a day and a half of
his week. During his speech, he attacked the Israeli media. The
next day, he appeared on the popular political talk show *Moked*.
The gloves were off. Sharon blamed members of the government
for inappropriate behavior, claiming that he was the only one who
was forced to pay the price, and again decried the results of the
Kahan Commission. "The commission did not delve into the real
facts," Sharon claimed. The National Union of Israeli Journalists
responded: "We denounce Ariel Sharon's anti-news-media strike.
It seems his hatred for the media has driven him out of his mind."

On July 28, 1983, Sharon appeared on the balcony of the post
office in Pardes Katz, which was known to be a Likud stronghold,
smiling broadly and waving to the crowd. They sang ecstatically,
"Arik, King of Israel." Sharon had come to help the campaign of a
Likud candidate for the Bnei Brak municipal elections. People
continued to chant and wave signs reading "Arik, We Love You"
and "Arik Sharon Is a Symbol of Security."

Suddenly, a long-haired young man jumped onto the stage,
yelling, "Arik, go home! My brother died in Lebanon." The police
escorted the protester from the scene, and the crowd responded by
shouting, "Arik, we want you as defense minister, we trust you."
Sharon swept the sweat from his brow and replied, "Thank you. I
also trust in you."

Sharon filled his schedule with appearances before Likud activists, discovering what would become the cornerstone of his intra-

party power: the local branches of the Likud. His star began to rise among the party's field workers in sleepy development towns in the far south and north.

Sharon spoke to a group of Likud activists in Ofakim:

> I hear the propaganda machine saying "Sharon got us stuck in this mud and now we're pulling ourselves out of the mud." Well, folks, what kind of mud are they talking about exactly? Are they referring to the unprecedented operation we led the IDF on to expel the terrorists from Beirut, the annihilation of the PLO's terrorist infrastructure in south Lebanon, the rescue of the northern villages, and the eviction of the Syrian troops from the Shouf Mountains? That was the situation when I left the defense ministry seven months ago. Now that I'm no longer in the critical decision-making slot, the Syrians and the terrorists . . . are returning to Beirut. That's the real mud, and I won't allow them to hold me responsible for that.

As Sharon grew close to his voting constituency, the former leader of the Likud was fading from view. Menachem Begin, limiting his public appearances and spending more and more time at home, crawled into a shell. The masses of Likud supporters in Israel's disenfranchised neighborhoods and towns, many of whom saw Begin as their spiritual mentor, were left leaderless. On September 19, 1983, Begin resigned as prime minister. He never told the Israeli public why. Most analysts attribute his retirement to the burden of fallen soldiers that he could no longer bear, to the heartbreaking daily protests of bereaved families outside his home. Some of his confidants blamed Sharon for his demise on account of Sharon's conduct during the Lebanon War, but those rumors were never validated by Begin. As the tragic results of the Lebanon War became known, Begin began to sink into a deep melancholy. Testifying before the Kahan Commission was one of the most traumatic experiences of his life. He left the public arena with his head hung low. It's impossible to say whether Begin fell prey to the depression that had haunted him since birth, as a new study by Dr. Ofer Grosbard contends; because he had been crushed by the human toll of the war; or because he had been devastatingly disappointed by his defense minister, whom he had so admired. He took the truth to his grave.

The Likud electoral authorities voted in Foreign Minister Yitzhak Shamir to replace Begin until the end of the term in July 1984. Sharon continued to troll through the different Likud branches, so much so that Gideon Samet, a political columnist for *Haaretz*, labeled him "Arik, King of the Streets."

But there was great aversion to Sharon outside of right-wing bastions. One of his most demeaning moments occurred in February 1984. Sharon pushed Shamir for an influential position, but the prime minister issued a series of vague commitments, until, one day, one of the prime minister's men told Sharon he might be nominated to head Aliyah (Jewish immigration to Israel; the word means to go up, as in spiritual elevation) for the Jewish Agency. Bored as a minister without portfolio, Sharon offered himself as a candidate for the menial position. The Jewish Agency turned him down. At fifty-six years of age, he had fallen for Shamir's ploy like a political newborn.

A person close to Sharon recalls "looking at Arik and seeing a truly humiliated man. He had been defense minister with the potential to be prime minister and suddenly he's dealt that kind of loss. I remember he said, very embarrassed, 'We need to check what happened here.' It was a breaking point. He'd fallen into a trap like a rookie. From there you either crash, go home, and forget you were ever in politics, or you begin the climb all over again."

One of the people closest to Sharon in those days was a young student leader named Yisrael Katz. Katz, pursued by Shamir, bet on Sharon despite the latter's predicament. Katz told Sharon he needed to stop leaning on cross-country support and start building a base in the party. Katz suggested he translate his widespread support in the Likud branches to representation and influence on the central committee. Sharon, who had been in, and disdainful of, the party's institutions, gave Katz the green light. Haim Aharon had a small but pivotal role in the founding of the Sharon Camp.

When the time came to choose the next Likud representative for prime minister, Sharon decided to test the strength of his

intraparty camp. Most told him it was suicidal to run and that he
wouldn't get more than 10 percent of the vote from the central
committee, but when the tallies were counted, Sharon shocked
everyone with 42.5 percent of the vote. The sitting prime minister,
Shamir, won with 56 percent, but the ringing message from the
primaries was that the downtrodden defense minister had returned
to the heart of Israeli politics. The rebound was incredible.

Hundreds of Likud activists from the Katz-orchestrated Sharon
camp huddled around Arik and Lily Sharon after the votes were
counted. The press called the achievement "Sharon's amazing victory." Uri Dan chimed in, telling everyone he saw that thirteen
months earlier, after the publication of the Kahan Report, he had
announced: "Whoever doesn't want Sharon as defense minister
will get him as prime minister."

During the next Knesset election campaign—the Likud's first
without the charismatic Begin—Sharon spoke at 180 conferences
and rallies. Inflation, the stock market crash, and the complex retreat to the security zone along the border with Lebanon were the
major issues being debated. Despite the disaster predicted in the
polls, the Likud managed to tie Labor on July 23, 1984.

The Likud lost 7 seats, from 48 in the previous Knesset to 41.
Labor, led by Shimon Peres—one of the few career politicians incapable of winning a popular vote—lost 3 seats, from 47 to 44. Together with other left-wing parties and the anti-Zionist Arab parties,
they were able to garner a 60-seat coalition. The Likud, along with
the other right-wing parties, the ultra-Orthodox and the National
Religious, were also able to collect 60 seats. The two sides were
deadlocked.

Sharon played a central role forming the 60-seat blockade during the thirty-nine-day period of coalition negotiations. He brought
the ultra-Orthodox and the National Religious parties together to
block Peres from forming a 61-seat majority. Sharon, a kippa on his
head, went from Bnei Brak to Jerusalem, persuading rabbis to adhere to their political and ideological pact with the Likud. Sharon
also initiated a secret meeting with Peres at the start of the negotiations, offering a national unity government based on equal representation for the two big parties.

The long months of silence, arising from a heated campaign and unresolved animosity over the Lebanon War, were broken. In Dani Korn's book *Time in Gray*, Sharon is quoted as saying, "The meeting was emotional, as Shimon and I have known each other for many years." The two discussed Labor-Likud equality. Sharon said to Peres, "Let's decide matters between the two big parties, and then the little parties will wait in line like at the medical clinic."

After thirty-nine days of negotiations, a national unity government was formed. The broad coalition was based on a rotation at the top: For the first half of the term, Shimon Peres would hold the prime minister's post and Yitzhak Shamir would serve as foreign minister and deputy prime minister; for the second two years they would switch. Yitzhak Rabin would serve as defense minister throughout, and Arik Sharon would be given one of the top financial ministerial posts.

At the time, Sharon was in New York. During one of the hearings at the *Time* libel suit, he received a message to contact Prime Minister Shamir. Sharon went into the judge's chambers to make the call. Shamir asked him whether he would be willing to accept the post of minister of industry and trade in the coming national unity government. Sharon answered yes and returned to the courtroom in high spirits—his dry spell was over.

CHAPTER 31

Minister of Industry and Trade

SHARON'S APPOINTMENT TO A SENIOR MINISTERIAL POST WAS NOT UN-contested. As the two sides neared a coalition agreement, Yitzhak Shamir told Shimon Peres that Sharon was his candidate. "We must give Arik the post of Industry and Trade," Shamir told Peres. "We can't leave him out in the cold." Peres invited the upper echelons of the Labor Party to the King David Hotel in Jerusalem and reviewed the proposed composition of the national unity government. When he got to Sharon's name, he lowered his voice and whispered: "We'll give Arik the ministry. We have no choice."

Future president Yitzhak Navon had his reservations about the appointment. Gad Ya'akovi warned: "This will be a historic blunder; we'll pay a heavy price." But Peres wanted to sit in the prime minister's chair and avoid another crisis in negotiations. On September 13, 1984, Israel's first national unity government was sworn into office. Sharon was appointed minister of industry and trade and, more important, a member of the Cabinet.

MK Yossi Sarid left the Labor Party in frustration. "It's ironic," he said on September 13, 1984,

> that Menachem Begin removed Ariel Sharon from his position as defense minister and made him minister without portfolio, and now Shimon Peres returns him to a post of honor and influence. This week I read in the papers that Sharon is willing to forgive the Laborites. I wanted to cry. I remembered the four hundred thousand people that came to the square and called for his removal from office. Shame

flooded me. Why did we call them? Why did we ask them
to assemble? Simply in order to crown him as a member of
the Cabinet two years later?

For several months. Sharon focused on the needs of the ministry, avoiding political squabbles and even managing a harmonious
relationship with Prime Minister Peres. "Sharonophiles" predicted
the utopia would be short-lived. Meanwhile his suit against *Time*
magazine demanded much of his attention. "The *Time* trial takes
up twenty hours of my day. Every day I sit with my lawyers till the
middle of the night," he said in December 1984, after two straight
weeks in which he was unable to return to Israel.

Lily, in New York with Arik, remarked that budget constraints
forced them to order room service; meals at the Regency, she said,
were too expensive. She spoke on the heels of vocal criticism in Israel regarding government funding for Sharon's crusade in New
York. Gastronomically, there was no reason to worry about the welfare of Arik and Lily Sharon. The two ate regularly at New York's
finest restaurants, under the watchful eye of American security
guards provided by the federal authorities. Sharon was accompanied by two Israeli-American friends, Arie Ganger and Meshulam
Riklis, along with his Israeli lawyer Dov Weisglass and the reporter
Uri Dan.

One night the group was eating at a famous New York establishment. At the end of the meal the waiter informed them that the
bill had been taken care of, pointing to a couple seated in the corner of the restaurant. Sharon went over to thank them. The man
said he had fought with him in the "Camel Commandos" in the
Southern Command, chasing down terrorists and infiltrators.
Sharon recognized him immediately. One thing, Sharon told him,
had been bothering him ever since: "During one of our chases, a
well-aged salami disappeared from my cooler. I've always thought it
was you who swiped it. Was it you?" The man went white and then
smiled. It was he, and he now wished to repay Sharon for the loss.

The suit against *Time* dragged on. The government had to approve a three-month leave of absence from office. On the witness
stand in New York and again on *Nightline* with Ted Koppel, Sharon

was asked whether he desired to become prime minister. Both times he answered that he did.

Sharon returned to Israel in January 1985 without a verdict. The federal court waited for word from the Israeli authorities. The judge wanted to see the secret appendix. Sharon said publicly that he would like the "document of contention" to be released, but the Israeli authorities decided it could not be declassified. Instead, Sharon was able to persuade Judge Kahan to write a letter stating unequivocally that there was no mention in the appendix of a Sharon meeting with the Gemayel family at which vengeance was discussed, thus refuting the *Time* report.

In order to further bolster his standing in the Likud, Sharon toured the party's branches in the first half of 1985, vociferously opposing his government's policies. Sharon's hawkish views fit well with the ideology of most members of the Likud Central Committee and the Herut Conference—the two groups that selected the Likud leadership. At first, Prime Minister Peres said nothing. But in August 1995, Sharon crossed the line.

Sharon spoke in Tel Aviv in front of an audience of Likud party members and veterans of the right-wing Lehi underground. He criticized the government's policies—rather tame stuff from Sharon during that period—but added a personal insult which translates literally as "Peres and his buddies can go jump" ("jump me" being a crude and well-known vulgarism). The prime minister was furious. Sharon stayed the course: "Peres is selling Judea and Samaria," he told journalists. The heads of the Labor Party demanded that Peres terminate Sharon's tenure, but Peres, determined to keep the national unity government in place, said he preferred to further the peace process rather than his feud with Arik Sharon. On October 22, 1985, Peres addressed the U.N. General Assembly. For Sharon, it was a signal to charge. Joined by Deputy Prime Minister David Levy, Sharon attacked Peres for agreeing in his speech to multinational, rather than bilateral, peace talks. The multinational umbrella, he claimed, would allow Soviet and European pressure on Israel. Peres's silence on the matter of negotiating with the PLO further enraged him.

The verbal darts thrown by Sharon and Levy were actually

aimed more at the foreign minister and chairman of the Likud, Yitzhak Shamir, than at Peres. Sharon and Levy were preparing for the upcoming Likud battle. Shamir and Arens were intent on preserving the coalition until 1986, when they would be given the reins; the two addressed all political disagreements with Peres behind the scenes. Peres told Shamir: "Sharon and Levy want to ruin you more than they want to ruin me."

In early November 1985, Sharon accused Peres of reaching a secret agreement with Saddam Hussein to convene an international peace conference. "The danger to peace is inflicted by the government's flimsy and flaccid stance as exhibited by the behavior of Shimon Peres," he said. In response, all the Labor ministers gathered at the prime minister's residence and demanded that Peres fire Sharon. On November 14, Peres issued an ultimatum: Either Sharon would turn in a letter of apology by the afternoon, or he would be fired. "I am not willing to let Sharon do to me what he did to someone else," Peres said, referring to Sharon's role in Begin's demise. Sharon capitulated. He sent a "letter of clarification" that same day.

In early January 1986, Sharon was vindicated. The jury in the *Time* case returned a guilty verdict on the counts of false allegations and defamation of character. The magazine was compelled to apologize, but not to pay the $50 million libel damages Sharon had sought from them, since American federal law requires that a jury find evidence of malice, or of reckless disregard for the truth, when a libel suit is brought by a public figure.

Sharon's libel suit in New York was filed against Time Inc. International, the American publisher of the magazine. He had simultaneously filed suit in Israel against Time Life International, the magazine's European publisher. As opposed to the United States, where a plaintiff must prove that a libelous report against a public figure is defamatory, false, and published with a malicious or reckless disregard for the truth, only the first two requirements must be met when substantiating a libel claim in Israel. Weisglass based his case on the American jury's findings that *Time* magazine had published defamatory and false allegations, which had not, though, been published with actual malice. Tel Aviv District Court judge Eliyahu Vinograd accepted the findings of the jury in New York and recommended that the two sides reach an agreement. That month, January 1986, the magazine submitted a brief to the court declaring that *"Time* Magazine recognizes the jury's decision in the Federal District Court in Manhattan, which the Israeli court has recently recognized as binding, that the matter of avenging the death of Bashir Gemayel was not discussed in the Kahan Commission Report and that Appendix B makes no mention of such an account. *Time* apologizes for the mistaken report. *Time* has agreed to pay part of the plaintiff's legal expenses, as pertains to the aforementioned article, in a sum total to be decided between the two parties."

Sharon was in high spirits. After a year and a half as minister of trade and industry he had established himself as the far-right marker on the Israeli political map, opposing what he called "Peres's yielding government" and "Shamir's surrender to that policy." As the Herut Conference approached on March 10, 1986, Sharon stood firmly in command of his own camp in the Likud Party. At the conference's first convention in eight years, the main branch of the Likud Party was poised to calibrate the balance of power in the party in the wake of Menachem Begin's sudden retirement. The strength of the Sharon Camp was hard to gauge.

In late January 1986, Benny Begin, the son of the now-reclusive former prime minister, appeared on *Moked*. Begin, a Ph.D. in geology and perhaps the straightest arrow ever to serve in the Knesset, was asked whether he was angry at Sharon for his behavior during the Lebanon War. He said, "It is improper to mix personal feelings into the public discourse. I have no intention of writing a novel, *My Life as a Vendetta*. My personal feelings toward Ariel Sharon are not the primary focus of our national agenda."

Benny Begin went on to assert that the two main camps in the Likud belonged to Shamir and Levy and that the two needed to cooperate in order to maintain the proper working order of the party. When asked about the Sharon Camp, he said, "Sharon himself has said . . . that there is no such camp."

Begin's words resonated deeply and were interpreted by the Israeli public as ultimately having come from his father, who never explained his retirement from political life. Begin's decision to speak out against Sharon just two months before the first Herut Conference in eight years, along with his own decision to join the political fray, were an attempt to stem the tide of Sharon's advance through the party his father had led.

In the days after the TV interview, it seemed as though Begin's move to stop Sharon had worked. But, ironically, Benny Begin's statements, while they sent the general public reeling, had the reverse effect on Likud activists. Sharon had spent the last three years attending forums and weddings, bar mitzvahs and brises. He knew thousands of Likud Central Committee members personally and was considered a friend by many. He and Lily had dutifully shown up at all of these affairs, and their efforts were about to pay off. "When Benny Begin said Arik had no camp," a Likud activist later recalled, "he had no idea how much that motivated us to prove that the opposite was the case."

A close-knit group of confidants and friends helped Sharon prepare for the Herut Conference. The group met twice a week, once on a weekday in Sharon's office and once on Saturday at the farm. The most influential adviser, as always, was Lily. She joined the meetings, had an opinion on everything, and intervened in her husband's nomination decisions. Many of his confidants found her involvement as pleasing as a hornet's nest in the bedroom, but none dared say a word.

Yisrael Katz, Sharon's aide, orchestrated a political deal with David Levy's camp. Levy, a leader of the Likud's working classes from the development town of Beit She'an, had a tempestuous relationship with Sharon. In 1982 their relationship hit rock bottom when Levy openly criticized Sharon's conduct and handling of the war. Levy, like Sharon, had gathered much of his power in the party from the field.

Both, for their own reasons, felt disenfranchised. The two reached a mutual understanding that they would join together to "stop the arrogant establishment," as they called it, of the Shamir-Arens Camp. By "arrogant establishment" they meant those known as the Likud Princes—Benny Begin, Dan Meridor, Roni Milo, and

Ehud Olmert—all sons of prominent hawkish politicians who now planned to skip over the next generation, Sharon and Levy.

On March 8, 1986, three days before the opening of the conference, Sharon and Levy met at the Plaza Hotel in Tel Aviv to plan and coordinate their moves. They would try to sink the Shamir-Arens Camp in two stages. First, Sharon, with Levy's help, would run against Benny Begin for the position of chairman of the Mandates Conference. Then Levy, with the help of Sharon and his camp, would run against Arens for the position of chairman of the conference that assembles the Likud Central Committee.

The ballots of the 2,081 members of the Herut Conference were tallied at 2 A.M. on March 12, 1986. "Arik won," MK Gidon Gadot of the Sharon Camp yelled into the microphone. Shock was stamped on Roni Milo's face. Sharon received 1,082 votes to Begin's 850. Again, Sharon supporters started singing "Arik, King of Israel." The next day's headlines: "Arik Sharon Trounces Benny Begin."

The next matter before the conference members was to choose between Levy and Arens. The contest grew heated. At the height of the drama, Sharon and Moshe Katzav, currently the president of Israel and then a member of the Shamir-Arens Camp, got into a heated shouting match that ended with Sharon jumping on stage and announcing that he thereby quit as chairman of the Mandates Conference. He left the stage to the shouts of his supporters trying to get him to take the statement back.

Levy took the stage and accused Shamir of hijacking the vote. Shamir began to respond, but conference members charged the stage and the foreign minister's security detail escorted him away. No decisions were reached, and the public watched on TV in amazement as the committee members threw chairs at one another. Political analysts spoke of a mass political suicide.

Sharon, more than anyone else, benefited from the fact that the conference closed with no decisions. His contest was the only one put to a vote, and he had won—against the man who had attacked him, the son of the former prime minister, backed by the Likud's main power brokers.

As the rotation in government approached, Sharon prepared

another surprise for Shamir, this time in the form of an assault on Peres that would threaten the stability of the unity government. After a terror attack on a synagogue in Istanbul, Sharon stated that the attack was a direct result of the groveling of the Peres-led government. Again, Peres demanded a written apology. After twenty-four hours of intense pressure, Sharon wrote the letter. On October 10, 1986, Peres vacated the prime minister's office as promised and assumed the role of foreign minister.

In March 1987, the Herut Conference convened for a second round. In order to avoid further chaos, all agreed in advance that Shamir would be chosen chairman of the Likud Party. All other positions within the party would be up for grabs. Sharon vied for the position of chairman of the Likud Central Committee, an influential post since the chairman directed the meetings of the party's legislative branch. Ovadia Eli, a member of the Levy Camp, ran against him. Sharon won with 66 percent of the vote to Eli's 34 percent.

Sharon had not defeated Levy's man unassisted. The Shamir-Arens Camp had backed him. In turn, Arens received Sharon's backing in his race against a Levy representative. Levy learned the hard way, but for hardly the last time, that it was best to keep his back against the wall when dealing with the velvet-fisted Sharon. The following day's papers told the story: "Downfall for David Levy, Great Victory for Sharon."

CHAPTER 32

First Intifada

THROUGHOUT HIS TERM AS MINISTER OF INDUSTRY AND TRADE, EVEN during the heated battles for Likud leadership, Sharon always returned home to the ranch and his family. His 120-pound dog, Juan, greeted him at the gate. Sharon was proud that the wildly affectionate dog never knocked him over. Frequently arriving home late, Sharon would sink into his couch and leaf through one of the art books on the table, listening to classical music for a while before heading upstairs.

At times he and Lily would speak all night about politics. Together they would decide who was in their corner and who opposed them, who should be brought in and who should be kept at bay.

The house was always fragrant with the aromas of Lily's cooking. In the corner of the living room stood an old dark piano. Above it, in small wooden frames, hung portraits of the Scheinerman family. There were photos of Sharon as a child and Sharon with Ben-Gurion during the War of Independence. All of the wooden furniture had an old-time, rustic feel to it. The staircase banister was adorned with saddles and reins. The house itself was alive with green plants. Oil paintings hung on the wall, and china dishes and silver cutlery were visible through the glass-fronted cabinets. The rugs were from Damascus.

Saturdays at the Sharon residence were always busy with friends and food and family. The day would begin early with horseback riding and four-wheeling around the ranch and end with moonlight walking tours. Sharon was a perfect host, always enjoying himself, happy to talk about any subject under the sun. Mozart and Hebrew folk music took turns on the stereo, and the food and drink always flowed freely.

These social gatherings were limited to a very tight group, and friends who disappointed them were never invited again. Arik and Lily had one strict rule: absolute, unconditional loyalty. Anyone who strayed from that was exiled.

The "ranch forum," as those closest to Sharon were known in the Israeli media, included his confidants and political advisers on weekdays. On Saturdays they were joined by apolitical friends like the artist Ilana Gur and the stage actress Gila Almagor (who was cut from the list after she took part in an anti–Lebanon War rally). Omri, working in the fields at the time, and Gilad, usually on leave from the army on Saturdays, also took part in the Saturday rituals.

All the members of the ranch forum held pragmatic right-wing views much like Sharon's, and all were devoted to the cause of guiding their leader to the prime minister's seat. The core group included Eli Landau, the mayor of Herzliya; Reuven Adler, an advertising executive; Uri Dan, a journalist; Dov Weisglass, the attorney; Oded Shamir, military secretary during the Lebanon War, who was nominated by Sharon to serve as director of investments at the Ministry of Industry and Trade; former Shabak and Mossad man Rafi Eitan, nominated by Sharon as chairman of the board of Israel Chemicals; and the former in-house counsel for the Shabak, Yossi Ginossar, named by Sharon to the position of chairman of the Israel Export Institute.

At eleven o'clock on each Friday morning the group would meet in Tel Aviv at Sharon's office in the ministry and analyze "Arik's week" while planning the week to come. During especially stormy periods, the group convened ad hoc in the minister's Jerusalem office. Sharon chaired the three-hour meetings. Issues were raised, examined, and analyzed from several different perspectives. Everyone weighed in—and Sharon decided.

Jokes and sarcastic comments always punctuated the discussions. After the Friday meeting, the group would continue on to the Olympia restaurant in Tel Aviv for feasts including smoked fish, onion rings, leek patties, prime red meat, wine, beer, pistachios, and cherries.

The forum consisted of independent minds from diverse backgrounds, people who would always tell Sharon the truth. When he made a mistake, fumbled a decision, or played a hand wrong, the feedback was immediate and blunt. Unlike many powerful politicians, Sharon never heard only what he wanted to hear.

Each member of the forum had an area of expertise. Uri Dan was deeply familiar with national and international news media. Dov Weisglass knew the law. Eli Landau knew Israeli local politics well and could get things done. Reuven Adler was the spin doctor. Rafi Eitan and Yossi Ginossar were specialists in Palestinian affairs and the war on terrorism. Oded Shamir was the financial wizard.

No one received any special pay for the long hours devoted to Sharon. But their proximity to his ear and their familiarity with the tentacles of the political and financial system in Israel helped each of them thrive in the private sector.

One of the forum's main missions was to guide Sharon through the two-headed national unity government, currently run by Shamir. Foreign Minister Peres spoke of a "land-for-peace" solution to the Palestinian conflict; Shamir immediately spoke out against the idea. Peres secretly met King Hussein in London and with him agreed on the terms for a multinational peace conference and direct peace talks between Israel and Jordan. Shamir shot that initiative down, dooming the London Document in May 1987.

The Jonathan Pollard affair further cracked the bonds of the national unity government. In March 1987, the U.S. Naval Intelligence officer was arrested and later convicted of spying for Israel. Harsh accusations were exchanged at a May cabinet meeting where the Pollard case was discussed. Sharon called on Peres to draw the necessary conclusions and step down. Enraged, Peres said, "You are responsible for the Pollard affair." Sharon replied, "I'd been at the ranch for a year and a half when Pollard was recruited. I was sitting at home because of the demonstrations you organized against me to aid the PLO." Peres: "You're not the pope! You're a tenth-rate, crappy politician! You're a cheap hack!" Sharon: "I won't compete with you in trading vulgarities."

Sharon kept his cool. Only Peres had been rattled. The soft voice and the placid face would from then on become one of Sharon's trademarks. He demanded the same of his assistants and advisers.

On August 11, 1987, Sharon shocked the government with a long speech to students in Tel Aviv University's Strategic Studies program. For the first time, he detailed his view of the Lebanon War with maps and documents. Sweating and growing pale as he spoke, Sharon gave his full account of the events of the war, reading from a 70-page document that he and Oded Shamir had culled from 170 pages over the course of two sleepless weeks.

Lily, Arie Ganger, and Uri Dan had accompanied Sharon to Tel Aviv University. The audience included deputy IDF chief of staff Ehud Barak, several generals who had fought in Lebanon, and Eli Geva, the armored brigade commander who had been stripped of his command for refusing to invade Beirut. A young left-wing protester burst into the hall in the middle of the lecture and yelled harsh accusations at Sharon before being dragged out.

"It has been five years since the expulsion of the terrorist personnel, staff, and headquarters from Beirut," Sharon said, beginning the lecture.

> In that, we achieved the central goal of a brutal war that was forced on us and claimed the lives of hundreds of IDF soldiers and injured thousands more. . . . It is my intention to present the facts of the war, the reason for its outbreak, the manner in which it was waged, the way we broke the back of the PLO infrastructure and expelled them from Beirut. But from the outset I'd like to say that this was a rescue war in the fullest extent of the term, a righteous war, and I'm proud to have been given the privilege of taking part in the planning and the direction of it as the defense minister of the Israeli government as led by Prime Minister Menachem Begin.

Sharon emphasized that the Lebanon War was the first of Israel's wars that had pursued specific goals, which were set months prior to the war, did not change during the conflict, and were attained without exception. According to Sharon, the goals of the war were perfectly clear to the government, the IDF, and the public well before the first shot was fired. It was the first and only war, he said, that was run by an ongoing series of ninety-three cabinet meetings, constant reports to the Knesset, and authorization for every move, small and large alike.

Sharon's version of events—in which Prime Minister Menachem Begin was a full partner in each stage and maneuver of the war, and leaders of the Labor Party supported the government's decision to invade Beirut—enraged many. Defense Minister Yitzhak Rabin responded on the Israel Broadcasting Authority's Channel 1: "The Lebanon War is one of those wars that never achieved its goals, so those responsible must work hard to justify their actions. . . . If Sharon thought the goals of the war had been achieved, he wouldn't be out searching for partners. People seek out partners for failures, not successes."

Ezer Weizman, soon to be the president of Israel, responded with ferocity: "Arik Sharon is a liar," he told *Yedioth Ahronoth* on August 12, 1987. "He takes things out of context. Ben-Gurion wrote in his book about Sharon's doubtful truths. When I heard Sharon on TV, I felt pity for him. Pity for a defense minister removed from office who now comes to justify a crooked war he waged. A war bathed in blood. His conscience must weigh on him; his soul must be heavy."

In late 1987, Sharon stirred up another controversy by buying a house in the Muslim Quarter of Jerusalem's Old City. The merchants in the Old City called a strike in protest of the housewarming party he threw in December, which required a massive city police and border police presence.

"We're not talking about a housewarming party," Sharon said with feigned innocence. "All we're doing is exactly what the Jew who built this house a hundred years ago did: We're lighting the first candle of Hanukkah in our humble home in the Old City." He added that he hated sleeping in hotels and that car rides from Jerusalem to the ranch were exhausting, making a place in the capital necessary. Sharon argued that other Jews lived in the area and that his house was adjacent to the Ateret Cohanim Yeshiva, so it was all much ado about nothing.

The idea of buying a house in the Muslim Quarter came to Sharon after several murders were committed in the area. Sharon believed that his move would encourage Jewish Israelis to return to the Old City. The Arab residents hated their new neighbor—for them, he was the very symbol of Israeli militarism and occupation—and the news media went on the offensive regarding the cost of the move to the Israeli taxpayer: 1.5 million shekels per year, eight times more than the cost of security for the prime minister.

The dovish MK Yossi Sarid spoke with the *Davar* daily about Sharon's new purchase:

> Yesterday, December 15, 1987, the country burned as Nero Caesar entered his new house in Jerusalem's Muslim Quarter and began playing the violin. The country burned and burned and he fiddled and fiddled. Along with him, with Sharon–Nero Caesar, were three hundred other flatterers and hypocrites, adventure-seekers and opportunists, the moonstruck and the hallucinating.

Labor cabinet ministers also called the acquisition "a provocation," but Sharon, seemingly pleased with the uproar surrounding him, answered that he in fact was the only minister in government who could play the violin and he was proud of that. Sharon rarely visited his apartment in the Old City, but although the criticisms regarding the security expenses continued, he never gave it up.

On December 9, 1987, an Israeli truck driver crashed into a Palestinian's car in Gaza, killing four people. The accidental deaths sparked an unprecedented people's revolt across the West Bank and Gaza. After the funerals in Gaza, hundreds of Palestinians stormed an IDF outpost. Before long, the territories were aflame. The *intifada*—"shaking off" in Arabic—had begun. Thousands of youngsters, many of them still children, poured out into the streets of Ramallah, Nablus, Hebron, and Gaza City, throwing stones at the soldiers that patrolled their streets.

The firm stand of the "RPG Boys" in the refugee camps around Tyre and Sidon as they battled IDF armor during the Lebanon War had made an impression on the Palestinians of the West Bank and Gaza. One of the unforeseen side effects of the expulsion of the

PLO men from Beirut and the thrashing of the militias and terrorists in Fatah-land was that the main thrust of PLO action had now
moved inside Israel's borders, into the territories. Since Arafat was
now based in Tunisia, the uprising was led by local leaders who
had grown up in the refugee camps of Jebalya, Khan Yunis, Rafah,
Jenin, and Balata.

The IDF and the security forces, caught unaware, were con-
fused and seemed helpless. Foreign Minister Shimon Peres sug-
gested withdrawing from Gaza. "That is an unsound suggestion,"
Sharon said, "which will lead to intensified violence from the
Palestinians, since it is impossible to hermetically seal off the Gaza
Strip. If we leave, the terrorists will fire mortars and missiles on
Sderot and Ashkelon, just as they did in Lebanon."

Sharon's men were busy telling everyone who would listen that
back in the seventies, Sharon had eradicated terrorism in Gaza.
But nowadays, the intifada pitted stone-wielding children, not
militias with AK-47s, against armed soldiers. Technology had altered the world, too. News media waited for IDF troops around
every corner, monitoring their actions.

Sharon, wanting more than anything else to return to being defense minister, suggested a solution to the new situation in January 1988: "The only realistic solution," he said,

> is a Palestinian state in Jordan. Israel has all the rights to
> the land of Israel. We should differentiate to as great a de-
> gree as possible between those who take part in the riots
> and aim to harm Israel and those who are uninvolved and
> merely want to work in Israel. The Arab movements should
> be outlawed. That requires legislation. The refugee camps
> should be demolished, and the Gaza Strip should be made
> into a planned urban industrial zone.

Sharon criticized, even belittled, the policies of Defense Minister Yitzhak Rabin. After three years of targeting Peres, Sharon
now aimed his criticism at Rabin and the prime minister who
backed him, Shamir. In late March 1988, Sharon demanded that
Shamir "transfer the authority over the territories to a ministerial
committee and not leave all power in the hands of the defense

minister, in light of Rabin's failure to reinstate peace and quiet."
Shamir refused.

In mid-June 1988, Sharon warned that Israel was not paying
attention to the PLO's cash flow, which moved through Israeli
banks. "I would like to remind my friends, the ministers who back
in the day commented on the damage inflicted by the Lebanon
War, that the damage here is far greater," Sharon said, sniping at
Rabin. "Israeli Arabs are joining the Palestinians' uprising, our
power of deterrence is diminished, and there has been great financial damage as well." Sharon called on Shamir to order the defense
minister to restore quiet in the West Bank and Gaza.

Speaking before Likud activists in Tel Aviv, Sharon said that
despite the respect he had for Yitzhak Rabin, the defense minister
needed to be replaced if he could not rein in the Palestinians. On
July 23, 1988, he was asked by *Haaretz* who should replace Rabin
if he were removed from his post. Without hesitation, he said,
"Had I been the defense minister on December 9, 1987, the riot-
ing in Judea, Samaria, and Gaza would not have erupted."

Sharon's campaign failed to weaken Shamir. In fact, it had the
opposite effect. Shamir's cooperation with the Labor defense minister brought him closer to the mainstream and heightened his
standing in the eyes of Likud supporters. Even in the forum discussions, it was widely agreed that although Sharon had won some
points among Likud supporters for his hard line, Shamir's popularity had been on the rise since he took office as prime minister.

On May 13, 1988, Sharon's mother, Vera Scheinerman, passed
away. She was eighty-eight. Vera had always refused to be known as
"Arik's mother," insisting she was her own woman. She rode Kfar
Malal's last mule to the fields every day. More than anyone else, she
shaped her son's character and personality. She was buried in a
small ceremony in the neighboring village of Ramat Ha'shavim.
Sharon, several friends, and the leaders of the country attended.
After the burial, friends and family went back to Kfar Malal to rem-
inisce. From there, Sharon went to the ranch to sit shivah.

"I shall miss her wisdom sorely," he said to the weekly *Ha'olam
Ha'ze*. "Her realistic view of life, her love of the land, all those I
shall miss. My first memory of my mother is of her working in the

cowshed. That's how I remember her: a woman of labor. Up until a year ago she worked eighteen hours a day. She planted orchards, grew tobacco, milked cows and goats, plowed, guarded. She never rested for a minute."

Sharon spoke of his mother's self-confidence and her refusal to accept authority. Regarding his childhood, he said, "Already at the age of ten I helped my parents with all the chores—in the fields, in the vineyard. It was not a home where love was heaped on the children as I do with my sons. Our bond with our parents was through work. A complimentary glance from them when I came back from a good plowing was worth more than a thousand kisses."

CHAPTER 33

The Night of the Microphones

IN THE SUMMER OF 1988, THE HERUT CENTRAL COMMITTEE convened to pick their Likud candidates for the coming fall elections.
Sharon, eager to best Shamir, Levy, and Arens, visited the different
Likud branches and spoke with central committee members, assuring them that as defense minister, he would crush the intifada.

Despite the flurry of activity, Sharon was well behind the pack
among the 2,081 voting committee members. The ranch forum,
anticipating a setback, put in many late hours preparing for the
July 6 internal elections.

Sharon tried convincing Levy that only an alliance between
them could keep their people from being trounced by members
of the Shamir-Arens Camp. Adding insult to injury was the meteoric rise of Binyamin Netanyahu—brother of Yonatan, the slain
heroic leader of the hostage rescue mission in Entebbe—who
had joined the Shamir Camp and threatened to leapfrog over
Levy and Sharon.

Tension and mutual accusations dominated the days before
the elections. A downhearted Sharon wrote a letter to Shamir asking him to put an end to the in-house rivalries. On July 3 he wrote,
"There must be a limit to our impulses, there is room for everyone." Farther down, he mentioned that it would be a mistake "to
try to divide . . . rather than establish internal unity."

July 6, 1988, Election Day, started out well for Sharon. His
deal with the Levy bloc seemed to be bearing fruit. The voting system ranked candidates for the party list in groups of seven. Levy
and Sharon came in first and second in the leading set, followed by

Moshe Arens, Moshe Katzav, Binyamin Netanyahu, David Magen, and Benny Begin.

But by five in the morning, Sharon was feeling dejected. With each successive "seven" his camp lost ground. Insubordination spread through the ranks as more and more candidates from the Sharon Camp realized they were in danger of losing their parliamentary positions. Central committee members voted as they saw fit, no longer abiding by Sharon's instructions. His deal with the Levy Camp collapsed. On November 1, 1988, the Likud secured 40 Knesset seats in the general election; Sharon and two loyalists, David Magen and Gidon Gadot, were the only representatives of the Sharon Camp in parliament.

In August 1988 Sharon suffered another setback. The Herut and Independent Liberal branches that formed the Likud merged into one homogenous party with a single constitution and governing body. Up until then, each faction had chosen its own Knesset members, who were then ranked in an agreed-upon order. The new three-thousand-member Likud Central Committee included a thousand people from the Independent Liberal Party, most of them from the Shamir-Arens Camp, weakening Sharon's standing.

Despite the poor showing in the internal elections and the strife in his own camp, Sharon kept his focus on important Likud activists and central committee members. Sharon had discovered the importance of the members of the Likud Central Committee after the Lebanon War. Previously, like most politicians, he had belittled the political insiders who ran the party and focused on charismatic appearances before the general public and key media performances; after the war, feeling like Cain, Sharon found a new pillar of support within the party organization. The Likud Central Committee, much like Sharon himself, was contrarian by nature: The more the media criticized Sharon, the greater their affection for him.

As opposed to the sick and suddenly reclusive Menachem Begin, and the trampled Yom Kippur War chief of staff David Elazar, who never recuperated from the Agranat Commission's report, Sharon refused to go quietly into that good night. Now, he realized, charisma and natural leadership, traits that had served him well as he rose from commander of Unit 101 to defense minister, would not suffice. Sharon's second assault on Israeli politics required a new, less savory approach: nepotism and Machiavellian maneuvering.

As the party geared up for the next general election, Sharon asked Shamir to appoint him campaign manager. Shamir refused. Sharon aimed to be defense minister by the end of his current term; this goal had become an obsession for him following the publication of the Kahan Report. By refusing to name him as campaign manager, Shamir was denying him access to the coveted position. In mid-August, eleven weeks before the election, Sharon called a press conference to announce his plan to formally annex parts of the West Bank in order to solve the problems raised by the intifada.

The unilateral proposition flew in the face of everything the party's strategic advisers had been preaching. The advisers had cautioned Likud members to refrain from hawkish statements—by their estimation, the elections would be decided by the teetering group in the middle of the political map. Sharon ignored this advice. A Labor Party cameraman filmed his press conference. Images of Sharon saying he intended to annex parts of the West Bank, where hundreds of thousands of Palestinians lived, played a central role in Labor's advertising campaign.

Sharon told *Haaretz* on August 19, 1988, that "to my dismay, I'm not part of the day-to-day activities of the Likud campaign headquarters. I very much wanted to be, but . . . someone apparently didn't want me there. I don't want to say the Likud lost out, but in my opinion regret is in order. As in the past, I'll form my own staff and work for the good of the party."

In September 1988, Sharon made clear to Shamir which ministerial position he would like. "The post of foreign minister is excellent," he said, "the post of minister of finance is difficult but very important . . . but there is one job I can do better than all the others—and that's in the ministry of defense." Five years after being evicted from office, Sharon waged a personal campaign to return to what he felt the Kahan Commission had stolen. In an interview with *The New York Times* he said that he was certain he could stop the intifada if he were appointed defense minister.

On November 1, 1988, the Likud beat Labor at the polls by the slimmest of margins, 40–39. But in effect the margin of victory was wider, since the right-wing and religious camps had grown; the Likud now controlled 64 seats.

Prime Minister Shamir had two options. He could form a narrow coalition with the religious, the far-right, and the ultra-Orthodox parties, or he could bond with the Labor Party, without a rotation at the top. Sharon understood that a coalition with Labor meant he would have no chance of gaining the defense minister position. Accordingly, he pushed for a narrow coalition with the religious, ultra-Orthodox, and right-wing parties, and at the same time stepped up his attacks on Defense Minister Rabin.

At the first postelection cabinet meeting, the rivalry between the two men grew personal. When discussing ways to stop the violent intifada, Sharon said: "I don't want to relate to Rabin's rude comments. That happens to him sometimes, especially when he's not clear-headed enough and loses his self-control." Rabin retorted, "Arik, your comments don't even reach my ankle."

Shamir formed his coalition with care. As time passed, Sharon understood that the ministry of defense was beyond reach. He began demanding one of the two other most senior posts—foreign minister and minister of finance. He made it known that if he didn't get one of the top three posts, he'd consider returning to the tractor and the ranch. He told Shamir, "I won't agree to being left back a grade."

On December 22, 1988, Shamir assembled a second national unity government. Shamir preferred a wide coalition with no need for support from each different Likud camp. He appointed Rabin defense minister, Peres minister of finance and vice prime minister, and Arens foreign minister. For Sharon it was the worst possible outcome. He remained at the ministry of industry and trade.

Levy, too, was held back. He remained minister of housing and construction. Three of the Likud Princes, Ehud Olmert, Dan Meridor, and Roni Milo, were promoted to ministerial positions. Sharon did not follow through on his threat to leave his Knesset seat for his tractor seat, but he felt increasingly frustrated. Sharon, Levy, and Yitzhak Moda'i, who wanted the post of minister of finance, formed an alliance of the embittered. The three co-ordinated their moves and waited for an opportunity to avenge Shamir's slights.

On May 14, 1989, Yitzhak Shamir returned from a meeting with President George H. W. Bush and presented a four-stage plan to the government: Israel would act to reinforce the peace with Egypt on the basis of the Camp David Accords; actions would be taken to make peace between Israel and the Arab states; solutions would be sought to the Palestinian refugee problem; and most important, Palestinians would democratically elect representatives in the West Bank and Gaza who would negotiate the terms of autonomous rule.

Despite Sharon, Levy, and Moda'i's opposition, the plan passed in a majority vote. Immediately after the decision was adopted, the threesome began campaigning against the plan, saying it strayed far from the ideological principles of the Likud. They demanded that the Likud governing bodies convene and vote on a number of principles, which, if passed, would restrict the Likud leaders in negotiations. The media dubbed the proposed restrictions "hoops" and the three who proposed them "hoopsters."

The threesome claimed that Shamir's plan would eventually lead to the establishment of a Palestinian state in the West Bank and Gaza. In response, they drafted a list of six impassible lines: no negotiations with the PLO; no Palestinian state under any circumstances; continued Jewish settlement in the West Bank and Gaza; no foreign sovereignty west of the Jordan River; cessation of the intifada as a condition for negotiations; and no participation in the Palestinian elections by the Arabs living in East Jerusalem.

On July 5, 1989, Sharon convened the Likud Central Committee, which he chaired, to discuss Shamir's plan. Shamir wanted the committee to vote yea or nay on his proposition. Sharon advocated two separate votes, one for Shamir's plan and one for his own. A vote in favor of Sharon's plan, which seemed bound to pass in the hawkish committee, would doom Shamir's plan.

Minutes before the meeting began, Shamir accepted the terms dictated by the three "hoopsters." The central committee unanimously adopted the six points, and the meeting ended with a display of unity as David Levy stood between Shamir and Sharon and they all raised their hands in the air while the crowd sang the *Ha'tikva,* Israel's national anthem.

Sharon, Levy, and Moda'i flashed V signs to their constituents in the crowd. Their beaming faces indicated just how sweet the victory over Shamir tasted. Their self-confidence soared. In the Knesset they spent hours in closed rooms plotting their moves before major meetings. The news media always waited outside the closed doors, anticipating the threesome's next new drama, which was certain to grab headlines and cast Shamir in the most unflattering light.

In Shamir's inner circle, Sharon was seen as the brains behind the threesome. The prime minister tried to bring Levy into the fold and alienate Sharon. On July 19, 1989, at a meeting of Likud ministers, Sharon complained that Shamir and Arens, the foreign minister, were conducting secret talks with the Palestinians without informing the other ministers. Shamir answered, "I, the foreign minister, and others are holding talks with the Palestinians. They are unofficial and I see no reason to do it in an official manner. I report back to Minister David Levy."

SHARON: "And I can't know?"

SHAMIR: "No, because you leak everything."

SHARON: "You leak the deepest secrets to the Arabs, but can't inform me?"

SHAMIR: "Everyone here in this room hears classified information from me and does not leak. You leak."

SHARON: "I resent the things you say."

SHAMIR: "I know you. You only foul the mood and [sow] hatred between us."

SHARON: "I laugh at those notions."

SHAMIR: "We'll see who has the last laugh. I don't want to talk to you."

Shamir announced that talks with the Palestinians would continue and did not conflict with the central committee's resolution. He quickly convened his confidants to discuss the matter of the rebellious, loose-lipped minister of industry and trade. Sharon met with Levy and Moda'i, sending a clear message to Shamir that firing Sharon would lead to a rift in the Likud that might tear the party in two.

Shamir feared Sharon would do more harm if he fired him. Less than a month later, while touring the northern part of the country, Sharon expressed his opinion that the Israeli government's main problem was an absence of leadership.

On October 1, 1989, as the intifada raged, the three "hoopsters" called a central committee meeting. This time they aimed their fire and brimstone at Rabin, Shamir's main partner in the political plan:

> The man known as the Israeli Churchill, a small and irrelevant imitation of the real Churchill . . . said there's no alternative, we must speak with the leaders of the intifada. That reminded me, while looking at this miniature, of the real Churchill, who said in June 1941 that Britain would never speak with Hitler and his henchmen. That should have been our response as well. But our Churchill, due to his utter and total failure, has a different solution: "We have no alternative; we must speak with the leaders of the intifada."

Sharon then moved on to Shamir, who, he claimed, had prevented him from convening the Likud Central Committee: "If there's no cooperation," he told the cheering crowd, "then we'll convene the central committee with no cooperation." The Likud Central Committee meeting was set for February 12, 1990. As chairman of the central committee, Sharon refused to consult with Likud chairman Shamir about the upcoming conference. Shamir intended for there to be one vote: a vote of confidence in him as chairman. His advisers let it be known that this time he would take a stand.

Sharon, a politician in the army and an army man in politics, prepared for the conference with military precision. He ensured that his people would be in charge of the amplifiers and the microphones. His new assistant, Uri Shani, replacing Yisrael Katz, who had left with a loud slam of the door, oversaw all the preparations.

Sharon's people were given instructions to arrive at the hall hours early and to fill the front rows of seats with "friendlies." Sharon suspected that Shamir would ask for a show of hands in the middle of his speech and, satisfied with victory, end the conference on the spot.

Sharon started the conference, announcing that they would begin by discussing the latest political developments, followed by the leaders' geopolitical suggestions and a confidential vote on those suggestions. When he finished, he asked for a moment to make a personal comment. Even someone as cool and calculating as Sharon had trouble sounding calm: "I would like to read from a letter I sent this evening to the prime minister: 'I hereby issue my resignation. I've decided to quit the government.'" The rowdy crowd fell silent.

His partners, Moda'i and Levy, were equally shocked. Moda'i leaned toward the man next to him and asked, "Did you hear what Arik said? Are you sure he said he's resigning from the government?"

Commotion quickly flooded the silent void. Sharon's supporters began chanting "A-rik! A-rik!" "I will continue my struggle as a member of the central committee and a member of the Knesset," Sharon announced, "for the attainment of our national goals, which are jeopardized by the very existence of this government. I've reached the decision that I can no longer, as a member of this government, stop the avalanche. It is a matter of national importance and principle. Mr. Prime Minister, under your rule, Palestinian terror is running wild through the land of Israel, claiming the lives of many innocent Jews. The government policy, under your command, has put Jewish lives up for grabs. I know and am convinced that we can eliminate this terrorism. In a relatively short period of time it is possible to restore law and order to the land of Israel and establish peace between us and the Arabs on the basis of our historic right to the land of Israel."

The hall went still again. "During your government's rule," Sharon's voice rang out through the loudspeakers, "Arab terrorism, murder, and violence have run rampant, even in the streets of our capital, Jerusalem. Terrorist leaders live comfortably in the eastern part of the city. The Israeli government has made its peace with that. Your political plan, Mr. Prime Minister, puts Israel on the path toward a Palestinian state. . . . Security must be addressed immediately, but . . . the Cabinet has ceased functioning and the government is paralyzed."

Sharon took a deep breath, scanned the audience, and went back to the printed words he had prepared. "There are moments when a man must rise out of his chair and start marching. There are moments in the life of a nation, in the lives of people, when they must awaken and fight before the onset of calamity. This may well be the final hour to do so."

As the audience and the millions of viewers on television digested his statement, Sharon, feigning nonchalance, called the next speaker, Shamir, to the stage. The prime minister had not seen Sharon's letter, since it had been timed to arrive after he left the office. "I have yet to receive the letter," he said in his opening remarks, "and only after I have received it will I comment."

Shamir then began reading his prepared speech about the pressing political issues of the day. When he finished, he looked up at the central committee members and, usurping Sharon's authority as chairman of the central committee, asked for an impromptu show of hands in favor of his leadership as chairman of the Likud Party. It was, as Sharon had foreseen, an attempt to circumvent the agreed-upon voting procedure.

Sharon was prepared for this eventuality. He had instructed Shani to bring a wire cutter to the conference. Shani told Sharon that he could control the volume of Shamir's microphone with the dials at his fingertips, but Sharon insisted, "Bring the cutter!" Sharon would not get up on the stage until Shani showed him he had the pliers in his pocket. In advance, Shani had raised the volume of Sharon's microphone, lowered Shamir's, and nailed Sharon's microphone to the table, so that only he could use it.

As Shamir spoke to the crowd, his microphone went dead. Then Sharon shouted: "Who's in favor of wiping out terror? Who's in favor of wiping out terror?" Shamir tried to overcome Sharon's booming voice, yelling, "Who supports me? Who supports me?" into his dead microphone. But Sharon, in a voice long accustomed

to making itself heard over thunderous noise, continued bellow-
ing: "Who's against allowing east Jerusalem's Arabs to participate
in elections? Who wants to wipe out terror?"

In the ensuing mêlée it was impossible to tell whether the
hands in the air were a show of support for Shamir and his political
plan or for Sharon and his demand that terror be eradicated before
proceeding with negotiations. The two politicians spent several
minutes on stage together, each trying to drown out the voice of the
other. It was perhaps the most shameful display in the history of Israeli politics. Disgusted, Shamir declared that his suggestion had
been passed by a majority of votes. As Likud chairman, he closed
the central committee session. By the time he left the stage, the
floor had been transformed into a mosh pit, the din deafening.

Each side claimed victory, but the Israeli public, treated to an
unadulterated view of its leaders' lowly behavior, seemed disgusted. The pathetic spectacle became known as the Night of the
Microphones, and all analysts agreed that Sharon had been the big
loser.

CHAPTER 34

Minister of Housing
and Infrastructure

TWENTY-FOUR HOURS BEFORE THE NIGHT OF THE MICROPHONES, Sharon had already decided to retire. He had made the decision alone, stepping down in order to advance, two weeks before his sixty-second birthday.

Some say that Sharon's tendency to make critical decisions alone was a product of ego. "Arik Sharon thinks," said a former confidant, "that Arik Sharon is the most important thing on earth; that he is the center of the world. That is the starting point when trying to understand anything related to Arik and the decisions he makes."

The microphone battle that followed Sharon's announcement cast him and Shamir in a negative light. The news media swarmed around him after the decision, interviewing him as sweat poured down his face.

The next morning Sharon held talks with some of his men. They tried to persuade him to reconsider. His departure would mean the end of their posts at key governmental positions controlled by the ministry. The daily financial paper *Globes* reported that twenty-seven board members of government offices under the auspices of the Ministry of Industry and Trade feared for their jobs. They were not alone.

On February 14, 1990, Sharon's resignation went into effect. From that moment on, he served only as an MK. He noted on several occasions that he had left office in order to return and that he saw himself as a natural candidate for prime minister in the future, but with the next elections two and a half years off, the talk had a hollow ring. He returned to the ranch, this time in high spirits, joking that the Likud MKs "were fighting for . . . my [government-issue] Volvo."

Sharon rented office space in central Tel Aviv. The funds for the bustling complex were provided by the Institute for Security and Peace, a right-wing NGO reportedly funded by Sharon's millionaire friends Arie Ganger and Meshulam Riklis. Sharon traded his government car for a new Chevy Caprice, equipped with a mobile phone and a driver.

The few visitors allowed into the new complex were surprised by the raw power of the place. Everything in the office gleamed, and a visitor had to submit to a physical pat-down and a background check before being let into the waiting room. Sharon sat in a capacious office, behind a gigantic, paper-free slab of mahogany—it seemed like he was running a parallel executive office, only there were no troops or ministers under his command.

During that period, he forged close ties with Robert Maxwell, a British Jewish billionaire who had recently purchased the Israeli daily *Maariv*. Maxwell even asked Lily to take charge of the interior design of his Tel Aviv apartment. Less than two years later, Maxwell was found dead in the Atlantic Ocean. Official reports asserted that he had suffered a heart attack and fallen off his yacht as he cruised near the Canary Islands, but speculation abounded. The mystery of his death endures to this day.

Sharon's break from government activity was brief. Although the next elections were slated for 1992, his nirvana on the ranch and in his palatial Tel Aviv offices was cut short by what Yitzhak Rabin memorably termed the Stinky Trick.

With Secretary of State James Baker and the rest of the Bush administration pushing hard for an international peace initiative, Foreign Minister Peres issued an ultimatum to a hesitant Prime Minister Shamir: Either agree to Baker's terms, or we'll resign and break up the national unity government. Sharon and the Likud "hoopsters" opposed the Baker initiative, which would include Palestinian representatives from the Diaspora and eventually necessitate territorial compromise. Shamir refused to comply with the American plans; Peres pulled the plug on the coalition.

In early March 1990, the Labor Party filed a no-confidence motion. On March 12, Shamir, realizing Peres was out to topple his administration, fired the foreign minister. In response, the Labor ministers resigned and joined the Opposition. Peres's main ally in the Stinky Trick was the head of the Sephardic ultra-Orthodox Shas Party, Aryeh Deri. On March 15, sixty MKs voted no confidence in the government; fifty-five were in favor, and five members of Shas were, as planned, absent from the hall during the vote. For the first time in the state's history, a government had been felled by a no-confidence vote.

On April 4, 1990, after much maneuvering and backroom dealing, Peres assembled a sixty-one-member majority and reached an understanding with Shas that they—ordinarily affiliated with the right—would join the government after it had been assembled.

Sharon recognized an opportunity to return to center stage. On March 18, 1990, the Likud Central Committee convened. Shamir had been weakened. But Sharon, the chairman of the central committee and Shamir's avowed adversary, surprised everyone by siding with Shamir. He called for all Likud members to put personal differences aside and form ranks behind their leader. That wholehearted support killed budding conspiracies to replace Shamir as prime minister.

Sharon supported Shamir for two reasons. Pragmatically, he hoped his support at this crucial juncture would be reciprocated in the future; ideologically, he feared Peres would return territory that was of critical importance. Sharon explains his decision in Dani Korn's *Time in Gray*: "I saved Shamir even though he was a political rival because he passed the Baker test [by refusing the peace initiative] while the rest of his friends wanted to chop off his head."

On April 11, 1990, leaders of the Labor Party came to the Knesset in their finest suits to take their oaths and assume control of the government. Peres, though, had not kept close enough tabs on Sharon, who had spent the last few days in the courts of the world's most influential rabbis, whispering into their ears. The Peres government, based on the support of left-wing and Arab parties, should not be supported by Jewish leaders, he said. Sharon flew to New York to meet the Lubavitcher Rebbe, Rabbi Men-achem Mendel Schneerson, and held ongoing talks with the Rebbe's personal assistant, Rabbi Dov Groner. Sharon also set his sights on two MKs from the ultra-Orthodox Agudat Yisrael Party, known to adhere to the authority of the Rebbe on all matters.

To ensure compliance, Sharon met the two MKs, Avraham Verdiger and Eliezer Mizrahi, and promised them all manner of jobs and responsibilities when the Likud formed the next govern-ment. Two days before the Knesset vote that would usher Peres's new government into office, the two MKs disappeared, seemingly swallowed by the earth. Verdiger and Mizrahi shocked Peres by not showing themselves until the Knesset deadline had passed; the or-ders from the Rebbe had been carried out.

Without the two MKs, the Knesset meeting dispersed. Without those two votes Peres lacked the necessary majority. Disgraced, yet tenacious as ever, Peres offered to form yet another national unity government with the Likud, which refused. On April 26, 1990, Peres reluctantly told the president he could not form a govern-ment. The task was given to Shamir.

Sharon again fought tooth and nail for the post of defense min-ister. Shamir, fearful of Sharon's ascendant influence and power in the party, appointed Arens defense minister and Levy foreign min-ister. He appointed Sharon minister of housing and infrastructure, a powerful post but not one of the top three ministerial positions.

Shamir offered Sharon an additional incentive: chairman of the Cabinet for the Absorption of Immigrants, a pivotal position. The Iron Curtain had fallen, and a mass influx of Jews from the former Soviet states was immigrating to Israel. With hundreds of thousands of Jews arriving, Sharon became a central figure in gov-ernment. Indeed, Shimon Schiffer, a senior political analyst for *Yedioth Ahronoth*, described Sharon as the axis of the new govern-ment, the man around whom everything revolved.

Sharon immediately put his own people in key positions and stripped Levy's employees of influence. After ten years in office, Sharon's people said, Levy had left "scorched earth" behind him at the ministry. Sharon spoke from the Knesset lectern about "Levy's inactivity." Two weeks later, Levy suffered a heart attack, and many of his associates blamed Sharon. After leaving the hospital, Levy said, "There's been an attempt to wipe away a life's work."

Sharon took the ministry by storm. The lights were on into the small hours of the morning. An enormous obstacle loomed: Close to a million people, more than 20 percent of Israel's population, had just immigrated and needed housing.

In late July, Sharon submitted hundreds of pages of plans to the Cabinet. He called for the construction of four hundred thousand new apartments over the next five years and, as a temporary solution, the import of fifty thousand trailers. The total cost of importing the trailers and establishing utilities in the trailer villages would come to roughly one billion dollars.

Finance Minister Yitzhak Moda'i claimed the plan turned a blind eye to the immigrants' true problem—employment. The clash between the two intensified, even spilling over into a personal battle. Moda'i claimed to have saved Sharon from certain death at Latrun; Sharon quickly made it clear that Ya'akov Bugin was the man who had rescued him.

Sharon spent most of his days touring construction sites. Although the majority of the construction was within the Green Line, Sharon decided to construct fifteen thousand new units in the West Bank in the area ringing Jerusalem. The decision caused a stir, as Foreign Minister Levy had promised the American administration that Israel would cease all construction in the territories.

In October 1990, Sharon arrived in Bat Yam, a relatively rundown city, to welcome the first immigrants to the trailer village. The new residents showered him with their displeasure, shoving him into one of the trailers to experience its inadequacies firsthand.

On January 17, 1991, the Gulf War began. Seven days before the American offensive, Sharon unnerved President Bush when he told the French newspaper *France Soir* that if Saddam Hussein followed through on his repeated threats to attack Israel, Israel would respond with force. The comments of the minister of housing and infrastructure stood in direct opposition to a secret understanding between Bush and Shamir.

Hussein followed through on his threats and fired dozens of

Scud missiles at Israeli population centers. Fearing chemical attack, the IDF handed out gas masks to all Israeli citizens and instructed everyone to prepare a sealed room in their house. But Hussein's salvos were conventional and largely ineffective; several citizens were injured, but most of the damage was to property. Sharon visited each missile crater. He spoke with worried civilians and castigated the Palestinians who "dance on the roofs to the sight of missiles falling on the heads of Tel Aviv residents." Sharon suggested asserting Israeli sovereignty on all West Bank and Gaza Strip areas settled by Jews.

President Bush pressed for Israeli restraint in the face of attack, fearing that a strike on Baghdad would cause irrevocable rifts in the coalition force, which included several Arab states. Sharon criticized Shamir. He felt Israel should respond on two counts: as the basic right of any state that had been attacked and as a means of preserving Israel's power of deterrence. (Ten years later, when he led the government, Sharon saw things differently, agreeing to similar terms from George W. Bush during the second American invasion.)

Shamir had to suffer Sharon's incessant sniping, and the Scuds, in silence. Sharon voiced his opinion freely. "It's idiocy. Let's say Israel defends herself, so then what—the Americans are going to stop the war and the Brits are going to go home? What, are they going to be offended?" Sharon also took pains to mention that he, along with Menachem Begin, had pushed for the 1981 strike against Iraq's Osirak nuclear reactor, which also drew international criticism across the board. Now, he said, ten years after the strike, people could see for themselves the wisdom of that decision.

CHAPTER 35

Fall from Power

AFTER THE FIRST GULF WAR, THE MINISTER OF HOUSING AND INFRA-
structure resumed construction in the West Bank. American secretary of state James Baker demanded that the prime minister
keep Sharon under control. In April 1991, *The Washington Post*
reported that Shamir had clashed with Sharon over the nature of
his reports on construction activities in the territories. Sharon
told the *Post* that he had not been building new settlements in the
territories; he had simply been expanding the existing ones in
order to accommodate the natural growth of the number of residents, a principle the Americans had agreed to. He added that
perhaps the Iraqi Scuds fired on Tel Aviv had caused many Jews to
leave Israel proper and move to the territories—hence the heightened pace of construction.

Senior State Department officials made it clear that the secretary was aware of Sharon's efforts to sink the peace initiative and
that the minister's actions would directly impact American willingness to act as a guarantor of the ten-billion-dollar loan Israel needed
from American commercial institutions. Having taken in three hundred thousand Jews—all entitled to citizenship under Israel's Law of
Return—the country desperately needed the funds.

Baker's diplomatic revenge came swiftly. In early May 1991,
Sharon visited the United States. With Sharon on his way to meet
Secretary of Housing and Urban Development Jack Kemp, Baker
put in a call to Kemp and asked him not to receive Sharon at his
office. In order to avoid a diplomatic fiasco, Kemp met Sharon at
the Israeli embassy in Washington. Sharon skirted American journalists' questions regarding whether he interpreted the change of
venue as a slight. He freely voiced his opinion on the matter of

Iraq, though, saying appeasement and abstention in the face of missile salvos had been a mistake. As for the loans, he said that the American administration seemed intent on enforcing a policy of "Land for Jews" by refusing to sign off on loans compensating for the influx of Jews until Israel stopped settling the territories.

In August 1991, Baker managed to secure the consent of all parties directly involved in the Middle East conflict to participate in an international peace conference. Shamir agreed, on several conditions: that the ceremonial aspects of the conference be international but the actual talks bilateral; that the Palestinian delegation be part of the Jordanian one; that the Palestinian people not be represented by the PLO; that Israel have the right to vet the Palestinian delegation members; and that Syria be willing to negotiate without any predetermined conditions.

Sharon claimed that Shamir and Foreign Minister Levy had hidden their agreement with the Americans. He attacked Shamir bitterly for agreeing to participate in a conference along with representatives of the United Nations and Europe, entities many Israelis considered biased. Sharon wondered aloud why Shamir had recanted his demand that negotiations begin only once the intifada had stopped.

"[They are] not able to demand anything, to stand firm on any demand," he told *Yedioth Ahronoth* on August 5, 1991. "As a member of government I felt misery and shame at the negotiation team's inability to handle negotiations properly." Levy responded, "Anything Sharon said borders on condescension and chutzpah."

As the conference date approached, Shamir distanced Sharon and brought in the ascendant deputy minister in the Prime Minister's Office, Binyamin Netanyahu. Far from the action, Sharon operated on a different front: Each time Secretary of State Baker visited, Sharon made sure to authorize the establishment of an additional settlement in the West Bank or the Gaza Strip. Many settlements were founded unofficially, but with official acknowledgment. The settlements of Bat Ayin, Avnei Hefetz, Talmon, and Ofarim were each born on the eve of a Baker visit.

In an attempt to attract young couples and new immigrants to the West Bank, Sharon announced that the ministry would be building thirteen thousand new housing units in the territories over the next three years. State land, for those who wanted to build their own homes, would be provided at no cost. The ministry issued low-interest mortgages for houses in the territories and established free water, electricity, and sewage services. The campaign both increased and diversified the seventy-thousand-strong settler population. Previously, only the ideologically driven had settled in the territories; now, with a slew of incentives, and many of the settlements situated but a few minutes drive from major cities, their appeal spread across a far larger swath of the population.

After the Gulf War, Sharon changed tactics. At one time he had done his settlement work in the shadows, but as minister of housing and infrastructure he openly diverted the ministry's budget to road building and home construction in the territories. Ya'akov Katz, known as Katzele, worked under Sharon at the ministry as a top adviser and aide. He, along with Ze'ev (Zambish) Hever, the director of Gush Emunim's settlement arm and a former member of the Jewish Underground—a group of settlers who carried out anti-Arab terror attacks—worked to dot the hills of the West Bank with dozens of settlements, with Sharon's support and encouragement.

The pace of construction rivaled that of 1977. In January 1992, *Yedioth Ahronoth* reported that eighteen thousand apartments had been built in the territories during Sharon's tenure, at a total cost of 3.5 billion shekels. The left-wing *Al Ha'mishmar* newspaper reported that one-quarter of all ministry-funded apartments had been built in the territories. Sharon said outright: Anyone who doesn't want to live in a trailer inside the Green Line can move to a house in the West Bank.

Katz described the modus operandi:

Each night we'd send a fax to Arik [explaining] what we did that day, what we had planned for tomorrow, what we needed. An hour later Arik would call and go over the things. Some of the communities owe their existence to James Baker. Each time he'd come to advance his peace initiative, we'd build another community. One visit? Revava. Another visit? A new neighborhood in Talmonim. Another visit? Nerya. In the evening we'd report to Sharon. He was in government at the time and we didn't want to embarrass him, so we'd write that there's another surprise for Baker. There's not another gentile in the world with James Baker's credits in Judea and Samaria.

On October 10, 1991, twenty days before the start of the peace conference, Sharon dropped another political bomb: He intended to run against Shamir for leadership of the Likud Party. No one had challenged Shamir since 1984. Levy, upset with Shamir for relying on Deputy Minister Netanyahu for peace conference coordination, joined the fray.

Although the Arab countries attending the conference chose to send foreign ministers rather than heads of state, Shamir represented Israel along with Netanyahu. Levy, dejected, stayed in Israel. The MIT-educated, media-savvy Netanyahu emerged as Israel's greatest spokesperson. The unequivocal view of the ranch forum was that Sharon needed to make a move for the top before Netanyahu surpassed him.

The American and Russian foreign ministers sent out joint invitations on October 18, 1991, twelve days before the opening of the conference. The following day, Sharon called on Shamir to step down, since the event he planned to attend was "not going to be a peace conference but a war conference." Shamir resisted calls to fire Sharon. The old Mossad man thought it was a good idea to keep your enemies in clear sight. On October 30, the peace conference began with speeches by Bush and Gorbachev, followed by remarks by Shamir, senior Palestinian representative Dr. Haidar Abdel Shafi, and the foreign ministers of Syria, Jordan, Lebanon, and Egypt.

The speeches bore no new tidings. After the opening ceremonies, the Israelis held bilateral talks with the Syrian, Lebanese, and Jordanian-Palestinian delegations. After the conference closed, Baker's plan moved to stage two, the initiation of bilateral talks in Washington in December. The Madrid Conference set the framework for all future bilateral talks between Israel and its Arab neighbors, excluding Egypt. From that point on, Israel negotiated one-on-one with each of the neighboring states.

After another long internal battle for control of the Likud, in which Shamir bested Levy and Sharon, the state comptroller shook the political realm with her annual report. Retired supreme court justice Miriam Ben-Porat found severe flaws in the management of the Ministry of Housing and Infrastructure. The timing of the report, just two months before the general election, was potentially disastrous for the Likud.

The state comptroller determined that the ministry had gone 1.5 billion shekels over budget. Regarding the trailer villages, she wrote that establishing them had been so costly, taken so long, and entailed so many planning snafus that it would have been easier and cheaper simply to have built permanent homes. She further determined that the villages frequently violated state planning and zoning laws.

Uri Shani played a leading role in the report. Sharon's close adviser and confidant, appointed by Sharon as chairman of the board of Amidar, a government construction company, had used his lofty position to charge luxury suites at hotels and other personal expenses to the government. The police subsequently investigated Shani, and in 1997 he was convicted of breach of trust, sentenced to six months' probation, and fined ten thousand shekels.

Shani resigned as chairman of the board of Amidar. Sharon, shocked by the severity of the report, asked Shamir to instruct the police to finish their investigations within a month so that they would not influence the June 23, 1992, elections. In his letter to Shamir he expressed his opinion that the state comptroller had acted improperly by not forwarding her report to the attorney general months earlier. In his opinion, the timing of the report was not coincidental.

In an interview for Channel 1 News, the taxpayer-funded TV channel, Sharon said, "I think it is a mistake and impudence of the highest order to come and assert that the Ministry of Housing and Infrastructure is stricken with corruption. It's hard to shake the feeling that in a non-premeditated yet intentional way there has been an attempt to meddle, and not delicately, in a tough, ongoing

election campaign." Ben-Porat responded, "I stand behind everything written in the report."

Sharon justified his actions:

> When I began as minister of housing and infrastructure,
> everyone complained about helplessness in the face of the
> mass immigration and that no one was building houses in
> Israel. That criticism was heard, written, and televised
> from morning till night, and even in political circles no one
> stopped talking about "the great debacle" of inaction. . . .
> Today I suggest that everyone go out and look at the thou-
> sands of apartments and houses established across the
> country, and the same for the trailers. I know what I'm
> doing and what I need to do. More than three hundred fif-
> teen thousand new immigrants arrived in Israel from the
> beginning of 1990 to the middle of 1991—and all of them
> have a roof over their head and none of them are hungry.
> What other country in the world has done something like
> that?

The publication of the report heralded a bitter end to Sharon's
tenure at the ministry. In less than two years he had initiated the
construction of 144,000 new apartments and the renovation of
22,000 more. The scope of development was without precedent,
and in the end further confirmed his reputation both as a man of
action—a bulldozer—and as Israel's most controversial leader.

Sharon's behavior, as documented in the report, was just one
link in a long chain of malfeasance by Israeli politicians, and the
Israeli public was growing increasingly disenchanted with their behavior. The Labor Party decided to base their campaign on
promises of change. Yitzhak Rabin was chosen to lead the party instead of Shimon Peres, the author of the Stinky Trick. The charismatic war hero ran under the slogan "Israel Is Waiting for Rabin."
The strategy paid off. On June 23, 1992, the Labor Party won
forty-four seats to the Likud's thirty-two. For the first time since
1977, the Likud returned to the Opposition.

One week after the elections, at a gathering of downcast Likud
ministers, Sharon felt sharp pains in his abdomen, which had been

plaguing him during the campaign. Immediately after the meeting he went to the hospital, where he was diagnosed with gallstones. Back on the ranch, the pain continued until he had his gallbladder removed. The nurses praised Lily's devotion to Sharon during his incapacitation. As for Sharon, they said, "He acted like an obedient soldier."

Sharon's integrity chart is full of alleged fluctuations. In May 1987, state comptroller Ya'akov Meltz sent a letter to Sharon, at the time the minister of industry and trade, regarding his relationship with Meshulam Riklis. Years before, Riklis had lent Sharon a significant interest-free sum. During Sharon's tenure as minister of industry and trade, he had been involved in approving a loan to Riklis, the joint owner of Haifa Chemicals. The state comptroller wrote, "The loan you received from Mr. Riklis [that is, the money Riklis had lent Sharon to buy the ranch] was substantial, long-term, and without interest. In that, of course, lies a significant benefit, which ties you to Mr. Riklis. . . . You should have stated your affairs, avoided making a decision, and passed the matter on to a ministerial committee."

Riklis responded:

> Arik, a man who has devoted his entire life to the state, has nothing else in mind but to help Riklis close out the month? True, fifteen years ago I lent him two hundred thousand dollars and said: "Sir, if you devote yourself to the State of Israel, I will help you buy the ranch, so that you won't have to grovel before anyone." He already paid me back! How is it possible to insinuate that a man like Arik is corrupt, especially after his *Time* trial?

In July 1987, the state comptroller took another look at Sharon. In 1984, during his term as minister of industry and trade, a professional committee had recommended that Israel import four hundred tons of frozen mutton. A panel of directors general had to authorize the recommendation before it could take effect. According to the state comptroller's report, the director general of the Ministry of Industry and Trade failed to convene the meeting for a full three years, ensuring that the meat would not be imported. Local mutton rose in price, and the minister, who raised sheep, gained significantly.

A famous shot taken in the 1980s. Sharon's youngest son, Gilad, warned him not to raise the sheep up on his shoulders in front of Yedioth Ahronoth photographer Yossi Rot. Sharon responded: "I trust this guy. He took my picture in October 1973 at the bridgehead along the Suez Canal."
(YOSSI ROT, *YEDIOTH AHRONOTH*)

December 1955. Ariel Sharon, paratroop commander, with IDF chief of staff Moshe Dayan during a period of reprisal raids.
(IDF & DEFENSE ESTABLISHMENT ARCHIVES, *BAMAHANE* MAGAZINE)

June 1970. Chief of Staff Haim Bar-Lev and
OC Southern Command Sharon briefing
the soldiers on the southern front.
(DAVID RUBINGER, *YEDIOTH AHRONOTH*)

January 1971. A visit from his patron.
David Ben-Gurion touring the southern border
with OC Southern Command Sharon.
(DAVID RUBINGER, *YEDIOTH AHRONOTH*)

October 16, 1973. Commanders reconnoiter
the western bank of the Suez Canal. From left: Haim Bar-Lev,
David Elazar, Sharon, and Rechavam Ze'evi (with glasses).
(DAVID RUBINGER, *YEDIOTH AHRONOTH*)

October 1973.
Chief of Staff David Elazar and
Major General Sharon on African
soil after crossing the canal.
(DAVID RUBINGER, YEDIOTH AHRONOTH)

October 1973.
Dayan and Sharon
on the banks of the canal.
(AVRAHAM VERED, IDF & DEFENSE
ESTABLISHMENT ARCHIVES)

June 1977. The Knesset. The new minister of agriculture with Prime Minister Menachem Begin.
(DAVID RUBINGER, YEDIOTH AHRONOTH)

September 4, 1979. Egyptian president Anwar Sadat and his wife, Jehan, with Minister of Agriculture Sharon during a visit to Haifa, Israel.
(SA'AR YA'ACOV, ISRAEL GOVERNMENT PRESS OFFICE)

September 1981. Sharon's mother, Vera Scheinerman.
(YOSSI ROT, YEDIOTH AHRONOTH)

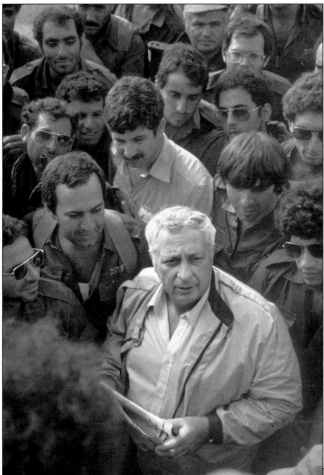

June 10, 1982.
Defense Minister Sharon
in Lebanon.
(DAVID RUBINGER,
YEDIOTH AHRONOTH)

September 1982.
The massacre in
Sabra and Shatilla.
(YOSSI ROT,
YEDIOTH AHRONOTH)

1984. The founding of the Sharon Camp in the Likud. Deputy Minister of Industry and Trade Yisrael Katz whispering into his boss's ear.
(Michael Kramer, Yedioth Ahronoth)

September 1984. Sharon and Minister of Defense Yitzhak Rabin discussing the National Unity Government.
(David Rubinger, Yedioth Ahronoth)

February 1986. Foreign Minister Yitzhak Shamir with Minister of Industry and Trade Sharon.
(David Rubinger, Yedioth Ahronoth)

March 10, 1986.
Sharon and Lily in the
audience during the Herut
Party convention at the
exhibition grounds in Tel Aviv.
(NATI HARNIK, ISRAEL GOVERNMENT
PRESS OFFICE)

June 1986.
Omri (left) and Gilad Sharon.
(SHAUL GOLAN, *YEDIOTH AHRONOTH*)

August 1987. Sharon during his famous Tel Aviv University lecture on the Lebanon War.
(DAVID RUBINGER, YEDIOTH AHRONOTH)

December 1998. Metzudat Ze'ev. Sharon with Prime Minister Binyamin Netanyahu and his wife, Sara.
(HAIM ZIV, YEDIOTH AHRONOTH)

September 1989. Lily lovingly offers Arik a taste of her cooking at their Sycamore Ranch home.
(DAVID RUBINGER, YEDIOTH AHRONOTH)

*September 1996. Minister of National Infrastructure
Sharon receiving a blessing from Rabbi Yitzhak Kaduri.*
(DANNY SALOMON, YEDIOTH AHRONOTH)

*January 1997. Lily straightening the minister
of national infrastructure's tie.*
(DAVID RUBINGER, YEDIOTH AHRONOTH)

*February 1997. With Lily during the
libel suit against* Haaretz.
(OREN AGMON, YEDIOTH AHRONOTH)

*March 1997.
Laying the cornerstone
at the Rabin Center.*
(EFFI SHARIR, YEDIOTH AHRONOTH)

October 1998.
Foreign Minister Sharon with
Lily and their first grandson,
Rotem, on an ATV at the ranch.
(HAIM HORENSTEIN, YEDIOTH AHRONOTH)

June 1999.
Family pictures
on the wall of the
Sycamore Ranch house.
(SHAUL GOLAN,
YEDIOTH AHRONOTH)

December 1999.
The ranch house on fire.
(DANNY SALOMON,
YEDIOTH AHRONOTH)

January 2000.
Sharon playing with
his German shepherd
at the ranch.
(MICHAEL KRAMER,
YEDIOTH AHRONOTH)

March 26, 2000.
Windflower Hill.
Gilad (listening to his father),
Arik, and Omri Sharon
at Lily's funeral.
(DANNY SALOMON,
YEDIOTH AHRONOTH)

February 6, 2001.
Front row, left to right: Uri Dan,
Cyril Kern, Arie Ganger, and
Sharon watch the election
results on TV as Sharon is
elected prime minister
for the first time.
(DAVID RUBINGER,
YEDIOTH AHRONOTH)

February 6, 2001.
Victory night. A celebratory
embrace from Omri
as Cyril Kern looks on.
(DAVID RUBINGER,
YEDIOTH AHRONOTH)

May 21, 2001.
Interior Minister Eli Yishai,
Rabbi Ovadia Yossef,
and Prime Minister
Ariel Sharon.
(SA'AR YA'ACOV, ISRAEL
GOVERNMENT PRESS OFFICE)

September 2001.
Cabinet meeting. Sharon
with Foreign Minister
Shimon Peres.
(DAVID RUBINGER,
YEDIOTH AHRONOTH)

September 2001.
Sharon with
Chief of Staff
Uri Shani.
(DAVID RUBINGER,
YEDIOTH AHRONOTH)

January 2003. Sharon with Education Minister Limor Livnat (left)
and Chief of Staff Dov Weisglass at an event for the
friends of the Weizman Institute.
(MICHAEL KRAMER, YEDIOTH AHRONOTH)

June 2003. Aqaba Summit. Abu Mazen (a.k.a. Mahmoud Abbas), President George W. Bush, and Sharon.
(AVI OHAYON, ISRAEL GOVERNMENT PRESS OFFICE)

July 14, 2003. Sharon meeting with Prime Minister Tony Blair at 10 Downing Street.
(AMOS BEN GERSHON, ISRAEL GOVERNMENT PRESS OFFICE)

February 2005. Shaking hands with Arafat's successor, Abu Mazen.
(AVI OHAYON, ISRAEL GOVERNMENT PRESS OFFICE)

April 2005.
Crawford, Texas.
Prime Minister Sharon
and President Bush
walking the grounds
of Bush's ranch.
(AVI OHAYON, ISRAEL
GOVERNMENT PRESS OFFICE)

April 2005. Crawford, Texas.
Sharon and Bush in the president's study.
(AVI OHAYON, ISRAEL GOVERNMENT PRESS OFFICE)

April 2005.
Condoleezza Rice visits
the ranch.
(AVI OHAYON, ISRAEL
GOVERNMENT PRESS OFFICE)

December 20, 2005. Sharon and the director general of Hadassah's Ein Karem hospital, Dr. Shlomo Mor-Yosef, speaking to reporters upon Sharon's release after his first stroke.

January 4, 2006. Sharon with Finance Minister Ehud Olmert at the ceremony marking the sale of Bank Leumi shares to a private investment group, at Sharon's office in Jerusalem. A few hours later he suffered his second stroke.

CHAPTER 36

Blunder in Oslo

HARDLY A DAY PASSED AFTER HIS SURGERY BEFORE SHARON HUSTLED out of bed to the Knesset, ignoring his doctors' advice to spend three weeks recuperating. Rabin's government, with Shimon Peres as foreign minister, was fast becoming all that he had feared it would become. In one of its first moves, the government vetoed Sharon's plans to build two hundred housing units in the east Jerusalem neighborhood of Sheikh Jarah. On August 25, 1992, Sharon filed a no-confidence vote, citing the government's "scheme against Jewish settlement in Jerusalem," but it failed to gain a majority or arouse any media interest. Labor leaders didn't even bother quarreling with him. Back on top, they were dismissive of his attempts to overthrow the government.

Shortly after the Likud's dismal showing in the general elections, Shamir gave up the chairmanship of the party, setting off a succession battle. Sharon and Levy each saw himself as the natural heir, but Netanyahu was quickly raising support. At a mid-November 1992 Likud Central Committee meeting, Netanyahu suggested replacing the deal-ridden election system with a full-fledged primary, in which all registered Likud voters could participate in choosing their leaders. When he addressed the crowd, they chanted: "Bi-bi! Bi-bi!" Sharon, sixty-six, was visibly irritated.

Political analysts saw Netanyahu's rise as the end of Sharon's career as a Likud leader. But Sharon, well versed in turmoil, didn't pay any attention to their predictions. On July 10, 1992, he took a swipe at Netanyahu, telling a *Yedioth Ahronoth* reporter, "The last elections weren't won by models. Yitzhak Rabin is seventy years old . . . people with real actions in their past were picked."

The primary contenders in the battle for control of Likud

were Levy, Netanyahu, and Benny Begin. Sharon was so far
out of contention he even joined Begin in an effort to block
Netanyahu's bid to change the electoral system. Nonetheless,
Netanyahu's suggestion passed with 80 percent support. "The
members of the Likud Central Committee want one leadership
that will unite the party and lead it to victory, not deals and rivalries," Netanyahu said.

All told, 216,000 voters had registered as members of the
Likud, making it the biggest party in the country. A new wind was
blowing, and it carried not a whiff of Sharon. On March 24, 1993,
Netanyahu was elected chairman of the party with 52 percent of
the vote. Levy, Begin, and Moshe Katsav trailed far behind with
26, 15, and 7 percent respectively.

Sharon was not even on the public's radar. He considered taking a stab at municipal politics and campaigning for mayor of
Jerusalem, but feared losing to the legendary Teddy Kollek. One of
his friends noted, "With Arik, when he's up, he's as up as possible,
the king of Israel. But when he's down, he's so down—his situation
seems pathetic and we're sad for him, because he's not a regular
politician, who lives off politics. Arik's a warrior and a rancher and
at heart a man of toil. He gets up in the morning and wants to
work. It kills him not to have real tasks. He's not built to wake up
in the morning and attend meetings where people just talk and talk
and nothing ever gets done."

The Likud Central Committee convened on May 17, 1993,
with Netanyahu as chairman. Sharon, the star of the stormy meetings of the eighties, sat in silence, far from the spotlight, as Netanyahu spoke. Sharon, though, kept his faith that the political
wheel of fortune would continue its natural rotation.

On June 4, 1993, Sharon told *Hadashot* that he didn't rule out
a future challenge for leadership of the Likud, but "I have far less
ambition than people think. That's my secret weapon. As opposed
to my friends, I suffer not even one moment of crisis when I'm not
in the government. But if there's a need, I'll contend. It depends. It
very much depends on the Likud and the line Netanyahu adopts."

In late August 1993, news sources broke the story of a secret
agreement reached in Oslo between Foreign Minister Peres and

his deputy Yossi Beilin, and Arafat and his confidant Abu Ala. While the official talks, an extension of the Madrid Conference, were at a dead end, low-level talks, unbeknownst to Sharon and Netanyahu, had been going on since January.

After fourteen secret sessions, Rabin was convinced that they were on track toward a historic reconciliation. On August 20, he formally briefed the Cabinet on the agreements reached in Oslo. On September 13, Rabin, Peres, and Arafat, guests of President Bill Clinton, found themselves in the White House Rose Garden, shaking hands for the cameras, Rabin's distaste for Arafat all over his face.

The Oslo agreement established mutual recognition between the State of Israel and the PLO and the transfer of Gaza and Jericho to autonomous Palestinian rule. For the first time, Israel recognized the legitimacy of the PLO and Arafat as the leader of the Palestinian people. Arafat, for his part, committed himself to the peace process. The chairman of the PLO promised to lay down the sword of terrorism as a tool to further his political goals, and also to alter the PLO charter, removing the lines that called for the destruction of the State of Israel.

Within weeks, the Israeli right had become an anachronism. The vast majority believed in Shimon Peres's vision of a new Middle East. Overland trips to Paris through Damascus's old city and across the Bosporus suddenly seemed imaginable to Israel's isolated citizens. Sharon, opposed to the Oslo Accords, sketched a plan of his own: It staunchly refused to recognize the legitimacy of the PLO, designated Jordan as the Palestinian state, and determined that all negotiations regarding the fate of the Palestinian residents of Gaza and the West Bank should be conducted between Israel and the leaders of the Hashemite kingdom. On October 2, 1993, Rabin invited Sharon to present his plan to the Cabinet. His real motive was to drive a wedge between Sharon and Netanyahu, weakening the opposition.

At the meeting, Sharon suggested that Rabin assert Israeli sovereignty over the areas settled by Jews in the West Bank and allow Palestinian autonomy in the major cities. Sharon underlined the need to deny the autonomous regions territorial contiguity, pre-

venting a future Palestinian state west of the Jordan River. Sharon
further suggested that Israel expand its settlement policy, creating
a stretch of Jewish population centers reaching from the Jordan to
the Mediterranean, or, as Palestinians say, "from the river to the
sea." Finally, he thought that Palestinian residents of the territories should be given Jordanian passports and be allowed to vote in
that country.

Sharon's plan was rooted in the geopolitical strategy that had
guided him since the seventies: Jewish settlement would lead to
the annexation of biblical Israel, granting it defensible borders and
historical legitimacy.

Sharon first mentioned the annexation of certain strategic
areas in November 1988. In late 1993, he suggested that Rabin
annex far more land, while making it clear that the right-wing
camp would not allow him to uproot so much as one settlement
from the Gaza Strip or the West Bank. On October 4, 1993, he
told a reporter for *Haaretz* that should the government try to withdraw from settlements, "we'll climb the mount." (At the time, he
meant that simply in the sense of "shout from the mountaintops."
The noise from the Temple Mount would come later.)

After Oslo, Sharon flew to the United States with Uri Ariel, the
director general of the Yesha Council, the quasi-leadership of the
communities outside the Green Line. The two spoke before major
Jewish philanthropists and warned them that uprooting settlements would endanger the existence of the Jewish state. When
asked why, after having overseen the withdrawal from Yamit, he
suddenly viewed such a move as an existential threat, Sharon said:
"That was a mistake, and I'm sorry I supported that mistake. It's
coming back to haunt us now."

Sharon explained that only Arafat's words had changed; his intent to destroy Israel, incrementally if necessary, remained. His
speeches raised millions of dollars for settlements. In fact, he was
such a successful speaker that Israeli ambassador to Washington
Itamar Rabinovich recommended to Foreign Minister Peres that
he send someone of equal stature to explain the government's support of the Oslo Accords.

CHAPTER 37

Rabin's Assassination

IN LATE MARCH 1994, TWENTY THOUSAND SETTLERS GATHERED TO protest the arrival of armed Palestinian policemen in Hebron. Binyamin Netanyahu addressed the crowd, decrying this latest manifestation of the Oslo Accords—Palestinian control over large parts of Hebron. Sharon, the next speaker, whipped up a political storm, calling Shimon Peres "the foreign minister of Palestine."

The foreign ministry responded sharply: "Sharon's pathetic insults are testament to the final shudders of the political demise of the architect of the Lebanon disgrace." Settlers held aloft pictures of Rabin as Pharaoh, the biblical enslaver of the Jews. "We survived him, we'll survive this too," the signs read. It was the beginning of the far right's incitement campaign against the prime minister.

One week later—and only six weeks after a Jewish extremist, the physician Dr. Baruch Goldstein, opened fire on Muslims as they knelt to pray in the Tomb of the Patriarchs, killing 29 and wounding 150—Hamas executed its first suicide attack. A recruit with a belt of explosives around his waist blew himself up in Afula, killing eight. On April 13, Hamas struck again, this time at Hadera's central bus station. The country was gripped by a nauseating mixture of rage, fear, and impotence. Right-wing protestors raged in the streets after each attack, and Rabin began losing public support for the accords.

On May 4, 1994, the two sides signed the Cairo Agreement, stage two of the Oslo Accords, which entailed an Israeli military withdrawal from Jericho and Gaza. Under the agreement, known in Israel as the Gaza and Jericho First Plan, the IDF would be replaced by armed troops under Yasser Arafat's command. Right-wing protests heated up. Sharon spearheaded the attacks.

Later that month, Sharon announced his plans to run for chairman of the Likud before the next national election in 1996. His announcement deepened the split with Netanyahu. "Sharon incessantly undermines," Netanyahu said. "Personal gains alone interest him. He undermined Begin, then Shamir, and now me. . . . The sum of his goals is to [create] and use contention. The time has come for this man of contention to leave the Likud."

On July 1, 1994, Arafat returned to Gaza after twenty-seven years of exile. On July 2, one day after Arafat's visit, thousands of right-wing supporters convened in downtown Jerusalem's Zion Square to protest. The densely packed, fiery crowd yelled, "Rabin's a traitor; Arafat's a murderer." In a preplanned move, Netanyahu and Sharon shook hands, reconciled. Speaking from a balcony above the square, Netanyahu said, "We will put aside all personal considerations, all quarrels and squabbles"—he extended his hand to Sharon—"and go forth together under a unified flag." Sharon grabbed Netanyahu's hand and declared, "This is the first time in Jewish Zionist history that a government of Israel is retreating from the most brutal and base of its enemies."

Neither the steady march of settlement building nor the wild-fire of suicide attacks halted the peace process. Once the IDF withdrew from Jericho and Gaza and Arafat established the Palestinian Authority (PA), Israel and Jordan sat down to talk peace. On August 3, 1994, the Washington Declaration, a prelude to a formal peace treaty, was signed by Prime Minister Rabin, King Hussein, and President Clinton, and brought before the Knesset. An uncommon unity prevailed in the Israeli parliament that day: The peace treaty with Jordan required no territorial compromise and was widely believed to be born of genuine goodwill.

Nonetheless, Sharon found fault with it. Before the vote in the Knesset, he asked Rabin to insert a clause into the treaty that proclaimed Jerusalem the unified and eternal capital of Israel. Rabin refused, saying he did not need to take a written oath to provide his dedication to Jerusalem and that at any rate there

was no place in the treaty in which to squeeze that kind of comment. Of the 96 Knesset members present, 91 voted in favor of
signing the peace treaty. Three far-right members of the Moledet
Party opposed the treaty, and Sharon, along with one other MK,
abstained.

Before signing the treaty, the Jordanians demanded the return
of 385 square kilometers of land confiscated by Israel under the
authority of the IDF OC Southern Command during the early seventies: Ariel Sharon. On October 26, 1994, after the matter had
been resolved, Rabin and Hussein, by now true partners and
friends, signed the treaty in the presence of a glowing President
Clinton.

Rabin remained active on multiple fronts, pursuing negotiations with Syria and the interim agreements of the Oslo Accords simultaneously. According to news sources, Rabin was willing to
withdraw from the entire Golan Heights in return for full peace
with Syria. Sharon, up until that time careful to attack Rabin's
policies and government rather than the man himself, now called
Rabin "the defense counsel of Syrian president Hafez Assad."
Sharon warned the residents of the Golan Heights that Rabin
would evict them. He said that the Likud, upon return to office,
would not abide by a withdrawal agreement.

On December 10, 1994, Rabin, Peres, and Arafat jointly received the Nobel Prize for Peace. A friend explained how Sharon,
deeply shocked, interpreted Rabin's willingness to accept the prize
along with the man responsible for the deaths of so many Jews:
"Over the years Arik felt disdain for what he called 'the red-carpet-
and-cocktail affairs.' He felt contempt for anyone willing to make
concessions in exchange for international celebrity. Arik told us
many times that he would never sell his convictions for such an
event, no matter how historic."

On January 22, 1995, two Hamas suicide bombers blew themselves up—one after the other, to increase the death toll by catch-
ing medical and rescue teams in the second explosion—at Beit Lid
Junction, north of Tel Aviv, killing twenty soldiers. Rabin's popularity plummeted, and Netanyahu's soared. In response, Rabin introduced the idea of a separation wall.

Plans for the wall dragged on. If it lay along the Green Line, satisfying American and international opinion, then terrorism would seem to have attained what negotiations could not: all of pre-1967 Palestine; anything less, and the barrier would seem like an illegitimate land grab. As politicians debated the merits of the move, terrorism inflicted an unprecedented toll on Israeli society. With buses, cafés, and malls under relentless fire, the Israeli public lost faith in the Oslo Accords.

Protests spread across the country. Activists held a permanent vigil outside Rabin's Tel Aviv home. Sharon and Netanyahu spoke out often against the policies of the Rabin government. Protesters shouted slogans like "With blood and fire Rabin will go." Ben Caspit and Ilan Kfir wrote in *Netanyahu: The Road to Power* that in July 1995, the head of the Shabak, Carmi Gilon, asked Netanyahu to tone down the protests out of fear of political assassination. Netanyahu passed word to Sharon. According to Caspit and Kfir, Sharon told Netanyahu that Gilon's request was "a Stalinist plot by the government."

On August 23, 1995, after yet another terror attack in Jerusalem, Sharon and twenty other right-wing politicians, professors, and leaders began a hunger strike outside the governmental offices. Thousands of supporters came to the Rose Park, near the Knesset, to show their support. On the fifth day, Sharon announced for only the second time that the withdrawal from Yamit had been a mistake. "The evacuation of Sinai," he said, "was a grave historic blunder, especially since this government sees it as a precedent and a propaganda tool."

Deemed to have served its purpose, the hunger strike was called off after a week. Sharon spoke vociferously at the closing ceremony. The government was collaborating with Hamas, he claimed. If he were prime minister, he would send the army into Jericho to wipe out the terror cells. "Once a nationalist government has been established after elections," he said, "all agreements with the Palestinians would be voided." Some people in the audience yelled "Rabin's the Engineer," equating the prime minister with Yehia Ayash, the most wanted Palestinian terrorist, the bomb builder known as al-Mohandeis, the Engineer.

In response to the signing of Oslo 2 on September 28, 1995, which granted the Palestinians self-rule in Hebron, Bethlehem, Jenin, Nablus, Qalqilya, Tulkarm, Ramallah, and some 450 villages in between, nine prominent rabbis published a halakhic ruling forbidding withdrawal from Jewish settlements in the Land of Israel. The ruling, in essence, granted legitimacy to the faithful who were intent on opposing the withdrawal with force. Talk circulated in far-right yeshivas about whether Din Rodef, the Law of the Pursuer—an edict commanding all Jews to subdue, even at the cost of death, a person pursuing another with intent to kill—applied to Rabin as he prepared to withdraw from areas of biblical Israel. Despite the absurdity of the statement, the talk refused to die down. Several rabbis also reportedly cast a Kabbalistic curse known as a Pulsa DiNura on the prime minister, begging God for Rabin's demise.

After Oslo 2 passed through the Knesset, activists and right-wing supporters returned to Zion Square. Leaders of the right-wing camp, including Sharon, crammed onto a balcony. Netanyahu, the evening's main attraction, said the government "was based on Arabs." Below, anti-Oslo activists handed out flyers depicting Rabin in Nazi SS garb. Police were accosted by protesters and called "Nazis" and "Judenrat." Some burned images of the prime minister. It is unclear whether the men on the balcony knew what was taking place beneath them as they spoke.

Oslo supporters broke a prolonged silence and organized a support rally, meant to show that the silent majority in Israel supported the prime minister and his policies. More than a hundred thousand people attended the rally in Tel Aviv's main square on November 4, 1995. The swell of support buoyed Rabin's spirits after months of political pressure and personal attacks. He participated in the festivities, looking bashful as he sang the Song of Peace. On the way to his car after the event, he was shot in the back. Shabak bodyguards piled on top of him as his car sped toward nearby Ichilov Hospital, where the doctors declared him dead on the operating table. For the first time in the country's history a prime minister had been assassinated. The murderer, Yigal Amir, a twenty-seven-year-old religious law student with no criminal record, admitted that his motive was to stop the Oslo peace process.

The nation mourned. Shimon Peres took office. Left-wing party officials, journalists, writers, and the Rabin family pointed their fingers at the right-wing leadership—primarily Netanyahu and various settler rabbis—accusing them of whipping their supporters into a frenzy and then deafening their ears to the unrest they had incited. Leah Rabin, Yitzhak's widow, refused Netanyahu's hand at her husband's funeral. Overnight, Netanyahu went from leading candidate to pariah.

Sharon learned of the assassination at the ranch. His first instinct was to jump in his car and drive to the hospital, but his PR adviser, Reuven Adler, persuaded him to stay put and, like the rest of Israel, watch the tragedy unfold on TV.

Over the years Sharon went to great lengths to direct his critical fire at the government rather than a single individual. That, along with the fact that he generally showed Rabin respect, helped him at this point. The family welcomed his condolences when he paid them a shivah call, remembering well the two generals' long history and common bond as protégés of Ben-Gurion. At the entrance to the house, Sharon hugged Yehezkel Shara'abi, Rabin's driver, as the driver burst into tears.

Two days after the murder, Sharon published a eulogy. He wrote that he had seen Rabin as a political adversary and a friend. He recalled the long road the two had traveled together, in uniform and out. In the same article, in the November 6, 1995, issue of *Yedioth Ahronoth,* he wrote:

> This is not the time to settle scores, [to see] who first incited against whom, who showed greater verbal violence, who came first to stand next to the signs [reading] "Murderer," who denounced, who tried to prevent those signs and who did not. I don't want to get involved in those questions. It is forbidden to get involved in them. [It is] too dangerous. [It] must stop immediately.

His words had no power over reality. Israeli citizens were asking how a Jewish assassin could kill a prime minister, and whether the murder could have even been imagined. The soul-searching did not focus on Sharon. But on November 17, 1995, Nahum Barnea, an influential political columnist, published quotes Sharon had given to a magazine of the ultra-Orthodox Chabad group two months before the murder. He compared the Oslo Accords to the capitulatory agreements between Marshal Pétain, ruler of Vichy France, and the Third Reich. He had stated that Rabin and Peres were "stricken by insanity" and needed to be brought to trial. When asked whether the news reports regarding threats to Rabin's life were mere provocations, he responded, "Of course they are."

"Look what happened in Stalinist Russia," he said. "In the mid-thirties the government authorities spread rumors of a plan to assassinate Stalin, and the matter served as grounds for wiping out the entire upper echelons of the Red Army. The same was the case for the Jewish writers and doctors who, Stalin claimed, were planning to poison him. That's exactly what Rabin's government is doing in Israel: media provocations regarding alleged intentions to assassinate Rabin. Its goals are plain to the eye. [We] must see where these things were drawn from. Only the left is capable of this type of provocation! . . . And I ask myself: Is everything permissible in the name of victory in the elections—the blackening of the nationalist camp, the abandonment of the settlers, and maybe even civil war?"

Despite the national mood of mourning, Sharon called on the Israeli public, almost immediately after the murder, to make sure that the horror of the act did not conceal the truth of Oslo—the government was still leading the country to a national disaster. Five days after the murder, Sharon demanded that Peres abandon the Oslo agreements. The Arab states had not demilitarized, he argued, and the Temple Mount, the Tomb of the Patriarchs, and the Golan Heights had become no less important to the State of Israel and to the Jewish people.

Five years later, Sharon, moved by the winds of political expediency, eulogized Rabin from the Knesset lectern. "We must decide how we are to reach the peace we all yearn for, knowing that peace is almost as painful as war. Because in peace, as Yitzhak Rabin,

may his memory be blessed, understood, there are painful concessions, tough concessions. . . . I miss Yitzhak Rabin, I miss having
the option of consulting even if there are differences of opinion,
and there were. [I miss] speaking plainly, simply, without slogans.
In Yitzhak's absence the responsibility on our shoulders is greater,
heavier. That's how I feel."

CHAPTER 38

Back in Office

ATTENTIVE TO THE POLLS, SHARON REALIZED THAT HE HAD NO CHANCE of replacing Netanyahu as chairman of the Likud. If Netanyahu stepped down, someone else would take the reins. Therefore, near the beginning of 1996, he rescinded his candidacy for chairman of the Likud and supported Netanyahu. In light of Netanyahu's tarnished image, a movement formed in the Likud to crown Dan Meridor, a Likud Prince, as chairman. Sharon, dead set against Meridor, threw all of his political weight behind Netanyahu. As far as Sharon was concerned, Meridor had wronged him in 1982 when, as secretary of the government during the Lebanon War, he had prominently opposed the defense minister.

After the assassination, Peres had to choose whether he wanted to form a new government from the sitting Knesset or go straight to elections. Netanyahu had crashed; Peres led him by 30 percentage points. His advisers urged him to set an election date as soon as possible in order to cash in on the public's sympathy and outrage. But Peres wanted to be voted in as a peacemaker, not merely as Rabin's replacement. For that, he needed time to create a bold peace initiative. Sharon seized on Peres's blunder. He understood that Netanyahu needed to put as much time as possible between the murder and the elections.

Netanyahu, certain that Sharon's political might had been sucked dry, learned the lesson that Shamir had learned in 1990: In times of trouble, Arik Sharon had the power to influence political elections. In the days after the assassination, as the buzz around Meridor intensified, the cadre of senior Likud officials surrounding Netanyahu disappeared. Only Sharon, his former adversary, remained. Sharon believed that his support at such a time would be

repaid with an appointment to one of the top three ministerial positions.

Sharon unified the right behind Netanyahu—a pivotal move,
since the electoral system had been changed during Rabin's
tenure. Under the old system, in place since the state had been established, a voter cast one ballot, for a party, and the leader of the
largest party formed a coalition of parties that represented a simple majority in the Knesset. Now the voter would be asked to slip
two ballots into the box: one for a party and another for a prime
minister. Hence the need to line the parties up behind Netanyahu
before the votes were counted.

Sharon suggested drafting two major political figures into the
Likud: Rafael Eitan, the leader of the Tzomet Party and former
IDF chief of staff during the Lebanon War, who had already declared his candidacy in the prime ministerial election; and David
Levy, who had branched off from the Likud several months before and planned to run from the Knesset as head of Gesher, a
new, socially active centrist party. Levy and Netanyahu were at
odds and held each other in contempt. Levy told Sharon that
there was no chance of his joining hands with Netanyahu. Netanyahu, doubting Levy's willingness to join the Likud, didn't take
part in the political wooing. But Sharon, the Bulldozer, kept
plowing straight ahead.

In early February 1996, Peres announced that the next general
election would be held on May 29. Peres still held a significant
lead in the polls, but Rabin's murder no longer dominated the
news. A wave of suicide bombings in all major cities had captured
the headlines.

The approaching election date spurred the right to close ranks
behind Netanyahu. Eitan, having been promised suitable positions
for his top seven Tzomet people on the Likud list, came first. Netanyahu showed Sharon a draft of the agreement, which granted
the second spot to Eitan, and received his blessing. Up next was
the truly difficult mission of reeling in Levy, who was in the midst
of negotiations with Peres over a joint list with Labor.

Sharon knew Levy well. He promised the Gesher Party an
arrangement similar to that reached with Tzomet, and although it

had already been given to another, Sharon, sure he'd convince Netanyahu and Eitan later, offered Levy the second spot on the Likud list, which he accepted.

Netanyahu arrived at Sycamore Ranch on a Saturday in late February. Sharon showed him a draft of the Levy agreement, and spelled out the implications: Either succumb to Levy's terms or forfeit the elections. Netanyahu pondered for several days before consenting. Once Levy had been confirmed in the number two spot, Netanyahu's poll numbers continued to climb.

The Hamas organization, fearing Peres and his willingness to make a historic peace settlement, and spurred on also by the assassination of Yehia Ayash, the Engineer, in early January, stepped up their terror attacks during the campaign months. On February 25, 1996, two terrorists blew themselves up, one at a hitchhiking post in Ashkelon and another on the No. 18 bus in Jerusalem, killing twenty-six Israelis. On March 3, another terrorist blew himself up on the No. 18 bus, taking twenty more lives. A day later, on Purim, another suicide attack occurred, this time in Tel Aviv, outside the Dizengoff Center mall, amid a crowd of parents and costumed kids. Thirteen men, women, and children were killed. Now fear spread in the streets. The economy froze. The news reported the ongoing savagery in graphic detail. Prime Minister Peres seemed helpless, his talk of a "new Middle East" a cruel joke.

On March 12, 1996, Netanyahu, Levy, and Eitan signed a unification agreement. At the signing, Sharon may have suspected betrayal. Netanyahu arranged for only three chairs at the heavily covered event, leaving Sharon, the force behind the arrangement, in the cold. Eitan and Levy protested, and a fourth chair was brought on stage.

In the March 26 primaries, Sharon came in second behind the newly retired general Yitzhak Mordechai, earning him the fifth spot overall, after Netanyahu, Levy, Eitan, and Mordechai. All agreed that Sharon's surpassing Benny Begin and the Princes was the comeback of the year.

Despite his high standing, Sharon felt slighted by Netanyahu. The Likud chairman chose Mordechai to head the party's election campaign and kept Sharon far from all campaign strategy meetings and advertising campaigns. His blind eye toward all Sharon had done to shore up support for his candidacy was an indication of the strife that was to come.

Netanyahu ran a brilliant campaign. With Arthur Finkelstein—a mysterious, seldom-seen political consultant who has guided numerous conservative candidates to office in America and Israel—as his adviser, Netanyahu ran under the slogan "Peres Will Split Jerusalem." A month before the elections, Peres's unassailable lead had been cut to single digits.

Netanyahu, still needing a few more points, turned to Sharon, who again sought to squeeze support from the cryptic leaders of the ultra-Orthodox world. With the election just two weeks away, Sharon met with Yitzhak Aharonov, the head of Chabad's youth wing. The Hasidic sect, active worldwide in spiritually assisting Jews, had more than two hundred branches in Israel and wanted to keep its standing as a politically neutral organization. But Sharon knew that one word from the rabbis would mean tens of thousands of volunteers out in the streets supporting Netanyahu heart and soul.

Sharon met with Aharonov and several senior rabbinical figures in Beit Rivka, an ultra-Orthodox girls' school, in secret. In the middle of the night, the rabbis received a state security lecture from Sharon. He told them that under Peres, countless holy sites in the West Bank would be lost. The rabbis demanded to speak with Netanyahu. Netanyahu was there within the hour, his head covered with a kippa.

Netanyahu conveyed his commitment to the entire land of Israel. The rabbis asked whether he would return any part of the West Bank or Gaza. He said he would not. Later, they asked him to put this in writing. He did, and earned their support.

Sharon also sought a written commitment from Netanyahu that he would receive one of the top three ministerial posts. Netanyahu was not forthcoming. Battle-hardened in Israeli politics, Sharon drafted an insurance policy: He and Levy agreed that if one of them didn't receive what had been promised him by Netanyahu, the other would threaten to crack the coalition until the prime minister relented.

The Chabad movement now introduced a surprising slogan: "Netanyahu: Good for the Jews." They flooded the country with hundreds of thousands of stickers and posters. Thousands of Chabad activists took to the streets along with settlers and other right-wing activists. Their massive campaign was funded by Australian millionaire Rabbi Joseph Gutnik, a strong supporter of both Chabad and the settler movement. The new support turned the tide in favor of Netanyahu.

The evening news, broadcast after the ballot boxes had been closed, predicted a narrow victory for Peres. That forecast held through most of the night, but by morning the true results were in: Netanyahu had won by one-half of one percent. Six months after Rabin's murder, Peres—learned, pioneering, and utterly detached from the voting public—was out.

Three of Sharon's initiatives had helped elect Netanyahu: his decision to rescind his own candidacy and support Netanyahu, dooming Meridor's bid; his ability to draft Levy and assist with Eitan; and his success in reeling in Chabad.

Sharon had contributed despite his growing feeling of alienation. The morning after the elections, Sharon waited by the phone. Levy had—rather curiously for a man who ran on a social agenda—secured the post of foreign minister; Sharon hoped for finance or defense.

Sharon stayed at the ranch, trying to cut down on the binge eating he had indulged in during the campaign, and waited for word from Netanyahu. It soon became clear that he was out of contention for any of the major ministries.

Netanyahu appointed Mordechai defense minister, Levy foreign minister, and Dan Meridor finance minister. At one point Netanyahu seemed poised to offer Sharon the Ministry of Housing and Infrastructure, a slight in and of itself, but in the end he kept that ministry for the ultra-Orthodox Agudat Yisrael Party. Sharon was elbowed out of the government entirely.

The newly elected prime minister was, at forty-six, by far the youngest leader in Israel's history, and seemed poised to reign over the right for years to come. But after fifty years of service in the army and in politics, the sixty-eight-year-old Sharon had no intention of allowing Netanyahu to push him out of the political arena. Sharon counted on Levy, and Levy, a man of honor, kept his word. The foreign minister and head of the Gesher movement refused to take the oath of office until a suitable ministerial position had been found for Sharon.

Under vast pressure from Levy, Netanyahu agreed to carve out a new position for Sharon: minister of national infrastructure. Sharon didn't attend the swearing-in ceremony, preferring to stay at home and draft a detailed document that outlined the parameters of the new post, assisted by the ranch forum.

Two weeks later, on July 3, 1996, members of the coalition convened to discuss the guidelines of the new government. Levy enumerated the promises Netanyahu had made and broken to Sharon, and announced in front of a crowd of stunned reporters that he would leave the coalition along with the other Gesher members if Sharon was not promptly sworn in as a minister. Sharon attended the conference, but said little, his face as unreadable as ever.

Netanyahu folded fast. The post was established, and the new ministry was given an annual budget of 20 billion shekels ($4.5 billion), as Sharon had asked. On July 8, 1996, Sharon's new post was authorized by the Knesset. His handshake with Netanyahu was cold, but he and Levy huddled and talked at length. "David Levy proved to me there is true friendship," Sharon said.

Sharon suddenly controlled Mekorot, the national water company; Israel Railways; the Eilat-Ashkelon pipeline; the Society for the Development of the Negev; the Society for the Development of the Galilee; the Israel Land Administration, which manages 93 percent of Israel's territory; the Energy Department; the national electrical company; the Kinneret Authority, which governs the Sea of Galilee; and the National Authority for Water and Waste. The other ministers looked on in disbelief. The new ministry suddenly controlled massive agencies and budgets. After weeks of frustration, Sharon was satisfied indeed.

CHAPTER 39

Minister of
National Infrastructure

ON JULY 30, 1996, THE NEW MINISTER OF NATIONAL INFRASTRUCTURE introduced his long-term plans for the ministry. The Israeli press headlined the show "The Return of the Bulldozer." Sharon looked loose and acted boisterous. With a 20-billion-shekel budget, he was one of the most influential ministers in the government.

He announced a full makeover for the Israel Land Administration; prioritized the development of the Negev and the Galilee; laid out infrastructure for a railway system; conducted negotiations with several countries about natural gas (so that Israel wouldn't be dependent on a single source); cultivated far-reaching plans for solving the country's chronic water-shortage problems, and authorized a 170-million-shekel road-building project around Jerusalem and the northern West Bank.

Sharon had more on his mind than natural gas. He wanted to dictate geopolitical strategy, to set Israel's permanent borders while bridging the Arab-Israeli rift. He prepared an alternative peace plan while Netanyahu prepared to restart the Oslo negotiations, to which he was bound by the previous government.

In August 1996, the Cabinet decided that Netanyahu should begin negotiations with the Palestinian Authority on the interim agreements, which had been halted after Rabin's death and included a scaled-back Israeli presence in Hebron. In early September, Netanyahu picked his "kitchen cabinet," the small group that would guide the peace process. Netanyahu included the defense minister, Mordechai, and the foreign minister, Levy. For Sharon, his exclusion amounted to a betrayal, but he did not threaten to quit.

Levy and Netanyahu continued to quarrel. The prime minister angered his foreign minister when he visited King Hussein alone, without Levy. The Clinton administration kept up the pressure to continue on the path Rabin and Peres had forged. Netanyahu tried to avoid a face-to-face meeting with Arafat, but on September 4, 1996, he yielded to American pressure and met the Palestinian leader at the Erez Crossing, along the Gaza border.

Netanyahu handed Arafat a new IDF deployment plan in Hebron. Sharon was furious. No one had shown him the plan. Sensing cracks forming around Netanyahu's throne, Sharon gritted his teeth and said nothing.

On September 23, 1996, Netanyahu, with the backing of Jerusalem mayor Ehud Olmert, decided to open the northern end of the Western Wall tunnel, igniting a holy fury in the West Bank and Gaza: Many Palestinians perceived the move as an attempt to undermine the foundations of the al-Aqsa mosque. The confrontation became violent; Palestinian police officers and IDF troops engaged in firefights, and sixteen Israelis and ninety Palestinians were killed.

The peace process threatened to collapse. The news media flogged Netanyahu for provoking the Palestinians and opening the tunnel against the better judgment of the Shabak. Worldwide condemnation followed. Suddenly, Netanyahu sought out Arafat rather than the other way around. At a cabinet meeting after the uprising, Sharon demanded that Netanyahu quit begging for a meeting with Arafat.

On December 24, 1996, the government convened to discuss a draft of the Hebron Agreement, which would allow Palestinian control over most of the city. Just before the meeting, Sharon met with Shimon Peres, leader of the Opposition, at his house to discuss the idea of a national unity government.

Peres and Sharon's relationship had known ups and downs over the years, but the two were drawn to each other, despite their ideological divide, owing to a common theme in their political lives: Both were being pushed aside by young stars in their respective parties, Ehud Barak in Labor and Netanyahu in Likud.

The peace process rolled on. Netanyahu met Arafat in Washington, and on January 17, 1997, he signed the Hebron Agreement, according to which the majority of the city would be handed over to Palestinian control, the few hundred settlers in the city and the forty thousand Palestinians in their midst remaining under Israeli rule. As a result of the agreement in Hebron—the burial site of Abraham, Isaac, and Jacob and the seat of King David's throne for several years—Benny Begin, a staunch ideologue, quit the government. Sharon voted against the Hebron Agreement but never considered resigning.

The Netanyahu-Sharon conflict flared during a February 18 meeting of the Ministerial Committee on Jerusalem Affairs. Netanyahu and Sharon clashed over planned building in the Har Homa neighborhood in south Jerusalem, beyond the Green Line. "Don't preach to me about Jerusalem," Netanyahu said, raising his voice. "I recommend you speak quietly," Sharon responded. From the first, Sharon refused to accept Netanyahu's authority; he waited to replace him at the first possible chance. As with Shamir, Sharon opposed the leader of the party when he felt he was being kept out of the inner circle. There was a difference, though: The conflict with Shamir had revolved around power and ideology; with Netanyahu, there was an element of disdain.

Netanyahu was further humiliated at the dedication of the Yitzhak Rabin Center in March 1997. The MC at the event asked everyone to rise when Netanyahu entered the hall, as a show of respect. Leah Rabin motioned for everyone to remain seated. They did, but Sharon was greeted with cheers when he made his way to the podium.

"We all want peace," Sharon said, "but it is hard to reach an agreement; therefore we'll all have to forfeit something. Although Yitzhak Rabin no longer marches with us, I would like us to follow in his path." That was the first hint at the dramatic changes to come in Sharon's approach to the Israeli-Palestinian conflict.

On March 19, 1997, Netanyahu announced that Israel was unwilling to proceed with the next three withdrawals in a two-year period as outlined in the Interim Agreements to the Oslo Accords. Instead, he suggested that Israel carry out one more withdrawal and then in September 1997 a final agreement be reached—a suggestion acceptable to the Cabinet, the Opposition, and Arafat. "I raised that idea many years ago," Sharon said. "In my opinion, going for a final resolution is the only way to proceed with the strategic assets still in hand."

In mid-June, Meridor clashed with Netanyahu and resigned from the government. The departure of Begin and Meridor and the rocky relationship between Netanyahu and Levy suited Sharon. Left with little choice, Netanyahu sought to reconcile with Sharon. Suddenly, Sharon was a viable candidate for minister of finance.

Sharon announced he would accept the post on one condition: that he be accepted into the so-called kitchen cabinet alongside Mordechai and Levy. "What more do I need to learn in order to sit there?" Sharon asked Netanyahu bitterly. Netanyahu refused to open the door to Sharon, and refused to appoint him minister of finance.

In June 1997, as Sharon and Netanyahu discussed Sharon's inclusion in the kitchen cabinet, the news media reported a secret meeting between Sharon and Mahmoud Abbas (known as Abu Mazen), Arafat's deputy, at Sycamore Ranch. The two holed up in Sharon's study and discussed different aspects of the peace process for over two hours. They found a common language.

Abu Mazen told Sharon: "I owe you a deep gratitude for pulling the PLO out of Lebanon when you were defense minister. Only then were we able to resist the influence of Syria, and in Tunisia we became truly independent and able to progress to the Oslo Accords." Sharon spoke of his Canton Plan, which advocated pockets of Palestinian autonomy rather than territorial contiguity. Abu Mazen said that the gulf between Sharon's vision and the PLO stance was too wide to bridge, but that perhaps he ought to meet with Arafat. Sharon declined.

The following day Sharon described the meeting as honest and good, adding that the two had pledged to meet again. Abu Mazen remarked how surprised he was by Sharon's hospitality and the warm atmosphere in the Sharon home. But Sharon was forced to deal with rising anger from the right regarding the meeting.

Settler leaders reminded him of his own statements. Circa 1974: "We must find a starting point for talks with the Palestinians, even though I say we should wipe out and destroy Arafat and the terrorist organizations." In 1982: "Terrorism is part of the Palestinian people's character. They have a deep desire to destroy the State of Israel." In 1985: "Our mistake in Lebanon was leaving Arafat alive." In 1994: "If the people vote Likud, that means they don't want an agreement with the PLO; the agreement with the PLO is a historic, moral, and practical error." And in early 1997, several months before the meeting with Abu Mazen: "Arafat is a war criminal by any law."

Only Netanyahu knew of the Sharon–Abu Mazen meeting—a move intended to bring Sharon closer to the inner circle. Mordechai and Levy learned of the meeting on TV and were stunned.

Levy tried organizing a large enough bloc to break away from the coalition and bring down Netanyahu's government. Once again he faced off against Sharon, who managed to speak with several of Levy's Gesher people and persuade them to remain in government, keeping Netanyahu afloat.

While Levy asked himself what had become of their "true friendship," Sharon pursued other objectives. In dealing with the upper echelons of the Palestinian leadership, he found himself, for the first time since 1983, at the center of the Arab-Israeli conflict.

Two terror attacks in Jerusalem on August 30, 1997, along the pedestrian mall and in the vegetable market, claimed twenty more Israeli lives. Netanyahu called a halt to the peace process, claiming the Palestinians were not holding up their side of the bargain by failing to combat terror. Sharon supported the move.

On September 25, 1997, two Mossad combatants were caught in Amman, Jordan, just after they slipped poison into the ear of Khaled Masha'al, the head of the political wing of Hamas. Evidence of a Mossad operation on Jordanian soil was a huge embarrassment to Israel and threatened to tear the two nations apart. King Hussein warned that he was prepared to try the two Mossad men and that the verdict would likely lead them to the gallows. Netanyahu sent the only envoy the king would receive, Sharon, who met with Hussein and averted disaster. Later, a senior Mossad officer, Efraim Halevy, met with the king and hammered out the terms of reconciliation: the combatants' freedom in exchange for the release of Sheikh Ahmed Yassin, Hamas's wheelchair-bound spiritual leader, from an Israeli prison.

Netanyahu repaid Sharon toward the end of the year, including him in the kitchen cabinet at last. In early January 1998, David Levy railed against the proposed annual budget—it slighted, he claimed, the disenfranchised who made up the bulk of his constituency. Levy quit the Cabinet in dismay, leaving Sharon the second most important minister in Netanyahu's government. The man who had squeezed into the Cabinet by the skin of his teeth was now the front-runner for foreign minister.

CHAPTER 40

Foreign Minister

IN MID-MARCH 1998, SHARON ISSUED A STUNNING PROCLAMATION: It was time, he said, for Israel to withdraw from Lebanon. The serving defense minister disagreed. Yitzhak Mordechai warned that Israel could withdraw from its security zone in Lebanon only if the move was coordinated with the Lebanese government. Barring that, Hizballah would occupy the void. Many asserted that the latest from Sharon was another ideological flip-flop. Sharon contended that the U.N. troops and the Lebanese Army served as a mere backdrop for unfettered Hizballah activity; an agreement with Beirut was worthless, as the marionettes in the capital took their orders from Damascus.

Mordechai prevailed. In April, the government authorized his plan for withdrawal. One year later, Sharon's plan would be approved, but it would be too late: The next prime minister, Ehud Barak, would lead Israel out of Lebanon.

The American administration stepped up pressure on Israel to execute a "double-digit" withdrawal from the West Bank, as mandated in the Oslo Accords. With Netanyahu in Washington, Sharon led a campaign against the proposed scale of the withdrawal. He claimed Israel could afford no more than a 9 percent withdrawal. Netanyahu and Mordechai leaned toward accepting the American demands. Sharon, operating from the far right corner of the political map, criticized the prime minister relentlessly. Netanyahu's people claimed Sharon's objections were merely a form of political blackmail—the Foreign Ministry in return for his silence. Sharon responded: "If Netanyahu were to offer me the position of foreign minister on condition that I alter my views, I would scorn the offer. I'll give no gifts." Sharon refused to meet with the administration's envoy, Dennis Ross, and Secretary of State Madeleine Albright. He accused Mordechai and Netanyahu of being too eager to please.

Sharon, though, still felt free to meet with Opposition leader Ehud Barak and dangle the bait of a national unity government. Barak, the new hope of the left, didn't want to breathe life into the Netanyahu government, and refused. Netanyahu viewed the meeting between the two as a betrayal.

In September 1998, Sharon flew to China. From there, he declared that "under certain circumstances" he would run against Netanyahu for prime minister. The two clashed over the extent of the next withdrawal from the West Bank. Netanyahu wanted to satisfy the American administration, which demanded a 13 percent withdrawal; Sharon met with Abu Mazen and Abu Ala, Arafat's top deputies, and tried to persuade them to accept a single-digit withdrawal, from 9 percent of the West Bank.

Sharon continued from Beijing to Mongolia, and returned to Israel full of stories about their wonderful mare's milk. Netanyahu, though, was certain that Sharon had spent his time far from horse country. Netanyahu reasoned that Sharon, armed with a satellite phone, had been feeding the rumor mill, which would explain the recent talk regarding the right-wing parties' plans to have Sharon contend against Netanyahu and Barak in the next election.

Sharon did nothing to quell the rumors. He made it known that a 13 percent withdrawal would lead to the collapse of the government. By October 1998, Netanyahu's wiggle room had run out. The American administration wanted results; the settlers and the right-wing factions of his coalition threatened to break up the government if he acceded to U.S. demands. He had only one place to turn: Sharon. Netanyahu offered him the post of foreign minister in return for his support.

The two signed an agreement drafted by former justice minister Ya'akov Ne'eman. After locking it in his ranch-house safe, Sharon demanded three additional months in his current post as minister of national infrastructure. Officially, he wanted to see certain projects through to conclusion; in truth, he wanted to keep an escape hatch open. Netanyahu also guaranteed Sharon the post of foreign minister in the current government and the next.

In early October, two weeks before the prime minister's trip to Washington, Netanyahu named Sharon as his foreign minister, praising Sharon's vast experience and his familiarity with war and with peace; he was, Netanyahu said, "a man worthy of admiration." The prime minister was engaging in more than flattery. He had realized the secret to subduing Sharon: inclusion. As soon as he was seated behind the foreign minister's desk, he ceased his opposition to the double-digit withdrawal.

After fifteen years of exclusion from the highest realms of Israeli politics, Sharon celebrated his victory with his family, then tore through the fields on his ATV for an hour. When he returned, he said he had seen his whole life play through his mind.

Cries from the left opposing the appointment were drowned out by waves of positive feedback from the Americans and the Palestinians. On October 20, 1998, Sharon and Netanyahu flew to the United States. Before signing the withdrawal agreement in Washington, the two sides met in Maryland at the Wye Plantation. For the first time in his life, Sharon shared a table with Arafat, a man he considered a war criminal, though he stood by his word never to take the man's hand. At Clinton's urging, the two spoke, but each used the third person to refer to the other.

On October 23, 1998, after a marathon negotiating session with King Hussein and President Clinton, Netanyahu and Arafat signed the Wye Agreement. Israel committed itself to an incremental 13 percent withdrawal in the West Bank. The Palestinian Authority would, in return, jail terrorists, attempt to foil attacks, and delete from the PLO's charter the articles that called for Israel's destruction.

Back in Israel, Netanyahu and Sharon faced stern criticism from the leadership of the settlers and the betrayed Chabad Hasidim. Arafat fanned the fires by announcing his intention to declare unilaterally the independence of the Palestinian state, with Jerusalem as its capital, on May 4, 1999. Nonetheless, the Knesset ratified the Wye Agreement. Abu Mazen met with the foreign minister and heard Sharon say that the agreement "wasn't easy, but the government had decided to make every effort to attain peace and I've adopted that attitude."

Sharon also said that if the Palestinians failed to keep their side of the bargain, there would be no withdrawal. During his next trip to Washington, National Security Advisor Sandy Berger expressed his displeasure with Sharon's threats. Clinton dropped in on the stormy meeting; he understood that the pragmatic general was the only one who could shield Netanyahu from the settlers and thereby allow him to carry out the withdrawal.

After the meeting, White House officials told the Israeli ambassador, Zalman Shoval, that the president was beginning to develop a fondness for the foreign minister such as he had felt for Rabin. Even Secretary of State Madeleine Albright acknowledged that Sharon was creative. Albright's comments reveal the extent to which the administration understood that Netanyahu's tenure was in Sharon's hands.

By early 1999, the Wye Agreement had ground to a halt and Netanyahu's government was in deep crisis. Caught between the settlers and the Americans, Netanyahu was forced to call elections for May 17, 1999.

Defense Minister Yitzhak Mordechai, yet another official at odds with Netanyahu, announced that the present government was leading the country toward war. On January 23, Netanyahu fired him, making Sharon the second most influential man in government.

On the advice of the enigmatic Arthur Finkelstein, Netanyahu nominated Moshe Arens to the position of defense minister, flanking himself with veterans. The stalemate with the Palestinians on the one hand and the American administration's frustration on the other had Netanyahu trapped. His adversary, Opposition head Ehud Barak, was rising in the polls while he and Sharon plummeted. After three-quarters of a term in office, Netanyahu's endless deliberations and lack of an overall policy toward the Palestinians had left the peace process at a frustrating standstill. The back-and-forth dance frayed the nerves of the Clinton administration.

During a visit to New York, Albright now refused an audience of any kind with Sharon. French president Jacques Chirac refused to meet him in Paris. *Le Figaro* reported that the German chancellor, Gerhard Schroeder, did likewise. European and American leaders, through the laws of diplomatic etiquette, were signaling which side of the aisle they preferred in power in Israel.

In February, Sharon's attention was refocused homeward when Lily was diagnosed with lung cancer. Sharon accompanied her to Boston for further tests. They returned again in April, and Sharon met with Albright. Ostensibly they discussed the Wye Agreement, but the secretary of state wanted to chastise the Israeli foreign minister for his comments on NATO attacks in Yugoslavia (Sharon had said that support for such actions could come back to haunt Israel).

With a nod in the direction of the nearly one million Israelis from the former Soviet Union, Sharon flew to Russia. Ze'ev Schiff wrote in *Haaretz* that Sharon sought Russia's help in brokering an Israeli withdrawal from Lebanon. According to the same article, Sharon passed word to Syria, through the Russian foreign minister, that a withdrawal from the Golan Heights would be on the table after the elections. Sharon claimed the article was outright false; Schiff accused Sharon of dangerous behavior in going behind the Americans' back, and noted that it was not the first time Sharon had issued a hollow denial of reported facts.

Ehud Barak opened a wide lead in the polls. Internal battles plagued the Likud. Netanyahu's campaign aired ads featuring only the prime minister or Sharon. Netanyahu tried shoring up support for the Likud from the religious parties, but the false promises of the last campaign were fresh in their minds.

On May 17, 1999, Barak defeated Netanyahu for the Likud chairmanship, 56 to 44 percent. That same evening, Netanyahu announced, "The time has come to take a break, to be with my wife and young children, and consider the future." Sharon, after decades of waiting, would slip straight into his shoes.

CHAPTER 41

Likud Chairman

NETANYAHU THANKED TWO PEOPLE IN HIS RESIGNATION SPEECH: HIS wife, Sara, and Ariel Sharon. Sharon was one of the few people to stand by him when he stepped down. Scrubbed and polished, Sharon remained stone-faced throughout the speech. By the next day, he was widely seen as Netanyahu's successor.

Sharon immediately set about rehabilitating the Likud, calling a meeting of the central committee and adopting a dignified demeanor. On May 27, 1999, Sharon was chosen as temporary chairman of the Likud. Netanyahu backed his selection, thinking that the seventy-one-year-old leader could keep the chair warm for him for a few years—a better option than opening the door to the up-and-coming Silvan Shalom and Ehud Olmert, who might seize long-term control of the party.

Sharon's first move was an attempt to broker a deal with Barak. Sharon calmed the ideological wing of the party, assuring them that the Likud would join the government only under certain agreed-upon terms, which included settlement expansion in east Jerusalem and the West Bank. For Sharon, a national unity government made sense. As temporary head of the Likud, he would snatch one of the top ministerial posts, putting him in pole position for the Likud chairmanship.

Barak, a former special forces commander and longtime admirer of Sharon's, knew that allowing him into the government would come at a steep price. "Ehud always thought highly of Arik," a person close to Barak says, "but he knew that bringing Arik into the government meant there would be many hoops to jump through during negotiations, and therefore he kept the door closed to the Likud. Barak worried that Arik would create an internal, religious-right opposition in the government."

In fact, it was Sharon who had insisted on promoting Barak to the rank of general years before. Then IDF chief of staff Rafael Eitan had thought Barak too young and lacking in command skills. Sharon had refused to back down. But after the elections, Barak was in no mood to show deference to his old champion.

In early June 1999, Ehud Olmert announced his intention to run for the position of Likud chairman. His staff began spreading word about Sharon's advanced age and the improbability of a seventy-five-year-old man contending against Barak in the next elections, four years down the road. Suddenly everyone talked about his age. Some reports had it that Sharon could hardly function in his day-to-day chores.

Sharon said a candidate needn't show his birth certificate; a lifetime of achievements should suffice. His staff made it known that Sharon was healthy and planned to follow in the footsteps of his Uncle Yossef, who died at a hundred and one, his Aunt Fania, who died at ninety-nine, and his mother, Vera, who died "early," at age eighty-eight and was lucid to the last.

Sharon prepared for the September 2, 1999, primary elections by appointing Uri Shani as director general of the Likud, and his son Omri as campaign manager. Within a month, Shani had Sharon's photo hanging on the walls of party headquarters, next to those of Begin and the father of Revisionist Zionism, Ze'ev Jabotinsky. Nearly all of the local Likud leaders, until recently firmly in the Netanyahu Camp, pledged their allegiance to Sharon.

Yet recently Sharon seemed changed. His age was all over his face. A stewing melancholy had replaced his quick wit and sharp tongue. Political achievements seemed to pale in the face of what was happening at home.

The cancer in Lily's lungs had been discovered by accident in February. The couple no longer listened to classical music on their stereo or dined extravagantly. Their home, which had always been a place of refuge for Sharon, now seemed cursed. "Lily was an integral part of Arik," a close family friend says. "She was like one of the organs in his body. Dealing with the disease was too much to bear for them both."

Lily refused to impose on Arik. "Lily always asked, 'What will it do to Arik?' or 'How will Arik get along without me?'" a close friend recalls. "That was part of her reckoning with the disease—worrying about Arik. One thing she wouldn't hear of was that he quit politics for her, or even cut back slightly during his race. Her whole life she preached to all of us that it was just a matter of time before he would be prime minister. To be by his side when he made it there was her life's work. She didn't want the disease to stop the realization of their joint desire."

In late June 1999, Lily went to the Memorial Sloan-Kettering Cancer Center in New York. It was her fourth time flying to the United States for treatment. Sharon, as always, accompanied her. Her friends described him as a perfect husband: gentle, sensitive, discussing all of his thoughts and plans with her. Sharon was on track to achieve his ultimate goals—the Likud chairmanship and the prime minister's portfolio—but he spent most of his time at Lily's side.

On the political front, his plan was to lull the race into a slumber, keeping the number of Likud members low and, as a result, predictably supportive. Olmert, the mayor of Jerusalem, began an assault on Sharon. In August he accused Sharon of approaching him during Netanyahu's term and suggesting a coup to oust "Bibi" from office. "If there is one person who has signified disloyalty for his entire career, it's Sharon," Olmert said on August 20, 1999, "since the days he openly and covertly opposed Begin, via the leadership of the 'hoopsters' against Shamir, and up to his comments against Netanyahu."

Reuven Adler ran a tight PR campaign for Sharon. Olmert's attacks were never dignified with anything beyond "That does not warrant a response." On the fund-raising front, things ran less smoothly. Campaign manager Omri Sharon raised funds far beyond the legal limit and then tried to bury the money in fictitious companies. (He was convicted in August 2005, sentenced to nine months' incarceration, and fined $65,000 for violating political fund-raising laws and providing false testimony. The money trail almost reached his father, who was but a step away from criminal prosecution.)

On the day before the elections, Olmert accused Sharon of hiring private investigators to plant false evidence against him. Adler released the usual statement, neither denying nor confirming. In fact, Omri Sharon had employed David Spector, the owner of Specurity, a security and strategic planning company, to investigate whether Olmert had illegally drafted members of the ultra-Orthodox community to the Likud Party. Spector brought his evidence to the media and the police, but neither found any prosecutable offenses. Olmert denied all allegations.

Sharon let out a sigh of relief on September 2, 1999, as he took 53 percent of the votes, compared with 24 percent for Olmert and 22 percent for Meir Shitreet. There would be no second round. After twenty-eight years in the army and twenty-seven years in politics, Ariel Sharon was at last the unrivaled leader of the Likud. Lily joined him that day for a helicopter ride up north, attempting to ignore her disease for a brief holiday.

CHAPTER 42

Lily

FOUR PEOPLE MADE DECISIONS CONCERNING SHARON'S 1999 CAM-
paign for Likud chairman: Arik, Lily, Omri, and Gilad Sharon.
From that point on, major decisions would be made by the family.
The influence of the ranch forum diminished.

For years, Lily had dominated Arik's decision-making process.
The two shared the same dream: to see Arik become prime minister. As her body withered and her interest in politics faded, her
sons stepped into the void. Gilad, quiet and introspective, handled
all of the family's internal affairs; Omri, robust in build and character, acted as "foreign minister," carrying out the political decisions reached at home. Gilad ran the ranch, and Omri ran the
Sharon Camp in the Likud. The "Forum of Four" replaced the
ranch forum.

Two days after Sharon won the Likud primary, Ehud Barak
reached an agreement with Yasser Arafat in Sharm al-Sheikh,
Egypt. Under the terms of the agreement, Israel would relinquish
control of parts of the West Bank and engage in final status talks.
Much like the Wye Agreement, the Sharm al-Sheikh Agreement
called for implementing Oslo 2 and addressing the true obstacles
on the path to reconciliation—Jerusalem, permanent borders,
refugees' right of return, and settlements—at a later stage. Some
people called it Wye 2. But Sharon, who had supported Wye, attacked the Sharm al-Sheikh Agreement.

He argued that Barak had forsaken the mutuality of the negotiations: He had agreed to release Palestinian prisoners and return
lands without receiving adequate compensation. He called the
agreement irresponsible and full of meaningless eye candy. The decision to allow a Palestinian port in Gaza, without security precau-
tions or measures guaranteeing Israel the right to inspect the

goods coming in from the sea, meant that terrorists could ship arms into the country at will.

Barak enjoyed the support of the majority. He promised to leap over all of the petty grievances and obstacles on the path to peace and hammer out a permanent settlement with the Palestinians within months. Aside from winning the allegiance of the settlers and other members of the ideological right, who flocked to him, Sharon's attacks failed to hurt Barak, but he kept up his anti-Oslo stance, even sharpening his views.

In early November 1999, Sharon called a Likud meeting to discuss the party's position on final status talks. Sharon drew two lines in the sand: Israel had to retain a strip of land between the Palestinian territory and the majority-Palestinian Hashemite kingdom of Jordan, ensuring the impossibility of a Palestinian state on both sides of the Jordan; and Israel had to protect the Temple Mount area from encroaching Palestinian populations. He marked his red lines on a map and went to the see the Sephardic chief rabbi, Ovadia Yossef, whose party was part of Barak's coalition, to explain the dangers.

On December 8, 1999, President Clinton announced the resumption of peace talks with Syria. It was another big coup for Barak, and Sharon was immediately critical, claiming that Barak had agreed to a full withdrawal back to the pre-1967 borders. Sharon claimed Barak had succumbed to American pressure, and he called on him to step down. "How did Barak fall into that trap?" he asked. "What brought a brilliant military leader, a son of this land, to such a degrading surrender?"

A week later, Sharon's house caught fire. Lily and Arik were at a relative's house when sparks from the heating system ignited the wooden roof; the blaze consumed the entire second floor. They hurried back, sick with worry. Lily was particularly concerned about the dove that had made a home outside their bedroom window.

The firemen were hard at work when they arrived. Pictures of Lily's mother and several of Samuel Scheinerman's paintings had already been destroyed. Lily refused to accept the loss. She picked through the ashes and found Samuel Scheinerman's wedding ring. Gone were the hundreds of pages of notes Sharon had taken since his first political meeting, with Ben-Gurion. Hundreds of books

were burned, including one from Ben-Gurion that had been in-
scribed "in friendship and expectation." Only the Bibles survived,
in which Sharon saw the hand of God.

Several of Lily's friends hurried to the ranch. "We came over
and saw a sad scene, truly heartbreaking," a close friend recalls.
"Arik and Lily stood on the firemen's crane and went slowly up to
the second floor to look for salvageable items. We brought Lily
clothes from home so that she would have something to wear,
since all of her wardrobe had been burned. Arik's clothes also went
up in flames, and it isn't easy for a man his size to find new clothes.
He had a meeting in the Knesset the following day, and I remember the first thing we did was go look for something for him to
wear. Many memories were buried that night at Sycamore Ranch."

Lily began planning the renovations the following day. They
moved in next door with Omri. Their oldest son filled the house
with flowers. As time passed, Lily left her bed less and less often.
Darkness spread throughout the house.

A hundred and fifty thousand Israelis ushered in the New Year
with a demonstration against Golan Heights withdrawal. Ehud
Barak was in Shepherdstown, West Virginia, negotiating with the
Syrians. Sharon was forbidden to speak at the event. His spirits
were lifted by the polls, though: Barak was losing ground.

Sharon figured that fifty years of experience with the Palestinians didn't lie. He was certain that the gap between Israeli and
Palestinian public opinion could not be bridged. Instead of final
status talks, he suggested an extended nonbelligerency treaty, a
test case of sorts.

On January 18, 2000, one month after the house fire, Lily was
brought to the hospital in critical condition. The doctors felt that
the smoke she'd inhaled had weakened her lungs and worsened
her disease. Sharon canceled all of his affairs and planted himself
by her side.

Lily was now confined to bed. Their lives became unbearable.
Sharon tried to breathe hope into her, promising her that as soon
as she was well again he would take her to see the Israel Philhar-
monic in Tel Aviv, where they would sit in their usual spot in the
fifth row. She continued to push him to seek the prime minister's
post, not allowing him to slow down on her account.

In March 2000, six months after his election as Likud chairman, Sharon was in dire straits: His wife was dying, his home was
in ruins, Barak's popularity was surging again after his promise to
extract all Israeli forces from Lebanon by June 2000, and many
were beginning to call for Netanyahu to return to the helm of the
Likud.

When friends asked how he was doing, Sharon replied uncharacteristically. "These aren't easy times," he would say. "I'm immersed in a type of longing," he told *Yedioth Ahronoth*.

A person grows used to living in a beautiful house for
twenty-five years, where each thing carries Lily's imprint:
every plant and tree and vase, and the pictures over the
piano and the knit towels in the bathroom and the mats in
every corner. I would come home at night and the music
Lily and I loved was always on, and I'd sit on the couch and
Lily would pour me a drink, and when I used to still smoke
cigars she'd light me a cigar and we'd sit and talk. We don't
have that now, and I really miss those moments.

Sharon was determined to fight the cancer in his wife's lungs.
"I didn't allow myself to break down for even a second," he told the
reporter.

I needed to make decisions immediately. It's a problem, but
do you break down and fold? I'm not built that way. Never
in my life have I surrendered to anything, and I hope I
never will. To my mind it's a struggle, something that must
be overcome. I've already seen the greatest victories and
the most bitter defeats and I've never broken, never. But if
you're asking me if I didn't choke on tears, then that's not
true. I did. I choked back tears.

Sharon was missing Lily in his political life, too. During meetings she couldn't attend, he would step outside every few minutes
and call her, explaining all developments in minute detail.

"It's a serious predicament," Sharon explained.

I especially need Lily when I'm in a battle. I need to see her
sitting in the front row, and she knows that. No matter how

busy she was, she always found the time to accompany me. I don't think there was ever a case where I went to an interview or a television show without her or to some battle in the Knesset or political campaign. . . . I need to see her sitting there, to share the feeling of victory with her. It's not that I need to share the pain—that I can bear alone—but I need the feeling of backing, the unified front. Only Lily could give me that.

During Lily's final days, Sharon either stayed by her side or called incessantly. Her approaching death brought him back to his previous tragedies—the deaths of Margalit and Gur. "The truly difficult blows," he once said, "were dealt to me personally, not in politics."

On March 25, 2000, Lily Sharon died. After thirty-seven years, one of the greatest love affairs in Israel had come to an end. She spent her final days in a Tel Aviv hospital. Sharon stayed in a hotel room adjoining the hospital complex. Each night he sat with her until her eyes closed and her pain subsided. On Friday night, March 24, she began suffering from an acute shortness of breath —she felt as though she were drowning, but she never panicked. "Arik," she mumbled, "the lapwings are chirping outside." On Saturday at seven in the morning she passed away, pictures of her grandchildren clasped in her hands.

During one of their final walks together, Lily had told Arik she would like to be buried on the grassy hill that overlooked the ranch house and, in spring, turned brilliant red with windflowers. In the presence of the prime minister, the president, family, and friends, Sharon wept softly as he eulogized his wife. "Till today I haven't done without you. From today it will all be without you," he said over her open grave. "It won't be easy, but I will continue along the path both of us believed in. Love from all of us."

After the ceremony, Sharon left a single yellow flower on her grave and turned from the hill. He opened his home to all during the shivah, and the people came in droves.

CHAPTER 43

Opposition Leader

HIS FAMILY PROVIDED SHARON WITH CONSTANT COMPANIONSHIP. His daughter-in-law, Inbal, Gilad's wife, slipped into Lily's role. She filled the house with flowers, brewed tea from the herbs in the garden, baked his favorite date cakes, bought his clothes, and prepared his food, just as his wife always had.

A silver lining formed around Sharon's melancholy as Inbal, mother of two-year-old Rotem, Arik and Lily's first grandchild, announced she was expecting another child. Gilad, an agricultural economist with a B.A. from Hebrew University, ran the ranch and began to dabble in business. He and Inbal set to reconstructing the ruined second floor and building an addition. Omri concentrated on politics.

Originally encouraged by his mother to enter politics, Omri now held a firm grip on many of the Likud's internal institutions. Unlike his brother, Omri never finished an academic degree. At the time of his mother's death he was in law school, but spending a lot of time partying in Tel Aviv.

Today, Omri splits his time between Tel Aviv, Jerusalem, and the ranch. Although he has not married his girlfriend, Tamar Netanel, or lived under the same roof with her for any extended period of time, the two have three daughters together—Denya, Aya, and Avigayil. Ideologically, Omri is the most liberal member of the Sharon family.

Gilad is to the right of his father politically. He met Inbal, at the time a high school student in Haifa, during his army service. After dating for seven years, they married, alone, at the local rabbinate, without prior notice. They let Arik and Lily know after the fact, so that there wouldn't be a big party. Gilad has always guarded his privacy jealously.

Sharon tended to treat his youngest son with great respect. After Lily died, Gilad influenced his father on matters of strategy, ideology, and economics, while party politics was Omri's forte. Omri was assertive, at times publicly chastising and yelling at his father; Gilad was always circumspect.

Sharon instilled the lessons of Kfar Malal in his sons. They worked in the fields, cared for the horses, and tended the crops, sometimes after school in the dark. Both of them knew the stories of the Scheinermans' struggles and stubbornness well. Omri, who, unlike his brother, has sat for numerous press interviews, has always prided himself on the nonconformist streak instilled in him at home.

After his mother's death, Omri, a captain in the IDF who once considered a military career, grew extremely close to his father. The two drew strength from each other. Everyone wanting to see Sharon went through Omri first. People in the Likud began referring to Omri and his entourage as the king's court. But Sharon knew one thing for certain: His son's loyalty would never waver.

Silvan Shalom, Ehud Olmert, and Binyamin Netanyahu all had their eyes fixed on replacing Sharon. Netanyahu, his most dangerous rival, waited on the sidelines for a verdict from the attorney general regarding a bribery allegation. If the attorney general decided not to recommend pressing charges, he would be ready to return. His PR people were already marketing a new, mature Netanyahu.

Meanwhile, Barak's grandiose plans began to crumble. The negotiations with the Syrians fell apart. His hold on the seventy-five member Knesset coalition began to slip. In response, Barak, who had won four of the country's top honors for valor, held a master's degree in economic engineering systems from Stanford, and was widely considered to be a brilliant tactician, announced his intention to solve the Israeli-Palestinian conflict once and for all—within one hundred days.

Barak promised Clinton he would make far-reaching territorial concessions. As a show of goodwill, he stated his intention to relinquish control of three towns on the eastern edge of the capital. That proclamation immediately ignited the most flammable topic in Israel and the Middle East—Jerusalem.

Barak's apparent willingness to put parts of Jerusalem—officially annexed to Israel in its entirety after 1967—on the bargaining table fissured the coalition government. Jews in Israel and around the world consider Jerusalem their holiest city. In Israel, emotions run high, particularly among the religious, when discussing the fate of the city: The al-Aqsa mosque, resplendent in gold, sits, many Jews believe, on the site of their ancient temples and on the grounds where Isaac was bound. (Muslims believe Muhammad ascended to heaven from the same spot of holy earth.) Sharon seized on the turmoil and immediately paid a visit to the spiritual leader of the ultra-Orthodox Sephardic Shas Party, Rabbi Ovadia Yossef. He came to him with a thick roll of maps.

In early May, Sharon met Barak in private and told him he had two options: Either hold early elections or suffer a relentless campaign to oust the government and bring elections by force. Sharon had two overlapping motives. He opposed any and all negotiations on the future of Jerusalem, and he desperately wanted elections to come soon, before Netanyahu had time to organize a run for chairmanship of the Likud.

Barak did not take Sharon's ultimatum seriously. On May 23, after eighteen years of guerrilla warfare, he pulled Israel out of Lebanon. The new border was recognized by the United Nations. Once again the Israeli public supported Barak. The withdrawal, carried out in a single night with zero casualties, increased Barak's confidence in his ability to forge a peace deal with the Palestinians.

Although Barak now stated that Jerusalem was not on the table, Sharon continued to hammer home the point that the holy city was in danger. In June 2000, Arthur Finkelstein met Sharon in Reuven Adler's Tel Aviv office. There, and again at the Sheraton in Tel Aviv in July, Sharon, Omri, Gilad, David Spector, and Finkelstein molded Sharon's campaign. Finkelstein advised Sharon to concentrate on a single point—Jerusalem. He instructed him to repeat this single line like a mantra: "An undivided Jerusalem is the capital of the Jewish people forever and ever." Sharon followed his orders.

Meanwhile, Barak prepared for Camp David. The setting for the final status talks was not lost on any of the participants. Clinton hoped to follow in Carter's footsteps and, from the wooded retreat in the Catoctin Mountains, create a lasting peace. Days before Barak's departure in July, the National Religious Party and the Yisrael Be'aliyah Party, sensing an untenable compromise on Jerusalem, resigned from the coalition. Shas was under pressure to follow suit. The party members asked Barak for a clear answer on the limits of territorial concessions. When an answer was not forthcoming, Rabbi Ovadia Yossef ordered his party out of the coalition.

Days before Barak's departure, Sharon had told a large crowd of supporters in Tel Aviv that no prime minister had the legal or moral right to concede parts of the unified and eternal capital of the Jewish people, just as Finkelstein had directed. Sharon called on Barak, now in charge of a crumbling coalition, to disband the government and call new elections. Sharon then led two buses of reporters to Jerusalem's Mount Scopus.

The Camp David peace talks, held from July 11 through 24, 2000, were a failure of historic proportions. Barak offered Arafat more than 90 percent of the West Bank—a territory representing a mere fraction of mandatory Palestine—and, under pressure from Clinton, parts of east Jerusalem; but Arafat turned his back on the offer. Barak proposed Abu Dis, a village on the edge of the Old City, as the Palestinian capital, but Arafat, who stressed Jerusalem in his speeches in Arabic as much as Sharon did in Hebrew, refused that as well. The sticking point was the Temple Mount: Barak proposed Palestinian autonomy; Arafat demanded full sovereignty. Neither would budge. Over the following weeks, both sides tried, but failed, to reach a compromise.

The Israeli left had reached a moment of truth. Barak had offered the Palestinians what they had long called for in exchange for peace, and Arafat had rejected it. Barak returned to Israel battered and bruised. He lost his majority in the Knesset and sent word to Sharon asking about the possibility of a unity government. But Sharon was no longer interested. He wanted elections, and fast.

Sharon realized that the right could easily prevail. The Knesset was preparing to vote for Israel's next president, a largely ceremonial position. Barak backed the veteran Shimon Peres, but with the support of Shas, the relatively unknown and unaccomplished Moshe Katsav prevailed. The 63–57 loss stunned Peres.

An aide of Katsav's spent the tense minutes before the vote in Knesset searching for Sharon. After combing the halls he found him in the cafeteria, hunched over a bowl of soup. Sharon assured him that everything had been taken care of. When he had finished eating, he walked into the general assembly hall, sat down in his seat, and smiled at Peres. After Katsav emerged victorious, Sharon said, "This is proof that with a unified nationalist camp we could switch the government."

The coming elections brought Netanyahu out of his self-imposed exile. Despite Sharon's standing as chairman of the Likud and head of the Opposition, all polls pointed to a preference for Netanyahu among voters nationwide. As Netanyahu prepared for the primaries, Sharon bad-mouthed him whenever possible, repeating to Likud leaders everything he had done to rehabilitate the party after Netanyahu's departure. The party had been carrying tens of millions of shekels of debt, and branches had been closing all over the country when Netanyahu departed, Sharon said.

Reuven Adler arranged a conciliatory meeting at his Tel Aviv advertising office. Speaking beneath the framed pictures of Sharon and the ranch forum, Sharon and Netanyahu decided to join forces against Barak.

Sharon flew to New York and met with Arthur Finkelstein. In September 2000, after he returned to Israel, Attorney General Elyakim Rubinstein ruled that the evidence against Netanyahu was insufficient to press charges. Sharon sent his rival a congratulatory card but realized that he would now face a tough challenge from within.

Two days later, Sharon castled his king: On September 28, 2000, he made an official pilgrimage to the Temple Mount, rocking Israel and the entire Middle East.

CHAPTER 44

The Temple Mount

FEW KNEW THAT SHARON INTENDED TO VISIT THE MOUNT. OMRI opposed the idea, Gilad was in favor, and Arthur Finkelstein tipped the balance. The intensely private American adviser felt the visit was a good idea because it framed Sharon's campaign for prime minister around the heart of Jerusalem. Omri Sharon was convinced it was a grave error and refrained from joining Arik and Gilad as they set out for the Temple Mount.

Sharon had trapped Barak between a rock and a hard place. As negotiations were ongoing, the last thing Barak needed was to have attention drawn to the holiest place in Jerusalem. But denying Sharon access would be seen as an admission that the Mount was on the bargaining table. Intelligence estimates indicated that the visit could be made without violence—and so Barak allowed it.

Sharon's visit fell on a symbolic date—the weekend before the Jewish New Year. The idea of Ariel Sharon visiting the Haram al-Sharif, the Noble Sanctuary, incensed Muslims worldwide. In 1967, Israeli forces flew the Star of David from the Temple Mount. Defense Minister Dayan, unpredictable as ever, had ordered the flag down, and out of deference allowed the Muslim *waqf* to maintain control over the sacred area.* Arafat's Fatah, along with other Muslim organizations, mobilized to prevent Sharon's visit. Fatah's elite Force 17 troops blocked the entrances to the sanctuary. Sharon was forewarned not to approach the mosque. As an Israeli, he responded, he had the right to visit the holiest site of the Jewish people. He would not be deterred by Palestinian threats.

*A *waqf* is a permanent endowment in which the proceeds (usually real estate) are used as specified by the benefactor, usually for a charitable or religious purpose. If a person makes property *waqf*, neither he nor anyone else can give or sell it to an individual.

That violence was in store was clear before Sharon even approached the Western Wall beneath the Temple Mount. More than a thousand policemen fanned out through the Old City. Snipers lay on top of tall ledges, and helicopters circled in the air. It looked like the scene of a high-budget movie. Israeli police had limited access to the area to Muslims over forty years old; nonetheless, an angry crowd was waiting. Among the throng of Hamas and Fatah loyalists were the Palestinian aristocrat Faisal al-Husseini and Israeli-Arab MKs Ahmad Tibi, Azmi Bishara (a Christian), and Taleb el-Sana.

At 7:55 A.M. Sharon walked through the Mugrabi Gate, and all hell broke loose. Palestinians rained rocks down on the police, who responded with rubber bullets. Sharon was accompanied by five Likud MKs and dozens of elite police officers. Gilad and his friend Roni Schayak stayed close to Sharon. The wide-bodied Schayak took it upon himself to watch Sharon's back and protect him from snipers.

Hundreds of Palestinians swarmed through the uniformed troops in an attempt to claw at Sharon, who, sweating profusely beneath his bulletproof vest, was busy explaining to journalists that he had come to the Mount with a message of peace. Cries rang out: "Sharon is a murderer," "We won't forget Sabra and Shatilla," "With blood and with fire we'll free al-Aqsa."

Sharon changed his tone when he learned that Arab-Israeli MKs were participating in the violent demonstrations. "The gravest matter is the incitement and hostility of the Arab MKs," he said. "They represent anti-Jewish and anti-Israeli parties. It's unacceptable that a Jew can't visit the holiest site to the Jewish people." When he reached the stairs leading to King Solomon's stables, the demonstrators lay down and blocked his passage. Sharon turned around, ending the visit, but not before he echoed Motta Gur's immortal words from 1967: "The Temple Mount is in our hands."

The forty-five-minute visit triggered the worst riots since the beginning of the first intifada in 1987. At first, the demonstrators threw stones and the police fired rubber bullets, injuring dozens on both sides. MK Ahmad Tibi broke his arm. The riots soon spread across the territories. Enraged youth pelted army troops with stones and hurled flaming Molotov cocktails.

Arafat released a statement accusing Sharon of starting a religious war in Jerusalem. Frustrated with the impasse in negotiations and certain he could command better terms with violence, Arafat called on his people to rise up and defend "the holy sites of Islam." The IDF killed seven Palestinians in the ensuing riots. The second so-called al-Aqsa intifada had begun.

The most famous casualty of those clashes was a twelve-year-old boy named Muhammad al-Dura, who died in a crossfire between Israeli troops and Fatah Tanzim (the armed wing of Fatah) in Gaza. A Palestinian cameraman recorded his death on film: His father is seen shielding his son with his own body as he waves to the troops in surrender; seconds later the boy goes limp. The images were relayed across the world, demonizing the callous Israeli troops. Investigations later questioned the veracity of Palestinian claims. Several credible independent sources, most notably James Fallows in *The Atlantic Monthly,* reached the conclusion that al-Dura had not been shot by Israeli soldiers who had been involved in the day's fighting.

Days later, Jewish Israelis' worst fears came true as Arab-Israeli citizens rose up in solidarity with their Palestinian brothers. A main highway connecting the center of the country to the lower Galilee became a battlefield. Youths swarmed onto the streets and clashed with police. Rocks were thrown on the country's main highway, killing one. With the country paralyzed, the police responded with alarming force: Thirteen Arabs, twelve of whom were Israeli citizens, were killed. The police had used live ammunition and deployed snipers against citizens. The Barak government was managing to look both brutal and ineffective.

In America, State Department spokesman Richard Boucher blamed Sharon for the uprising; Madeleine Albright concurred. Sharon blamed Arafat, saying the riots were premeditated. History sides with Sharon. In a September 2005 article in *The Atlantic Monthly,* David Samuels spoke with Mamduh Nofal, the former military commander of the Democratic Front for the Liberation of Palestine and member of the High Security Council of Fatah, the key military decision-making body during the beginning of the intifada. He had known Arafat since the Battle of Karamah, in 1968. Nofal said that Arafat told them to prepare to fight both before and after Camp David. Once Sharon announced his plans to go up to the Temple Mount, Arafat said, "Okay, it's time to work." In private conversations, former prime minister Ehud Barak, who was defeated in elections largely as a result of the violence that erupted on September 28, 2000, and had plenty of reasons to blame Sharon, has also fingered Arafat.

Despite American pressure, Barak refused at first to blame Sharon. He told close advisers that Sharon's visit was merely an excuse. But two weeks later, with the violence still unabated, Barak admitted that allowing Sharon to go to the Temple Mount had been an unfortunate decision. It was the beginning of the end of Barak's time in office.

On October 16, 2000, Barak met Arafat in Sharm al-Sheikh, Egypt, to try to reach a cease-fire. Final-status negotiations were well beyond the pale. Before leaving, Barak approached Sharon and offered to include him in an emergency unity government. For Sharon, the offer was a major achievement. He would join, he said, if Barak agreed to withdraw everything that had been on the table at Camp David and renew negotiations only with Likud approval. Forced to choose between Sharon and Clinton, Barak went with the American president.

As time ran out, the Clinton administration applied massive pressure on Barak to reach a settlement. The talks faltered, though, and Arafat announced his intention to declare Palestinian statehood unilaterally on November 15, 2000. Sharon called on Barak to capture all of the territory controlled by the Palestinian Authority. Barak's popularity began to spiral downward. The gap with Sharon was narrowing, but the overall favorite, by far, was Netanyahu.

A new wave of terror attacks swept the country. Sharon set up a protest tent outside the Knesset. In November, right-wing supporters assembled in Zion Square for a protest entitled "Let the IDF Win." Sharon told the crowd of a hundred thousand that "once the area calms down, we'll have to strive for a different political plan: a multistep peace plan, a plan based along the lines of nonbelligerency and spread out over a long period of time."

On November 28, Barak announced his willingness to move toward general elections—for the Knesset and for prime minister.

He accused Sharon of pushing the country toward yet another election and promised that he would regret his agitation. Sharon blamed Barak for the fact that there was no unity government, adding that his main problem was inexperience. In fact, Sharon needed a unity government at this point to save him from the seemingly inevitable return of Netanyahu.

Likud leaders waited for Netanyahu to return from a speaking tour in America. Everyone assumed that he would announce his candidacy, dooming a Sharon bid for prime minister. Netanyahu's supporters had already arranged to rent the biggest soccer stadium in Jerusalem for the celebration. But Barak changed his mind. On December 9, 2000, he announced his resignation—a move that, by law, necessitated direct elections for prime minister (and only for prime minister) within sixty days. In order to run, a candidate had to have been an MK at the time of the resignation. Netanyahu did not qualify.

Barak believed that with the front-runner out of the way, he'd have little trouble handling Sharon, the dreaded architect of the Lebanon War. At the time, Barak and Sharon were tied at the polls with 39 percent. Netanyahu commanded a hypothetical 52 percent.

Netanyahu's backers introduced what was to be known as the Netanyahu Law in the Knesset, allowing a non-MK to run for prime minister after the standing one resigned. Netanyahu seemed like a lock for the December 19 Likud primary elections. Public opinion was overwhelmingly in his favor. All other contenders dropped out of the race. Sharon braced for defeat but kept his demeanor even-keeled.

Suddenly, almost miraculously, Netanyahu announced he would run for prime minister only on condition that a general election (that would include elections for the Knesset) was declared. Barring that, he said, the Likud would remain a nineteen-seat party with its hands tied. Netanyahu's announcement shocked even his closest advisers. The Likud and the prime minister's seat had seemed his for the taking.

Netanyahu's decision remains a mystery. Yet we have learned that Sharon's ally, Arie Ganger, spoke with Netanyahu before the announcement and tried to persuade him not to run. According to one version of events, Netanyahu told him to get lost. Both Netanyahu and Ganger have refused to discuss the matter.

On December 18, 2000, the Knesset passed the Netanyahu Law but rejected the proposed legislation for general elections. Netanyahu stood by his word and announced that he would not run against Sharon, or for prime minister. He politely wished the seventy-two-year-old Likud candidate, Ariel Sharon, good luck.

CHAPTER 45

Prime Minister

SHARON WOKE UP ON THE MORNING OF DECEMBER 19, 2000, TO THE call of roosters. Elections were less than two months away. He decided to take the morning off and visit Lily's grave. Energized by the walk to the top of Windflower Hill, he set off for Tel Aviv and Reuven Adler's office. One more miracle was needed—the transformation of Ariel Sharon.

Based on a system devised by Arthur Finkelstein, Adler and his associates placed Israeli politicians on a sliding scale that measured their positions on geopolitical issues. Those at the far left were a 1, and those at the extreme right were a 5. Arik Sharon weighed in at 4.7. Adler's main pollster, Kalman Gayer, determined that the majority of the Israeli population was between 2.6 and 3.2. Finkelstein decided that Sharon needed a 2.7 on the scale to emerge victorious from the coming elections—just twenty days shy of his seventy-third birthday.

The campaign team consisted of Finkelstein, Adler, Gayer, media consultant Eyal Arad, Uri Shani, and Omri and Gilad Sharon. Gayer kept daily tabs on Sharon's progress along Finkelstein's scale. Adler cooked up the campaign slogan: "Only Sharon Will Bring Peace."

Meanwhile, Sharon established the Hundred-Day Team, a group charged with plotting his first moves as prime minister. Under the current system he would have only two years in office before the next general elections, and with the intifada raging, the incessant terror attacks, and the peace process stalled, Sharon realized that he would have few days of grace once he took office.

A week after Netanyahu announced his decision to sit out the race, polls had Sharon leading Barak 49 to 38 percent. The campaign portrayed Sharon as a kindly grandfather who, in his late years, was willing to make "painful concessions" for peace. The substance of those concessions was not revealed, but Adler says Sharon knew exactly which concessions he would make. The campaign jingle spoke of "security," "experience," "Jerusalem," "leadership," "hope," and "peace"—all things Barak had promised, but failed, to deliver.

Sharon and Barak had agreed not to include personal attacks in their campaigns. As Sharon's lead grew, Barak reneged. His campaign ads implied that the wolf was dressed in lamb's clothing. Posters of the dead from Sabra and Shatilla were displayed nationwide. Hints were dropped regarding prior atrocities, along with whispered fears over what would happen if Sharon were made commander in chief. Barak claimed the posters had been put up without his knowledge and ordered them taken down, but the damage had been done.

At Sharon's campaign headquarters, a debate raged over how to react to the Barak attacks. Adler argued that silence was the best tactic, as Sharon was in the lead and the issue would soon subside. Lebanon, he said, was part of the distant past and had no bearing. Everyone but Sharon agreed. Lebanon was still an open wound for him. Nonetheless, he took his PR team's advice and merely issued a short statement about how Barak had violated the agreement between them.

As the elections approached and Sharon's lead solidified, the left began to concentrate on Qibiya, the Rafah Salient expulsion, and the defense minister's "unstoppable" march toward Beirut. As the patron saint of the settlements, he was portrayed not only as someone who refused to consider territorial compromise—the standard land-for-peace solution—but as someone whose leadership would assuredly implode.

Sharon kept himself in check. The "good grandpa," once forceful and outspoken, clung to cliché and consensus. Internal campaign polls showed that with each day he drew nearer the vaunted 2.7 mark.

Toward the end of the campaign, the staff changed Sharon's slogan from "Only Sharon Will Bring Peace" to "I Have Confi-

dence in Sharon's Peace," which had an intentional double meaning, since the Hebrew word for "confidence"—*bitachon*—also
means "security." The polls had shown that the Israeli public,
weathering both the intifada and terror attacks, was concerned
more with security than with peace. Sharon toured the Jordan
Valley, the area that divides Jordan from the hill country of the
West Bank, and announced that it would remain in Israeli hands
forever. By early January 2001, Sharon led by twenty points.

Sharon stayed behind the scenes, following his staff's instructions dutifully. Arik, Omri, and Gilad had all had a hand in hiring
the staff, but once they were chosen, Sharon put his full trust in
them. Finkelstein, Adler, Arad, Omri, Gilad, and Arik Sharon held
daily meetings. Sharon listened carefully and occasionally wrote
notes in a spiral notebook in his neat, rounded hand. The team decided that Sharon should concentrate on three things: the people's
desire for unity, their need for personal safety, and their craving for
peace.

A focus group of young people revealed that few of the younger
voters were familiar with his feats as commander of Unit 101 and
almost all were ignorant of the Battle of Abu Ageila during the Six
Day War. Sharon began speaking about his role in crushing the terror cells in Gaza in the seventies, and his heroic crossing of the
canal during the Yom Kippur War.

Fatigue took a toll on the seventy-two-year-old Sharon. On occasion he lost his train of thought or forgot people's names—both
rare occurrences for him. Barak's campaign staff zeroed in on that
weakness. The news media began carrying stories about his age.
Anonymous charges in the media asserted that he suffered from
forgetfulness, did not appear in public because he was no longer in
full control of his faculties, and was a marionette in the hands of
his staff.

Sharon's staff decided not to respond, but Omri felt compelled
to refute the claims. No one had ever been able to decide for his
father, he said, and as far as his health was concerned, the doctors
call him a "tiger."

Sharon labeled the charges infantile, but his most convincing
backing came from his physician, Dr. Goldman, who had been

with him as far back as Beirut. From Cambodia, he told the press that Sharon had been given a clean bill of health.

Adler was worried about Sharon's appearances in front of the camera. He came off as labored and insincere. Adler learned from American experience: During his campaign, George W. Bush spoke to the camera while doing something else, like driving. Sharon, who came across even worse than Bush when speaking from a script, never addressed the cameras except while "working," or "touring" the country.

On January 16, 2001, twenty-one days before the elections, state-sponsored TV campaign ads began to run nightly. Sharon was featured playing with his grandson, Rotem. The message seemed clear: The good grandpa, the family man, was not about to lead the country to war.

Barak's ads stressed the point that he had extracted the Israeli forces from Lebanon, while his adversary had entangled them there nineteen years earlier. His advisers pushed him to go on the offensive and attack Sharon personally, but Barak refused, a move many say cost him the elections.

On the campaign trail, Sharon was caught off guard by a sixteen-year-old high school student in Beersheba. At a question-and-answer session with the candidate, she charged Sharon with responsibility for the fact that she had grown up with a shell-shocked father, who had served in Lebanon during a needless war. Because of that Sharon shouldn't be allowed to serve as prime minister, she said. Sharon blushed. He had been caught unprepared. He said he was sorry for her pain, and that back in 1982 he had asked to withdraw from Lebanon but no prime minister had been willing to heed his advice.

The American administration released the Clinton peace framework, which rendered roughly 90 percent of the West Bank and Gaza to the Palestinians, including the Arab neighborhoods of Jerusalem. Sharon responded by unveiling the so-called Sharon Political Plan, according to which the Israelis and the Palestinians would sign a long-term interim agreement—a state of nonbelligerency that would, over time, lead to a Palestinian state on the 42 percent of the West Bank and Gaza lands that they already controlled. The plan was meant to nudge him farther in the direction of Finkelstein's 2.7 mark, but the public did not take it seriously. It was clear no Palestinian would sign such an offer. Barak labeled it a recipe for war.

Sharon's plan called for Israel to maintain control of the Jordan Valley, Jerusalem, and, in particular, the Temple Mount. The right of return would never be extended to Palestinian refugees, and Jewish settlements would stay in place—even expand—but not multiply. Sharon emphasized that he would not negotiate with Arafat under fire and that he did not feel bound by Barak's concessions.

Finally, he said that he would not shake Arafat's hand until the Israeli-Palestinian conflict had come to a complete and final end. His advisers tried to sway him on that, saying it damaged the campaign, but Sharon was adamant.

After making the plan public in January, he received the backing of his former adversary Dan Meridor, a politician who singularly is strongly identified with the center. As a former opponent and staunch humanist, Meridor's backing put Sharon in the mainstream for the first time in his career. The bulk of the business sector, previously behind Barak, also swung to Sharon's camp.

Seven days before the elections, the news media reported that Omri Sharon and Dov Weisglass had met with Arafat's financial adviser, Muhammad Rashid, in Vienna. The meeting, held at the home of Martin Schlaff, one of the owners of the casino in the Palestinian city of Jericho, reportedly revolved around matters of state. Barak complained that Sharon was usurping him and violating his own principal of no talks with Arafat under fire. The meeting raised other questions: Why the urgency? What was Omri Sharon's role? Why wouldn't the Palestinians give a straight answer about what had been discussed in Vienna?

One thing the secret meeting did reveal was that the greatest fear of Sharon's team was that there would be a last-minute agreement between Barak and Arafat. Such an agreement would give Arab Israelis a reason to go out and vote, tightening the race. Sharon's campaign team concentrated on bringing three different population groups out to vote: the settlers, the ultra-Orthodox, and the immigrants from the former Soviet Union.

Six days before the elections, Sharon's daughter-in-law, Inbal, gave birth to twins, Yoav and Uri. By custom their circumcision fell seven days later, on Election Day, a coincidence the Sharon family considered a sign from heaven.

Three days before the elections, Sharon opened his house to journalists. The hospitality backfired when one of the journalists discovered that the Thai cook in his home had a visa that permitted her to do only agricultural work, not housework. After a flurry of articles, Sharon's campaign handlers decided that from that moment on, the campaign was closed.

The campaign had deeper worries than slips of the tongue and gaffes—the pressure had increased Sharon's facial tics to the point that a public appearance was out of the question.

On February 5, the day before the elections, he released a statement indicating that he planned to pursue a unity government when chosen to lead the country. It was clear by then that he was going to win.

At 10 P.M. on the evening of the sixth, even Sharon was shocked· He had taken 62 percent of the vote to Barak's 38 percent. 1,698,077 citizens had voted for him and 1,023,944 for Barak. No one had foreseen that kind of defeat for the left.

Sharon kept his composure, making the rounds and shaking hands, saying thank you to all who came to congratulate him. Just before midnight he got up on the podium and told the ecstatic crowd that he had just gotten off the phone with the president of the United States. "He asked me to present his best wishes to you," Sharon said. "He told me that they want to cooperate very closely with the government under my leadership. He reminded me of the trip I took with him through Samaria and the Jordan Valley.* And he said to me, 'No one believed then that I would be president and you would be prime minister. But as things turned out, despite the fact that no one believed us, I have been elected president, and you have been elected prime minister.' "

After that he took a personal moment and thanked the woman

---

*In 1999, George W. Bush, then governor of Texas, had visited Israel and been treated to the usual helicopter tour by then foreign minister Ariel Sharon.

who had stood behind him for so many years. "Since my youth, I have devoted myself entirely to the country, to consolidating and building its security. In all of my positions, at all times, whether difficult or joyful, I was accompanied by my dear late wife, Lily, who supported me wholeheartedly. At this moment, when the Israeli people have expressed their confidence in me to lead the country in the coming years, I miss her, and she is not standing here by my side."

CHAPTER 46

Policy of Restraint

SHARON STOOD ON THE BALCONY OF HIS HOTEL UNTIL FOUR IN THE morning, looking out at Tel Aviv and the shoreline below. Habit woke him again an hour and a half later. He drove down to the ranch and asked the Shabak secret service agents to wait for him at the bottom of Windflower Hill as he climbed up to Lily's grave.

He spent a long time at her gravestone before turning to the nearby landing pad and the waiting helicopter. He had planned to fly straight to Jerusalem to pay his respects at the Western Wall, but bad weather forced him to take an armored car into the capital, through the donkey-cart-sized streets of the Old City and into the open plaza before the Western Wall. Supporters welcomed him with a series of blasts from a shofar. Sharon put a kippa on his head, laid his right hand on the old stones, and, uncharacteristically, prayed.

As opposed to his two immediate predecessors, Sharon kept his guard up after winning the elections. He didn't gloat or show any outward signs of satisfaction—the support and affection of the Israeli public, he knew, could slip though his fingers like water.

Likud leaders flocked to his office, looking for prominent positions. Sharon thanked them personally for their support and wrote down their wishes. Sharon adopted a princely manner. He no longer clashed with or belittled rivals. His first goal: to establish a unity government.

Time was short. Sharon had a two-year mandate. Worse, he had only forty-five days to form a coalition; if he failed to assemble a majority in the Knesset by then, general elections would be called, and Netanyahu would return to the political arena. Ehud Olmert, mayor of Jerusalem at the time, Ya'akov Ne'eman, and Uri Shani headed his negotiation team.

It took just three weeks to assemble the coalition. Beneath the surface, Sharon hadn't changed at all. "He was a champion manipulator, a genius at it," a close associate from those years recalls. "Everything was always planned, even the slips of the tongue. I'll never forget how one day, as he orchestrated the resignation of one minister in order to replace him with another, he said, 'Iago pulled the strings.' He was referring to himself."

Sharon ignored calls to form a 61-seat coalition of right and center parties. He wanted a stable unity government consisting of Barak's Labor Party (26 seats), Shas (17 seats), Yisrael Be'aliyah (6 seats), and Likud (19 seats). Everything rested on Barak's willingness to serve under Sharon as defense minister. He wavered. Sharon explained that the true art of politics was not the upstream crawl but the career-saving float. Barak agreed—then changed his mind. Dogged primarily by his own party, he announced his plans to retire. Sharon stuck to his conciliatory script and said that "what happened to Barak weighs on me personally." His empathy paid off. Barak agreed to serve on occasion as Sharon's unofficial envoy to Washington.

Sharon assembled his stable coalition. He gave the Foreign Ministry and the Defense Ministry to Shimon Peres and Binyamin Ben-Eliezer of Labor, the Interior Ministry to Eli Yishai of Shas, the Ministry of Housing and Infrastructure to Natan Sharansky of Yisrael Be'aliyah, and the Ministries of National Infrastructure and Tourism to Avigdor Liberman and Rechavam Ze'evi of the Yisrael Beitainu–National Union alliance. In just three weeks' time, he had put together a 68-seat coalition. The National Religious Party, Gesher, and the Center Party, left out of the coalition, were ready and willing to negotiate.

Sharon nominated Silvan Shalom of the Likud as minister of finance and Limor Livnat and Reuven Rivlin, also of the Likud, as ministers of education and communications. To David Levy, his old ally, who had played a leading role in ousting Barak, he offered a minor position in government as a minister without portfolio. Offended, Levy refused.

Netanyahu's camp complained that Sharon had not kept his campaign promise to appoint Netanyahu to a ministerial post.

Sharon called Netanyahu overseas and asked outright if he would like to serve as a minister in his government, but the former prime minister realized that the offer was empty—everything of worth had already been distributed. The facetious offer was the first of a series of moves meant to marginalize Sharon's last real threat.

Even before the new government was officially sworn in, Sharon passed two laws through the Knesset, as he had promised on the campaign trail: The first changed the voting law back to its original form, in which citizens voted only once, for a party, and the second effectively extended the ultra-Orthodox exemption from army service.

On March 7, 2001, the government was sworn in and the prime minister recited the standard oath: "I, Ariel Sharon, son to Samuel and Devora, may their memory be blessed, hereby commit to be faithful to the State of Israel and its laws and to faithfully fulfill the decisions of the Knesset as prime minister."

In his first speech, Sharon reiterated his commitment to peace and the need for "painful concessions," which, however, would come slowly—once the Palestinians had stopped dealing in terror. "The verdict, for both our peoples, is to live together, side by side, on the same sliver of land," he said. "We have no power to change that reality, but we can stray from the path of blood."

After a short changing-of-the-guard ceremony with Barak, Sharon moved into the Prime Minister's Office. Officially, Uri Shani was the prime minister's chief of staff, but Omri Sharon, who, as an immediate family member, could not be officially employed, handled a great deal of his father's business.

The international press greeted Sharon's election with alarm. Newspapers across Europe and parts of America expressed concern for the future of the Middle East now that a man of such extreme opinions had been elected to lead Israel. The French paper *Libération* ran a headline that read "Sharon the Terrible" over a caricature of him, as a butcher, selling Palestinian flesh. Sharon sent envoys to capitals all over the world, but abroad, his image had not changed an iota since Lebanon. He was seen as forceful, militaristic, and extremist.

Sharon took office at around the same time as the new Ameri-

can president, George W. Bush. Sharon's two primary goals were
to establish a strong relationship with Bush and to stop the latest
wave of terror.

Arafat was one of the first leaders to congratulate Sharon. In
fact, he congratulated him twice, first on the victory and again on
the birth of his twin grandsons. Arafat asked Sharon to loosen the
Israeli closure around the territories and to release the Palestinian
workers' tax money. Sharon said both of those conditions would be
met when the terror stopped. Two days later, an Israeli was shot
while driving; three days after that, eight people were killed by a
Palestinian truck driver; two weeks after that, a suicide bomber
blew himself up on the way to the Netanya central bus station,
killing three more civilians. To Sharon, Arafat was sending a message of his own.

Arafat denied responsibility. Sharon reiterated that he would
not negotiate under fire. The two locked horns. From that first
telephone call until Arafat's death in a French hospital during
Sharon's second term, they never met. Sharon did, however, send
Omri to deliver and receive messages—a tactic that drew a howl of
criticism from concerned Israelis who felt that Sharon had learned
too much from Israel's despotic neighboring regimes, where only
blood could be trusted.

Sharon asked his staff not to mark his seventy-third birthday.
Without Lily, he had no desire to celebrate. Nonetheless, on February 26, 2001, they sent him a large bouquet. (He didn't like it,
and they did not continue the custom.) On March 14, 2001, one
year after Lily's death, family and friends gathered atop Windflower Hill. A rough stone monument was unveiled. It said simply
"Lily Sharon."

Later that month Sharon flew to Washington for his first official meeting with President George W. Bush. He prepared with
care, certain that the nature of their relationship would have lasting implications on his tenure as prime minister. Sharon covertly
sent Arie Ganger to Capitol Hill with a clear message: He had mel-
lowed, and was willing to make territorial concessions. The message was received with skepticism.

Arafat, though, was already perceived as the real villain in the

Israeli-Palestinian conflict. The second intifada had been raging for six months, and he was widely seen as the man fanning the flames. On arrival in Washington, Sharon spread the word that he was willing to make territorial compromises in order to move the peace process forward. He had also decided to leave requests for monetary aid aside during this first meeting. His main goal was to establish a friendship with Bush, who was close to him ideologically. Sharon came with only one condition: No negotiation under fire. The two hit it off.

A new wave of terror attacks struck Israel. The far-right members of Sharon's government, led by Avigdor Liberman and Rechavam Ze'evi, called for a forceful response. In late March, Shalhevet Pas, a ten-month-old infant, was shot and killed by a Palestinian sniper in Hebron. In response, Ze'evi suggested blowing up Arafat's home. The American administration urged restraint.

Although the attacks continued virtually unabated through mid-April, Sharon kept his word to the president and maintained a position of restraint. He issued orders to the IDF to fire only when fired upon. Although the Palestinian uprising continued, Sharon authorized Israeli officials to hold talks with midlevel Palestinian diplomats, and he sent Omri, who held dovish views compared with those of his father, to talk to Arafat. Sharon claimed that this contact with the Palestinians did not qualify as negotiations, but rather were solely about a cease-fire. No one on the right believed him.

In mid-April 2001, Palestinian militants fired mortar shells at Sderot, a city close to Gaza and Sycamore Ranch. Sharon sent the IDF into Gaza, violating Palestinian autonomy in what was called Area A. Intense American pressure forced him to recall the troops.

Although terror ran rampant during his first one hundred days in office, by May 2001, 70 percent of Israelis polled viewed Sharon as reliable; 65 percent thought he handled the uprising in the territories well or very well. For the first time since 1973, Sharon enjoyed widespread public support. The Kadosh family in Haifa named their twins, a boy and a girl born in May 2001, Ariel and Sharon.

A large part of Sharon's high approval rating can be attributed to the "targeted killings" of Palestinian terrorist leaders. Although Peres had coined the phrase and Barak had institutionalized the policy, Sharon fashioned it into Israel's most potent weapon against terrorism.

Sharon took care to maintain his 2.7 on the Finkelstein scale. In May 2001, he authorized Peres to open a back channel with the Palestinians, but simultaneously declared that he would never withdraw from the territories. Arafat continued to promote violence in the territories, enabling Sharon to dance between the raindrops and keep everyone happy without truly lifting a finger on the political front.

The Mitchell Report, based on an investigation headed by former U.S. senator George Mitchell into the causes of the second intifada, was released in May. Among other things, Mitchell, who had successfully served as chairman of the peace negotiations in Northern Ireland, examined Sharon's role in inciting violence when he visited the Temple Mount. Sharon had criticized Barak for allowing the foreign commission to operate in Israel and judge its affairs, calling it surrender. But in the end he benefited from the report. Mitchell found that Sharon's visit angered Palestinians but was not, as Arafat had claimed, the primary cause for violence across the territories.

The Mitchell Report recommended that both sides announce an end to violence and pledge their willingness to abide by previously signed agreements, and, later, to work to build mutual trust: the Palestinians by jailing terrorists and preventing attacks, and the Israelis by scaling back their responses to nonviolent protests, ending the closures of Palestinian cities, and releasing the tax money owed to the Palestinian Authority.

For Sharon, the report was both bad and good news. Mitchell concluded that all settlement activity, including expansion for natural growth, had to cease, but that peace talks should resume only after the first two stages of recommendations had been met.

Immediately after the report's release, Sharon unilaterally declared an Israeli cease-fire, but Arafat refused to call unambiguously for an end to terrorism. On June 3, 2001, a suicide bomber blew himself up next to a line of teenagers waiting to get in to a nightclub near Dolphinarium Beach in Tel Aviv, killing twenty-one people. For the first time since he took office, right-wing protesters, angered by Sharon's perceived restraint, took to the streets. They rallied under a banner that read "Let the IDF Win"—a slogan Sharon had used during his campaign against Barak.

The American administration, recognizing Sharon's difficult position, stepped up pressure on both sides to reach an agreement. Bush sent CIA director George Tenet to Israel to draft an immediate cease-fire plan. Both sides signed the Tenet Agreement, but the attacks continued. Twenty-four hours after the IDF removed the hermetic seal around Palestinian cities, hostilities flared up again. In June, twenty-nine Israeli civilians were killed. Israel could not continue to abide by a policy of restraint.

At the end of the month, Sharon visited Washington again. Sharon turned to his maps, spreading them out like an old general and presenting the American president with his plan: a long-term interim agreement under which Israel would maintain control of greater Jerusalem and the Jordan Valley while holding certain "security zones" in the West Bank. This time, Bush gave him the cold shoulder. They disagreed over Sharon's overriding condition, which he repeated incessantly: No talks until Arafat stopped the terror.

Bush wanted Sharon to renounce his policy of targeted assassinations. He suggested that Sharon accept a two-week period of quiet as evidence of Arafat's goodwill. Sharon wanted six. Back in Israel, Sharon sent Omri to meet with Arafat again. The procedure was always the same: Sharon wrote out detailed instructions on a pad of paper; Omri reported these to Arafat verbatim. This time Omri relayed that Israel would not launch a full-scale attack against the Palestinian Authority. Frustrated that he was meeting only the messenger, Arafat told reporters that Omri was just a genetic improvement on his father—a typically enigmatic Arafatism.

The Likud's dominant right-wing camp called for the central committee to convene and decide on political guidelines for Sharon. Netanyahu had called for legislation that would nullify the Oslo Accords and had criticized the policy of restraint. Sharon said the policy would remain in place, as would the targeted killings. Sharon, pressured by Netanyahu, issued a direct threat—Israel, he noted, was fully capable of smashing the Palestinian Authority.

On July 22, the central committee members welcomed Netanyahu like a returning king. His fiery speech criticizing Sharon's policy of restraint drew loud applause. Sharon was greeted by a hostile crowd that interrupted his speech repeatedly, many of them shouting "Resign!"

In early August, a suicide bomber—explosives-laden guitar case in hand—blew himself up at a Sbarro's pizza place in downtown Jerusalem, killing fifteen civilians. The Schijveschuurder family lost both parents and their three oldest siblings. The attack shocked the nation and further energized the right. Arafat condemned the attack, but in the same breath added that Sharon was responsible because it was he who had not adhered to the Mitchell Report's recommendations. In response to the attack, Sharon sent the IDF into Jenin, the city the terrorists had set out from, and took over the Orient House, the Palestinian Authority's diplomatic center in east Jerusalem.

Sharon announced that the takeover of the Orient House was permanent. European officials had long frequented the Old City building and, Sharon felt, thereby undermined Israel's claims to sovereignty over the entire city. Peres, close to many European Union officials, announced that the takeover was temporary. The strife between the two grew when Sharon refused to allow Peres to meet with Arafat for cease-fire negotiations. Peres threatened to pull out of the government, thus destabilizing the coalition. The two old men of Israeli politics met over lunch at the prime minister's office and reached a compromise: Peres could talk with Palestinian officials, but not with Arafat.

Later that same month, Peres opposed Sharon's move to send troops into the Palestinian town of Beit Jallah, just south of Jerusalem, after weeks of incessant sniper fire on Gilo. Ben-Eliezer, also of Labor, supported the invasion. In late August, Israel assassinated Abu Ali Mustafa, a Popular Front for the Liberation of Palestine (PFLP) leader. It marked an escalation; until then, Israel had targeted only terrorist operatives, not their bosses. Peres, who had opposed the assassination of Mustafa, listened to the news of the killing over the radio, furious.

In early September, Israelis prepared for Rosh Hashanah with little fanfare. Day-to-day-life had become unbearable. Tourists and businesspeople stayed away from the country. Hotels were empty, the real estate market slumped, and unemployment soared. The economy was limping along.

By early September 2001, Sharon had not yet made up his mind how to proceed. Netanyahu pushed for a military solution, while Peres and the Americans called for negotiations. On September 11, Muslim terrorists flew two planes into the World Trade Center's twin towers and a third into the Pentagon, while a fourth was brought down by its passengers in a Pennsylvania field en route to another target. The political landscape of the Middle East was about to be shuffled like a deck of cards.

CHAPTER 47

9/11

NEWS OF THE ATTACKS REACHED SHARON DURING A CABINET MEETing. Uri Shani pulled him aside and walked him back to the Prime Minister's Office, where they watched events unfold. Suddenly two Shabak agents entered and asked the prime minister to accompany them to a secret base for safety. Sharon refused.

After the brutal al-Qaeda attacks, the American administration was intent on establishing a coalition to fight its "war on terror." Saudi Arabia and Egypt, potential allies, demanded that Bush force Israel's hand on the Palestinian problem. The administration pressured Sharon to proceed with negotiations. Secretary of State Colin Powell pushed for Peres to meet with Arafat.

Sharon complained to Powell that it was absurd to allow Arafat, a man who had made a living from terrorism, to benefit from the terror attacks in America. Aware, however, that the giant had been roused from its slumber and was in no mood to be toyed with, Sharon submitted to the American demands. At home, he was on shaky ground. The intifada churned on. Each week the country counted its fallen. The gap between the rich and poor continued to grow. Increasingly, the public began to feel that Sharon had no solutions.

Bush's pressure bore fruit on September 23, 2001, when Sharon became the first Likud leader in history to promote the idea of a Palestinian state west of the Jordan River. In his historic speech at Latrun, Sharon said, "Israel wants to give the Palestinians what no else ever has: the opportunity to establish a state of their own."

The message conflicted with the Likud charter, which explicitly opposed a Palestinian state. A new movement within the party

called for Sharon's ouster from the Likud. Many central committee members viewed the Latrun speech as a betrayal.

In the speech's aftermath, Sharon began to lose the backing of
the Likud Central Committee. The speech had etched a fault line
between the party and its leader, one that would grow with time.
Sharon's move toward the center could no longer be seen as a
gimmick.

When addressing the issue of the growing rift within his party,
Sharon repeatedly contended that it was he, rather than the party
leadership, that had been entrusted with serving the people.
Sharon was, in fact returning to his political roots: Only after the
Lebanon War, when he lost public support, was he forced to use
the party bureaucracy as leverage against Shamir and Netanyahu.
As prime minister, he divorced himself from party politics and be-
came, once again, the darling of the public.

Under pressure from Colin Powell, Sharon, recognizing the
need to appease potential allies and allow America to form a coalition for the invasion of Afghanistan, allowed Peres to meet with
Arafat. After the meeting, he complained that Peres, rather than
helping him isolate Arafat in the post-9/11 world, had bestowed legitimacy on the Palestinian leader by rushing to meet him.

Until the attacks on America, President Bush had kept his
focus far from the intractable problems of the Middle East. Now
that they had been thrust to the center of his agenda, Sharon
hoped Bush would take a tough stand against Arafat and the Palestinian Authority, which he saw as an organization that supported
terrorism. Instead, on October 2, 2001, Bush announced his support for a Palestinian state.

Several days earlier, on September 30, riots marking the anniversary of the al-Aqsa intifada had spread through the territories,
resulting in dozens of exchanges of fire, ten wounded Israelis, and
eleven dead Palestinians. On October 4, two days after Bush's remarks about the need for a Palestinian state, Sharon leveled the
harshest criticisms any Israeli prime minister has ever made to an
American president: "I call on all Western democracies, and first
and foremost the leader of the free world, the United States," he
said, "not to repeat the terrible mistake of 1938 when the enlight-

ened democracies of Europe decided to sacrifice Czechoslovakia
for a temporary solution. Do not try to placate the Arabs at our expense." Then he issued a veiled threat: "The Palestinians have hindered all of our attempts to achieve a cease-fire . . . we will use all
measures necessary to provide security for the people of Israel.
From today forth, we will count only on ourselves."

The day after the "Czechoslovakia speech," two terrorists
opened fire indiscriminately in Afula's central bus station, killing
three civilians. The deaths didn't dampen the American administration's rage at Sharon, who had likened Bush to Neville Cham-
berlain. Sharon was forced to apologize but he never recanted his
statement.

On October 7, 2001, Bush called Sharon to inform him that
the war in Afghanistan would begin in half an hour. Although the
timing of his call may have reflected his displeasure, the two spoke
at length without mentioning Sharon's speech. The administration, concerned with its coalition in Afghanistan, kept up the pressure on Sharon to comply with the recommendations of the
Mitchell Report.

Sharon was under domestic fire, too. American demands to
allow Peres to negotiate had opened Sharon to attacks from the
right, a slot Netanyahu was all too happy to fill. Suddenly Netanyahu's popularity soared. Right-wing parties were threatening to
overthrow the unity government.

On October 13, 2001, Bush said that "the world should cheer"
the way Arafat had tamped down the al-Qaeda support rallies in
the territories. (Arafat, it seemed, had learned at least one of the
lessons of the first Gulf War: Palestinians dancing on their roofs to
the tune of Saddam's falling missiles had done his people no good
internationally.) That same day, the leaders of the National Union
and Yisrael Beitainu parties, Rechavam Ze'evi and Avigdor Liberman, demanded that Sharon prevent Peres from negotiating with
Arafat. They further announced that they would abstain from attending cabinet meetings until the policy of restraint had been
reevaluated. Sharon refused to bend to their demands, saying that
the unity government was of national importance. The two resigned.

Their letters of resignation were to take effect within forty-eight hours. Before that happened, Rechavam Ze'evi, returning to his room from the breakfast buffet at the Hyatt Hotel in Jerusalem, was gunned down. The PFLP killers fled to the autonomous Palestinian Authority areas. The PFLP explained that the assassination had come in response to the IDF's killing of Abu Ali Mustafa.

Sharon, a friend of Ze'evi's for decades, was told of his death as he was about to begin a defense cabinet meeting. He asked Peres and Ben-Eliezer to join him in a moment of silence. After the meeting, he persuaded Liberman to rescind his letter of resignation in light of the tragic circumstances. Paradoxically, Ze'evi's death had given breathing room to the government he had sought to bring down.

The right reacted strongly to Ze'evi's murder. Netanyahu called for all-out war against the Palestinian Authority and the terror organizations operating under its auspices, and for the exile or death of Yasser Arafat. Tens of thousands of activists returned to Zion Square to honor Ze'evi and protest Sharon's policies. All of the speakers called on Sharon to dethrone Arafat and crush the PA.

The killing of a government minister seemed to demand a response. Sharon issued Arafat an ultimatum: Hand over the wanted men, or we will consider the PA a terrorist entity and topple it. Arafat refused to hand over the killers. Sharon sent troops into the Palestinian cities of Jenin, Nablus, Bethlehem, Qalqilya, Tulkarm, and Ramallah.

Sharon's attempts to present Arafat as "the Osama bin Laden of the Middle East," though, fell on deaf ears. Bush, afraid the coalition in Afghanistan would collapse if America condoned the Israeli invasion, demanded that Israel leave the Palestinian cities immediately.

In November 2001, Sharon was instructed to pull IDF troops out of the cities before his scheduled visit to Washington. Left with little wiggle room, he delayed the visit. Officially, "security reasons" prevented him from leaving the country.

Beyond its demand to withdraw from the Palestinian cities, the American administration also insisted that Sharon rescind his condition of a seven-day stretch of terror-free silence before implementing the recommendations of the Mitchell Report. Powell sent a special envoy to the Middle East, Marine general (ret.) Anthony Zinni. Sharon took Zinni, a four-star former U.S. CENTCOM commander in the Middle East, on his usual helicopter tour of the region—pointing out Israel's slender, vulnerable waist and the topographic dominance of the Golan Heights.

In December, Sharon set out for Washington for what was shaping up to be a harsh meeting with Bush. The American administration wanted Sharon to implement the Mitchell recommendations immediately and to move in the direction of final status negotiations—forcing his hand on Jerusalem, settlements, and territorial concessions to the Palestinians. Word from Washington was that the people around the president were talking about a Palestinian state that would include almost all of the West Bank and Gaza. Certain heavily settled areas would be swapped for other unsettled lands on the other side of the Green Line.

Arafat stopped the initiative in its tracks. Israel was hit with four deadly terror attacks during the days leading up to the meeting. Within a week, thirty-three Israeli civilians had been killed—teenagers on a Saturday night in Jerusalem and citizens on a bus the following afternoon in Haifa. Bush had no choice but to pay condolences and share in the grief of the visiting prime minister. He did not restrict Sharon in his response to the attacks. Arafat, Zinni reported, had a credibility problem.

That week was a turning point in the relationship between Bush and Sharon. Sharon's restraint, especially during the war in Afghanistan, along with a strong anti-Arafat campaign in Washington, Sharon's attempts to find favor in Bush's eyes ("Czechoslovakia speech" notwithstanding), and the sudden vulnerability of Americans to attack after 9/11, all led Bush to reassess his position. His stance on Arafat began to change. In a meeting with Jewish Republican contributors shortly after Sharon left the capital, the president said that if he were in Sharon's shoes, he would act exactly as Sharon had.

In mid-December, a Palestinian terrorist opened fire on a civilian bus near the settlement of Emanuel, killing ten people. This time Bush gave Sharon the green light to respond with overwhelming force. His only condition was that Israel spare Arafat's life.

The president's demand may well have been the only thing that kept Arafat alive. Sharon had despised Arafat since Beirut in 1982 and was eager to kill him or, at the very least, see him exiled. Aware of Sharon's sentiments, Bush forced him to give his word that he would not harm or exile the Palestinian leader. After terror attacks, Sharon would often complain that he had made a mistake when he made the promise.

Instead, Israel confined Arafat to Ramallah's city limits. According to Sharon's new policy, Arafat was no longer "relevant" to the peace process. Rather than complain of his hypocrisy in supporting both terrorism and peace, Israel simply ignored the Palestinian leader and urged others to follow suit.

In January 2002, Israeli naval commandos captured the *Karin A* on its way to Gaza. Hidden beneath bags of rice, the boat carried a wide array of weapons, including surface-to-air missiles, explosives, and other implements of the terrorist trade. Arafat categorically denied any knowledge of the arms shipment. Israel showed several Western leaders proof to the contrary.

On January 14, 2002, Sharon spoke at the annual foreign correspondents' meeting:

> I'll be seventy-four in a few weeks. I have no other political ambitions in life. I've done everything; all I want is to achieve a political arrangement that will lead to peace with the Palestinians and the Arab world. That is the last thing I want to do in my life. After that I'll go back to the ranch and ride horses and herd sheep. Right now the Palestinians are wasting precious time.

Sharon also discussed his relationship with Arafat: "I have no personal grudge against him. I'm too busy to waste my time on that type of thing. Arafat embraced a terror strategy before I was elected prime minister." Sharon said Arafat would not be allowed to leave Ramallah until he arrested Ze'evi's killers and those responsible for the *Karin A*.

That same day, Sharon authorized the assassination of Ra'ad Karmi, whom Israel held responsible for a series of attacks that had originated in Tulkarm. Karmi, a Fatah man, was considered a Palestinian national hero. After his death, all of the Palestinian terrorist groups vowed as one to respond. The subsequent wave of attacks did not push Sharon off course. He still planned to topple Arafat's regime and begin negotiations with his hopefully more moderate replacement, who would denounce terrorism.

Sharon felt that Arafat's confinement was beginning to pay off. His people in positions of power in Hebron, Nablus, Jenin, and Gaza were demoralized, their funds depleted. Sharon explained his rationale to *Maariv* in 2002: "He opens the window in Ramallah, sees tanks, and knows there's nowhere for him to go. He's dying to travel, to fly; he's getting sick just from sitting in his cell." Sharon often referred to him as "the dog."

In February 2002, Sharon met Bush again and asked the American president to call publicly for Arafat's removal from office and to close the Washington offices of the PLO. Bush made clear that both options were beyond the pale; instead, he expressed displeasure at the continued closures in the territories and support for Peres's talks with Abu Ala, Arafat's right-hand man.

Bush asked that Israel keep a low profile while America formed a coalition against Iraq. Although the mood was positive, Bush also told Sharon that the siege of Arafat was only contributing to his appeal in Europe and across the Middle East, as Arafat remained the sole representative of the Palestinian people. Bush's stance took Sharon back to square one. His attempts to strip Arafat of all legitimacy had failed.

Sharon stopped off in New York and fell ill with the flu. He had resisted his doctors' advice consistently ever since taking office. Although they cautioned him to rest, Sharon was always at his desk by 6 A.M. and hardly ever in bed before midnight. Once he got back to Israel, he took another day off. He secluded himself in his tower study, just as he had done almost seventy years before in the barn in Kfar Malal, and considered his position.

Along with tricky allies and enemies, Netanyahu was also at his heels. Ever since the Latrun speech, Sharon had felt that the former prime minister was on a campaign to replace him. In February, Omri Sharon and Uri Shani listened in on a direct cell phone feed from one of their supporters as Netanyahu criticized Sharon in front of a crowd of two thousand Likud members. His allies,

Likud MKs, hailed Netanyahu as "the once and future prime minister." Moreover, Sharon had begun to realize that while 9/11 was a common tragedy to all like-minded nations, and may have cruelly elucidated some of the points Israeli leaders had been making in vain for decades, it was not going to solve his country's problems. On the contrary, Israel, that small thorn in the side of the Middle East, now demanded the world's attention.

CHAPTER 48

Defensive Shield

AFTER THE ASSASSINATION OF RA'AD KARMI, THE TERROR ATTACKS came in rapid succession. In February 2002, twenty-eight civilians were killed; March was worse—one hundred dead. The public was increasingly feeling that Sharon had no answers. Stickers ridiculing his campaign slogan—"Love the Peace, Digging the Security"—began to crop up in public. Netanyahu continued to rise in the polls. Toward the end of February, Sharon sent the IDF into the refugee camps of Jenin and Nablus—for the first time since the Oslo Accords in 1994.

In early March 2002, the IDF laid siege to Tulkarm. "It's all clear now," Sharon said. "It's either us or them." The operation in the northern West Bank did not quiet Sharon's detractors. Eighty thousand protesters gathered in Rabin Square in Tel Aviv and called on the prime minister to crush the Palestinian Authority.

At his father's behest, Omri Sharon called Arafat's chief of staff and delivered a succinct message: If the terror didn't stop, Ramallah was next. On March 11, the IDF invaded. Under pressure from Bush, Sharon was forced to allow Arafat freedom of movement. He complained that the American president didn't see eye to eye with him on the matter of Arafat.

In March 2002, Sharon's approval rating dropped to 50 percent, 25 points below the rating he had enjoyed for most of his first year in office. On March 14, Avigdor Liberman finally left the government. Sharon, he said, wasn't doing enough in the fight against terror. (The National Religious Party took his party's place in the coalition.)

Passover came at the end of a deadly month. On March 27, Sharon's seder was interrupted by bad news: A suicide bomber had blown himself up during a holiday seder at the Park Hotel in Netanya. Thirty Israelis were dead. For Sharon, the time of restraint was over.

At the following day's cabinet meeting, Sharon wanted to pass a motion to exile Arafat and declare the Palestinian Authority a terrorist entity. All Likud ministers were in favor, all from Labor opposed. The directors of both the Mossad and the Shabak felt exile would be a mistake. Avi Dichter, the well-spoken head of the Shabak who had grown close to Sharon, persuaded the prime minister that Arafat abroad would inflict far more harm than Arafat at home, imprisoned in his office. Sharon tightened the siege around Arafat's compound and labeled him an enemy, but left him in place.

On March 28, twenty-four hours after the terror attack in the Park Hotel, the Cabinet authorized Operation Defensive Shield. For the first time since the Lebanon War, Israel instituted an emergency call-up of the reserves. Thousands picked up their phones and heard an automated voice summon them to what seemed a doomsday scenario: a massive invasion of all of the West Bank's major cities and refugee camps.

The goals of Operation Defensive Shield were to flush out the terrorists and apprehend them, particularly the higher-ranking officials; to find and confiscate arms and explosives; and to locate and destroy factories used to create explosives and other implements of terror. The orders were to kill anyone with a weapon, but to use utmost caution with civilians.

On the morning of March 29, the IDF invaded Ramallah and surrounded Arafat's headquarters, the Muqata, where he lived and worked. From that moment on he lived under Israeli siege. The Paratroop Brigade invaded Nablus, advancing from all sides through the narrow streets of the ancient city. Amazingly, this most defiant and difficult stronghold fell within days. Seventy Palestinian combatants were killed.

Jenin proved more difficult. As in Nablus, the militants in Jenin had laid dozens of trip wires in the alleyways, preventing the soldiers from progressing door to door. Not willing to launch an air assault, the IDF ordered its soldiers to drill holes through the walls in order to move forward. On April 9, the seventh day of the operation, a platoon of reservists were trapped in an ambush; fourteen of them were killed.

Taking no more chances, the IDF moved into the city with armored bulldozers and rammed through the last bastion of resistance in the camp. Realizing that the battle had been lost, hundreds of wanted men came out of the densely populated refugee camp and surrendered.

The IDF had sealed the area, and journalists were unable to gain firsthand access. Palestinian sources claimed there had been a massacre of monumental proportions—Sabra and Shatilla revisited. Many respectable branches of the international news media parroted what they had heard, ignoring official Israeli denials.

Under international pressure, U.N. secretary general Kofi Annan assembled a commission of inquiry. Sharon resisted the initiative, saying Israel would not stand trial. Under American pressure, he was forced to submit to the commission and allow them access to Jenin. The final report negated all charges of a massacre: fifty-six Palestinians had been killed, twenty-seven of whom were armed, along with twenty-three Israeli soldiers.

Amnesty International also cleared Israel of charges of a massacre, but faulted the IDF for using overwhelming force, ruining neighborhoods with bulldozers, and preventing civilians from receiving medical care. The IDF pointed out that it had refrained from an aerial bombing campaign and risked its soldiers' lives in order to avoid civilian deaths.

The results of Operation Defensive Shield were favorable for Sharon. The gunfire aimed at the town of Gilo had stopped; impressive amounts of ammunition and arms had been seized; the symbol of Arafat's rule, the Muqata, was surrounded by tanks; dozens of terrorists and wanted men had been arrested; the IDF was free to move in and out of Area A; and terror attacks, at last, subsided.

Defensive Shield also reaped a diplomatic victory: Palestinian Authority papers seized by IDF troops revealed Arafat's direct involvement in terror attacks. Sharon later used that proof to convince Bush that Arafat was not a partner for peace, and that as someone who had not renounced terrorism, he needed to be physically and diplomatically isolated.

Operation Defensive Shield, despite thirty-four fallen Israeli soldiers, was perceived as an unprecedented victory against terrorism. Sharon did not let up. He initiated another IDF operation weeks later and ordered the Shabak to step up its "targeted killings."

On June 23, 2002, the IAF, acting on solid intelligence, dropped a one-ton bomb on the home of Salah Shehadeh, the most wanted man in Hamas at the time. The IDF claims to have allowed Shehadeh to slip through their fingers many times because of the risk of civilian casualties. The bomb, dropped in a densely populated area, killed Shehadeh, his wife, his son, and thirteen other civilians, provoking international condemnation. Sharon remained convinced of the justness of the assassination policy.

Fifteen wanted men were holed up in Arafat's quarters in Ramallah, including those accused of killing Rechavam Ze'evi. Three Israeli tanks had their cannons trained on Arafat's offices. Sharon allowed for the provision of food, water, and electricity. Beyond that, nothing; No one could come or leave. His home had been rendered a prison.

Immediately after the siege on the Muqata, American officials warned Israel not to attempt a charge on the offices in order to arrest Ze'evi's killers. Sharon said he was willing to go to elections if that's what it took, but he would not relax the siege until the men had been turned in. The American administration facilitated a compromise whereby Arafat would turn over the killers to an American-British contingent, which would jail them in Jericho. In return, Israel would loosen the siege on the Muqata.

By now, Sharon had a 70 percent approval rating. Two-thirds of the country felt Defensive Shield had been warranted. In early May, Sharon met with Bush for the fifth time as prime minister. He laid out his plan for the president: a long interim agreement, during which the Palestinians would be given an independent state, whose borders he refrained from clearly defining, on condition that Arafat play no role in the negotiations or ever lead the fledgling state. He, Sharon insisted, had founded "an empire of terror and a corrupt regime."

The plan Sharon presented to Bush had three stages: a regional peace conference under the auspices of the American government; a rebuilding period for the Palestinian Authority under strict international supervision of their weapons and security services; and the beginning of negotiations for final status talks. Bush liked the plan, but demanded that the Israelis implement all three stages at once, in order to expedite the process. Sharon felt that the president's condition rendered the plan unfeasible. It could never be passed through the government and was untenable in terms of security.

Sharon returned to Israel days before the May 12, 2002, Likud Central Committee meeting, which he had been preparing for since the beginning of the year. Peres's staff had been saying that Sharon's decision to stray from the path of restraint had been dictated by Netanyahu's internal party maneuverings. The main point on the evening's agenda was Sharon's speech at Latrun and the issue of Palestinian statehood.

Sharon stopped off at Reuven Adler's office before the meeting to review his strategy against Netanyahu. The state of affairs in the central committee was clear to both of them: An overwhelming number of members, including many Sharon supporters, opposed the idea of a Palestinian state. Sharon invited Likud ministers and MKs to meet with him in the VIP room of the Mann Auditorium in Tel Aviv. Almost no one seemed to support his initiative for a state—all of them knew that the Likud Central Committee was against the idea, and the committee members were the ones who would rank the Likud members running for the Knesset at election time.

The meeting began, almost ceremonially, with a barrage of taunts and insults. Netanyahu spoke first. He attacked Sharon's policies and called on the central committee members to make their opposition to a Palestinian state clear to the prime minister. Sharon, speaking next, mentioned that it was Netanyahu who had shaken Arafat's hand and not he, and, unable to pass up another chance to snipe at Netanyahu, he noted that terrorism was fought with calmness and responsibility, not lectures and book tours. Sharon warned the committee members not to enforce limits on the public's elected officials.

A small cluster of people booed Sharon throughout the speech, pausing only to take up the chant "Bi-bi! Bi-bi!" Netanyahu got up and asked for quiet during Sharon's speech, but the cries of "Old man, go home!" only intensified. Sharon shouted over the jeers and asked the central committee to vote in favor of the leadership or against it, and to leave the issue of a Palestinian state for a later date.

According to Likud Party rules, a prime minister's motion must be voted on first. Tzachi Hanegbi sent the members out to take a confidential vote, telling them to consider Sharon's request first and then reassemble for a second vote on the matter of Palestinian statehood. The results of the first vote were stark: 60 percent of the Likud Central Committee members voted no confidence in the government.

"I respect all democratic decisions taken by the Likud Central Committee," Sharon said, "but I want to tell you tonight that I will continue to lead Israel with the same considerations that have guided me in the past—the security of the State of Israel and its citizens, and the common goal of true peace." As instructed by Adler and Omri, he left immediately, not wanting to be present for the certain defeat in the second vote.

Sharon left under a hail of boos and whistles. The entire affair had been broadcast on TV. Hanegbi then introduced Netanyahu's motion, which, if passed, would force Likud leaders to oppose the establishment of a Palestinian state. A sea of hands went into the air. Only five people voted against the measure.

It seemed that Netanyahu had scored a big victory against Sharon, but in essence he had merely served as the prime minister's foil. With Netanyahu now on the far right, the majority of the Israeli public supported Sharon. European and American leaders waited in line to congratulate him on his brave commitment to peace. For the first time, he was accepted by the leaders of the European Union. Netanyahu was portrayed as a small-minded politician who was concerned with scoring points with his party while Sharon was willing to fight valiantly for his principles. The defeat in Tel Aviv had in effect turned into Sharon's first major victory over Netanyahu.

At one in the morning, as he was being driven back to the ranch, Sharon called Arie Ganger and asked him to pass word to the White House that he had no intention of straying even the slightest bit from his commitments to the president. Pleased with himself, Sharon told Shimon Schiffer and Nahum Barnea of *Yedioth Ahronoth* that "they say I'm a lame duck and it's true I have been limping for fifty-four years, ever since I was injured at Latrun and then again when I was a battalion commander in the paratroopers. Lame, yes; duck, no."

Sharon stayed at the ranch the next day, resting while his associates worked on presenting Netanyahu to the voters as a meddlesome and overeager heir to the prime minister. Sharon left the ranch in the afternoon and arrived at the Knesset in time to attend the Likud meeting, where he announced that no one would dictate policy to him. As MK Yossi Sarid walked in to congratulate him on his stance, Sharon surveyed the chaos around the table. He smiled and turned his attention to the bowl of cornflakes in front of him.

CHAPTER 49

The Road Map

SHARON'S STRICT CHIEF OF STAFF, URI SHANI, MENDED HIS BOSS'S ways, putting an end to Sharon's lengthy phone conversations with friends. There was no time in his pressure-filled eighteen-hour days for idle chats and distractions. All incoming calls went through Shani. Without his authorization, nothing passed through to the prime minister. He also decided to exclude Sharon's old secretary from the staff. Sara Shama'a knew all of Sharon's cronies— with her in the office they'd always have access to the prime minister. Shani brought in Marit Danon, the formidable secretary to Prime Ministers Rabin, Peres, and Shamir.

Before Shani's arrival, the prime minister's office space had been accessible to drivers, secretaries, and aides from all floors of the building. Shani sealed it with glass walls. Each day at 6 A.M. Sharon would arrive at a quiet, sterile office and meet with Shani and several aides for a briefing on the issues of the day. Shani took his cues from George W. Bush's chief of staff, who ran an administration where timeliness and godliness were closely related.

Shani managed the office on a strict need-to-know basis, rarely informing Omri Sharon, his old friend, of developing matters. Omri, though, kept very much involved in politics. From the prime minister's residence, Omri handled party politics and embarked on a campaign to run for the Knesset, actively courting many Likud Central Committee members and frequently deciding which committee members would receive public sector appointments. For a while it seemed as though Shani was also planning a run for the Knesset. Despite his denials, the rumors fueled the rivalry between the two men. The prime minister believed that Shani was in fact preparing for a campaign run.

Under Shani, all of the prime minister's conversations were

recorded, and private meetings were prohibited. Either Shani or a political or military aide sat in on all of the prime minister's meetings and conversations. Having weathered the controversies over Qibiya and the Lebanon War, among others, Sharon adhered to Shani's terms religiously. When people are being taped, Sharon often said, they speak differently. The procedure allowed Shani to keep track of all conversations, tightening his hold on the prime minister.

The only facet of Sharon's behavior Shani couldn't control was his eating impulses. He overate in the prime minister's office just as he had during wartime. It was the only battle he admitted to losing.

Sharon's former secretary, Sara Shama'a, had been Lily's ally in her campaign to keep her husband reasonably healthy. The two of them ran a tight ship, supervising all he ate. They often had him on a diet of tomato juice, which, like everything else, he salted heavily.

At times, when his former secretary was not vigilant, Sharon would send an aide out to the street to pick up two falafel sandwiches, which the aide would smuggle in under his blazer. Sharon would ask his secretary not to disturb him for the next ten minutes. Watching Sharon eat falafel, his favorite food, was quite an experience. Visibly elated, he attacked the pita, splattering tahini everywhere.

At times, Sharon could grow agitated without the food he wanted. One time in Washington, just moments before a meeting with President Bush, he sent one of his aides out on a mission to find some quality salami. Only after he had cut it up and begun eating did he relax.

Days later, when they landed in Lod, Sharon began campaigning for falafel. Shani sent an aide to bring the boss a few sandwiches, but Sharon didn't want takeout. "Uri, I miss eating falafel standing up, in one of those shacks in Jerusalem's Bukharin neighborhood, pouring tahini and spices as necessary," he said. "Don't keep me from that pleasure." Shani knew that when Sharon set his mind on a certain food, there was simply no way to move forward until he'd gotten what he wanted.

The Shabak secret service agents opposed the idea, but the prime minister was adamant, and the chief of staff seemed willing to please him after a stressful yet successful trip to the United States. Sharon was taken in his armored car straight from the airport to the narrow streets of the old Bukharin area, where he ate two falafel sandwiches one after the other. Sharon chatted amiably with the salesperson, asking permission before using the spices and salads on the countertop. He was unaware that the rest of the customers were all in the employ of the Shabak.

During his campaign for prime minister, the press caught Shani whispering into Sharon's ear and speculated at length whether Shani was feeding him his lines. In truth, Sharon couldn't hear in one ear, and Shani, who kept the hearing loss a secret, told him not what to say, but what was being said. Once Sharon realized how the whispering was perceived, he decided to rely on notes, a system he maintained all of his days as prime minister.

Sharon often communicated in note form. Since his days as a young commander he had kept records of meetings and always had a notepad in his pocket. The system allowed him to put his acting skills to good use. One confidant recalls, "It could say that the meeting needs to end right away, or that the person opposite him had been badmouthing him, or that a military mission had failed. With Sharon's poker face it was impossible to know. He could read a note with terrible information about one of the people in the room and respond to it with 'Thank you, but I don't care for tea right now.' "

His favorite notes were the daily ones from Gilad about the news on the ranch—the livestock births, the new crops, the rainfall. One time, during a particularly heated discussion with David Levy, Sharon read a note and smiled broadly. Levy was sure it was just another twist in the plot, but in fact a calf had been born.

In late May 2002, Uri Shani quit as chief of staff. Tension with Omri and some of Sharon's other friends, along with the feeling that the prime minister no longer backed him without question, led him to the decision. As often with Sharon, the departing aide kept the dirty laundry in-house.

Dov Weisglass took over as chief of staff, changing the tone and operating procedure immediately. The easygoing Weisglass took little interest in the strict running of the office and far more in foreign affairs. Weeks later, Weisglass was handling matters of state.

Like Shani and other key aides and advisers, Weisglass was an old Sharon hand. But for Sharon's circle, he was a liberal. Although Omri Sharon also held political views that were considerably to the left of his father's, Weisglass lived in that world and acted as a bridge between the liberal media and judicial establishment and Sharon, a man they had long abhorred. Weisglass and Omri, friends and partners, reigned over the prime minister's office—a union many settlers would fault for what they came to call the "Disengagement disaster."

Weisglass accompanied Sharon on his next trip to Washington in June 2002. Shortly before departing, Sharon listed three terms for renewing the peace talks: replacing Arafat with new leadership, instituting reforms in the Palestinian Authority, and reaching long-term agreements prior to final status talks. Bush intended to launch an international peace conference. The Palestinian delegation would be headed by Arafat—an untenable position for Sharon.

The analysts who predicted Bush would compel Sharon to agree to his terms proved mistaken. Instead, the two agreed that Arafat, as leader of the Palestinian people, precluded any hope of a settlement. After twenty months of armed conflict with the Palestinians, Sharon, who more than any of his predecessors believed in the singular supremacy of the Israel-America alliance, succeeded in convincing the White House of his contention that Arafat was irrelevant to regional peace.

In June, Bush worked on a Middle East policy speech. Sharon, directing another antiterror operation in the West Bank, stayed in close contact with the administration, through official channels and otherwise. He sent the most sensitive messages through his friend Arie Ganger, who spoke directly with Vice President Dick Cheney, National Security Advisor Condoleezza Rice, and Secretary of State Colin Powell. Ganger wore shades and evaded journalists.

Sharon invested a great deal of effort in convincing Bush that

Arafat was no different from other terrormongers. He instructed Shabak director Avi Dichter and Mossad chief Efraim Halevy to produce concrete examples of Arafat's involvement in terror attacks. The intelligence agencies also provided examples of collaboration between Arafat and America's looming enemy, Saddam Hussein.

Arafat claimed to have had no knowledge of the *Karin A* arms boat; Sharon passed documents on to Washington that proved otherwise. Documents seized from the offices of Jibril Rajoub, the director of the Preventive Security Service in the West Bank, tied the Palestinian Authority to terror attacks. Days before a major presidential address, the Prime Minister's Office provided documentary proof that Arafat had paid $20,000 to the terrorists who carried out a shooting attack in Jerusalem's French Hill neighborhood earlier that week. The president's advisers argued that he would be hard pressed to fight terror and back an Arafat-led Palestinian state at the same time. Convinced, Bush gave up faith in Arafat.

On June 24 it became apparent that the direct line to Washington had paid off: Bush announced that the United States would support the Palestinian desire for statehood only after the Palestinians elected a leadership that did not support terror. On the flip side, he demanded that Israel draw its forces back to pre-September 2000 lines and stop all settlement building as outlined in the Mitchell Report; but the call to remove Arafat from the stage was an outright victory for Sharon.

There was, however, one line Sharon would rather not have heard. "The Israeli occupation," the president said, "that began in 1967 will be ended through a settlement negotiated between the parties, based on U.N. Resolutions 242 and 338, with Israeli withdrawal to secure and recognized borders." The meaning was clear: Israel would have to enter final status negotiations with 1967 borders as a given.

After a much-needed rest in August, during which he read war novels and hosted his Jerusalem staff at the ranch, Sharon confided in ranch forum member Eli Landau. The Arab-Israeli conflict, he said, would not end until the Arabs recognized the Jews' basic right to live in a sovereign state in their ancestral land. "Show me one other people that has been willing to concede land without losing in war. No one would do that. I managed to work out a plan with the Americans by which an agreement will be reached in stages. Why stages? Because each step is permanent. What you have given will never be returned."

According to Sharon, the terms he hammered out with the Americans were an agreement in stages; no negotiations under fire; PA reform; Arafat conceding control of the state security apparatus and state finances; PA security forces acting under American supervision; the tracing of all money donated to the PA to ensure it did not finance terrorism; and the complete cessation of anti-Israel incitement in the media and in schools. Only once those reforms had been put in place would Israel proceed with negotiations.

In September 2002, Saddam Hussein threatened to launch missile strikes at Israel if his country came under American attack. Sharon ordered the IDF Rear Command to produce millions of chemical and biological weapon protective kits and distribute them to the public.

As the American attack drew near, the pressure on Sharon to play ball and keep a low profile increased. On September 20, though, six civilians were killed by a suicide bomber on a Tel Aviv bus. Sharon tightened the siege around Arafat's quarters. Israeli Army troops flattened several buildings, including the adjacent convention building and the bridge that joined Arafat's compound to the rest of the government buildings. Arafat and the 250 people confined with him watched as Israeli soldiers walked over the rubble.

The IDF's proximity to Arafat, holed up in his third-floor bedroom, set off alarms in Washington. If Arafat were harmed, the plans in Iraq would potentially be shelved. American ambassador to Israel Dan Kurtzer visited Sharon at the ranch and expressed his concern. From TV footage, he said, it looked as though they might "drop the whole building on him." Sharon said that the terrorists who blew up the bus in Tel Aviv were responsible for the bad timing, but also promised not to harm Arafat.

Bush sent a stark message: Discontinue the siege and refrain from hindering our prewar plans. Sharon quickly sent Weisglass to Washington to soften the White House's stance. In a meeting with Rice, Weisglass was told that America would not stand for Israel's doing anything that hindered America's effort to draft support for the war.

The siege of Arafat made U.N. Security Council approval for a strike in Iraq difficult. The destruction of his offices and the PA government buildings returned Arafat to the headlines and, as in the past, made him a popular international cause. Israel seemed to be unduly oppressing the leader of a people. Sharon succumbed to American demands, but said the decision did not constitute surrender since he had ordered the tanks to withdraw only five hundred meters, leaving the siege intact.

In October, Sharon met with Bush again. The two agreed that the United States could use Israel's airspace and air force bases during the coming war. Bush pledged to destroy all Scud launching sites in western Iraq promptly and to provide Israel with Patriot surface-to-air missile defense batteries. Sharon promised to keep a low profile and to warn America in advance if Israel decided to attack Iraq.

Russia, China, and France, three of the seven permanent members of the U.N. Security Council, opposed a declaration of war with Iraq. Bush and British prime minister Tony Blair decided to wage war without U.N. approval, calling their hodgepodge of allies a "coalition of the willing." During the months leading up to the March 20, 2003, invasion, the American administration drafted a far-reaching plan to settle the Israeli-Palestinian conflict. The plan, associated with the American president, would grant him international legitimacy in his efforts to rectify the wrongs of the Middle East. The plan was called the Road Map.

According to the time schedule of the Road Map, by 2003 all terror attacks would stop, a list of reforms would be enacted within the PA, and Israel would freeze all settlement building; by 2004, the Palestinians would hold elections for prime minister, after which America would organize an international peace conference at which the issue of a Palestinian state would be decided; by June 2005, the two sides would hold talks along with other representative Arab states over final status agreements. The two thorniest problems would be solved there: Jerusalem, and the Palestinian refugees' right of return.

Once the Road Map was formally unveiled, Israel had to withdraw to September 28, 2000, lines, freeze all settlement construction, and ease restrictions on the three million Palestinian civilians who suffered from the collective punishment of closure.

As far as Sharon was concerned, the plan was rushed, and terribly dangerous for Israel. The timetable deviated sharply from his plan to proceed incrementally. Sharon, already very familiar with the operating procedure of the Oval Office, couldn't flat out refuse the president's plan, certainly not as America readied for war in Iraq. He said that Israel was willing to talk the plan over but that it could not agree to it all exactly as presented. After the war, and elections in America and in Israel, there would be time to toss this plan too in the trash bin of history, on top of all the other well-intentioned peace papers that had been floated down to this region.

CHAPTER 50

Recession

SHARON'S GREATEST LIABILITY AS PRIME MINISTER WAS, WITHOUT doubt, the economy. Polls taken during the summer of 2002 indicated that over 90 percent of Israelis felt that Sharon had failed in his handling of the country's economy, which had been in recession since the second intifada. Terrorism crushed the tourism market and scared off many potential investors. Unemployment had gone up to 11 percent, the shekel had gone down, and hundreds of businesses and factories had closed. From September 2001 to April 2002, the country's GDP decreased by 5 percent, a nominal value of 25 billion shekels.

The Sharon government was caught in a budgetary crisis. Operation Defensive Shield and subsequent IDF operations had added eight billion shekels to the planned annual budget. Sharon and his minister of finance, Silvan Shalom, declared "an emergency economic recovery plan."

Sharon realized an unchecked deficit could lead to double-digit inflation, high interest rates, a weakened stock exchange, soaring unemployment, and a lowering of Israel's credit rating. Professionals at the Bank of Israel assured Sharon that drastic measures were necessary. Sharon, no expert in economics, called the campaign an "economic war."

The goal of the economic plan was to cut government spending by six billion shekels and increase its tax revenue by three billion shekels. To attain those goals, the government had to freeze government salaries, levy a tax on stock profits, slash government subsidies to families with children, reduce social security payments by 4 percent, lower unemployment compensation, raise the rate of value-added tax, scale back tax breaks for those living in areas of national importance, and raise taxes on cigarettes and gas.

The proposed measures faced opposition from all across the political map. Although Sharon had authorized the measures in principle, he knew there'd be an uphill battle to implement them as scheduled on January 1, 2003. The first hurdle approached on May 20, 2002. Sharon needed his coalition partners, the ultra-Orthodox Shas Party, to vote in favor of the plan on its first call in the Knesset. But the seventeen-seat party opposed the measures that would scale back government benefits to their largely low-income constituents.

Sharon offered certain concessions but refused to tinker with the reduction in social security payments, the housing subsidies, the unemployment benefits, and, most importantly for Shas, the drastic cuts in government benefits for military-exempt families with children—a measure aimed to cut the soaring birthrates of the ultra-Orthodox and Arab populations. Sharon did not want a power struggle with the ultra-Orthodox, but he was willing to fire all the Shas ministers if they refused to fall into line on this issue. No one took his threats seriously. Shas had been successfully dictating its own terms in government for years; their weight in the coalition could force a prime minister out of office.

All seventeen Shas MKs voted against the bill, which was defeated 47–44. Several Labor MKs disappeared from the Knesset floor during the vote. Even Education Minister Limor Livnat of the Likud, whose ministry would have suffered serious budget cuts and been forced to fire scores of teachers, absented herself from the vote. Furious, Sharon huddled with his staff. It was clear to him that his leadership was being tested.

A few minutes later, Sharon walked out of the conference room and announced on live TV that he was firing all Shas ministers from the Cabinet. At once Sharon was transformed from a powerless leader unable to garner a simple majority in the Knesset to a brave and principled prime minister who stood up to the extortive demands of Shas and responded to necessity rather than courting popular favor. The resemblance to the Likud Central Committee vote was intentional.

Sharon drafted the termination letters that night. In high spirits, he repeatedly asked Government Secretary Gidon Saar, "Nu, did you send the letters out yet?" Stunned, Shas leaders tried to soften their demands and stave off Sharon's decree, but with popular support swelling, Sharon was suddenly unreachable.

Congratulatory cards, e-mails, faxes, and telegrams flowed into the Prime Minister's Office, and his approval rating took off. Paradoxically, his recent defeats made him more popular. Finally, the person in the Prime Minister's Office had shown some spine.

While Shas MKs openly declared their willingness to go to the polls, it was clear that they would be hard pressed to duplicate their success of the previous elections. The party's spiritual leader, Rabbi Ovadia Yossef, complained of Sharon's ingratitude and appealed to President Moshe Katsav to change Sharon's mind. But for the next forty-eight hours, even Katsav had a hard time reaching the prime minister.

Sharon, visibly delighted by the spectacle, reintroduced the bill. This time, Livnat and all Labor MKs voted in favor; Shas abstained, and the bill passed 64–25.

The director general of the Prime Minister's Office, Avigdor Yitzhaki, revealed the prime minister's thinking at a management seminar broadcast on Army Radio. Sharon fired the Shas ministers, Yitzhaki said, "for no other reason than to change the next day's headline. This country has a stock exchange and a foreign currency market and they were sensitive. . . . The purpose was to forestall any type of collapse. All we wanted to do was change the headline on the front page and we knew the headline would change only as a result of one thing—if the prime minister fired the Shas ministers. The fact that there was a successful political ploy behind that was just an outcome of the other issue."

Sharon was furious. His office released a clarification: "With all due respect to Yitzhaki's comments, the prime minister made the decision and showed leadership of the highest order. The fact is, the Shas ministers have been fired, and everything else is nonsense."

Yitzhaki's revelation could not have come as a surprise to anyone familiar with Sharon's methods of operation. He was Israel's king of spin. The voyage to the Temple Mount, the firing of the Shas ministers, and the timing of the Disengagement from Gaza announcement were all born of a need to manipulate a political reality.

In early June, after multiple promises to reform their ways, Sharon allowed Shas to rejoin the Cabinet. They promptly voted with the prime minister in support of his economic bill.

On August 13, 2002, Amram Mitzna, a retired major general and mayor of Haifa, announced his intention to run for head of the Labor Party. Ben-Eliezer, Mitzna said, was merely carrying out Sharon's orders. The policy of targeted killings and collective punishment against the Palestinians during Ben-Eliezer's tenure were blurring the line between Likud and Labor.

Needing a drastic move to try to even the race against Mitzna, Ben-Eliezer decided to pull out of government: The economic bill, he said, was far too generous with the settlers and too stingy with the needy. But Sharon, as in 2001, was more worried about Netanyahu than about Labor.

The Labor ministers turned in their resignation letters on October 30. Sharon could either call new elections or build a new, narrow coalition. Choosing the latter, Sharon had to face down the temptation to right what he still saw as a historic wrong and name himself defense minister. Realizing that Israel needed a full-time minister in the position, and not wanting to antagonize the public, he appointed the newly retired IDF chief of staff Shaul Mofaz. Ideologically in tune with Sharon, Mofaz, one of the fathers of Israel's assassination policy, had no political base, and, more important, as a rising Likud figure, he could keep Netanyahu at bay.

Netanyahu arrived at Sycamore Ranch with his friend and adviser Dr. Gabi Picard. Sharon jokingly asked if he had brought the doctor because he felt sick, and, still laughing, happily informed Netanyahu that his own health was better than ever. After the meeting, Netanyahu announced that he would join the government on the condition that Sharon change the date of elections. Proper governance, he argued, was impossible with such a narrow coalition. Sharon said elections would be held within ninety days, and he offered Netanyahu the post of foreign minister.

Many analysts interpreted Sharon's move as unwise: Netanyahu now had a podium on which he could stand during the prime ministerial race. Sharon, however, reasoned that with Netanyahu close and involved, his hands would be tied. He couldn't criticize a government of which he was a part. On November 6, 2002, Netanyahu walked into the gilded cage Sharon had crafted for him.

Sharon kept Netanyahu immersed in the realm of diplomacy and far from economics and the treasury. Unlike Sharon, Netanyahu brought to government a well-formed economic ideology. For years he had been calling for free-market ideals—demanding that Israel open its market to competition, utilize its advantage in the high-tech sector, and privatize the state monopolies that ran the telephone and electrical companies, the railways, and the ports, among other major utilities. One of his main calling cards was that he alone could lift Israel from its recession.

Netanyahu based his primary campaign on the economy. One million citizens lived beneath the poverty line, he said, and the standing prime minister knew next to nothing about the modern economy, nor had any semblance of a clue as to how to extract the country from its predicament. The American-minded Netanyahu promised to reduce government involvement and allow the invisible hand of the marketplace to reign. He spoke frequently of emulating the success of Ireland.

Sharon sought help in Washington, telling Bush that the intifada had taken a toll on Israel's economy. Bush issued a public call of faith in the Israeli market, to no avail. Israel was on the verge of seeing its credit rating drop, which would raise the interest rate on the country's loans. Sharon asked Bush to help Israel, as his father had done, by signing as a guarantor for a multibillion-dollar loan package that would help the country out of its recession.

Sharon figured that the loans would keep Netanyahu off his back and allow him to concentrate on his main battle, against terrorism. He assigned Weisglass to the case.

Sharon's staff, led by Finkelstein and including his two sons, Adler, Shani, and Arad, had marked three major dates, November 28, December 8, and January 28—the Likud primaries, the partywide internal elections, and the national elections.

Surprisingly, the dates dominating Sharon's mind were the ones in November and December; the premiership, he was sure, would be decided within the Likud. In the post-Oslo age, no one gave Mitzna, who had prevailed over Ben-Eliezer in the Labor primary, a fighting chance.

Sharon's campaign handlers again advised him to make no waves and coast to the finish line on his lead in the polls. Accordingly, he refused to participate in a televised debate against Netanyahu. He responded to all attacks by reading a prepared text that blandly refuted his opponent's claims and methodically introduced the twin issues of peace and security. In general, the campaign focused on Sharon rather than on the issues. He was presented as a responsible, judicious leader, the beloved elder of the tribe who had softened over the years and now captained the ship of state as it sailed through the straits to the promised land. The key phrases of the campaign were "national responsibility" and "sound judgment."

Sharon's campaign staff portrayed Netanyahu as a man willing to divide and conquer the Likud even at the cost of the party's continued rule. They stressed that the current structure, the triangle of Sharon as leader, Mofaz as security chief, and Netanyahu as financial wizard, was a strong lineup that was certain to crush anything Labor could present. Adler came up with the campaign slogan: "The People Want Sharon."

On the morning of the Likud primaries, the only question was the margin of victory. Sharon won handily, by 56 to 40 percent, but his success was equivocal. Netanyahu still drew widespread support within the party. His hopes of crushing his rival and wiping him off the political map had been dashed.

CHAPTER 51

Landslide Victory

SHARON'S CAMPAIGN WAS OFF TO A ROCKY START. AS USUAL, THE Likud primaries were (in keeping with the circus atmosphere of the fairgrounds where they were held) a carnival of backslapping and backstabbing. A host of new characters were vying for spots on the Likud list, including Ruchama Avraham, Binyamin Netanyahu's flashy former secretary; Inbal Gavrieli, the niece of a casino owner, who had been working as a waitress since dropping out of law school; Gila Gamliel, a fiery student leader from Ben-Gurion University; and, of course, Omri Sharon. The prime minister walked into Tel Aviv's teeming exhibition grounds and immediately caught sight of Ofakim mayor Yair Hazan's campaign workers. In an attempt to generate support for their boss, who was running against Omri, they wore T-shirts that read "Daddy, get me a job in the Knesset. —Omri."

Although Sharon and Netanyahu had saved for themselves the first and second spots on the party list, Sharon had little reason to gloat. At the end of the day, his people had performed miserably. Shaul Mofaz came in twelfth, Omri Sharon beat Hazan but still came in only twenty-seventh, and Ehud Olmert, Sharon's campaign manager, came in thirty-third.

Worse, the police soon began investigating Likud member Naomi Blumenthal, the deputy minister of infrastructure. She was suspected of having paid for central committee members' rooms at the City Tower Hotel in Ramat Gan before they went to vote at the primaries. Blumenthal exercised her right to silence when questioned.

Sharon sensed the public's growing disgust with the dirty politics of the Likud. He sent Blumenthal a letter: "A person whose credibility has been called into question while seeking public office not only loses the right to silence but has an absolute duty to reveal the circumstances surrounding their decisions," he wrote. If she clung to her right not to incriminate herself, Sharon said, he would fire her. She claimed the matter was under investigation and that her lawyers had advised her not to make public comments. On December 31, 2002, Sharon fired her and appointed a committee to investigate all claims of wrongdoing at the Likud primaries. Blumenthal fell victim to Sharon's political ambition. Within days of her public castigation, the polls showed that the Likud's slip in popularity had stopped.

Faced with a weak contender on the left—Mitzna had voiced the type of dovish views that guaranteed Sharon control of the political center—he seemed to be on cruise control. The economy hardly played a role in the campaign. Israeli voters were concerned primarily with security and the possibility of peace, and Sharon sat, kinglike, on the 2.7 spot Finkelstein had marked.

On January 7, 2003, three weeks before elections, *Haaretz* revealed that the police were investigating Gilad Sharon, who had reportedly received a $1.5 million loan from his father's old friend Cyril Kern. The police suspected that Sharon had used the money to pay back donors who had illegally contributed to his father's primary election campaign in 1999. The front-page revelation brought other instances of suspected malfeasance to the fore. At the time, the police were investigating not only the Cyril Kern loan, but also the Annex Research shell company, which had funneled money far beyond the legal limit into Sharon's 1999 campaign, and allegations of bribery and conflict of interest in what came to be known as the Greek Island affair.

News of the latest affair threatened to pull the rug out from under the Likud and Sharon. Mitzna came to life, gaining traction. For the first time, Sharon seemed rattled, sending his adviser Eyal Arad, along with Omri and Gilad's lawyer, Yoram Rabad, to deflect the growing criticism.

Eyal Arad agreed that many of the facts were as presented, but maintained that the prime minister was innocent of any wrongdoing. "What we're dealing with here," he said, "is a concerted effort by the prime minister's rivals to switch the government." Arad called on the police to investigate who had leaked the matter to the press, and charged the Labor Party with blowing the affair out of proportion. Rabad produced documents proving that the loan was for personal use and had nothing to do with bribery.

The performance was unconvincing. The news media demanded that the prime minister explain himself in his own words. With three investigations pending, the stench of impropriety began to spread. The Likud's enormous lead had nearly evaporated.

Sharon's campaign team was panic-stricken. As usual in tense moments, Sharon remained calm, weighed his options, and then seized the initiative. He realized he had to address the public directly or forgo his candidacy.

He canceled all meetings and went down to the ranch to work on his defense. Finkelstein, Adler, and Arad joined him, and the four played a no-holds-barred game of interrogation. During the simulation they decided that their main defense would be to accuse rivals of "setting up" Sharon in order to evict him from office.

After hours of role-playing, Sharon, who often wrote his own speeches, shut himself in his office until the small hours of the morning. At 8 P.M. sharp, Israel's news hour, Sharon began his speech, broadcast live from the Prime Minister's Office, with a rousing attack on Mitzna and the Labor Party.

"What we are dealing with here is a despicable false charge against myself and the Likud that has been woven together with the intention of overthrowing the government," Sharon read from the page.

> They're out on a witch hunt against the Likud, trying, out of political motivations, to turn us into the Mafia. Worse affairs have been revealed from within the Labor Party, and they are under police investigation . . . but compare: I acted immediately and announced I'd expel anyone from the Likud who had acted improperly. Mitzna has done nothing.

Sharon claimed that neither he nor his sons had violated the law, and that his sons had handled the matter of the loan without his knowledge. All claims of corruption or bribery were false, he said. While speaking, he raised his voice often. Pounding on the wooden lectern, he asked over and over: "This is a Mafia? Have you gone crazy? Are you out of your minds?"

Supreme Court justice Mishael Cheshin, chairman of the Central Elections Committee, listened to the speech for the first ten minutes. Dismayed that Sharon seemed to be using his platform for a campaign speech rather than addressing issues of state—a violation of the law in Israel, where each party is allotted a specific amount of "campaign propaganda" time during the month leading up to elections—Justice Cheshin pulled the plug.

No one expected him to stop the prime minister in the middle of his defense. Even Sharon was shocked. But the move played in his favor. He had been given time to say that he felt the whole investigation was a witch hunt, but had been cut off before the speech trailed off into hollow protestations of innocence.

By the next morning it was clear that the presentation had been a success. The aggressive part of the speech, during which he lashed out at Mitzna and the Labor Party for framing him and presenting his two innocent sons as members of organized crime, had satisfied large swaths of the public. Moreover, Justice Cheshin's decision had played right into Sharon's hands. The next day's headlines focused on his decision rather than on Sharon's defense; freedom of speech and Supreme Court arrogance dominated the talk of the day.

From that point on, Sharon's PR men kept Omri underground and forbade the prime minister to talk about the loan. If asked, he was instructed to harp on the so-called conspiratorial aspects of the revelation. Mitzna tried, unsuccessfully, to keep the momentum of the scandal alive.

Two days after the press conference, a majority of Israelis felt that the Cyril Kern affair had been leaked to the media in order to harm the prime minister in the final days of his reelection campaign. Sharon reveled in the outpouring of support. He never mentioned the affair again during the campaign, and his PR men continued to pump the line that the investigation was baseless and the leak premeditated and timed to damage Sharon.

The attorney general ordered an inquiry panel, including a representative of the Shabak, to investigate the identity of the whistleblower. Within days, they had pinpointed a high-level lawyer at the state prosecutor's office, Leora Glatt-Berkowitz, who, in her confession, conceded that she leaked the information in order to inform the public of the allegations before they went to the polls.

The exposure of the informant as "ideologically motivated" seemed to prove just what the prime minister's camp had been contending. By now, no one cared about the criminal investigation. Sharon was seen as the victim rather than the suspect.

As the elections approached, Mitzna's campaign, under the slogan "We Believe in You, Mitzna," began to look pathetic. Sharon's slogan, "The People Want Sharon," was cast between two royal-blue stripes, like the flag. Polls predicted that the Likud would take thirty-four seats to Labor's nineteen, but on January 28, 2003, the tally was even more favorable: thirty-eight to nineteen.

At 12:45 A.M. Sharon walked into Likud headquarters. The crowd burst into song, replacing the words to a soccer chant with gleeful verses describing Mitzna's demise. Sharon silenced them with his hand. He sat Netanyahu on his right and looked out at the international cast of reporters. Elation was written all over his face. He spoke of the need for a national unity government, and ended with a quote from Yitzhak Rabin: "We are all brothers, we are all Jews: our fate is one."

CHAPTER 52

Police Investigations

THREE POLICE INVESTIGATIONS INTO SHARON FAMILY AFFAIRS CAST A dark pall over Sharon's political career. In the Annex Research and Greek Island scandals, Attorney General Menachem Mazuz decided that the police had insufficient evidence to indict Ariel Sharon. The third criminal investigation, the Cyril Kern affair, which is linked to Annex Research, is ongoing.

Sharon's political career was saved by Mazuz's decision. He would have been hard-pressed to continue serving while facing criminal charges. In neither case, though, was he deemed completely clean.

Sharon came treacherously close to indictment in the Greek Island affair. State Prosecutor Edna Arbel recommended indicting him for accepting bribes from businessman and Likud activist David Appel, but Attorney General Mazuz decided not to indict, thereby repealing the already-issued indictment against Appel. Mazuz also recommended closing the case against the prime minister in the Annex Research affair, but in the same case he ruled in favor of indicting Omri Sharon.

The Annex Research Affair

On February 17, 2005, Attorney General Menachem Mazuz charged Omri Sharon with violation of campaign finance laws, fraud, breach of trust, and perjury for his role in funding his father's campaign in the Likud primaries in September 1999. That same day, he terminated the investigation into Ariel Sharon's role by reason of a lack of evidence.

In 1999, after Netanyahu's loss to Barak, Sharon had been

nominated temporary Likud chairman. Party leadership elections were set for September 2, and Sharon nominated his son Omri to run his campaign against Ehud Olmert and Meir Shitreet.

On March 3, 1999, Dov Weisglass, responding to a request by Yoram Oren, a fund-raiser for Sharon and the Likud in the United States, officially registered Annex Research, Inc., in Israel. In August 1999, Omri Sharon and Yoram Oren asked Weisglass to nominate Gavriel Manor, a close friend of Omri's, as director general of the corporation. The official address of Annex Research, Inc., was Manor's home address.

During the next seven months, $1.5 million poured in to the company. The contributions came from the American Israel Research Friendship Foundation, Inc. ($815,000 from August to October 1999); the Center for National Studies and International Relationships ($150,000 from August to December 1999); and the Center for National Studies, Inc. ($520,000, from September 1999 to February 2000).

The attorney general concluded that Omri Sharon funneled contributions to his father's campaign through two separate tracks. One, aboveboard and legal, went straight into a special bank account listed as "Ariel Sharon—Primaries 1999." The other, covert track led to Annex Research, Inc., which paid for campaign-related services and workers' wages. Those funds, mostly from overseas corporations, were not lawfully reported and were, with the help of Gavriel Manor, disguised.

The attorney general wrote that from July 1999 to February 2000, Omri Sharon received six million shekels from local and international corporations—a sum that significantly exceeded legal limits. The majority of the funds went straight to Annex Research, Inc., and were used to pay campaign service providers. According to Mazuz, the front company served as a pipeline for funds from corporations abroad to Sharon's campaign in Israel.

The Israeli Political Parties Law requires all contenders in the primaries to submit full financial reports to the party authorities, who pass them on to the Ministry of Justice. Sharon's signed report declared a total expenditure of 962,000 shekels, 130,000 of which had come from donations. The attorney general determined that that sum represented the money raised and spent aboveboard and did not include the funds donated through the back channels.

The decision to prosecute Omri Sharon was based on recordings, reports from service providers, documents, and handwritten checks found in his house, and on his own testimony. On October 24, 2004, during questioning, he denied any criminal wrongdoing but also shouldered all responsibility, exonerating his father. The Israeli press reported that he had "taken the fall" for his dad.

Omri claimed that he was the one who had seen the signed financial report before it was submitted and that his father had signed it without reading it. Omri stressed that his father had thought he was signing a completely truthful document. He had acted out of a desire to see his father win. "It's possible I made a mistake," he said, "but that was what I chose."

On August 28, 2005, Omri Sharon was indicted on charges of violating campaign finance laws, fraud, breach of trust, and perjury.

Questions regarding Ariel Sharon's role in the affair remained unanswered. Was he aware at the time of Omri's actions? Was he aware of the back channel? Did he know that he was signing a falsified document? What, if any, was his role in the financial side of the campaign?

On three occasions, the police questioned Sharon at the prime minister's official residence in Jerusalem: in April 2002, October 2003, and February 2004. Asked about his role in campaign fundraising, he said: "I didn't handle financial matters. I didn't raise money for my election. That was Omri's responsibility. He handled it. . . . The main parts of the campaign, I would say, concerned politics, economics and education. . . . I never handled financial affairs for the primaries."

During the course of the investigation, written correspondence was found in Omri's house that indicated he was updating his father daily on campaign matters, although not necessarily relating to finances. "I took care to insulate him from that type of thing," Omri testified. "I made sure that nothing would disturb my father's candidacy. I made sure he wouldn't know about and wouldn't be involved in money and organization."

In his decision not to indict Ariel Sharon, Mazuz wrote, "You can assume that Omri did his best—in real time as in the police investigation—to help his father and protect him from bearing responsibility." Mazuz added that the "need-to-know defense" was supported by the testimony of others. Therefore, he concluded that there was insufficient evidence tying the prime minister to the fund-raising and financing of the campaign. The attorney general found no evidence that Ariel Sharon had known anything about Annex Research or the covert back channel. Mazuz also found no proof that Ariel Sharon personally took part in any fund-raising endeavors.

There is no doubt that Sharon had filed false reports, but whether he had knowingly done so could not be proved. Omri told the police that his father knew only about the aboveboard fund-raising channel, because he informed him only on a need-to-know basis. Therefore, "those were the only donations and expenditures he [Ariel Sharon] was aware of, and from his perspective there was nothing false about it. He knew nothing different from what he signed . . . as far as he was concerned, he had signed properly." Based on that testimony, the attorney general decided that despite lingering suspicions, Ariel Sharon could not be implicated beyond reasonable doubt.

"I have therefore decided," the attorney general wrote, "to close Ariel Sharon's file due to insufficient evidence."

The Cyril Kern Affair

The Cyril Kern affair came to light just three weeks before the general elections of January 28, 2003. On January 7, *Haaretz* reported that the police were secretly investigating Ariel and Gilad Sharon for accepting a $1.5 million loan from Cyril Kern, an old South African friend of Ariel Sharon's, in order to pay back the illegally raised money funneled through Annex Research, Inc. At the time of this writing, the investigation is ongoing, and therefore all the following information is alleged.

The affair began on October 1, 2001, with the state comptroller's report, which "looked into the running accounts of the different parties in the Fifteenth Knesset." State Comptroller Eliezer Goldberg first revealed the Annex Research affair.

Goldberg ruled that of the 5.9 million shekels donated to Annex Research, Inc., 1.2 million shekels had gone to the Likud Party and 4.7 million had gone to Ariel Sharon's campaign. Goldberg included an August 27, 2001, letter written by Sharon in response to a first draft of the state comptroller's report, which reads in part:

> The August 20, 2001, first draft that was sent to me for response clarified that . . . a company by the name of Annex Research, Inc., received 4.7 million shekels, which served as finances for the campaign to promote my candidacy in the internal Likud elections in September 1999. Since it has been decided in the first draft of the comptroller's report that those funds were unlawfully raised, I intend, in the coming days, to return the money to Annex Research, Inc., in order for it to be returned to the donors.

On October 4, 2001, three days before the official publication of the report, Sharon transferred an initial installment of half a million shekels of his own money, half of which was on credit, to Annex Research, Inc. His two sons set about the task of raising the remaining 4.2 million shekels. On October 22, Gilad Sharon went to the nearby Leumi Bank in Sderot and asked for a 4.2-million-shekel loan. He offered to mortgage the ranch.

The Leumi Bank authorized the loan. Gilad paid Annex Research the full sum the following day. Later, the bank realized that for procedural reasons, the ranch, jointly owned by Gilad and Omri, could not be mortgaged. They asked for the funds to be returned.

An August 2002 document sent to the South African Justice Department from the Israeli Ministry of Justice requests information about whether three months after receiving the loan from the Leumi Bank in Sderot, Cyril Kern, a South African businessman and personal friend of Sharon's, transferred $1.49 million from his account in Austria to the joint account of Omri and Gilad Sharon in the Discount Bank in Tel Aviv. The sum was given to the Sharon brothers as a loan with a 3 percent interest rate.

The money traveled the following route: Cyril Kern's $1.49 million arrived in Tel Aviv on January 17, 2002, and served as collateral against a 4.2-million-shekel loan* Gilad Sharon had taken in April 2002 from the Discount Bank in Tel Aviv in order to pay back the Leumi Bank in Sderot. Gilad then returned the original loan.

When Ariel Sharon was questioned by police on April 22, 2004, it was known that he could not mortgage the ranch. Nonetheless, when asked by the police how he had managed to pay Annex Research such a significant sum, he said that mortgaging the ranch had generated the capital. He made no mention of Cyril Kern.

The police suspect that Cyril Kern's loan, used to repay unlawfully raised campaign money, was also illegal. The Ministry of Justice requested permission from the South African authorities to question Kern, in South Africa, about the nature of the loan.

The Ministry of Justice sent a similar request to the Austrian authorities, revealing that during the months of November and December 2002, Gilad and Omri Sharon received three million dollars in their Tel Aviv account from the Austrian Bank für Arbeit und Wirtschaft (BAWAG). On December 17, 2002, Gilad Sharon used those funds to pay back his loan to Cyril Kern.

The Ministry of Justice requested an investigation of the identity behind the loans. An Austrian court ruled that Israel could not conduct an investigation on their soil or gain access to the BAWAG accounts. Cyril Kern's $1.49 million had come from another account in the same bank.

Gilad Sharon exercised his right to silence during police questioning and embarked on a long legal campaign to prevent the police and state prosecutor's office from accessing documents that might reveal the source behind the three-million-dollar loan. During the legal proceedings, Gilad Sharon acknowledged that he was, in fact, the owner of the Austrian account and he had transferred the funds to the Discount Bank in Tel Aviv. He testified that he had received the three million dollars from Cyril Kern in a joint business venture.

*At the time, the exchange rate was 4.47 shekels to the dollar.

Unlike Gilad, Ariel Sharon and Cyril Kern—who was questioned in South Africa—both spoke to the police. "Over a year ago," Sharon said,

> the state comptroller discovered that unlawful funds were raised and he alerted me to it. I was shocked by his discovery. I went home to the ranch and talked to the boys and said, on my own initiative: "We must give the donors all their money back immediately. Even if we have to once again mortgage our house. We have to do it." As far as I know, I'm the only one who acted in that manner. . . . [Ehud] Barak hasn't done that to this day. . . . Only I returned the money, of my own volition, without being forced.
>
> We're dealing with a large sum of money, almost five million shekels. I have no financial means. Back in 1989 I stopped running the ranch . . . as demanded by law. When the boys came back from the army, they took over the ranch along with their other business interests. These days Gilad runs it successfully, and I don't intervene—that's what the law demands. [Therefore,] I withdrew my and Lily's (may her memory be blessed) savings and gave half a million shekels, half of which was on balance. Gilad took it upon himself to draft the rest of the funds. And shortly thereafter he transferred the rest of the sum to me, just over four million shekels, and I paid the donors back and informed the state comptroller. That's where the story ends as far as I am concerned.

Later, he said:

> I want to state clearly here: I did not know precisely how the money was raised. We spoke of mortgaging the ranch and as far as I know that's what was done. When asked by the police, that's what I said, that I don't know exactly but that the boys took care of the matter and as far as I know the ranch was mortgaged. If it turns out another way was found—great. Gilad, my son, is a very successful businessman. His business interests are widespread. He's success-

ful and earns profits and I'm very proud of him. I know everything was kosher and legal, and everything was reported properly. He has documents that prove everything.

Sharon said that Kern was a close personal friend who had come to Israel from Britain at age seventeen to fight as a volunteer in the IDF during the War of Independence. They met while serving in the Alexandroni Brigade and had fought side by side. Since then, despite the geographic distance between them, the two had remained friends. Kern had gone into the textile business and headed the British Fashion Council. He emigrated to Cape Town, South Africa, in the 1990s along with his second wife, the Swedish-born Annalina Johnson. Kern frequently came to Israel over the holidays and celebrated with the Sharon family. He had known Gilad and Omri since they were born.

"He loved us," Sharon said of Kern.

He loved the land, the nation, and yes—we are friends. It's a friendship that's decades old. During the Yom Kippur War he showed up . . . came to my forces west of the canal. I ask you: Look what they are trying to do just because he is my friend. And I ask you, how can you treat people like this? . . . So Gilad received a loan from him, with interest, and then paid it back, with interest, and paid taxes. Is that bribery? Is that undue benefit? I could give him something? What is this? Have you gone totally nuts? . . . There's no bribery, no cheating, no nothing.

The Greek Island Affair

In the Greek Island affair, the police suspected Ariel Sharon of bribery, fraud, and breach of trust. In January 2004, the state prosecutor's office indicted businessman and Likud member David Appel on charges of bribery. The state charged that he had agreed to back Sharon in the Likud primaries and pay Gilad Sharon a handsome salary in return for Ariel Sharon's support and influence in securing a giant development deal on the Greek island of Patroklos and the promotion of his real estate deals in the Israeli city of Lod.

In March 2004, State Prosecutor Edna Arbel recommended indicting both Ariel and Gilad Sharon for accepting bribes from David Appel. Arbel prepared a first draft of the indictment. She wrote that Ariel Sharon, "as minister of national infrastructure and foreign minister, accepted bribes in return for activities relating to his official role, in that he received political support from David Appel and large sums of money into his Sycamore Ranch account, knowing that those were being given by Appel in return for actions as minister of national infrastructure, who is in charge of the Israel Lands Authority, and as foreign minister."

Nonetheless, Menachem Mazuz, the attorney general, reviewed the evidence and decided on June 15, 2004, to reject Arbel's recommendation. He closed the case by reason of insufficient evidence to support criminal charges. Sharon had avoided a disgraceful end to his political career.

Section 290 of the Israeli criminal code states that a public servant convicted of bribery can be sentenced for up to seven years. Sharon was suspected of accepting bribes on two accounts: in return for Appel's support during the Likud primaries, and for Appel's employing his son Gilad and paying him to promote the Patroklos development project.

All told, Appel paid Gilad Sharon $640,000 for a period of employment from March 1999 to June 2001. He promised him three million dollars of financial incentives during and after the development of the project. Their arrangement never advanced to that stage. Police, though, suspected that the business venture between Appel and Gilad Sharon was so unique "as to be fictitious."

Police suspected that in return for Gilad's position, Ariel Sharon had used his connections as foreign minister and minister of infrastructure to assist Appel in his negotiations with Greek authorities. On February 12 and July 28, 1999, Sharon had accepted Appel's invitation to dine at his home with the deputy foreign minister of Greece and with the mayor of Athens, respectively. From 1997 to 1999, Sharon, as minister of infrastructure, had helped Appel with his real estate transactions in Lod, the police alleged.

The police questioned Sharon twice about the Greek Island affair, on October 30, 2003, and February 5, 2004. Sharon told the investigators that he had known Appel for many years, both through politics and as a family friend, but categorically denied that Appel had assisted him in his Likud campaign in exchange for political favors. According to Sharon, his conversations with Appel, two of which were recorded by police taps on Appel's home phones, were within the bounds of normal political relations.

The attorney general sided with Sharon. He determined that there was no evidence indicating that Appel had supported Sharon in internal Likud elections or in his bid for chairman. On the contrary, in the race for Likud chairman and candidate for prime minister, Appel had supported his rival, Ehud Olmert.

Gilad's work for Appel was at the center of the bribery allegations. In late 1998, Appel began promoting his idea of building a string of vacation villages on three thousand dunams* of land on the island of Patroklos, fifty miles southeast of Athens. The project would include a hundred thousand rooms, fifteen casinos, several golf courses, malls, entertainment centers, amusement parks, and sports facilities, and an underground railway tunnel that would convey visitors straight from the Athens airport to the island. The sum total of the investment was $16 billion.

Appel knew Gilad Sharon long before the investment plan in Greece came to life. The families were close, and Appel had on several occasions invited Gilad to Bible study classes in his house. In March 1999 he offered him the position of director of marketing, publicity, and sales for the project. From March to October 1999, Gilad Sharon worked on the project intensively.

Appel never signed any papers with Gilad, and up to that point had not paid him. Gilad turned to David Spector, the owner of a security and investigations company, for advice. Their conversations, which were taped by Spector and eventually made their way into the hands of the police, played a major role in uncovering the agreement between Gilad Sharon, who refused to speak with the police, and Appel.

---

*A dunam is an area of land roughly equivalent to one-quarter of an acre. Three thousand durams is equivalent to approximately 741 acres.

In May 2000, after weeks of negotiations, David Appel and Gilad Sharon settled the financial terms of their deal. Sharon would receive $400,000 for services already rendered plus a steady salary of $20,000 per month. Upon receipt of their first building permit, he would be paid an additional $1.5 million, minus the sum already paid him in salary, and an additional $1.5 million once the project was operational.

Sharon continued working for Appel until June 2001, at which point the two were no longer contractually bound to cooperate. Sharon received $400,000 and an additional $240,000 for twelve months' work. The project stalled and Sharon did not receive any bonuses. Although the pay was high, the attorney general ruled that it corresponded to the salaries of other employees of the project.

Gilad Sharon, a graduate of Hebrew University's School of Agriculture, an economics major well versed in marketing, has been running the ranch since 1989. He has also developed and marketed real estate locally and internationally. When speaking to the police about his son, Sharon said: "I say this not only because he is my son, but he is a very talented young man . . . capable of extraordinary work. Moreover, he's serious. I mean, if he takes something on, then he works. . . . I've seen him burning the midnight oil . . . he has a great mind and he is very methodical and organized." Sharon added that Gilad "does business in all kinds of places around the world," but could not tell his questioners exactly where. He said that Gilad refused to bring him into the fold and that he used to tell his father, "You deal with the Arabs and the Americans and I'll deal with the business. Everyone will do his part."

Sharon's version is supported by the transcript of a September 17, 1999, phone conversation the police recorded between Ariel Sharon and David Appel. Sharon seemed totally unaware of the particulars of the project. Appel tried steering him toward the matter. "So, how far is it from the beach over there?" Sharon asks. Appel: "Eight hundred meters." Sharon: "That's it? . . . It's not a long sail out to sea?" Appel: "He [Gilad] hasn't gotten you caught up in the excitement of the project yet?" Sharon: "Our boy is discreet, just so you know . . . he has never revealed business matters."

Later in the conversation, which the police taped six months after Gilad began working on the project, Appel told Sharon that Gilad had been doing a great job and stood to be paid very well for his labors. Appel asked Sharon whether "we'll be graced with your presence . . . in our new estate, just let us invite you once, you and Lily, but truly for real honest enjoyment." Sharon thought he meant to Tel Aviv, but Appel explained, "to the new house in Greece," when it is built. Sharon responded: "Yes, but I will pay."

Attorney General Menachem Mazuz ruled that Gilad's position and the quality of his services, along with the scale of the development plans and the high salaries across the board, all flew in the face of the accusations that Appel's payment to Gilad was a fictional deal drafted only as a means to bribe his father. Mazuz further ruled that there was no mention of the development project during the dinner party at Appel's house with Sharon, foreign minister at the time, and the deputy foreign minister of Greece. During the second dinner, with the mayor of Athens, Sharon was already serving in the Opposition, as a simple MK, and in that instance as well there had been no mention of Patroklos.

"It seems that the fact that the project was not presented or spoken about during the two dinners," Mazuz wrote in his ruling, "narrows Sharon's role at the two dinners to merely favoring the guests with his presence, a matter that, the investigation has revealed, Appel felt was important. From Sharon's perspective, it will be difficult to contradict him that his willingness to accept Appel's dinner invitation was based on their friendship and not in return for gifts given by Appel."

Appel's development project in Lod included a construction project in the northwest part of the city, on roughly 350 acres of agricultural land Appel had bought from nearby Moshav Ginaton for $24 million. Sharon was suspected of promoting Appel's interests while serving as minister of national infrastructure from September 1997. The attorney general ruled in this case that it would have been best for Sharon to have recused himself from handling any of Appel's affairs, since they were close. However, he wrote that no one disagreed that from the moment that the Israel Land Authority refused to allow Appel's project, Sharon accepted their decision. Mazuz wrote that he decided to shut the case because during the years 1997–99, when Sharon served as minister of national infrastructure, he did not aid Appel in his real estate ventures and did not act in any way unlawfully.

Of the Greek Island affair, the attorney general wrote: "The evidence is weak in every kernel of the offense and does not coalesce into a self-standing structure." Therefore, "there is not a sufficient framework of evidence to bring Ariel Sharon or Gilad Sharon to trial, and therefore I have decided to close the case against both of them due to insufficient evidence." In the wake of his decision the state prosecutor's office, on April 14, 2005, wiped David Appel's slate clean of all suspicion of bribing Ariel Sharon.

CHAPTER 53

Trapping Netanyahu

IN OCTOBER 2002, AS BINYAMIN BEN-ELIEZER PULLED LABOR OUT OF the coalition, Shimon Peres, the outgoing foreign minister, offered Sharon a word of advice. The oldest member of Knesset told the prime minister that the time had come for him to make the move from the annals of politics to the annals of history. If he did not act soon, Peres cautioned him, he would be forgotten by both.

The complex relationship between Sharon and Peres had known many undulations over its forty years. They were the last of the old generation—the only ones left who had witnessed the establishment of the state and worked with Ben-Gurion, Dayan, Begin, and Rabin. Although they had always seemed at odds ideologically, Sharon's worldview was closer to Peres's than to that of many of their heirs, such as Netanyahu and Barak. Sharon didn't follow Peres's advice, but he kept it in mind.

It is impossible to tell whether Sharon embarked on the Disengagement Plan because he wanted to change his entry in the annals of history from warmonger to peacemaker, or whether he was responding to the mounting police investigations, on the one hand, and the American pressure to implement the Road Map, on the other. What is certain is that in January 2003, Sharon, at the start of his second term as prime minister, was a changed man. In 2001, Sharon seemed interested only in staying in power; Sharon in 2003 was focused on bringing about dramatic political change.

Sitting with his sons around the table at the ranch, he told them he felt that after many years of toil, he had been given a historic mission that only he could fill: to change the face of the Middle East and move toward a diplomatic solution. Having served the land for the better part of a century, Sharon had a proprietary feeling about the country. He could lead Israel to the best possible peace deal. Anyone else, he was certain, would have to settle for far less. The dimming of his days induced a sense of urgency.

From the first day of his second term, he faced pressure to act. On January 29, 2003, Bush congratulated Sharon but also reminded him of his commitment to the Road Map. Sharon assured the American president that he would remain true to Bush's vision.

The Americans used their nine-billion-dollar loan package and additional one-billion-dollar signing bonus as leverage to ensure Sharon's compliance with the president's political plans. By stressing the importance of the Road Map, the Bush administration was silently able to dictate the terms of Sharon's coalition. Sharon understood the American message, and did not even consider establishing a center right–far right coalition.

The Likud, along with Natan Sharansky's Yisrael Be'aliyah, held a stable forty seats. Sharon offered Mitzna and Labor (nineteen seats) a place in the coalition. The unity government, he promised Mitzna, would return to the September 28, 2000, borders, evacuate illegal settlement outposts in the West Bank, and, later, partially freeze settlement construction. Mitzna wanted more. He demanded that Sharon commit to a complete cessation of settlement expansion and the evacuation of, and withdrawal from, isolated settlements like Netzarim, a settlement of six hundred people that had been sandwiched between the sea, Gaza City, and the al-Bureij refugee camp.

Toward the end of his first term, Prime Minister Sharon had gone on record as saying that "the fate of Netzarim is the fate of Tel Aviv." He rejected Mitzna's conditions out of hand. Mitzna left that meeting jolted by Sharon's hawkish views. Sharon had lectured him on the importance of Netzarim. "Arik didn't even leave a crack in the government's door," Mitzna said, reminding the public that Labor had promised to withdraw from the Gaza Strip and all isolated settlements. Without Sharon's consent to those terms, there was no way to share the seats of government, he said.

Instead, Sharon formed a sixty-eight-seat government along with the secular Shinui Party. He abandoned the ultra-Orthodox for the first time, mostly because he knew the government would have to pass economic measures that would take a toll on this largely poor constituency.

Sharon intended to focus on the economy. In his previous term, he felt, he had neglected the economy in favor of the intifada and the grave security situation. Ehud Olmert, who had pieced together the terms of the coalition, expected Sharon to name him to the post of finance minister. Yet after three weeks of negotiating with coalition partners on Sharon's behalf, Olmert found himself without a role.

Sharon wanted to oust Silvan Shalom from the post of finance minister, but did not want a confrontation with the third strongest man in the Likud. Instead, he surprised everyone by moving Shalom to the Foreign Ministry, leaving Finance open, and pushing Netanyahu, his old nemesis, deep into the corner. The foreign minister often pops up in the newspapers grinning and clasping hands with world leaders; the minister of finance is often invisible if things go well—as the prime minister's ratings soar—and wears a set of prominent horns when the economy takes a turn for the worse. Netanyahu was forced to choose between sitting on the sidelines and taking over the most thankless job in Israel's government.

Sharon, Israel's greatest political tactician, pushed Netanyahu out of the spotlight on the stage of foreign affairs. Any advance on the peace front would be his success alone. As minister of finance, Netanyahu would need not only the prime minister's full cooperation to have a chance at success, but also quiet along Israel's borders, making it impossible for him to outflank Sharon from the right.

Sharon sent Weisglass to offer Netanyahu the job. If he accepted the post, it was his; if not, it would go to Olmert. Netanyahu saw the trap Sharon had set, and impulsively refused the offer. Twenty-four hours later, he changed his mind. If Sharon agreed to back his far-reaching economic plan and give him the type of autonomy that would make him "the prime minister of finance," he would take the job. Once Sharon had given his word and guaranteed that he would handle all matters pertaining to the American loans, Netanyahu took office.

Olmert felt betrayed. Sharon tried to placate him. Omri bridged the gap between the two: Sharon would make him minister of industry, trade, and labor, minister of communications, and, pivotally, vice prime minister.

MK Omri Sharon's power was boundless. Ministers, party leaders, CEOs, lobbyists, and journalists all waited in line outside his small Knesset office. Ariel Sharon was to a great extent under Omri's influence. "He's the kind of person who loves to help," Sharon told *Yedioth Ahronoth* on April 16, 2003. "He likes talking to people. Not like me. I don't have that need. All talk of Omri as the state's director general has no grounding in reality . . . there's one person who calls the shots. You know who that is? It's me."

In early March 2003, the American and British armed forces prepared for the invasion of Iraq, and Israel braced for missile strikes. Bush asked Sharon to keep a low profile in the days before war. "We need to stay quiet," Sharon told the Israeli public, "no howling or crying. This is not the time."

Some twelve thousand reservists were called up. On March 19, the IDF ordered all civilians to prepare sealed rooms in their homes and pick up gas masks. The front stayed silent, though. Gulf War II would not reach Israel.

The invasion began the next day, March 20. Within a month, the entire country of Iraq had been ripped from Saddam Hussein's iron grip. In July 2003, American forces found and killed the dictator's two sons, Udai and Qusai. On December 13, 2003, American troops found Saddam Hussein cowering in a hole in the ground outside Tikrit.

Terror attacks intensified across Iraq. The Bush administration had been unable to prove that Hussein had amassed weapons of mass destruction. Nonetheless, in November 2004 the American public returned George W. Bush to a second term in office.

From Israel's perspective, the war in Iraq realigned the balance of power in the Middle East. One of the country's main threats from the east had been nullified, and the militants within the territories had been cut off from a major source of funding. The pitiful way in which Saddam Hussein's regime had crumbled was a blow to the morale of Palestinians, who largely supported him.

While the crushing power of the American military sent a daunting message to the Arab world, the Israeli public watched the early stages of the war with delight. For the first time since the outbreak of the second intifada, there was reason to celebrate.

It was a time for change. On March 19, 2003, Arafat appointed Abu Mazen (Mahmoud Abbas) Palestinian prime minister. His hand had been forced by American and European pressure. They hoped that Abu Mazen could institute change in the Palestinian Authority and present himself as a viable peace partner. Abu Mazen soon found, however, that Arafat had not left the stage, but maintained control over all of the state security apparatuses, neutralizing the new prime minister.

British prime minister Tony Blair, Bush's primary ally in the Iraq War, urged the American president to release the Road Map before going to war. He needed to silence domestic criticism with a Middle East quid pro quo. A third draft of the Road Map was prepared well before the war, but Sharon, still unhappy with the American peace plan, pushed hard to postpone its official publication.

The Israel lobby worked overtime in Washington. They urged the president not to force an agreement on Israel. Sharon angered many at the State Department and the White House by returning a draft of the agreement with more than a hundred changes. Nonetheless, he prevailed. The president postponed the release of the Road Map until after the American elections.

Sharon spent the spring holiday of Passover with his family. The pre-Passover toast at the Prime Minister's Office, ordinarily a lavish affair, was celebrated in 2003 with syrupy Kiddush wine and a few bowls of fruit. The Knesset vote on the economic plan was just around the corner.

The budget was to be cut by eleven billion shekels. Retirement age would be raised from 65 to 67 for men and from 60 to 62 for women. Government-funded child support would be reduced, tax breaks for those living in settlements and development towns would be cut, thousands of public sector workers would be fired, tax reform aimed at inducing the unemployed to return to the workforce would be enacted, and government ministries across the board would face cuts, including a three-billion-shekel cut to the defense budget.

Sharon supported the plan, but stayed out of the spotlight, leaving Netanyahu out in front. But by April 2003, before the plan went to first call in the Knesset, Amir Peretz, then chairman of Israel's General Federation of Labor, threatened a general strike if certain cuts were not rolled back. Under intense criticism from Netanyahu supporters, Sharon called on Peretz to rescind his threats, asserting that a strike, heaped on top of Israel's other problems, would bring the economy to its knees.

At the end of April, Peretz shut down the public sector. Suddenly, Netanyahu and Sharon were in the same leaky boat. On April 27, as the Knesset met to vote on the budgetary measures, Sharon announced that the vote was tantamount to a show of confidence in the government. Outside, thousands of single mothers, senior citizens, the unemployed, and physically impaired people railed against the plan.

The bill passed through the first of three "calls" necessary to make it into law. In mid-May, Netanyahu and Peretz reached an agreement that ended the strike. Netanyahu reduced the number of workers to be fired and scaled back certain measures that restricted workers' rights. At the end of the month, the bill became law.

In mid-April, Sharon had a malignant tumor removed from his left temple. The procedure was performed at Sheba Hospital in Tel Aviv. Sharon stressed the low level of the tumor's malignancy and the unlikelihood that it would metastasize. It had been caused, he said, by overexposure to the sun. In interviews he noted that many people in Israel had had similar growths removed and they were fully capable of living to the age of 120. After a few hours' rest, he was released from the hospital. That same day, he showed up at the office, his sound health and fitness on display.

Abu Mazen's government was sworn in on April 29, 2003; the next day, he and Sharon were shown the final draft of the Road Map. According to the document, a "Quartet" consisting of the United States, the European Union, Russia, and the United Nations would guide the two sides along the path laid out in the Road Map. By 2005, Israel and the Palestinian Authority were to sign a final agreement.

The first stage, to be implemented by May 2003, called for a complete cessation of violence on both sides. Israel was to improve humanitarian conditions, lift curfews, and ease restrictions on the movement of people and goods. The PA would institute far-reaching democratic reforms and call for an immediate end to violence against Israelis everywhere. Each side would issue an unequivocal declaration affirming the other side's right to live in peace and security, and Israel would announce its commitment to a two-state solution.

As the security situation quieted, the IDF would return to September 28, 2000, lines and the Palestinian security forces would assume control over the areas Israel had vacated. Still in the month of May, Israel would evacuate and destroy all illegal outposts established after March 2001 and freeze all settlement building in the West Bank and the Gaza Strip.

The second stage, to be implemented by December 2003, would focus on the establishment of a Palestinian state, with temporary borders, symbols of sovereignty, and a democratic constitution. First, the Road Map dictated, the Palestinian leader would have to tamp down terrorism and institute a liberal democracy. The Quartet would decide whether the sides had fulfilled their obligations and could progress from stage one to stage two. If all went as planned, the second stage—general elections in Palestine and the establishment of a state with temporary borders—would be implemented by the close of 2003.

In early 2004 an international peace convention would meet and sign a declaration of Palestinian statehood. In addition to the parties of the Quartet, Syria and Lebanon would also attend the conference, in an effort to achieve peace with all of Israel's neighbors. The agreement would lead to a final settling in 2005 of the remaining differences: sovereignty over Jerusalem, Palestinians' right of return, and the Jewish settlements.

The second to last paragraph of the Road Map reads:

Parties reach final and comprehensive permanent status agreement that ends the Israel-Palestinian conflict in 2005, through a settlement negotiated between the parties based

on UNSCR 242, 338, and 1397, that ends the occupation
that began in 1967, and includes an agreed, just, fair, and
realistic solution to the refugee issue, and a negotiated resolution on the status of Jerusalem that takes into account
the political and religious concerns of both sides, and pro-
tects the religious interests of Jews, Christians, and Muslims worldwide, and fulfills the vision of two states, Israel
and sovereign, independent, democratic, and viable Palestine, living side by side in peace and security.

Although he kept his displeasure to himself, Sharon had a
hard time accepting Bush's plan. There were positive aspects,
particularly in the emphasis on defense in the first stage. But the
plan moved along at what he considered an alarming pace. American demands to stop all settlement building—and the penulti-
mate paragraph, which spoke of ending "the occupation that
began in 1967," finding "an agreed, just, fair, and realistic solution" to the issue of Palestinian refugees, and the ominous-
sounding "negotiated resolution on the status of Jerusalem"—left
Sharon sick. The ideological right in Israel, his political home,
utterly opposed any concessions whatsoever on the matters of
Jerusalem and the return of Palestinian refugees.

Two days after he had been given the American president's
Road Map, Sharon spoke at the annual Memorial Day service in
Jerusalem. After acknowledging the unbearable sacrifice of the bereaved families, he said, "It is my duty to rid the land of war and
usher in peace and security."

CHAPTER 54

From Aqaba
to Geneva

Up until the last minute, Sharon had hoped that his reservations about the Road Map would sway the American president, but this time their friendship was not enough. The U.S. position remained firm. At first Sharon pushed for a trade: the Road Map in exchange for Palestinian capitulation on the right of return. After that tactic was rebuffed, he told Secretary of State Colin Powell he would have no chance of passing the plan through government with the clauses calling for a freeze on settlement construction still intact. Snidely, he asked Powell whether all the female settlers should have abortions in order to curtail their natural rate of reproduction. The remark did not exactly open the secretary's heart.

Sharon sent Weisglass to Washington to try to persuade National Security Advisor Condoleezza Rice to include some of the Israeli points in the final draft of the document. She, too, was unrelenting. At last, President Bush announced that the United States would consider some of the Israeli reservations about the plan after implementation had begun. Sharon sent word through Weisglass that Israel wouldn't be able to ratify the agreement so long as the freeze on settlement construction and the Palestinian right of return remained stations on the president's path to peace. He also demanded that the United States and not the Quartet supervise the implementation of the plan, and that the Palestinians be required to strengthen their previous security measures.

At the "G8" foreign ministers' meeting in Paris, Secretary of State Powell announced that despite Bush's remarks regarding Sharon's reservations, the president had no intention of seriously altering the document that represented his vision for peace in the region. Although the plan still troubled Sharon, on May 23, 2003, he was forced to accept it "in principle."

Before Sharon brought the plan to the Cabinet on May 25, both the National Religious Party and the National Union announced that they would vote against it even if it meant bringing down the current government. Sharon, along with Weisglass and Omri, spent the better part of the weekend on the phone trying to persuade Likud ministers and others to fall in line and vote with the prime minister.

Sunday the twenty-fifth was an especially exhausting day for Sharon. Concerned about the prospect of humiliation at the 9 A.M. meeting, he gathered the Likud ministers around a table at an early hour to see which way the wind was blowing. The mood was grim. Uzi Landau, Yisrael Katz, and Natan Sharansky said they'd vote with the NRP and the National Union; Tzachi Hanegbi, Limor Livnat, Danny Naveh, and Binyamin Netanyahu stayed on the fence.

Sharon was short-tempered and rude at the meeting, cutting the ministers off in midsentence. At one point Sharon wondered aloud whether some of the people around the table were acting on principle or for political gain. Everyone knew he meant Netanyahu. From there, they went to the government complex. The cabinet meeting took six hours. Outside, right-wing protesters were calling Sharon a traitor.

Sharon was not at his best that day. He carried his short temper from meeting to meeting as he pushed everyone to vote in favor of the Road Map even while maintaining that the plan, in its current form, was unsatisfactory. Livnat suggested the government announce that it "accepts the stages laid out in the plan but determines that there will be no compromise on the right of return, no return to 1967 borders, no concessions regarding Jerusalem, and no agreement on a Palestinian state until the terror cells have been uprooted entirely." Realizing that Bush would interpret such a declaration as a slap in the face, Sharon batted down her proposal. At the end of the marathon session, twelve ministers voted in favor of the plan and four abstained—Netanyahu, Livnat, Hanegbi, and Naveh.

Sharon was forced to compromise. The Cabinet's decision read: "The Israeli government announces that it accepts the prime minister's declaration regarding the adoption of the steps of the Road Map, and asserts that the plan will be implemented in accordance with the fourteen comments Israel submitted to the Americans."

Regarding Palestinian refugees, Sharon wrote: "The Palestinian state should serve as the sole solution to the problem of the refugees and their absorption."

Sharon took even more flak at the next day's Likud meeting in the Knesset. "The Road Map is even tougher than Oslo," Gila Gamliel said. "It's as though the Labor Party is still in power." Ehud Yatom said it was as if they had "crossed off" forty members of the Knesset. Furious, Sharon set off another feud with his response. "We must reach a political agreement. It is not known whether we will succeed, but I'll tell you clearly: I will make every effort to reach an agreement because it is imperative. I also think that the notion that it's possible to keep three and a half million Palestinians under occupation—you may not like the word, but it is under occupation—is bad for Israel, the Palestinians, and the economy of Israel. We must free ourselves from controlling three and a half million Palestinians, whose numbers are not diminishing, and reach a diplomatic agreement."

The phrase "under occupation," more commonly heard from the lips of Peace Now supporters than of the general who founded the Likud, caused a stir. At the following day's meeting of the Committee of Foreign Affairs and Security, Attorney General Elyakim Rubinstein recommended that Sharon instead use the phrase "disputed territories."

Sharon explained that his sentiment was simple: He did not want to rule over another people. He disregarded Rubinstein's advice and repeated, almost verbatim, the previous day's statement.

Before the two sides could internalize the demands of the Road Map, President Bush, just a month after landing in front of his "Mission Accomplished" banner on the USS *Abraham Lincoln,* organized an international convention at King Abdullah's summerhouse in Aqaba, Jordan. Bush, Sharon, Abu Mazen, and Abdullah

sat for many pastoral photos on the lawns overlooking the bay. The
June 4, 2003, Aqaba summit was little more than a congratulation
ceremony for a job well done in Iraq.

Bush found Sharon pliable, though. He was able to secure his
promise to demolish all illegal outposts in the territories and a
commitment from the prime minister to a future Palestinian state
on a contiguous stretch of territory in the West Bank. In his
speech, Sharon stressed security:

> As the prime minister of Israel, the land which is the cra-
> dle of the Jewish people, my paramount responsibility is
> the security of the people of Israel and of the State of Is-
> rael. . . . There is now hope of a new opportunity for peace
> between Israelis and Palestinians. Israel, like others, has
> lent its strong support for President Bush's vision, ex-
> pressed on June 24, 2002, of two states—Israel and a
> Palestinian state—living side by side in peace and security.
>
> We can also reassure our Palestinian partners that we
> understand the importance of territorial contiguity in
> Judea and Samaria, for a viable Palestinian state. . . . We
> accept the principle that no unilateral actions by any party
> can [predetermine] the outcome of our negotiations. In re-
> gard to the unauthorized outposts, I want to reiterate that
> Israel is a society governed by the rule of law. Thus, we will
> immediately begin to remove unauthorized outposts.

Abu Mazen promised to put an end to the "military intifada"
and anti-Israel incitement. He said that President Bush's plan represented a true opportunity for peace, and then, after speaking of
the generations of Palestinian suffering, Abu Mazen, as encouraged
to do by the Americans, noted that he was not oblivious to Judaism's
historical travails—a bit of a feat considering that his Ph.D. disser-
tation had denied all accepted versions of the Holocaust. President
Bush said, "The Holy Land must be shared between the state of
Palestine and the state of Israel, living at peace with each other and
with every nation of the Middle East."

Sharon's acceptance of the plan shocked the Israeli right. The
settlers were stunned to see the man who had pushed so hard for

Jewish settlement turn his back on them. Almost everyone had a theory about the prime minister's motivations. Some felt the view from the top had changed his perspective, others posited that the Middle East had changed, and still others felt that Sharon was making a conscious effort to move to the left, toward the largely liberal Israeli media, in exchange for their silence on the corruption front.

People close to Sharon denied any correlation between the prime minister's willingness to uproot outposts and the heat he was feeling from the corruption scandals. According to them, since 2001 Sharon had come to believe that he alone could secure a peace agreement that would provide generations of peace for the Israeli people. He saw himself as a shepherd, a biblical metaphor for leadership.

Sharon was unwilling to partition the land before all traces of terrorism had been eradicated. According to Weisglass, Sharon had felt certain, upon taking office, that he could secure a twenty-five-year interim peace deal with the Palestinians. By the end of his first term, he had concluded that he could approach the well but not drink. Weisglass says Sharon contended that the Palestinians would never relinquish terror, even after a national homeland had been established, because the majority, in their society, had no control of the minority and many of the terror cells, religious rather than national in their affiliations, would never lay down their arms. Sharon decided to annihilate terrorism first, and only then move forward on the diplomatic front. The swamp of terror, he contended, had to be drained.

"President's Bush's speech on June 24, 2002, expressed that concept exactly," Weisglass told *Haaretz*. "We didn't write it, but it expressed our beliefs in the best possible way. That's why Sharon accepted the principles of the speech immediately. He saw it as a historical turn of events. He saw it as a diplomatic prize of the first order. For the first time, a new principle had been established: When you go into the negotiating room, you leave the guns at the door."

Tens of thousands of protesters waited for the prime minister in Zion Square after he returned from Aqaba. Their slogan was

"Oslo Proved It: Don't Give Them a State." At the rally, Aqaba was described as "a degrading ceremony celebrating the Israeli government's surrender to Palestinian terror." The Road Map was portrayed as a direct descendant of Oslo. The evening was punctuated by taped speeches by Sharon in which he had praised the settlers for their fortitude and explained why he opposed a Palestinian state. Far-right protesters held placards that read "Sharon Is a Traitor," "Sharon Needs to Follow Rabin," and "The Road Map Leads to Auschwitz."

Sharon was greeted at a June 6 Likud Central Committee meeting with deafening boos. Netanyahu declared that Israel must resist the establishment of a Palestinian state. Instead, he suggested, the Palestinians should live under autonomous rule with security operations remaining in Israel's hands.

Sharon spoke last. He quoted Menachem Begin, saying the prime minister carried "just a tiny bit more" responsibility, and as such he had taken on fateful decisions. Sharon reminded everyone that he had promised a huge victory in the elections, and the forty MKs seated in the hall were testimony to that. Just as he had delivered on that promise, so too would he deliver on the promise of peace and security.

During the months of May and June, Hamas joined hands with Arafat in an effort to hinder Abu Mazen's attempts at a cease-fire. Terror attacks plagued Israeli cities. On June 10, just days after returning from the saccharine affair in Aqaba, Sharon authorized the IDF's assassination of Dr. Abdel Aziz Rantisi, the leader of Hamas at the time.

The targeted killing missed its mark, and Abu Mazen called the attempt on Rantisi's life an effort to "eliminate the peace process." Hamas intensified their efforts to carry out attacks within Israel. In mid-June, a Hamas suicide bomber exploded on a bus in Jerusalem, killing seventeen people. Sharon belittled the heads of the Palestinian Authority and called Abu Mazen "a chick that hasn't yet grown feathers." At a cabinet meeting, he said, "We'll take care of terror until he grows some feathers."

Sharon decided to eliminate the entire Hamas leadership at the first possible opportunity. Until then, the spiritual leader of

Hamas, Sheikh Ahmed Yassin, had not been targeted. As they had done with Arafat in 2002, the Israeli intelligence services passed along information about the Hamas leadership's involvement in terror to the Americans. Several days later, National Security Advisor Rice said that the war on terror had to continue and that Hamas was an obstacle on the path to peace.

In late June, the U.S. Congress voted on the measures Israel could take to defend itself from terror. Three hundred ninety-nine representatives voted in favor of allowing preemptive killings; only five were opposed. Sharon got his wish: American approval to assassinate "ticking bombs," that is, terrorists on their way to an attack.

Immediately after the vote, Sharon authorized the assassination of Abdullah Qawasmeh, the leader of Hamas's military wing in Hebron. According to Israeli intelligence, Qawasmeh had been responsible for the deaths of forty Israelis. His death roused the Palestinian street. By July, though, Abu Mazen had roped the Islamic terror groups into a *hudna*—an Arabic term for "truce" that originated with Muhammad and, to the faithful, connotes an armistice that eventually led to the conquering of Mecca. Hamas's Izz al-Din al-Qassam Brigades, Islamic Jihad, and Fatah's al-Aqsa Brigades all committed to a six-month cease-fire. In return, they demanded that Israel cease all "targeted killings" and release a large number of Palestinian prisoners from Israeli jails.

After a thousand days of fighting, claiming eight hundred Israeli and twenty-two thousand Palestinian lives, it seemed that a small window of hope had been opened. Sharon's iron-fisted policy had brought the PA to its knees. He began demolishing illegal outposts, as he had promised Bush. During the first weeks of the hudna, Israel took down roughly ten outposts. The epicenter of settler resistance to that policy was in the hard-line outposts around Yitzhar.

On TV screens, the violent confrontations between the security forces and the settler youth looked like the beginning of a major shift in Israel's settlement policy. In essence, though, it was a charade in which all the players knew their parts. After the dust settled, the settlers moved back in and the army returned to its usual routine, which included protecting the settlers. When presented with American satellite photos depicting the outposts back in full swing, Sharon ordered them evacuated again.

The Palestinians were not fooled by Sharon's tactics: "eye-pleasing techniques," they called them. Although Sharon vowed to follow the Road Map without any "winks or deals," the settlers failed to take him seriously: they called one of the outposts built during those days "Ariel Hill" in his honor.

The IDF also began its retreat to September 28, 2000, lines. They left Beit Hanoun in Gaza and Bethlehem in the West Bank. As the hudna continued, the army began pulling out of more urban areas.

On August 19, at nine in the evening, a Hamas suicide bomber activated a ten-pound explosive device on a bus, killing twenty-three people, many of whom were on their way home from prayers at Jerusalem's Western Wall. The hudna had ended. Sharon called a cabinet meeting and ordered an immediate halt to diplomacy. No one was to meet with any PA members at any level. Sharon and Bush were aware that the recent attacks had been carried out by Hamas, but Arafat was blamed. Sharon, certain of both Arafat's power throughout the occupied territories and his successor's impotence, refused to hear talk of a renewed hudna.

Sharon ordered the IDF to resume its policy of targeted killings. In late August, top-level Hamas military leader Muhammad Kadah was assassinated while riding on a donkey cart in Khan Yunis. On September 6, Abu Mazen resigned, claiming that Arafat, in maintaining control of the security forces, had set him up for failure. He blamed President Bush too, asserting that the American president had refrained from pressuring Sharon to grant the Palestinian people tangible rewards in exchange for their gestures of peace.

A spate of terror attacks claiming fifteen Israeli lives followed Abu Mazen's resignation. Sharon considered sending troops into Gaza to strike back at the Hamas strongholds there, but right-wing ministers in his government urged him, in his pursuit of revenge, to look northward, toward Arafat's Ramallah headquarters. They demanded that the besieged leader be slain or exiled. A cabinet vote favored the latter option. Avi Dichter, head of Shabak at the time, argued that an exiled Arafat would be far more detrimental to Israel. He would, Dichter assured them, tour the world's capitals and charm the media as in the days of old. Dov Weisglass, Sharon's chief of staff and special envoy to Washington, spoke with National Security Advisor Condoleezza Rice before the cabinet meeting. She made it clear that Bush opposed exiling Arafat. The U.N. Security Council, backed by many world leaders, warned Israel not to pursue a policy of forced relocation. Labor launched a campaign against the proposed exile, which Sharon characterized as "hypocritical."

Arafat appointed a new prime minister, Abu Ala. A representative more clearly under Arafat's thumb, Sharon refused to meet him. As far as Sharon was concerned, Arafat's involvement in Palestinian affairs of state doomed President Bush's Road Map. Instead, he initiated a campaign of assassinations, targeting top-level terrorist leaders throughout the territories. The assassinations, based on an impressive level of real-time intelligence and carried out by attack helicopters and fighter planes, reached a record level of efficacy during the second intifada, enabling the IDF to kill terrorist leaders, who sleep in a different bed every night, almost at will.

Despite the perceived success of the targeted killings, Sharon had few reasons to rejoice. It seemed as though he was back where he had started during his first term in office: Terror attacks were rampant and showed no sign of slowing; peace negotiations were stalled; the hudna had failed; Arafat still ruled the PA; Sharon's relations with the American administration were at their nadir; and Israel's economy was suffering. Sharon saw no light at the end of the tunnel.

A growing chorus of voices in the Bush administration questioned Sharon's commitment to peace, arguing that in order to move forward, Sharon needed to do more than mouth the words "painful concessions." Chill winds were blowing out of Washington. Senior administration officials began leaking to the press that American ties with Israel were not as deeply rooted as they seemed. The annual loan package, they said, needed reexamination. Dov Weisglass, sent to the United States to mend relations, returned empty-handed. President Bush, he relayed, had taken Sharon's half-hearted treatment of the Road Map personally.

When asked about the apparent failure of the Road Map, Sharon encouraged anyone with a better solution to come forward. Yossi Beilin, former deputy foreign minister and architect of the Oslo Accords, along with Avraham Burg and Amram Mitzna of the Labor Party and Yasser Abed Rabbo of the PA, did exactly that, constructing an alternative peace plan—the Geneva Initiative. The goal of this plan was to show that peace was attainable, even with Arafat in the picture.

The nonbinding settlement hammered out by Abed Rabbo and Beilin went well beyond the Road Map, offering, for instance, Israeli concessions on the Palestinian right of return and a massive withdrawal from settlements. The Geneva Initiative was closely followed in the media. Even the administration in Washington, eager for any progress in the peace talks, responded positively to the content of the initiative. Colin Powell invited the principals of the Geneva talks to meet him in Washington; Sharon, aware that the president must have signed off on the invitation, understood the ominous message.

The meeting between Beilin and Abed Rabbo, which was instigated primarily to exert pressure on Sharon, had the prime minister seething. He lashed out at Beilin and the Labor Party, charging them with collaboration. He contended that the Geneva Initiative was a cynical political move aimed at overthrowing the government in "illegitimate ways while in the midst of a fierce fight against terror. . . . They do not hesitate to use any move; there are even those [in the Labor Party] who coordinate their moves with the Palestinians, behind the government's back."

The Geneva Initiative was creating a buzz. With the Road Map stalled, the Geneva Initiative, abhorred by Sharon, threatened to morph from an exercise in diplomacy into reality. In early December, the Geneva Accords were signed by Abed Rabbo and Beilin with great fanfare in Zurich. Two weeks later, Sharon announced the Disengagement Plan.

CHAPTER 55

Declaring
Disengagement

IN LATE 2003, ISRAEL WAS MIRED IN A DEEP RECESSION. WITH UNEM-
ployment on the rise, Finance Minister Binyamin Netanyahu had
to cut ten billion shekels from the 2004 budget, on top of the
eleven-billion-shekel slash already approved by the Knesset in
2003. Previously, the majority of citizens had stood behind Netanyahu in his battle with Israel's General Federation of Labor, but
this time a genuine cry arose from the swelling lower classes. Viki
Knafo, a single mother from the small desert town of Mitzpe
Ramon, walked the 125 miles from her home to the center of
Jerusalem in order to protest outside the Knesset. Her march
sparked widespread dissent. Israel's poor, sick, elderly, crippled,
and disenfranchised minorities erected a tent city near the main
entrance of the Knesset.

Personally, Sharon was in trouble. Three separate corruption
investigations were coming to a head. The Sharon family was
under siege by the media. Each new leak led the day's news. On
October 30, 2003, the police formally questioned Sharon; his two
sons had faced similar interrogations two months before. "It certainly isn't easy," Sharon said at the time. "I keep saying to myself
that it's lucky Lily isn't around to see this. It would definitely have
hurt her."

On September 1, 2003, Omri Sharon was questioned about
both the Annex Research and Cyril Kern affairs. He did not cooperate with police investigators, offering evasive answers at best.
Two days later, Gilad Sharon, brought in to answer questions regarding the Greek Island affair, exercised his right to silence. For-

mer MK Yossi Sarid railed against the prime minister. Speaking from the Knesset podium, he joked that Sharon was currently out of the running for Father of the Year. Sarid suggested that Sharon learn from former prime minister Yitzhak Rabin, who, during his first term in office, in the mid-seventies, had stepped down after the media revealed that his wife, Leah, kept money in a foreign bank account. "There is no choice but the suspension of the prime minister from his post," Sarid concluded.

David Spector, the owner of a security firm and a former adviser to Sharon, taped multiple conversations with Arik, Omri, and Gilad Sharon. Spector, once a regular at the ranch who had fallen out of favor with the Sharon family, provided the police with sworn testimony. Four employees at the Prime Minister's Office were brought in for questioning about their role in Omri Sharon's illegal fund-raising. None of them was charged with a crime, but the publicity surrounding their interrogations did little to enhance the prime minister's prestige.

On October 29, 2003, Sharon holed up in his office and prepared for the following day's questioning. He spoke with his lawyer at length and reviewed the relevant documents, refreshing his memory of the Greek Island affair. At nine o'clock the following morning, five police investigators arrived at the prime minister's official residence in Jerusalem. The seven-hour interrogation was largely futile. As one police official said, "He gave answers, but said nothing new. Most of the time he said, 'Ask Gilad' "—who had again exercised his right to silence.

Several hours after the exhausting investigation, Sharon participated in an economic forum in Tel Aviv. He announced that secret talks with the Palestinians, approved by Prime Minister Abu Ala, had been under way for some time. A diplomatic breakthrough was imminent. The media, still focused on the family's criminal investigations, treated his declaration as a gimmick.

The police investigations woke a number of old Likud enemies from their slumber. After five years of Sharon's iron-fisted rule, his adversaries began to organize. The media suddenly aired stories about Sharon's well-being, noting that he appeared to be in an abysmal mood. Sharon responded by saying that he was in perfect health, adding, "I do not think this is a good time for wars of inheritance. I wouldn't want anyone to spend time and money unnecessarily."

On November 2, 2003, more than a hundred thousand people showed up at Yitzhak Rabin's eighth annual memorial service. Their presence, despite the dwindling popularity of the Labor Party, seemed to underline Sharon's predicament. Shimon Peres, chairman of the Labor Party, speaking from a podium above Tel Aviv's central square, addressed the deceased prime minister as he attacked the standing one: "Those who castigated you have now adopted your path as their own, but they are tardy and they stammer shamefully." In previous years, the Rabin family had been careful not to dwell on Sharon's criticism of the prime minister during the days leading up to his murder. This time, Yuval Rabin, Yitzhak's son, demanded an apology.

Hoping to change the extreme right-wing perception many held of him, and to deflect the increasing pressure from Viki Knafo and others, Sharon tried, unsuccessfully at first, to convince Peres and the Labor Party to join him in a unity government.

At Peres's eightieth birthday party, Sharon, speaking in front of a crowd of people that included former president Bill Clinton, who had come to Tel Aviv for the occasion, said, "Shimon, maybe the two of us could join hands again toward a common goal. . . . Shimon, my friend, I wish you many more years of fruitful activity. Your achievements are great and you should take genuine pride in them. Please, let us share in your success." Peres responded, excited: "It is possible to renew the hope of peace. Arik, I want to tell you that it's closer than you think and closer than I believe. It can be done."

But just days after the festivities, the negotiations between the two major parties hit a rough patch. Speaking ten years to the day after the historic signing of the Oslo Accords, Sharon said Peres had made a "grave error" when he put his name to those documents and rolled out the red carpet for Yasser Arafat. Peres, upset, responded that Sharon ought to concentrate on his own errors. In an interview on Israel Radio, Peres said Sharon might have saved the country sixty million dollars by recognizing a Palestinian state twenty years earlier, rather than funneling money to the settle-ments.

On November 19, 2003, Sharon suffered yet another blow, this time from the U.N. Security Council, which unanimously ac-cepted Russia's proposal that the Road Map serve as the basis for resolving the Israeli-Palestinian conflict. The Russian proposal called on both sides to fulfill their commitments as outlined in the Road Map on the path toward "two states for two peoples." The measure passed despite Sharon's vehement opposition and his early-November trip to Russia to try personally to persuade Presi-dent Putin to relent.

A day later, on November 20, 2003, the Bush administration announced it would cut back on loans to Israel in the face of "on-going building in the settlements." Sharon felt a political noose tightening around his neck. He was under pressure across the board—Peres, Bush, Arafat, police investigations, the economy, the political quagmire, the persistent terror attacks, and, of course, the sudden vigor in the camp of his in-house rival, Netanyahu. It was his worst predicament since taking office in 2001, and it was from this soil that the Disengagement sprouted.

The people closest to the prime minister—Dov Weisglass, Reuven Adler, Eyal Arad, and his two sons, Omri and Gilad—offered advice in spades. They concluded that the Israeli public, above all else, wanted a significant peace proposal. The two people most active in pressing the prime minister to move toward a unilat-eral withdrawal from Gaza were Dov Weisglass and Omri Sharon.

On October 8, 2004, Weisglass explained Sharon's decision-making process. Weisglass told Ari Shavit of *Haaretz* on October 8, 2004, that Sharon's decision to "disengage" was rooted in both American and Israeli disappointment with Abu Mazen in the days following the Aqaba Summit. "The Americans were here for four months in 2003," Weisglass said in the interview.

> They were intimately involved in the process. The instruc-tional value of those four months was vast. The Americans saw for themselves the meaning of even the most festive Palestinian pronouncements. They saw the detailed work

plans and the beautiful charts, and they saw how nothing ever comes of it. Nothing. Zero. When you combine that with the trauma of 9/11, and their understanding that Islamic terror cannot be broken down and differentiated, you then realize that they came to their own conclusions. They didn't need us to help them understand what they were dealing with. Therefore, in the end, when we came to them and said we have no partner for dialogue, there was no problem. They already knew that as things stood, there was no partner.

We reached that point after years of thinking otherwise, after years of attempting dialogue. But once Arafat doomed Abu Mazen to failure in the summer of 2003, we came to the sad conclusion that we had no partner. There was no one to negotiate with, hence the Disengagement. When you're playing solitaire and no one is sitting opposite you at the table, you need to deal your own cards.

On November 21, 2003, Israeli TV's Channel 2 reported that Sharon intended to withdraw from certain West Bank and Gaza Strip settlements by the close of summer 2004. His goal, the news agency reported, was to reignite the peace process and move toward an independent Palestinian state. An anonymous source in the Prime Minister's Office would not confirm the report in full, but did note that discussions about withdrawing from certain settlements were under way. The source, acting under the prime minister's directives, said that the plan for withdrawal would be presented to the public shortly. The source stressed the fact that the Disengagement would not clash with the tenets of the Road Map.

The following day, in a meeting with the press, Sharon played his cards close to his chest. "Thus far I have not revealed the particulars to anyone," Sharon said of the burgeoning plan. "I just want the public to know that their prime minister has not stopped thinking of ways out of the quagmire with the Palestinians."

Two days later, on November 24, during a Likud Party meeting in the Knesset, Sharon kept the rumors simmering. He made clear that the upcoming meeting with Abu Ala was of no great urgency to him and that he would offer no prizes to the Palestinian prime minister so long as he refrained from fulfilling the first stage of the Road Map. He told Likud Knesset members:

> I informed the Palestinians that they do not have an endless amount of time. . . . Our patience has its limits. It's possible that we will reach a point where we will need to forgo the preferred option of negotiations. If I'm convinced that there is no point in waiting for another Palestinian government, then I will not be able to rule out unilateral action. It will be a move that serves our purposes.

Several days earlier, in a meeting with Elliot Abrams in Italy, Sharon told the White House envoy to the Middle East about his idea of unilateral withdrawal from Gaza. Abrams, who had come from Washington expressly to hear Sharon's urgent news, was shocked. He listened as Sharon detailed his plan and explained that Israel would dismantle a significant number of settlements. Subsequently, Sharon recounted his conversation: "I described the situation to him, explaining that without a partner for dialogue it seemed dangerous for Israel to proceed, and therefore Israel needed to break free of the Road Map and proceed according to a different plan." Sharon reported that the Americans initially didn't fully understand his intentions.

On November 27, 2003, Sharon held a long meeting with the editors of Israel's major daily newspapers. "It is possible I will come to the conclusion that it is not worth it to wait for another Palestinian government. . . . Unilateral steps must be taken. They should have understood already that what they were not given today may well not be on offer tomorrow."

The Yesha Council, the local government of Israeli settlers, recognized the brewing storm well before Sharon made any public announcement. On November 25, already fearing for the future of Jewish settlement in the occupied territories, the council began campaigning against the withdrawal. At the same time, they rallied their forces in the Knesset, preparing to bring down the Sharon government rather than have the withdrawal voted into law. Their slogan was "No nation should retreat from the history of its people."

In early December 2003, Ehud Olmert, vice prime minister at the time and one of the ministers closest to Sharon, sat for an interview with *Yedioth Ahronoth*. Citing the demographic danger of holding on to the Gaza Strip, he backed a unilateral withdrawal. Olmert's opinions were seen as a trial run for Sharon. On December 8, Sharon took another step closer to declaring his intentions, announcing that he would soon publicize his plans and explain his stance on the unilateral steps Israel was poised to take. "As you know," Sharon said, "I have announced that I have not ruled out unilateral measures if we find that our Palestinian partners are not willing to eliminate terrorism or conduct negotiations based on the Road Map. Over the past few days I have been conducting a series of consultations. I expect to present my intentions to the public during the coming weeks."

The maneuver, a classic Sharon flourish, rendered complete the manipulation of the media, the Knesset, and the public. Suddenly, at the nadir of his career as prime minister, as the economy and the security situation worsened, the peace process stalled, and criminal investigations raged, Israel held its collective breath, awaiting word from the prime minister. For a moment, the country forgot Viki Knafo, Cyril Kern, Yasser Arafat. Likud members, settlers, heads of the Labor Party, journalists, and ordinary citizens waited for the plan's unveiling. His confidants spread the word that he intended to outline his strategy in ten days' time at the annual Herzliya Conference on the Balance of Israel's National Security. The stage was set for the great spin.

On December 17, 2003, Sharon sat alone in his room at Sycamore Ranch and worked on the following day's speech. Dov Weisglass had relayed nearly every word to Condoleezza Rice and President Bush for approval. Certain Israeli government ministers were given morsels of the text. Shimon Peres received a few hints at the content of the speech, but said he wouldn't believe that Arik Sharon would promise to withdraw from the settlements until he heard it with his own ears.

Sharon began the next day, as all others, by putting on the clothes chosen for him by his behind-the-scenes adviser and make-up artist, Merav Levy. Levy, thirty-eight, began working for Sharon during his 2001 campaign as a makeup artist, but soon started choosing his clothes, preparing his food, and taking over many of Lily's other old chores. She adjusted all TV shots to make sure they were flattering, and she could often be seen riding beside the prime minister in his car. After four years at his side, she had become one of the most influential people in his life.

On December 18, 2003, Sharon, with his usual mask of makeup, arrived at the Dan Acadia Hotel in Herzliya. Zalman Shoval, a Likud member and former ambassador to Washington, called Sharon to the podium at eight o'clock sharp, just as the nightly news began. After several long minutes, he reached the word "disengagement." Some of those present had begun to feel that the ten-day wait had been in vain, but Sharon was finished with gimmicks.

> Like all Israeli citizens, I yearn for peace. I attach supreme importance to taking all steps which will enable progress toward resolution of the conflict with the Palestinians. However, in light of the other challenges we face, if the Palestinians do not make a similar effort toward a solution of the conflict, I do not intend to wait for them indefinitely.
>
> Seven months ago, my government approved the Road Map to peace, based on President George Bush's June 2002 speech. This is a balanced program for phased progress toward peace, to which both Israel and the Palestinians committed themselves. A full and genuine implementation of the program is the best way to achieve true peace. The Road Map is the only political plan accepted by Israel, the Palestinians, the Americans, and a majority of the international community. We are willing to proceed toward its implementation: two states—Israel and a Palestinian state—living side by side in tranquillity, security, and peace.
>
> The Road Map is a clear and reasonable plan, and it is therefore possible and imperative to implement it. The concept behind this plan is that only security will lead to

peace—and in that sequence. Without the achievement of full security—within the framework of which terrorist organizations will be dismantled—it will not be possible to achieve genuine peace, a peace for generations. This is the essence of the Road Map. The opposite perception, according to which the very signing of a peace agreement will produce security out of thin air, has already been tried in the past and failed miserably.

Sharon took a deep breath, looked up, and got to the heart of the matter. "We hope that the Palestinian Authority will carry out its part. However, if in a few months the Palestinians still continue to disregard their part in implementing the Road Map, then Israel will initiate the unilateral security step of disengagement from the Palestinians." The audience was completely still.

The purpose of the Disengagement Plan is to reduce terrorism as much as possible and grant Israeli citizens the maximum level of security. The process of disengagement will lead to an improvement in the quality of life and will help strengthen the Israeli economy. The unilateral steps which Israel will take in the framework of the Disengagement Plan will be fully coordinated with the United States. . . . The Disengagement Plan will include the redeployment of IDF units along new security lines and a change in the deployment of settlements, which will reduce as much as possible the number of Israelis located in the heart of the Palestinian population. We will draw provisional security lines, and the IDF will be deployed along them. Security will be provided by IDF deployment, the security fence, and other physical obstacles. The Disengagement Plan will reduce friction between us and the Palestinians.

This reduction of friction will require the extremely difficult step of changing the deployment of some of the settlements. I would like to repeat what I have said in the past: In the framework of a future agreement, Israel will not remain in all the places where it is today.

The relocation of settlements will be made, first and foremost, in order to draw the most efficient security line possible, thereby creating this disengagement between Israel and the Palestinians. This security line will not constitute the permanent border of the State of Israel. However, as long as implementation of the Road Map is not resumed, the IDF will be deployed along that line.

Settlements which will be relocated are those which will not be included in the territory of the State of Israel in the framework of any possible future permanent agreement. At the same time, in the framework of the Disengagement Plan, Israel will strengthen its control over those same areas in the Land of Israel which will constitute an inseparable part of the State of Israel in any future agreement. I know you would like to hear names, but we should leave something for later.

The next day he sent the list of names to Washington.

CHAPTER 56

Referendum Blues

SHARON COULD NOT HIDE HIS INNER TURMOIL WHEN HE STEPPED down from the platform. He said he felt fine, though, and had done what was necessary. The majority of the public remained incredulous. Over the past three years he had spoken at length of painful concessions; in reality, the number of settlers had gone up by 16 percent, to a total of 236,000.

After the Herzliya declaration, Labor MK Dalia Itzik called Sharon "the prime minister of verbiage." Peres termed the plan a deception. Skepticism was the order of the day in Washington, too, but Bush was willing to wait and see whether the unilateral plan revived the peace process.

The settlers' leadership—perhaps owing to their decades-long acquaintance with Sharon and their lurking fear that he supported them but was in no way *of* them—were the first to recognize the sincerity of his intentions. The Yesha Council published an announcement: "A new Arik, who turns his back on his brothers, the settlers, has been revealed. The Disengagement Plan is a disengagement from reality." Through their tight connections with the Prime Minister's Office, they learned that people close to the prime minister were already drawing up a list of settlements that would be erased from the map.

The Yesha Council organized a mass rally in Tel Aviv. On January 12, 2004, 120,000 people protested in Rabin Square under the banner "Arik, Don't Fold." Nonetheless, the polls showed that the majority of Israelis supported the notion of a unilateral withdrawal.

On January 21, 2004, State Prosecutor Edna Arbel indicted David Appel on charges of bribery relating to the Greek Island affair. This amended indictment stated that Appel "told Ariel Sharon that Gilad was likely to earn a lot of money." The businessman's indictment made it seem likely that Sharon himself would soon be charged with accepting bribes.

The media circled Sharon with pitchforks in hand, awaiting the signal to attack. Only the attorney general could decide whether to indict the prime minister. Arbel held the attorney general's post temporarily, because Elyakim Rubinstein had retired and been named to the Supreme Court.

A few days before the identity of the new attorney general was announced, Channel 2 News revealed that Arbel had recommended indicting the prime minister within the next two weeks. The ground beneath Sharon's feet was on fire. After consulting with his inner circle, he released a statement: He had no intention of resigning; if indicted, he would prove his innocence while in office.

Sharon's people made sure to tell reporters that according to the "Basic Law: The Government," a prime minister could be impeached only after he had been convicted of a felony. They also stressed that Sharon was certain Arbel had included his name in Appel's indictment as the result of a personal grudge. The next day he spoke at a Likud youth gathering and told the crowd he planned to stay in office until at least 2007.

Shortly afterward, the state prosecutor hinted that an indictment against a public servant should lead to dismissal. At the Herzliya Interdisciplinary Center, Arbel said: "If a public servant is indicted, he should suspend himself even if the 'Basic Law: The Government' does not say so explicitly." Arbel's comments came just a day after Menachem Mazuz had been named attorney general and before he had formed a legal opinion of the allegations against Sharon.

Less than a week after taking office, Mazuz called a staff meeting to discuss the Sharon scandals. Sources close to the attorney general let it be known that he was displeased with Arbel's attempts to force him to indict. The fact that she had voiced her opinion publicly left Mazuz with the impression that she was overly keen.

Sharon felt the pressure escalate as he waited for Mazuz's decision. He was scheduled to be questioned by the police later in the week. Even the legendarily composed Sharon could not conceal the stress. People close to him saw the ordinarily garrulous Sharon crawl into a shell. So long as indictment seemed likely, the

Greek Island case overshadowed the Disengagement Plan. The media were interested only in the corruption scandals.

That changed on January 29, 2004. Col. (Res.) Elhanan Tannenbaum was released from Hizballah captivity along with the bodies of three slain Israeli soldiers—Benny Avraham, Adi Avitan, and Omar Souad—in exchange for hundreds of Lebanese and Palestinian prisoners. Negotiations with Hizballah had been ongoing for three years. Throughout, the public had been kept from knowing the particulars of Tannenbaum's past. Sharon, the final arbiter of the hostage exchange, attempted to increase public sympathy for the retired colonel by saying his teeth had been extracted during torture. When Tannenbaum returned, however, he seemed to be in good health, his teeth in place. After so many lopsided deals with Arab armies and militias in which Israel returned hundreds of live prisoners for a few bodies of their own men—a policy that only heightened the Palestinians' desire to capture Israelis—many wondered why Sharon, a cunning negotiator, had agreed just then to swap a drug dealer and three fallen soldiers for hundreds of prisoners, offering Hassan Nasrallah, the leader of Hizballah, yet another opportunity to emasculate Israel.

Sharon's fate remained in the hands of one man: Menachem Mazuz. On February 2, 2004, before Mazuz issued his ruling, Sharon made another attempt to spin the focus of the media. He had breakfast with Yoel Marcus, a senior member of *Haaretz*'s editorial board, and dropped a hot story in his lap.

Sharon sat Marcus down and drew the exact contours of the withdrawal. He told him he had decided to withdraw from all settlements in the Gaza Strip and three in the northern West Bank. None of them would be part of Israel, he said. Marcus ran back to his computer and posted the story on the on-line edition of the paper, tilting the axis of public debate.

The story spoke of a unilateral withdrawal from twenty settlements, including all of the Gaza Strip, within a year or two. Marcus also wrote that Sharon had ordered the Prime Minister's Office to begin planning the operation and searching for new housing options for the displaced settlers.

Sharon went straight from breakfast with Marcus to the Knesset, where a storm awaited him. Sharon told the shocked Likud MKs, "We must take the initiative. Due to security and demographic issues, some of the Jewish communities in the Gaza Strip will no longer be able to exist. In the long run it would be wrong to continue Jewish settlement in Gaza. We need to explore the option of transferring certain communities. There are civilians there who are third generation. Their presence weighs on Israel. It's a heavy burden, and the friction is constant." Sharon looked pleased with the bubbling commotion around him.

His showing at the Likud meeting in the Knesset, along with his breakfast with Marcus, the representative of Israel's most liberal daily, which had criticized Sharon on every front for years, radically altered the perception of his Disengagement Plan. Politicians, journalists, average citizens, Palestinians, and Americans all understood, now that the plan had been outlined, that Sharon was truly going to throw his weight behind a unilateral withdrawal. The exposure also changed the media's attitude toward Sharon. The majority of the Israeli news media support a two-state settlement. Over the years, many had taken aim at Sharon as the most prominent figure on the far right. That changed dramatically once the Disengagement Plan took form.

On February 4, he addressed the allegations that the withdrawal and the corruption scandals were related. "There is no connection between the withdrawal from Gaza and the investigations," Sharon told a crowd of reporters. "It's not because of, but despite." To critics, his comments remained unconvincing.

In truth, Sharon did plan to withdraw from the settlements. He had declared his willingness at Latrun, and had demonstrated it by accepting the Road Map, by meeting with Elliot Abrams, in his speech at the Herzliya Conference, and as far back as 1979 when he called Begin at Camp David and told him he supported withdrawing from territory and from settlements in exchange for true peace. Undoubtedly, though, his decision to release the plans of the withdrawal on the pages of *Haaretz* was a brilliant tactical move.

In late February, police investigators, following the money trail on the Cyril Kern loan, flew to the Caribbean, where they learned that the case would demand months more research, which meant that Mazuz would rule on the Greek Island scandal first. Sharon tried to project calm, but the fact that his political future was in someone else's hands gnawed at his serenity.

In the meantime, the turmoil in the Likud turned into an uprising. In a letter to Sharon, a group of Likud antiwithdrawal lobbyists wrote that they would vote no confidence if he did not formally present his plan for a party vote. Sharon knew full well that the central committee and the majority of Likud MKs opposed the Disengagement Plan. "As the person on whose shoulders the responsibility rests, I don't have the luxury of choirs," he wrote in response. In a show of support for the antiwithdrawal groups, the NRP and the National Union Party abstained from votes of confidence in the government.

The Shabak began picking up threats on Sharon's life from far-right extremists. Sharon dismissed the threats. After fifty years of devotion to Jewish security, he said, he was not about to fear Jews. But those in the Protective Security Wing of the Shabak remembered Rabin's murder all too well.

Abu Ala, the Palestinian prime minister at the time, was unable or unwilling to stop another spate of terror attacks. Sharon met with his defense cabinet and decided to resume the targeted killings. On March 22, 2004, he authorized a helicopter missile strike against the hate-spewing quadriplegic leader of Hamas, Sheikh Ahmed Yassin. He was killed, along with his two sons and two personal escorts, as he left a Gaza City mosque.

The Arab world raged, and the European Union condemned the strike in the strongest possible terms. The U.N. Security Council met to consider a formal condemnation, which was barred by an American veto. Bush spoke of Israel's right to self-defense. In Israel, the assassination of the second greatest proponent of terror attacks after Arafat was widely supported.

Less than a month later, on April 17, Israeli missiles struck Yassin's replacement, Dr. Abdel Aziz Rantisi, as he was riding in his car in Gaza. Hamas, reeling, decided to keep the identity of its next leader secret. Rantisi's assassination completed a round of targeted killings that left all of the terror organizations leaderless. Only Arafat, living by the grace of Sharon's promise to the Americans, remained unharmed.

In late March, Arbel again called for Sharon's indictment. In the Likud, a party that still saw itself as an underdog despite years of rule, the state prosecutor's opinion strengthened Sharon's standing. Many central committee members viewed her stance as just another expression of arrogance from the elite left-wing aristocracy. Thanks to her, Sharon walked into a Tel Aviv Likud meeting on March 30 to cheers.

Yisrael Katz, the chairman of the conference, turned to Sharon while addressing the hall, and said, "We have complete faith in your honesty and leadership. All of us here and across the country are with you." Thunderous applause followed. Sharon tried to hide his satisfaction.

Arbel could carry him only so far. When he mentioned Disengagement, the boos rained down. Sharon surprised the central committee members, though, when at the end of his speech he announced that he accepted Katz's call to take the decision to the people. Sharon, who knew he had no chance to pass the plan through the Likud Central Committee, decided to put the withdrawal to a vote among all Likud Party members. "The results of the Likud members' referendum," he said, "will be binding on all Likud representatives, myself foremost."

Sharon's decision came just days after he had refused to put the plan to a nationwide referendum. Although it was clear to him that the plan would command a solid, favorable majority in a nationwide vote, a referendum required legislation, and a quick tally proved that without the dissenting Likud MKs, he would lack the necessary majority in the Knesset.

Opinion polls showed that 60 percent of Likud members supported the plan. Nonetheless, Adler and Arad vehemently opposed a partywide referendum. They argued that a standing prime minister had too much to lose. Omri and Shani recommended committing the plan to a vote.

Sharon heard reports that the settlers' leadership was pressing Netanyahu to lead the dissenters. Netanyahu, stuck between his principled opposition to the plan and his need for Sharon's and the Americans' support in his role as minister of finance, delayed his verdict. Sharon wanted the vote to take place before the settlers were able to mount a serious campaign within the party. MK Zvi Hendel of the NRP, a strong backer of settlements, coined the phrase that became the settlers' rallying cry: "The Disengagement will go as far as the investigations go."

Sharon planned to visit Washington in mid-April and then, with the president's approval for the withdrawal in hand, face the Likud on May 2, 2004. Mazuz may well have been on his mind, too. If the American administration and the European Union backed the move, it would be hard for even the attorney general, a powerful and independent figure in the Israeli system, to stand in the way of an internationally sanctioned peace initiative.

Bush's blessing for the plan could not be taken for granted. He was concerned that its unilateral nature might damage the Road Map and that the evacuees might leave Gaza only to settle in the West Bank. In return for the withdrawal, Sharon wanted the Americans to grant official acceptance to the existence of three settlement blocs—Ariel, Gush Etzion, and Ma'aleh Adumim.

The chairman of the NRP, Minister of Housing Effi Eitam, said that "it is not acceptable for a prime minister under investigation to go to the United States and commit to a plan that is crucial to the future of the country without first receiving backing from his government." MK Yossi Sarid created a stir when he asked Sharon in the middle of a Knesset Committee on Foreign Affairs and Security meeting whether Arbel's recommendation prevented him from functioning as prime minister. An uncomfortable moment passed, but then Sharon looked straight at Sarid and said, "I deal with it well."

Sharon sat for the usual Passover interviews with all the major newspapers. Aluf Ben of *Haaretz* asked Sharon why he had turned his back on his former supporters, the settlers. He said: "In our region not everything stands still and only my opinions change. There are developments and situations, and I, as the bearer of responsibility for the nation and its future, must weigh [the options] and choose the one that is the least dangerous to Israel."

According to Sharon, he weighed four different options once he came to the conclusion, in the late days of Abu Mazen's first term, that there was no Palestinian partner. The first option entailed ending the Palestinian Authority's rule. In that case, Israel would have to resume direct control over three million Palestinians—a long-term disaster. The second was a Geneva-type settlement, which Sharon deemed unsafe. The third was to remain inactive, which would trigger an increase in violence, and the

fourth was a unilateral move. His friends asserted that all allegations about the ties between the police investigations and the decision to withdraw were ridiculous. They said that he always felt the
weight of the country's future on his shoulders, and that as soon as
he found a path that allowed him to sidestep Arafat and delay the
Road Map, he pounced.

In conversations with Likud ministers who opposed the withdrawal plan, Sharon explained that the move would be a harsh
blow to the Palestinians. They would be forced to delay plans to establish a state and would have to wait for leadership that truly battled terrorism. He equated the plan to his earlier designs for a
long-term interim agreement. Sharon, who firmly believed that
forestalling a final settlement was the best course for Israel, told
the Likud ministers that he intended to execute the Disengagement Plan and then enjoy a long period of silence before moving
on to the next stage in the peace process.

Those opposed to the plan answered that the Golem might
well turn on its creator and seize control of the process. They contended that immediately after the withdrawal, the Americans and
the Europeans would bring immense pressure to bear to enact the
Road Map. If not he, then certainly the next prime minister would
be brought to the table of final status talks with far fewer cards.

Before leaving for Washington, Sharon called Netanyahu to
the ranch. Netanyahu said he would back the plan on three conditions: if Bush came out against the Palestinian right of return, if Israel maintained border control in Gaza, and if the three main
settlement blocs were brought inside the separation wall. Sharon
agreed, although he noted that the president might not be as ac-
commodating.

Bush, in the midst of an election campaign, also had his back
against the wall. With Iraq providing scant good news, he needed
a breakthrough of sorts in the Middle East. Sharon decided to
market the withdrawal as a stop on the Road Map, which suited
the interests of both leaders.

On April 14, 2004, Bush received Sharon at the White House
for a meeting billed as the "Disengagement Summit." Bush handed
Sharon a document that described America's updated stance on the

path to peace. It reaffirmed the president's conviction in the two-state solution as outlined in the Road Map and congratulated Sharon on his withdrawal initiative. Farther down it listed several concessions to Israel. The Palestinian right of return, which had been affirmed in a troubling way in the last draft of the document, was now "part of any final status agreement, which would include the establishment of a Palestinian state, and the settlement of Palestinian refugees therein, instead of in Israel." To the dismay of Palestinians and Arab leaders worldwide, the American doctrine now held that "in light of the new reality on the ground, including the existence of sizeable Israeli settlement blocs, it is unrealistic to expect that the result of final status talks will include a complete withdrawal to the 1949 armistice lines."

Bush made a large concession to Sharon on the separation wall. He expressed his opinion that it would be best if the wall were defensive, impermanent, and apolitical. He mentioned nothing about its legitimacy. He insisted that the Palestinians elect leadership that was committed to democratic reform and the peace process. He even approved Netanyahu's third condition, regarding Israeli control of the Gaza border.

Bush threw Sharon a lifeline with his concessions. "These are commitments we have never before received from America," Sharon said upon leaving the meeting. He was correct. In the weeks leading up to the meeting, Bush had been under pressure from Egyptian president Hosni Mubarak and British prime minister Tony Blair, who argued that such an American stance would be the final nail in the coffin of America's objectivity in the Israeli-Arab conflict. The Arab world reacted bleakly to the new American position.

Back in Israel, Sharon learned that the American willingness to side with Israel on the matter of Palestinian refugees and the large settlement blocs was not enough to put out the fire in the Likud camp. Ehud Olmert, Sharon's strongest supporter in the Likud, called the opposition to the withdrawal "a move meant to topple Sharon." The "Bush Document" did not guarantee Sharon victory in the referendum. His lead in the polls was shrinking, and his advisers offered a grim prognosis.

Ten days before the referendum, Netanyahu announced that

he supported the withdrawal. Other Likud ministers followed suit, including Foreign Minister Silvan Shalom, but the opposition went door to door with an effective campaign. Sharon's lead shrank from 15 percent to 4 percent. Sharon's camp, run by Omri, was caught up in an uncharacteristic panic. Three days before the referendum, all newspaper polls put the antiwithdrawal camp ahead by 3 to 9 percent.

At an emergency meeting, Sharon and his advisers decided to focus on the economy and the nature of their ties with the American administration, both of which, they wanted the Likud voters to believe, would be ruined if Sharon lost. Sharon called Netanyahu for help, but he said he had done all that he could. Those close to Sharon called the minister of finance "Trojan Horse."

Sharon devoted the weekend to press interviews. He warned that a loss in the referendum would irrevocably harm Israel. In private conversations with his staff, he seemed stressed and even revealed that he feared a loss would end his tenure as prime minister.

In a last-ditch effort to turn the tide, Sharon made certain that the question put to the voters would relate to his role in the withdrawal and not to the act itself. On May 2, 2004, all Likud members were asked to answer one question: "Are you for or against Ariel Sharon's political plan?"

Sharon believed until the end. A terror attack on the morning of the vote shocked the country and hurt Sharon politically. Tali Chatuel, a pregnant woman from Gush Katif, was shot while driving with her four daughters to meet her husband in Ashkelon. Under fire, she swerved and lost control. The terrorists shot everyone in the vehicle, including a two-year-old girl, at point-blank range. In the evening, Sharon learned he had been trounced, 59.5 to 39.7 percent.

Sharon huddled with his advisers. They decided that the first order of business was to announce that the prime minister would remain in office. As they spoke, a message from Washington came through. It said that Sharon had to abide by his commitments despite his loss in the referendum. That night he released a statement that signaled his intention to ignore the democratic decision of his party: "The people of Israel did not choose me to sit still," he said.

CHAPTER 57

Victory in the Knesset

AFTER THE REFERENDUM, SHARON WENT STRAIGHT TO DAVID CHA-
tuel's house in Gush Katif to offer condolences. He told the father
who had just lost his wife and four daughters, "I understand your
pain, but even in the face of such anguish, we must proceed with
the Disengagement." Later on, he said, "I am not afraid to look any
settler in the eye. I am determined to carry out the Disengagement." Five days after the loss in the Likud vote, he shrugged off
the referendum results entirely, telling the EU ambassador, "I'll
continue with the Disengagement despite the referendum. I don't
see any other plan that will restart the process. I don't plan to make
any major changes."

Eager to wipe away any remnants of the loss, Sharon announced that he would bring a revised withdrawal plan to the government for authorization by the end of May. This time Netanyahu
actively resisted him. The Likud had spoken, he said at the May 9
cabinet meeting, and "a political plan is not a pair of socks that are
changed daily."

On May 15, more than 150,000 supporters of the withdrawal
plan came to Rabin Square carrying banners reading "Arik, the
People Are with You" and "Majority Rules: We're Leaving Gaza."
Sharon did not attend. Many of the speakers were Opposition
leaders like Yossi Beilin and Shimon Peres, the men who had engi-
neered Oslo. More than a revival of the long-dormant left, the rally
signaled overwhelming support for the Gaza withdrawal. The next
day, President Moshe Katsav, a Likud man, conceded that the majority of Israelis wanted to pull out of Gaza.

On May 11 and 12, Palestinian forces in Rafah and Gaza City attacked two IDF armored personnel carriers, killing eleven soldiers. The ambush in Rafah, along a sandy route that divides Gaza and Egypt and is frequently used by tunneling arms smugglers, was so violent that IDF soldiers had to crawl in the sand to find the body parts of their fellow men. Pictures surfaced, shocking the public.

After meeting with his defense cabinet, Sharon authorized "Operation Rainbow." On May 18, 2004, a force of tanks and bulldozers moved into parts of Rafah and, in an effort to unearth some of the smuggling tunnels along the "Philadelphi Route," destroyed dozens of houses, including the one purportedly used by the terrorist who killed Tali Chatuel and her daughters. IDF shells mistakenly killed a group of protesters as well.

In the midst of the operation in Gaza, Shinui leader Tommy Lapid, Sharon's largest coalition partner (fifteen seats), announced that his party had no business in the coalition without a forward-looking peace plan. Lapid, like many other Israeli politicians, feared that Sharon, facing stiff criticism from within his own party, would back down from his stated goal and just play a game of survival.

Sharon made his intentions clear on May 23, 2004, at a memorial service for the fallen of the Alexandroni Brigade. "Lacking a partner on the other side, we must execute a unilateral plan that includes parting from Gaza and a small number of communities in Samaria." He said he would bring the plan to the Cabinet for authorization in a week. Speaking to the families of the men he had fought with in Israel's War of Independence, he said, "You know me, and you know that when I fight for something that is right and just, I see it through."

First he needed the Cabinet's approval. At the next week's session, he announced that everyone would get "unrestricted time" to air their opinions. He wanted a tally of friends, foes, and those still wavering. By the close of the meeting, perhaps his most tense as prime minister, Sharon realized he was in the minority. He delayed the vote by a week.

Articles about a possible Likud breakup began appearing in the papers. Netanyahu, Livnat, and Shalom, Israel's finance, education, and foreign ministers respectively, were the backbone of the resistance. Minister of Immigrant Absorption Tzipi Livni shuttled back and forth between the Prime Minister's Office and the Likud rebels' headquarters at the Tel Aviv Carlton Hotel in a desperate effort to placate the ministers and keep the integrity of the plan intact.

On June 3, seventy-two hours before the vote, Sharon called off the demeaning negotiations. He decided to solve the problem in a different way: He would "disengage" from the far-right ministers of the National Union Party, Benyamin Elon and Avigdor Liberman. At any rate, he knew the two of them were not long-term partners, certainly not with the withdrawal on the horizon.

Sharon called Liberman and Elon to his office on Friday morning. He needed to issue the termination letters before the Sabbath so that they would be in effect by the Sunday morning cabinet session. The two of them, sensing the trap, refused to show. Sharon was able to find Liberman on Friday and serve him notice; Elon had also disappeared. Sharon contacted Attorney General Mazuz a few hours before the Sabbath and asked whether notice could be served via fax. At 4:25 in the afternoon he sent a fax to Elon's office and informed him over the phone that he had been fired.

On Sunday, Sharon announced that the Cabinet would be asked to make a historic decision. There would be no more delays, he said. That was not entirely true. Elon had petitioned the High Court of Justice to weigh the legality of his firing. Elon arrived at the cabinet meeting while Supreme Court justice Edmund Levy deliberated whether he could participate in the vote. Many mocked him for his behavior on Friday. Sharon did not even look in his direction.

Justice Levy criticized Sharon for his handling of the affair but rejected Elon's petition. Although he was forced to bow to some of Netanyahu's demands, Sharon was still able to carry the vote, 14–7. The Cabinet had decided "to authorize the altered Disengagement Plan—but not to evacuate settlements." A commission would be established to plan for the evacuation of settlements, but the Cabinet "would meet again in order to decide whether to evacuate settlements or not, which settlements, and at what pace, dependent on the situation at the time."

Despite the verbal dance, the Cabinet had set the ball in motion. Sharon had forced them to support a plan that most Likud voters and central committee members opposed. Moments after the meeting, he said, "The government accepted my plan. The Disengagement is under way. . . . By the end of 2005 we plan to have left Gaza and four communities in Samaria."

Still, Sharon's future was in the attorney general's hands. Labor refused to join Sharon in a unity government before Mazuz had issued his ruling. Without them, any no-confidence vote could topple the government. On June 15, 2004, at five in the afternoon, Mazuz called a press conference. Wanting to avoid leaks, he delivered the news himself. As indicated in the seventy-eight-page document he had written, the evidence in the Greek Island scandal was deemed insufficient to indict the prime minister. "I would like to stress that my decision in this case was not born of an overly lenient attitude in general or toward the prime minister. In this matter, as I have said, each link in the chain of evidence is weak. . . . I have reached the unequivocal decision that the structure of the evidence cannot support a likely conviction."

While battling the Likud Party internal apparatus at every turn and working to include Labor in his government—a move opposed by the hawks for political reasons and by the doves for financial ones—Sharon found time in August to name Yonatan Bassi, a religious kibbutznik, to head the Disengagement Authority, more commonly known by its Hebrew acronym SELA, which stands for "Help for Gaza and Northern Samaria Evacuees." The Yesha Council, recognizing that Sharon had officially moved from words to action, stepped up their protests and organized a human chain from Gaza to Jerusalem.

On September 13, 2004, protesters filled Zion Square in Jerusalem yet again. With the Disengagement vote in the Knesset six weeks away, the atmosphere in downtown Jerusalem had the desperate feel of the Oslo days. Protesters held signs reading "Sharon the Dictator." They marched from Zion Square to the prime minister's residence a few blocks away, their torches flickering in a long procession. The steady backbeat of threats left many with the feeling of a coming civil war.

Modern Orthodox Jews (or religious-Zionist Jews, as they are known in Israel) do not take their orders verbatim from the mouths of their rabbis, but they do seek their advice on a wide array of matters. Many of the settlers belonged to this strain of Judaism and believed that the establishment of the State of Israel was not merely the newfound existence of "a nation like all others" as Herzl had dreamed, a remedy for the plague of anti-Semitism, but the beginning of their collective redemption. Therefore, tension thickened when, just weeks before the critical Knesset vote, the current head of the Mercaz Harav Yeshiva, Rabbi Avraham Shapira, ruled that it was forbidden to take part in the eviction of Jews from Gaza and Samaria. It was, he said, equivalent to eating pork or desecrating the Sabbath. Many rabbis agreed with him, and many refused to quarrel publicly with the former chief rabbi and leading light of a generation.

In the meantime, the army had its hands full in Gaza. Palestinian militants were firing Qassam rockets into the settlements of Gush Katif and the town of Sderot. In late September, the rocket fire killed two children. Sharon authorized an operation in the northern Gaza Strip, sending troops into the refugee camps of Jebalya, Beit Lahiyeh, and Beit Hanoun—Hamas and Islamic Jihad strongholds. Dozens of homes were destroyed; hundreds of armed men were killed. The operation ended in mid-October, although, as Hamas had vowed, the Qassam rocket fire continued, albeit to a lesser degree.

As the operation continued, Sharon's special envoy to the White House, Dov Weisglass, caused a stir in Washington. In an interview for *Haaretz* he said that the Disengagement Plan had been developed in order to freeze Bush's Road Map and postpone its implementation. Sharon had to come forward and deny what he had said.

At home, he was gearing up for the showdown in the Knesset. On October 25, 2004, Israel's parliament would vote on the Disengagement Plan. The Likud "rebels" were far from conceding the battle. Netanyahu pushed for a referendum, but Sharon refused, claiming it was merely a stall tactic.

Sharon, aware of the settlers' ability to mobilize and their relative political strength, called several Yesha Council members to a meeting. They demanded a referendum and warned Sharon that if he refused, the responsibility for civil war lay with him. The settler leaders demanded that the results of the referendum be tallied in a way that excluded the votes of the one million Israeli Arabs. Sharon refused and implored them to keep control of the fringe elements within their ranks. The outposts were harmful to the State of Israel, he said. The meeting ended on a sour note.

The head of the Binyamin Local Council, Pinchas Wallerstein, a longtime member of the Yesha Council and one of the leaders who remembered "the old Arik" well, came out of the meeting on edge. He noted that Sharon had batted down their request for a referendum with "very harsh phrases." Yesha Council spokesman Yehoshua Mor-Yosef said that Sharon was "determined to lead the country to a split." He said that from that point on, the settlers would lead a battle to topple Sharon. While they pressured right-wing MKs to vote against the withdrawal, Sharon warned all ministers and deputy ministers that they would be fired from the Cabinet if they voted against the plan.

Polls showed that 65 percent of the people supported Sharon's plan and 26 percent opposed it. In the days leading up to the vote, many settlement schools closed down. Fifteen thousand children and youths poured into Jerusalem and set up a protest village on a hill opposite the Knesset. Many of them, evoking Joshua and the Battle for Jericho, circled the building.

On the day before the vote, word got out that the United Torah Judaism Party was on the fence. Sharon fought for every vote, even arranging special medical facilities in the Knesset so that MK Eli Aflolo of the Likud could attend while he recuperated from surgery.

Unhappy with the drafts his speechwriters had provided, Sharon slaved over the text of the next day's speech:

> I am accused of deceiving the people and the voters because I am taking steps which are in total opposition to past things I have said and done. This is a false accusation. Both during the elections and as prime minister, I have re-

peatedly and publicly said that I support the establishment of a Palestinian state alongside the State of Israel. I have repeatedly and openly said that I am willing to make painful compromises in order to put an end to this ongoing and malignant conflict between those who struggle over this land, and that I would do my utmost in order to bring peace.

On the day of the vote, Livnat, Netanyahu, Agriculture Minister Yisrael Katz, and Health Minister Danny Naveh huddled in Livnat's Knesset office. They clung to their demands for a referendum, but they knew that a vote against the prime minister would cleave the Likud in two. Before entering the hall, they asked for a last-minute meeting with Sharon. He refused, taking his place in the Knesset and staring at their empty seats. The foursome walked in at the last minute. The vote began in alphabetical order. No one knew which way they would swing. Katz came first. He mumbled his "in favor" vote, setting off a celebration among the Labor MKs. All four Likud rebels voted in favor of the plan, which passed 67–44. Two months of frustration and political small ball ended in victory.

Sharon was pleased by the achievement, but left with a lonely feeling. He had beaten his old teammates—the settlers, the Likud Central Committee, and the MKs devoted to Greater Israel. His old adversaries from Labor and the Arab parties jumped up and pumped his hand warmly, while many of his friends stormed out of the hall.

CHAPTER 58

Traumatic
Disengagement

THE RIFT BETWEEN NETANYAHU AND SHARON THREATENED TO SINK
the 2005 budget bill. The finance minister's ultimatum was set to ex-
pire on November 9, 2004. The rest of the Likud ministers had fallen
in line behind Sharon. The prime minister's people made clear that
they would pass the budget through the Knesset with or without Netanyahu. Sharon stepped up contacts with Shimon Peres and Labor.

Casting aside Netanyahu would not be simple. He had easily
escaped from Sharon's gilded cage, even managing to lift Israel out
of its recession. Under his economic plan, unemployment had
gone down, the average salary had risen, and the Tel Aviv Stock Exchange had soared to unprecedented heights. If he retired now, the
economy would be rocked back on its heels. The two senior ministers in government faced off against each other.

The last thing Sharon wanted to do was tinker with the economy. For the first time since October 2000, it seemed to be on the
right track. Aside from the economic plan, the Israeli market benefited from a drastic reduction in terror attacks, a reality Sharon
had created by ordering Operation Defensive Shield, which allowed Israel freedom of movement within the Palestinian urban
centers, instituted an unremitting policy of targeted killings, and
called for the construction of a long separation wall between Israeli population centers and the West Bank.

At first Sharon was opposed to the separation barrier. It flew in
the face of his most basic ideologies. Ever since his mother had cut
the wire fence in Kfar Malal, he had fought against partitioning his
own land. It did not help that the barrier concept had originated
with Rabin and had been carried on by Netanyahu and Barak (with

disputes over placement, of course). At the time, he had said he couldn't see why Israel needed a partition fence.

Even in the early days of the second intifada, Sharon vocally opposed building a barrier, but he changed his mind after Operation Defensive Shield. Polls showed that the Israeli public increasingly favored a barrier. From then on he promoted the project and personally pored over the maps, determining exactly where to lay its serpentine path to make it most effective—keeping most of the Palestinians behind it, encompassing the most populous settlements, and not delving so far beyond the Green Line as to render it unacceptable internationally.

In late October, in the midst of the Sharon-Netanyahu battles, Arafat's health took a turn for the worse. His condition deteriorated day by day, but the circumstances of his illness remained enigmatic. Sharon received constant medical updates. Understanding that Arafat's condition was probably terminal, Sharon ordered Israel's security service to approve any and all Palestinian requests pertaining to Arafat's health. Sharon did not want to be blamed for his death. He made clear that Arafat could leave the Muqata and would be allowed to return.

At first Sharon approved a request made by Abu Mazen to transfer Arafat to a foreign hospital, but the Palestinian leader refused to be moved. His wife, Suha, and several close aides persuaded him to seek care in France. Sharon announced that he would be allowed to return to Ramallah, but thought to himself that this was the end—the man with nine lives was finally dying. On October 29, 2004, Arafat, looking ashen, was brought out of the Muqata in a wheelchair and flown to France. It was his first departure from the compound since Sharon had trapped him there in December 2001.

Rumors throughout the Arab world blamed Israel for Arafat's condition. Doctors were investigating whether his low white blood cell count was the result of poisoning, they said. When he landed in Paris, Colin Powell asked Arafat to pass his authority on to Abu Ala, but even as the Palestinian leader flickered in and out of consciousness, he refused to relinquish his hold on authority. He had always thought of himself as the only true Palestinian leader, encompassing within one body the full spectrum of Palestinian lore and life.

The settlers viewed Arafat's worsening condition as a sign from

God. They petitioned Sharon to wait and see who the next Palestinian leader would be before moving ahead with the withdrawal. Sharon rejected their suggestion out of hand. On November 1, 2004, the first call of the Evacuation-Compensation Law sailed through the Knesset, 64–44. Two days later, Bush emerged victorious from the American elections. Sharon congratulated him and said it was a victory for ideology and faith in a certain path. Bush praised Sharon for promoting the withdrawal.

On November 9, moments before his ultimatum expired, Netanyahu informed Sharon that he would stay in his post. In his open letter to the prime minister, Netanyahu wrote that he based his decision in large part on Arafat's dwindling influence on local politics, which demanded a reexamination of the merits of the Disengagement Plan. The NRP, on the other hand, resigned from the coalition, leaving Sharon as a minority prime minister who needed the Labor Party to keep him afloat.

On November 11, 2004, after Arafat had spent ten days in a hospital on the outskirts of Paris, his death was announced. The most pressing issue now was his burial. Sharon made his stance clear at a cabinet meeting on October 31: "So long as I am here—and I have no intention of leaving office—Arafat will not be buried in Jerusalem." Sharon would not even allow Arafat—who had claimed to have been born in Jerusalem, though authoritative sources listed Cairo as his birthplace—to be buried in Abu Dis for fear that his tombstone would become a pilgrimage site that could lead to claims of sovereignty.

Abu Mazen understood from Sharon that Jerusalem was out of the question. He asked to bury Arafat in the Muqata. The security services recommended that Sharon deny that request, too, out of fear that an impassioned mob would march the coffin to Jerusalem. In their nightmare scenario, tens of thousands of Palestinians would force their way into the Old City and lay "Abu Amar" to rest in the Haram al-Sharif sanctuary. They recommended Gaza, the birthplace of Arafat's father, as a suitable spot. After some deliberation, Sharon agreed to Abu Mazen's request, on condition that the Palestinian Authority provided all security.

Sharon masked his delight at Arafat's passing and projected a proper calm. The only crack in his veneer of decorum came during the live TV broadcasts of the funeral, when he observed, "A normal people would not set aside a full day of broadcasts for the man who murdered so many of its sons and daughters, women, children, and aged." When the analysts filled time with discussions about "Arafat's legacy," Sharon snapped, "What groveling. How ludicrous. . . . Who are we dealing with here? A terrorist, a murderer of Jews second only to Hitler."

On November 14, 2004, Arafat was buried in the Muqata in Ramallah. As the Egyptian helicopter carrying his body approached, the crowd of one hundred thousand erupted. Shots were fired in the air and hundreds of people crowded around the helicopter, preventing the removal of the flag-draped coffin. A security vehicle plowed a path through the throng, but the coffin was passed overhead on people's palms and masked, armed men climbed on top of it. Finally, the security services regained control of the coffin and Arafat's body was whisked off for burial. The senior Islamic authority in Palestine, Sheikh Tayseer al-Tamimi, recited verses from the Quran, and Arafat was hastily buried, Jerusalem earth poured over his cement tombstone. His wife, Suha, did not attend, and no eulogies were spoken.

For Sharon, the event passed without incident. Arafat was relegated to history, the Palestinians were mired in succession battles, and Israel was not being blamed for his death. In September 2005, a medical report was made public that determined he had died from either AIDS, poison, or infection. The cause of death remains ambiguous.

Sharon turned his attention back to the home front. He had to pass the budget bill through the Knesset and stabilize his coalition. He negotiated simultaneously with Labor and United Torah Judaism, promising the five-seat party 290 million shekels for ultra-Orthodox schools and religious establishments. Shinui leader Tommy Lapid told the prime minister he would pull his fifteen-seat secularist Shinui Party out of the coalition if he followed through and slated those funds for ultra-Orthodox schools.

Lapid's ultimatum forced Sharon to choose between, on the one hand, a left-wing government of Labor, Shinui, and Likud, which would make the Likud the most conservative party in the coalition and surely tear the party in two, and on the other hand, an alliance with Labor, Likud, and the ultra-Orthodox.

Sharon lost two no-confidence votes in late November. Both revolved around the widening gap between rich and poor in Israel, but neither totaled the requisite sixty-one MKs in opposition necessary to topple the government. Sharon realized, though, that Labor's security net was faulty at best, and that the National Union, NRP, and Likud "rebels" would prevent the budget bill from passing in the Knesset.

Sharon threatened to fire anyone who voted against party lines, and he proclaimed his willingness to go to elections. Although he had tried to convince Shinui that the 290-million-shekel package to the religious party was no reason to quit the government, they voted against the budget, and without Labor backing, the bill was defeated.

Sharon was beaming after the loss. Few could recall a prime minister as happy to lose a budget vote. Sharon could now offer the Likud Central Committee a choice: They could either sanction a unity government with Labor, or go to elections.

He fired the five Shinui ministers immediately after the vote. Within a span of four months, ten cabinet ministers had either resigned or been fired. Sharon's relationship with Lapid also came to an unpleasant end. The two were close in age and passionately loved literature, music, and food. Sharon could not understand why Lapid had chosen to take a stand on the issue of the 290 million shekels, forfeiting a role in the historic withdrawal from Gaza.

Sharon had a week to prepare for the Likud Central Committee meeting on December 9, 2004. As they deliberated whether to join forces with Labor or go to elections, Sharon took pains to state that he personally would be happy to go back to the polls. His hint was clear: He would win, but the Likud would be hard-pressed to duplicate their forty seats. The committee members would find themselves distanced from the halls of power.

As Sharon grew closer to Bush and showed his resolve to push toward a withdrawal, Egyptian president Hosni Mubarak suddenly warmed to the Israeli leader. After Arafat's death, Mubarak went so far as to say that only Sharon could bring peace. Four days before the central committee vote, the Egyptian president released Azam Azam, an Israeli Druze imprisoned in Egypt on espionage charges, in exchange for six Egyptian students who had sneaked into Israel to carry out a terror attack. Azam, a member of the Galilee's Druze population, who serve in the IDF and adhere strictly to a pact with Israel made in 1948, thanked Sharon profusely for his tireless work on his behalf.

On the eve of the central committee vote, Sharon promised his four most senior ministers—Foreign Minister Silvan Shalom, Finance Minister Binyamin Netanyahu, Defense Minister Shaul Mofaz, and Education Minister Limor Livnat—that they would keep their posts in the unity government. He also promised Netanyahu that he would insist that Labor back the budget and his economic reforms. Sharon won handily, 62 to 38 percent. The new government would include Likud, Labor, Shas, and United Torah Judaism.

At the annual Herzliya Conference, this year held on December 16, Sharon said he had paid a "steep personal and political price" for his decision to withdraw from Gaza and back the establishment of a Palestinian state. President Bush told a group of Jewish leaders who came to meet with him at the White House that the Disengagement Plan was brilliant.

On January 15, 2005, after free elections, Abu Mazen (Mahmoud Abbas) was sworn in as the new chairman of the Palestinian Authority. During his campaign he had taken a stand against terror attacks, saying they harmed the legitimate aspirations of the Palestinian people. On February 8, he met with Sharon in Sharm al-Sheikh at a summit hosted jointly by King Abdullah of Jordan and Egyptian president Mubarak. With Arafat gone, peaceful winds blew through the region. Sharon released hundreds of Palestinian prisoners from Israeli jails.

But as preparations for the withdrawal swung into a higher gear, so too did the settlers' resistance to the move. A right-wing fringe group circulated stickers that read "Sharon—Lily's waiting for you." They threatened to drag his wife's body from her grave. Sharon hired a security company to guard Windflower Hill.

In February 2005, Defense Minister Mofaz announced that IDF chief of staff Ya'alon's term would not be extended for the customary fourth year. Sharon and Mofaz did not want Ya'alon, who was known to speak his mind, commanding the army during the Disengagement.

Sharon frequently pulled the strings behind the scenes. In essence he picked Dan Halutz as the IDF's first air force–bred chief of staff. In May 2005, he ended Shabak director Avi Dichter's term, replacing him with Yuval Diskin. Although Sharon thought highly of Dichter, he had not fully endorsed the Disengagement Plan.

On February 16, 2005, the second and final calls of the Evacuation-Compensation Law passed the Knesset 59–40. All that was needed was for the Cabinet to vote on the matter.

One day later, Attorney General Menachem Mazuz announced that he intended to indict Omri Sharon in the Annex Research scandal, but not his father—an unpopular decision among the judiciary branch.

Before the February 20 cabinet meeting, Netanyahu announced his intention to vote against implementing the Disengagement Plan. With the new government in place, his vote was immaterial—17 voted in favor, 5 against. Natan Sharansky, who voted with Netanyahu, resigned his ministerial post, unable to condone the evacuation of Jews from their homes. Later that day, Sharon signed the withdrawal notices for twenty-four settlements—all the Gaza settlements and four in the northern West Bank—to be evacuated by July 20, 2005.

From the cabinet meeting the prime minister went on to attend the Jewish Federation's Conference of Presidents in Jerusalem. On February 20, 2005, a week shy of his seventy-seventh birthday, Sharon, just an hour after signing away a vast part of his life's work, told the group of American leaders, "Today I made the toughest decision of my life."

I arrived here today directly from the meeting of the government, a meeting in which an historic decision was made to implement the Disengagement Plan. Today, the State of Israel took a decisive step for its future. The government of Israel approved my proposal, and resolved to relocate the Israeli communities from the Gaza Strip and four communities in northern Samaria. Sixty years have passed since I began to serve the people of Israel, from when I served as a company commander in B Company of the 32nd Battalion of the Alexandroni Brigade until I gained the trust of the people when I was elected prime minister four years ago. During all those years, I made hundreds, if not thousands, of decisions. Many of them were fateful ones; some were life-and-death decisions. However, the decision regarding the Disengagement Plan was the most difficult one of all.

I accompanied the settlers of the Gaza Strip when I served as head of the Southern Command, and then as a minister in the governments of Israel. I was privileged to see the first greenhouse erected, the first field planted, homes built, and children born. I was with them in their difficult moments, in their daily security concerns, in their courageous stand when faced with mortar fire and terrorist attacks. As prime minister, as a citizen of the State of Israel, as a farmer—I am proud of them for their accomplishments, I am proud of them for their courage, I am proud of them for their great love of the land. However, there are moments which demand leadership, determination, and responsibility, even if it is not popular, even if the decision is difficult.

Weeks later, Sharon decided to postpone the withdrawal to August 15. The original date would have put the Disengagement in the midst of the three weeks of mourning before Tisha B'Av, the day the Jews' first and second temples were destroyed.

The IDF and the Israeli police trained for the mission for six months. During that time many settlers clung to the hope that Sharon—the only member of government whose audacity and conviction they feared—was merely playing out another spin and would find the opportunity to back down before entirely, and perhaps eternally, uprooting Jewish settlement in Gaza. But as the ides of August approached, reality began to manifest itself: The police had cordoned off the entire Gaza Strip, and tens of thousands of soldiers massed near the border and waited for orders. Many of the less religious settlers took the compensation offers and began packing their things.

On August 7, 2005, Netanyahu took a page from Sharon's book. Without forewarning he went into that day's cabinet meeting and handed in his resignation. The prime minister was stunned. "I carried out the [economic] measures and now I am acting as my conscience dictates," Netanyahu said at a press conference shortly thereafter. "I cannot take part in a move that is dangerous, divides the people, entrenches the notion of a withdrawal to 1967 borders, and threatens the future unity of Jerusalem."

As usual, Sharon rebounded quickly, appointing Ehud Olmert to the post of finance minister five hours later. Although it is quite likely that Netanyahu's decision was rooted in ideology, the public perceived it as yet another political party play, an attempt to out-flank Sharon from the right and position himself for another run for prime minister. At any rate, his resignation had no bearing on the looming withdrawal.

At midnight on August 15, 2005, the IDF officially closed the Kissufim border crossing in Gaza and began the evacuation. The following morning the IDF attempted to hand out eviction notices to the residents, granting them forty-eight hours to leave. The residents of Dugit, a small secular settlement by the sea, left of their own volition. The army provided movers, supplies, and support. On August 17, the IDF and the police, unarmed, moved into the settlements of Neve Dkalim, Bdolach, Ganei Tal, Tel Katifa, Kerem Atzmona, and Atzmona. The soldiers and police officers, both men and women, went door to door under a hail of epithets and refuse, to the accompaniment of pleading teenage girls in tears. Residents of Pe'at Sade, Nisanit, Alei Sinai, Netzer Hazani, Gan Or, Gadid, Kfar Darom, Shalev, Shirat Hayam, Kfar Yam, Katif, and Rafiah Yam were removed from their homes.

On Monday, August 22, the last and most isolated of the Gaza settlements was evacuated—Netzarim. The physical resistance was far less than expected. Most of the residents were simply un-willing to leave of their own accord. Soldiers and police officers dragged them from their homes and from the synagogue. Some wore prayer shawls, some sang and danced, some prayed, and some wailed in anguish.

The only true violence occurred in Kfar Darom on August 18. Hundreds of settlers, many from ideologically hard-line settlements in the West Bank, barricaded themselves on the roof of the syna-gogue. They stood behind coiled barbed wire, pushed the government forces off their ladders with long poles, and hurled lightbulbs filled with blue paint at the police, as well as buckets of other blue liquids. Eventually, the police officers huddled in a shipping container, used a crane to place it on the roof, and subdued the protesters. Despite this one minor flare-up, the soldiers and police officers comported themselves with remarkable grace and sensitivity.

Sharon stayed in close contact with the commanders in the field before and during the operation. He involved himself in everything, down to the smallest detail, but he took care to keep a low profile. During the days of Disengagement, as all of Israel sat glued to their TV sets watching the often heartbreaking footage of families being dragged from their homes, Sharon kept silent, almost invisible.

Only briefly was he shaken. During the early stages of the eviction from Kfar Darom, he was moved by footage of soldiers carefully boxing up a child's teddy bear, and he said he could see the pain on the stolid faces of other soldiers as the settlers berated them. That was early in the day. In the evening, after having watched the showdown on the roof of the synagogue, he called those resisting eviction "barbarians."

"When I saw the youngsters on the roof of the synagogue who tried to hurt the forces, my emotions swung from sadness to rage," he told *Yedioth Ahronoth*.

> I saw that group of wild men trying to injure police officers, border police guards, and soldiers, and I said to myself, What we have here is a crime, plain and simple. We're dealing with a mob of savages who were sent to Kfar Darom by a bunch of eye-rolling people in an attempt to overturn the decisions of the Cabinet and the Knesset by force. All of that stood in stark contrast to the honorable exit of the permanent residents of Kfar Darom.

The Disengagement took a total of six days. On August 23, the settlements of Homesh and Sanur, in the northern West Bank, were evacuated. Ganim and Kadim residents left on their own. All told, twenty-four settlements were evacuated. None of the doomsday prophecies materialized. As far as Sharon was concerned, the operation had been a great success.

CHAPTER 59

The Big Bang

THE DISENGAGEMENT CHANGED SHARON FROM A TIRED POLITICIAN fighting to keep his government afloat to a visionary leader, his popularity soaring. Yet Likud rancor deepened as the public's regard for him grew. The "rebels," a large group of Likud MKs and central committee members led by Netanyahu, hobbled him.

The next general election was to be held in November 2006, and Likud primaries were slated for April of that year. Days after the completion of the Disengagement, in late August 2005, Netanyahu and the rebels called a central committee meeting in order to pass a measure that would move the primaries back to the end of the year. Sharon, rightly, saw the move as an attempt to topple him. "They want to send me back to the ranch," he said, "but I won't give them that pleasure. I don't intend to go back to herding cattle."

The Israeli right feared that Sharon's unilateralism would spread to the West Bank. Most of the central committee members opposed any further territorial compromise. They expected Sharon to return to his old hawkish stance. Instead, he operated on two separate planes, calling for the continuation of the peace plan when speaking to the general public, and insisting, with the aid of an Omri-led party campaign, that he commanded a majority in the Likud Central Committee.

It was no use. Sharon's detractors dominated the public discourse in Israel, attacking him in the headlines. They cast Sharon as a tired old man who no longer came to the office regularly, and when he did, was worked like a marionette by Omri and other top staff members. Their attacks widened the rift between Sharon and the rebels, adding personal insult to ideological difference.

Sharon, realizing that a loss in the central committee vote on September 25 would drastically limit his power, began covertly to explore the option of forming a new centrist party.

People close to Sharon sent out feelers among the Likud's forty MKs; thirteen of them said they would join Sharon if he split off from the party. Senior Labor MKs and other high-profile public figures were similarly propositioned, and again, Sharon received positive responses. Sharon's plan to abandon the Likud was not seen as a means of escaping intraparty differences, but as a bold move made necessary by his need for autonomy while leading the country.

Sharon's strategy of leaving the party he had founded in 1973 and establishing a new centrist party that would loom over the two traditional powers came to be known as "the Big Bang." One of the main people behind the plan, Labor MK Haim Ramon, joined Sharon in his efforts to lure the seemingly eternal leader of Labor, Shimon Peres, a move that would bestow unrivaled seniority on the new party and lend it the legitimacy necessary to end the Palestinian conflict or at least achieve a long-term settlement. Sharon also spoke with Avi Dichter, the outgoing Shabak director, to see whether he might be interested in joining.

On September 15, 2005, Sharon spoke in front of the General Assembly on the sixtieth anniversary of the United Nations. The international body welcomed him as a man who had made history. Speaking in front of 160 world leaders, he made clear his intention to continue the policy of territorial compromise. Arab leaders, conditioned to leave their seats in defiance when an Israeli leader addressed the General Assembly, largely stayed put.

Sharon did not disappoint. "It is our duty to compromise for the sake of implementing peace with the Palestinians," he said. Senior staff members later said that he intended to execute a mass withdrawal from large swaths of the West Bank, setting Israel's final borders.

The U.N. speech did not, however, help his chances in the Likud Central Committee, and he knew it. The speech he prepared for the September 25 committee meeting was aimed over their heads, at the Israeli public. Omri Sharon, Uri Shani, Dov

Weisglass, Ehud Olmert, Tzipi Livni, and Haim Ramon began laying the groundwork for departure.

Sharon had written,

> The vote is not a formality. It is a move aimed at toppling me and a no-confidence vote in the way the Likud has led the nation. It represents a yearning for revenge and unbridled personal ambition. . . . We have an unprecedented opportunity. The world has accepted our view that without security there will be no diplomatic progress. That is what the Road Map, which was approved by a majority of Likud cabinet ministers, says.
>
> The truth must be told. Everyone knows that when we come down to it, not all of the territory will remain in our hands. We have a dream, and it is good and it is just, but there is also reality, and it is harsh and demanding. We cannot maintain a Jewish and democratic state while holding on to all of the land of Israel. If we demand the whole dream, we may end up with nothing at all. That is where the extreme path leads.

Sharon planned to end his speech with a call to the committee members to use their common sense and support him. "The decision," he wrote in his draft, "is yours, the committee members', to choose which path the Likud will take: a small, extreme, Opposition Likud, or a large, strong, centrist Likud that leads the nation responsibly."

That is the speech he had in his pocket on September 25. The first day of the meeting was to be devoted to speeches, the second to votes. At 8:30 P.M., after three hours of bruising speeches, Sharon walked up to the stage on the Tel Aviv Exhibition Grounds. Cheers and jeers mingled. As he began to speak, his microphone went dead.

Sharon waited, tapped the microphone, then returned to his seat. He climbed back on stage, but yet again the microphone stopped working. An invisible hand had silenced the prime minister. Sharon turned on his heels and left. The crowd was stunned.

It is unclear who disabled the microphone. A look at the electrical cabinet after the speech showed that someone had doused it with water. Sharon's people claimed that Netanyahu's people had wanted to prevent him from addressing the crowd. Netanyahu's people claimed that the electrical closet was in the "sterile security area" and that only Sharon's people had access to it. Moreover, they claimed that only Sharon had benefited from the fiasco. He came out looking like an innocent victim, while Netanyahu, the primary suspect, appeared to have pulled a dirty trick. Sharon's people claimed that the "rebels" were intent on silencing the prime minister.

Either way, Sharon, who had notoriously silenced Prime Minister Shamir back in February 1990, was the main beneficiary of "Night of the Microphones II." Standing in front of the lights and waiting to resume his speech, the prime minister seemed even more likable in his vulnerability. The next day, 90 percent of the central committee members voted in what turned out to be an upset for Sharon, who won by 104 votes.

Expecting to be publicly humiliated, Sharon skipped the results ceremony. His face lit up, though, when he learned of the victory. He was seen as a winner while Netanyahu was portrayed as a loser, a label that would stick to him in the months to come. Sharon, charismatic as ever, proved yet again that he outshone his peers as both a statesman and a politician. He had even managed to prevail over the opposition-minded, right-wing central committee.

Sharon knew the Likud rebels would hound him. The Knesset would be choked with in-house resistance. Until the April 2006 primary, his battle for supremacy in the Likud would be long and trying. His close advisers urged him to seize the moment to break away from the party. He hesitated. Sharon was all too familiar with electoral disappointment, having barely squeezed into the Knesset at the head of the short-lived Shlomtzion Party. Israel's brief parliamentary history was full of top-level politicians like David Ben-Gurion and Ezer Weizman who had left their parties, looked good in the polls, and bombed on Election Day.

On October 11, Sharon attended a Rosh Hashanah celebration in Ramat Gan along with fifteen hundred Likud supporters. He shook Netanyahu's hand and said, "The time has come to heal the wounds. Although I know it will be difficult, we will have to get used to the party supporting the measures passed in the Cabinet. I regret that we will not be able to continue in the current state." He told Netanyahu he intended to hold general elections, as planned, on November 7, 2006. Netanyahu said nothing. He had an earlier date in mind.

Sharon soon realized that reconciliation within the Likud was out of the question. Likud MKs joined hands with the Opposition to block Sharon's appointment of Olmert as minister of finance. Eventually, Sharon bent the wills of several Likud ministers, but the damage had been done. "The MKs' move to block the ministerial appointments will have consequences," he said from the Knesset lectern, without elaborating. To his aides he said, "I will not be humiliated," and he instructed them to hasten the preparations for establishing a new party. His confidants point to that moment as the hour in which his new party was born.

On Saturday, November 12, 2005, much of the old ranch forum met for a marathon session. They played out different scenarios, including funding for the new party and the number of Likud MKs willing to follow Sharon. He needed at least thirteen other MKs, more than one-third of the total number in the Likud, in order to make the new party eligible for state funding.

On November 15, Omri Sharon, in an amended indictment that had been purged of several of the original charges, pleaded guilty to charges of keeping false corporate records, perjury, and violating political fund-raising laws. After the plea bargain, he awaited sentencing. His father took the news badly, particularly disheartened by the fact that the prosecution made it clear they would not settle for an admission of guilt and community service, but would demand that time be served. Sharon also recognized that his son's political life had come to an end.

On November 19, the ranch forum met again to decide once and for all whether to break away from the Likud. They were almost unanimously in favor. Only Eyal Arad warned Sharon not to trust the polls. Sharon sent the group home late that night. As always, he listened to everyone and then sat down to decide. The thought of leaving the party he had founded did not go down smoothly, and the certainty that he would win in the general elections, were he to gain his party's nomination, gnawed at him.

Sharon was still on the fence on November 20. He had two different speeches ready and little time to decide. Ten days earlier, Amir Peretz had bested Shimon Peres in the Labor primaries. Within twenty-four hours he planned to send Sharon resignation letters from each of the Labor ministers, thereby ending the unity government. Officially, Labor had supported Sharon so long as he was in the midst of the Disengagement. Now that the plan had been carried out, Peretz wanted to set his own social and political agendas. The resignations would bring early elections; the only question was on which ticket Sharon would run?

A poll of the central committee revealed that even if Sharon beat Netanyahu in the primaries, the Likud Knesset list was shifting to the right. The rebels were heading for the top of the list, while Sharon's loyalists would be pushed out of contention. That was the final straw.

Sharon concluded that he had no chance of leading the nation as chairman of the Likud. He had to choose: He could stay in the Likud, easily secure another term in office, and forgo any further withdrawals, or he could take a chance and start a new party, which, if successful, would free him of the shackles of the central committee. After a long day of deliberation, Sharon decided to make the break. He notified Finance Minister Olmert and Defense Minister Mofaz and asked them to join him. The former, one of the architects of the move, immediately accepted; the latter said he needed to consider the matter.

On the evening of November 21, 2005, Sharon called a press conference in the eastern wing of the Prime Minister's Office. He seemed sharp and energetic, and his high spirits were contagious. His aides folded their Likud membership cards into paper airplanes and began sailing them through the conference room. They felt liberated at last from the restraints of the Likud Central Committee. Sharon summarized the reason for his departure: "Life had become impossible in that body. You are faced with endless difficulties and obstacles. There's no way to lead."

Thirteen Likud MKs followed Sharon. The split, and the public's outright adoration for Sharon, threatened to destroy the Knesset's largest party. People were fleeing the Likud like a sinking ship. Initial polls predicted incredible results: 30 seats for the new party, only 14 for the Likud.

Sharon wasted no time. He went straight to the president and asked him to declare new elections. After a vote, the Knesset was dispersed and elections were called. March 28, 2006, was the new date.

Sharon's new party lacked but one thing: a name. At first he considered "National Responsibility," but decided on the catchier "Kadima," which means "forward." The establishment of Kadima gave Israeli politics its greatest jolt in decades. People from across the social spectrum joined and issued calls of support. On November 30, nine days after Kadima's founding, the coup was completed: Shimon Peres, the strongest link in Labor's dynastic chain, joined the new party.

On December 4, Sharon and Peres held a joint press conference to announce Peres's decision. "Any party in the world would be blessed to have a man like Shimon," Sharon said, adding that Peres would have any ministry he pleased in his postelection government. Peres said, "Arik is the most suitable person to stand at the head of a coalition with a new agenda."

Reporters asked Sharon whether he was worried that Peres would drag him too far to the left. "Look at the two of us," Sharon said, to pealing laughter. "Can you see Shimon dragging me?" The unification between the last of the old guard, the only two active politicians left from the 1948 generation, symbolized the end of two-party hegemony in Israel. The Big Bang had succeeded.

ISRAEL, WEST BANK, AND GAZA STRIP AFTER THE DISENGAGEMENT, 2005

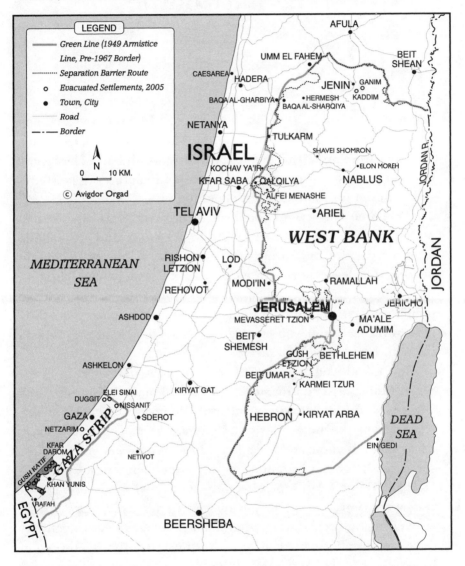

LEGEND

- Green Line (1949 Armistice Line, Pre-1967 Border)
- Separation Barrier Route
- ○ Evacuated Settlements, 2005
- ● Town, City
- Road
- Border

N
0   10 KM.

ⓒ Avigdor Orgad

AFULA

BEIT SHEAN

UMM EL FAHEM

CAESAREA · HADERA

JENIN · GANIM
○○ KADDIM
· HERMESH

BAQA AL-GHARBIYA ·
BAQA AL-SHARQIYA

NETANYA ·

TULKARM

ISRAEL

SHAVEI SHOMRON

KOCHAV YA'IR · · ELON MOREH
KFAR SABA · QALQILYA NABLUS
· ALFEI MENASHE

TEL AVIV ● · ARIEL

WEST BANK

MEDITERRANEAN SEA

RISHON LETZION · LOD
· RAMALLAH
REHOVOT · MODI'IN ·

JERICHO

JERUSALEM
ASHDOD · MEVASSERET TZION · MA'ALE ADUMIM
BEIT SHEMESH ·

GUSH ETZION · BETHLEHEM

ASHKELON · BEIT UMAR · KARMEI TZUR

ELEI SINAI
DUGGIT ○○ NISSANIT KIRYAT GAT
GAZA · ● · SDEROT HEBRON · KIRYAT ARBA
NETZARIM ○

KFAR DAROM
NETIVOT EIN GEDI

GUSH KATIF
○○ ○ ○○
· KHAN YUNIS

· RAFAH

EGYPT

BEERSHEBA

JORDAN R.

JORDAN

DEAD SEA

GAZA STRIP

CHAPTER 60

The Last Battle

SHARON'S STRATEGIC AND CREATIVE TEAM, LED BY REUVEN ADLER and Eyal Arad, began preparing for the March 28, 2006, elections. The polls were promising, and the campaign staff had a clear game plan: to pull away from either extreme and capture Finkelstein's vaunted spot just a notch right of center.

This time, the actions could speak for themselves. Sharon had pulled off the Disengagement with startling ease and presented a clear forecast for the future: progress on the diplomatic front and peace (or at least long-term calm) with the Palestinians. Sharon took care not to be specific about any future withdrawals, but the public understood his intentions. Reuven Adler spoke frequently of a "winning brand," an easy sell. He stressed "Sharon's way" as the path Israel needed to take.

Top Likud leaders joined Sharon, including Defense Minister Shaul Mofaz, Justice Minister Tzipi Livni, Finance Minister Ehud Olmert, Tourism Minister Avraham Hirchson, Tzachi Hanesbi, chairman of the Likud Central Committee, and others. Shimon Peres, Haim Ramon, and Dalia Itzik of Labor were joined by Professor Uriel Reichman, founder of the Interdisciplinary Center in Herzliya; Ronit Tirosh, the director general of the Education Ministry at the time; and several city mayors, to name just a few.

During his second term, Sharon had managed to drastically reduce the number of Israeli terror victims, and the relative calm brought social and economic differences to the fore of his campaign for a third. The former head of Israel's General Federation of Labor, Amir Peretz, having bested Peres in the primaries, made Israel's growing economic inequality the highlight of his campaign. Luckily for Sharon, Likud leader Binyamin Netanyahu was the

man most closely associated with the capitalistic economic reforms. His stiff economic measures had pulled the Israeli economy
out of its recession and put it on a path of growth, at the expense
of a widening gap between rich and poor. The divide created antag-
onism toward the architects of the plan.

Kadima campaign leaders aimed to brand Netanyahu as insen-
sitive to the plight of the lower classes and Peretz as ignorant in
matters of security and state. Sharon was portrayed as the "tribal
elder," a natural leader with vast experience, who had a deep sense
of responsibility to the nation and was capable of judicious decision making and statesmanlike behavior.

The Sharon campaign was buoyed by popular support. The
country had decided they wanted him to lead them; the only question was the margin of victory. Anything above thirty seats guaranteed him the premiership, and the polls were showing as many as
thirty-eight or even forty.

The elation surrounding Sharon showed its first crack on December 18, 2005. As on all Sundays, his schedule was particularly
full. He arrived at his office early, held a few meetings, and then
presided over the weekly cabinet session. He seemed sharp
throughout, and, as he had been doing since his departure from
the Likud, he cracked jokes freely, at times at the expense of the
other ministers.

After another series of meetings, he attended a 4 P.M. discussion on poverty reduction. The new finance minister, Ehud Olmert,
and the governor of the Bank of Israel, Professor Stanley Fischer,
were present. Sharon seemed alert and active during the meeting
and asked that an antipoverty plan be drawn up and presented to
the public before elections so that he could offer a worthy alternative to Peretz's economic agenda.

After the conference ended at 6 P.M., Sharon met with Peres to
discuss matters of state and their campaign plans for Kadima. Despite the long day, Sharon remained upbeat. After the meeting,
Peres said, "Sharon was in high spirits and both of us joked around."

The session ended after 7 P.M. His day over, Sharon planned
to leave for the ranch. Suddenly his head started to spin. Marit
Danon, his secretary, first noticed his altered condition and called

Gilad at the ranch. In the meantime, Sharon went downstairs to his car. The convoy drove onto the Jerusalem–Tel Aviv highway and headed toward the ranch. As they went, the paramedic accompanying the prime minister noticed that he seemed woozy. He ordered the convoy to make an immediate about-face and race to the closest hospital, the Hadassah University Medical Center in Ein Kerem.

Sharon remained conscious throughout the trip to the Jerusalem hospital. The convoy arrived at 8:05 P.M., and, under Shabak orders, the hospital went into emergency mode. Sharon's advisers claimed he got out of the car and walked through the hospital doors, but eyewitnesses reported that Sharon, unsteady and bewildered, had to be carried from the car on a stretcher. He was taken to the trauma unit and examined immediately.

Hadassah's top doctors were summoned. Gilad and Omri came quickly. "I'm sorry for causing you so much trouble," Sharon said to his doctors. "I didn't mean it. I'm okay, and I hope to leave you as soon as possible." When he caught sight of Dr. Boleslav Goldman, he teased, "I'm surprised at you. How long can it take to get here? Only now you've come?"

Israeli TV stations canceled their regular programming and went to live broadcasts from outside the hospital. Two hours after Sharon was admitted, the hospital released a statement: "Initial tests indicate that the prime minister suffered a mild stroke. During the course of his examination, his condition improved. The prime minister was fully conscious and remained so throughout the examination. The prime minister required no invasive procedures and will be released shortly."

Sharon's staff quickly briefed the press, telling them that the mild stroke would have no bearing on the campaign. Sharon will recover in a day or two, they said, and everything will be fine. That night Sharon met with a group of political reporters and told them, in his calm, reassuring voice, "We're going forward." The quote, using the Hebrew word *kadima* for "forward," was sprawled across the next day's front pages.

Sharon spent the night in the hospital. The next day, December 19, 2005, he was up early in the morning and feeling well. He joked with staff members and family: "I'm sorry I forced you to come so early. Usually I can only find you on the telephone at this hour." The hospital released another statement: Sharon had suffered a mild stroke, which would not interfere with his work as prime minister.

Professor Tamir Ben-Hur, head of Hadassah's neurology department and one of the doctors who treated Sharon, said, "At no point did the prime minister lose consciousness. He was not groggy, he suffered no paralysis, and, professionally speaking, he was not confused. His problem was very specific—not in the realm of memory or other neurological or cognitive functions, but in speech alone. That problem went away without a trace." According to Ben-Hur, "the matter was caused by a small blood clot that blocked off a cranial artery and restricted the flow of blood to the brain. The clot dissolved quickly, and we can say that the flow of blood in the brain has resumed, the blood vessels are open, and blood is being supplied to all parts of the brain."

Doctors began to suspect that Sharon's cardiovascular functioning had had something to do with the blood clot. Ben-Hur explained: "In an ultrasound performed on Sharon, we found an overabundance of heart movement along the wall that divides the two atria. That is a common condition among healthy people, found in a rather high percentage of the population, but it can also be related to the development of a blood clot and can lead to a stroke. In light of this finding, the prime minister is receiving anticoagulant treatment, and in a few weeks he will be called back for additional tests and evaluation."

Sharon was kept behind screens, far from the eyes of the public, the media, and other patients. Thousands of people stood vigil outside the hospital. Omri and Gilad took turns sitting by his side while Sharon held discussions about the next stages of Kadima's campaign. One of his staff members said, "At the rate he's returning to work, they'll have to hospitalize *us*."

According to *Yedioth Ahronoth*, President Bush called to wish him a quick recovery and advised him to lose weight, quit eating junk food, start working out, and cut back on his work schedule. Bush did not mask his concern. On a personal note, he told Sharon: "Be careful, my friend. I see in you a true partner and a courageous leader with a vision for peace. In order [for us] to defeat terror together, the Prime Minister of Israel can't be in the hospital. I need you healthy, Ariel."

After two days of hospitalization, Sharon was released. Kadima projected business as usual. Behind the scenes, though, the winds of stress whistled. During the first hours of his hospitalization, when Sharon's status remained unclear, many of the politicians who had recently transferred to Kadima were panic-stricken. They suddenly realized they had left promising careers for an uncertain political future that seemed increasingly unstable. Senior Kadima leaders were downright hysterical that evening—the party didn't have a Knesset list, basic party institutions, or a deputy leader. They were entirely dependent on Sharon, and he kept his secrets with him.

They heaved a sigh of relief when Sharon was sent home. Knowing that strokes tend to occur in waves, several senior Kadima members began quietly to prepare for the eventuality that Sharon would not be with them in March. They decided to shine immediate media attention on several other high-profile members of the party. Ehud Olmert, Tzipi Livni, and Avi Dichter were chosen.

In the days after the stroke, Sharon posed for pictures and handled party and state politics as deftly as always. His staff rebuffed requests to make their candidate's medical files public. His two personal physicians, Dr. Boleslav Goldman and Dr. Shlomo Segev, announced that Sharon was a healthy seventy-seven-year-old. At one point his weight was made public: 260 pounds before the hospitalization and 253 pounds afterward. More than a few disbelieving eyebrows were raised at those flattering figures.

Other details from his files, such as the positive results of the blood tests done weeks before the stroke, were criticized as merely a sliver of the full picture of his health, which, they said, the public had the right to know before casting its votes. But with Sharon as lively as ever, in meetings and before the media, his staff had no difficulty turning down the request, claiming that the demands sprang from a desire to undermine the prime minister's reelection campaign.

At Sharon's insistence, on December 26, 2005, one week after his release from the hospital, his two personal doctors and several physicians from Hadassah's Ein Kerem staff held a press conference. They released a few more details from Sharon's file, and announced that he was scheduled to have a cardiac catheterization on January 5 and that in the meantime, they had advised twice-daily shots of a blood-thinning medicine—Clexan—to prevent further blood clots.

On January 3, 2006, two days before the scheduled procedure, Sharon saw his son Omri resign his post in the Knesset. He had been convicted of crimes relating to the Annex Research affair and was awaiting sentencing. That same day, the prime minister decided, after much deliberation, that while under anesthesia he would transfer his powers to Vice Prime Minister and Finance Minister Ehud Olmert. Omri played a role in his father's decision. For years he had pushed for Olmert's advancement. They were close friends and ideological mates, both past members of the dovish wing of the Likud.

Sharon wanted to know exactly what Olmert's plans were for the duration of his hospitalization. He handed down specific orders for the time he would be under anesthesia. Although he had been assured that the procedure was simple and the recuperation period rapid, Sharon felt uncharacteristically distressed. On the night before the operation, January 4, 2006, Sharon, reclining on a couch after a long day, suddenly felt a sharp pain in his chest. At just after eight in the evening, Dr. Shlomo Segev was summoned to the ranch from Tel Aviv. He determined that the prime minister needed to be evacuated to a hospital immediately.

At 9:45 P.M. Sharon was taken back to Hadassah's Ein Kerem Hospital in an intensive care ambulance. The situation seemed hopeful: Sharon spoke steadily and was fully conscious. Gilad and his physician, sitting by his side, hoped he would be examined and promptly released. But minutes before the ambulance reached the hospital, Sharon's situation took a dramatic turn for the worse. Panic broke out.

The ambulance came to a stop outside the hospital and Sharon was wheeled to the trauma unit, where he was again hidden behind screens and lines of security personnel. Concerned citizens and an international troupe of reporters once again gathered.

The doctors put the prime minister under anesthesia and connected him to a respirator before transferring him to the imaging unit to gauge the extent of the damage. The MRI revealed a major cerebral hemorrhage, which necessitated brain surgery. At 12:10 A.M. Sharon was brought into the operating room in critical condition. The country held its breath.

As the hours passed, it became clear that Sharon had suffered a devastating stroke. His chances of recovery to the point where he would be able to serve as prime minister again appeared to be negligible. Still unconscious, Sharon was moved from the operating room to the seventh-floor neurosurgery intensive-care unit and the public went from nerve-racking worry for the prime minister's well-being to a state of national mourning for his sudden and tragic political death. The demise of the man who had symbolized strength, who had been able to hurdle all obstacles on the battlefield as well as in politics and life, left the Israeli public feeling as if they had lost a father.

The man who had exasperated many with his far-reaching settlement plans in Gaza and the West Bank, who had led Israel into the bloody conflict in Lebanon and been forced from his post as defense minister as a result of the massacres in Sabra and Shatilla, who had been perceived around the globe for nearly fifty years as a symbol of militaristic might left the stage of history a short while after carrying out the Disengagement, slipping through the back door into the middle of the mainstream. All the major television channels in Israel offered eulogies that placed him among the great leaders of the Jewish people.

Meanwhile, Ehud Olmert continued to assume his role as Sharon's replacement. Despite predictions that Kadima would sink without Sharon, the polls showed steady support. The campaign staff, led by Adler, regularly employed the phrase "Sharon's way" in order to turn the party itself into Sharon's heir and the upcoming election into a vote of confidence in Sharon's political path. Olmert, a seasoned and cool-headed politician, conveyed the message that he intended to fulfill Sharon's political will to the letter, primarily with regard to the peace initiatives. He took care not to sit in the prime minister's seat during cabinet meetings, leaving it empty as a gesture of respect.

The message was heard. The polls predicted Kadima would

take forty seats in the elections. In late January 2006, the big question was whether the Sharon touch would hold for the two months until elections. One month after his surgery, his condition was still reported as serious but stable.

Sharon remained unconscious and unaware of his surroundings. Although he could breathe on his own, he had suffered the deadliest type of stroke. Cranial hemorrhaging had led to severe intracranial pressure, damaging mostly the right side of his brain. Experts defined his state as "vegetative" and reported that his chances of ever regaining consciousness were slim. His doctors inserted a breathing tube into his throat and a feeding tube into his stomach.

On February 11, 2006, five weeks after he was hospitalized, Sharon's condition worsened. He now suffered from restricted blood flow to his bowels. Over the course of a four-hour operation, doctors removed seventeen inches of his large intestine. His condition remained serious.

On February 14, three days after the surgery, Omri Sharon was sentenced to nine months in prison, nine months' suspended sentence, and a fine of 300,000 shekels. The sentence, far stiffer than his lawyers had expected, added to the Sharon family's dismal mood when, two weeks later, on February 26, they met to mark the birthday of Ariel Sharon.

In the meantime, the Israeli news media had begun criticizing Sharon's medical treatment. Some of the reports focused on the fact that no outside expert had been allowed to examine his case. Some said that the public had not been properly informed of the prime minister's condition after his first hospitalization. Only after the second stroke had the media learned that Sharon suffered from a blood vessel disease affecting the brain, known as cerebral amyloid angiopathy (CAA). Many wondered why the presence of that condition had not been revealed during the December 26, 2005, press conference.

A second line of criticism concerned the doctors' decision making. Sharon was given a high dosage of blood thinners during the weeks leading up to his scheduled cardiac catheterization. The Clexan shots were prescribed in order to avoid further blood clotting and another stroke. He'd received his last shot on Wednesday morning, half a day before the second stroke and a full day before the procedure.

Some experts were concerned that the blood-thinning medicine may have caused the intracranial bleeding that led to the second stroke. In certain medical texts it is argued that administering blood-thinning medicine to someone with CAA can heighten the risk of cranial hemorrhage.

Many questions lingered: Why was the cardiac catheterization not performed immediately after the first stroke? Why, after the first stroke, was Sharon allowed to go home to his distant ranch and not kept in Jerusalem, close to the hospital, until the surgery? Why had a senior doctor not been assigned to him so that immediate treatment could be provided? Why had he been taken all the way to Hadassah Ein Kerem and not to the closer Soroka Medical Center in Beersheba? Why was he not flown to the hospital in a helicopter?

American neurologists raised tough questions regarding the treatment given Sharon. In the January 2006 issue of *Neurology Today*, a journal published by the American Academy of Neurology, several world-renowned neurologists discussed the central issues relating to Sharon's care, including the decision to administer the blood-thinning medicine and the decision to allow Sharon to return to his home, more than an hour away from his hospital in Jerusalem. "VIP Syndrome," a condition that causes physicians to treat famous people differently, was raised as a possible culprit.

Dr. Shlomo Mor-Yosef, the director of Hadassah's Ein Kerem Hospital, firmly rejected all of the criticisms, maintaining that Sharon received "the most proper and apt treatment for his medical condition and was treated by the best experts." Mor-Yosef asserted that the blood-thinning medicine was given in proper doses and under the proper medical supervision. It had been, he said, a judicious decision to rush Sharon to Hadassah's Ein Kerem Hospital (which was better equipped and where he had previously been treated) rather than to the closer Soroka Medical Center.

The differences of opinion surrounding Sharon's medical treatment from December 18, 2005, to January 4, 2006, have not been settled. To date, no independent commission has investigated the matter.

While Sharon lay in a coma on the seventh floor of Hadassah Hospital, his replacement, Ehud Olmert, managed to keep the numbers up in the polls. Nonetheless, as March 28 approached, Kadima began to slip. On Election Day, Olmert and Kadima received twenty-nine seats—enough votes for Ehud Olmert to become prime minister and form a government, but nowhere near Kadima's figures under Sharon.

Olmert hurried to the hospital to thank the unconscious leader who had, in essence, won him the elections. Although he had yet to form a government, there were no threats to his leadership in sight. Peretz-led Labor had secured nineteen seats; the Likud, under Netanyahu's leadership, had crashed, garnering just twelve seats.

The Sharon era officially ended on April 11, 2006. According to the "Basic Law: The Government," the term of an unconscious prime minister automatically ends after one hundred days. Attorney General Mazuz ruled that the Cabinet had to choose a new prime minister before the coming government was formed. The Cabinet authorized Olmert as acting prime minister. Olmert formed a government along with Labor and appointed Peretz to the post of defense minister. Netanyahu, battered, was left in the Opposition.

Sharon's personal items were taken from his office and his official residence and, by his sons' wishes, taken down to the ranch. Among them were the briefcase he used to take documents from the office to the ranch, pictures of his grandchildren, and a collection of notes from his time in office.

On May 28, 2006, Sharon was transferred to Sheba Hospital, east of Tel Aviv, where his wife Lily had died. He was placed in a wing for long-term comatose patients. Doctors estimated that his chances of returning to consciousness were negligible. In the summer of 2006, Omri and Gilad, his sons and legal guardians, still clung to the hope that their father would perform the impossible—as Ariel Sharon always had—and spring back to life.

ACKNOWLEDGMENTS

We would like to thank the hundreds of interviewees, sources, and experts who helped us with this project over the past four years. Since they cannot all be listed by name, we would like to extend special thanks to certain individuals whose roles were invaluable.

Pazit Ben Nun, Osnat and Chanoch Bloom, Orit Hefez, Noam and Omer Hefez: Your support, advice, patience, and forbearance carried us through the long days and nights we spent working on this book. We are grateful to Arnon Mozes, the publisher of Yedioth Ahronoth Group, and Dov Eichenwald, the CEO of Yedioth Ahronoth Books, for their backing and support.

Our translator, Mitch Ginsburg, did far more than render this book into English. His work, originality, and talent are evident throughout. We are grateful to Deborah Harris and Flip Brophy for their guidance and assistance in publishing this book internationally. Special thanks to the wonderful staff at Random House, and to our editor, Will Murphy, whose magic touch graces every page of this book.

BIBLIOGRAPHY

MEDIA SOURCES

Globes Archives
Haaretz Archives
Hadashot Archives
Maariv Archives
Yedioth Ahronoth Archives
YNET Archives

OFFICIAL SOURCES

IDF Archives
Knesset Archives
Ministry of Justice, www.justice.gov.il
Prime Minister's Office, www.pmo.gov.il
State Comptroller Report, www.mevaker.gov.il

BOOKS

Adan, Avraham. *On Both Banks of the Suez*. Jerusalem: Idanim, 1979.

Ansky, Alex. *The Selling of the Likud*. Tel Aviv: Zmora-Bitan-Modan, 1978.

Arens, Moshe. *Broken Covenant: American Foreign Policy and the Crisis Between the U.S. and Israel*. New York: Simon and Schuster, 1995.

Arian, Asher, and Michal Shamir, eds. *The Elections in Israel: 1996*. Israel: Israel Democracy Institute Press, 1999.

———, eds. *The Elections in Israel: 2001*. Israel: Israel Democracy Institute Press, 2002.

————, eds. *The Elections in Israel: 2003*. Israel: Israel Democracy Institute Press, 2004.

Avnery, Arieh. *David Levy*. Israel: Revivim Publishing House, 1983.

————. *The Liberal Connection*. Tel Aviv: Zmora-Bitan Press, 1984.

————. *Ha'tvusa: Kach Hitporer Shilton Ha'likud*. Israel: Midot, 1993.

————. *The Israeli Commando: A Short History of Israeli Commando, 1950–1969*. Tel Aviv: Madim, n.d.

Bar-Tov, Hanoch. *Daddo: 48 Years and 20 More Days*. Israel: Dvir Publishing House, 2002.

Bar-Zohar, Michael. *Ben-Gurion*. Tel Aviv: Am-Oved, 1977.

Benziman, Uzi. *Nothing but the Truth*. Jerusalem: Keter Press, 2002.

————. *Sharon: An Israeli Caesar*. Tel Aviv: Adam Publishers, 1985.

Caspit, Ben, and Ilan Kfir. *Ehud Barak: Israel's Number One Soldier*. Israel: Alfa Communication, 1998.

————. *Netanyahu: The Road to Power*. Tel Aviv: Alfa Communications, 1997.

Dan, Uri. *Sharon's Bridgehead*. Tel Aviv: A. L. Hotza'a Meyuhedet, 1975.

Dayan, Moshe. *Avnei Derech: An Autobiography*. Tel Aviv: Dvir Publishing House, 1976.

————. *Yoman Ma'arechet Sinai (Sinai Campaign Diary)*. Tel Aviv: Am Ha'sefer Publications, 1965.

Dayan, Yael. *Sinai, June 1967*. Tel Aviv: Am-Oved, 1967.

Druker, Raviv, and Ofer Shelah. *Boomerang*. Jerusalem: Keter Press, 2005.

Eban, Uri. *Arik Sharon: A Patch of a Fighting Man*. Tel Aviv: Bustan Publishers, 1974.

Eitan, Rafael, with Dov Goldstein. *A Soldier's Story*. Israel: Maariv-Modi'in Publishing House, 1985.

Eldar, Akiva, and Idith Zertal. *Lords of the Land*. Israel: Kinneret, Zmora-Bitan, Dvir Publishing House, 2004.

Gai, Carmit. *Bar-Lev: A Biography*. Tel Aviv: Am-Oved, 1998.

Har-Zion, Meir. *Pirkei Yoman (Memoir Chapters)*. Tel Aviv: A. Levine Publications, 1969.

Korn, Dani, and Boaz Shapira. *Coalition Politics in Israel*. Israel: Zmora-Bitan Press, 1997.

Korn, Dani. *Time in Gray*. Israel: Zmora-Bitan Press, 1994.

Margalit, Dan. *Commando 101*. Tel Aviv: Moked, n.d.

Meir, Golda. *My Life*. Tel Aviv: Maariv, 1975.

Miller, Anita, Jordan Miller, and Zetouni Sigalit. *Sharon: Israel's Warrior Politician*. Chicago: Academy Chicago/Olive Publishing, 2002.

Milstein, Uri. *Milhamot Ha'tzanhanim*. Israel: Ramdor Inc., 1968.

Neuberger, Benyamin. *Political Parties in Israel*. Israel: The Open University Press, 1997.

Morris, Benny. *Israel's Border Wars, 1949–1956: Arab Infiltration, Israeli Retaliation, and the Countdown to the Suez War*. Oxford: Clarendon Press, 1993.

Oren, Elchanan. *Toldot Milhemet Yom Ha'kippurim (The History of the Yom Kippur War)*. Israel: History Department of IDF General Staff, 2004.

Oren, Ram. *Latrun*. Tel Aviv: Keshet Publishing House, 2002.

Rabin, Yitzhak, with Dov Goldstein. *A Service Notebook*. Israel: Maariv, 1979.

Rubinstein, Danny. *Arafat: A Portrait*. Israel: Zmora-Bitan, 2001.

Schiff, Ze'ev, and Ehud Ya'ari. *Milhemet Sholal (Israel's Lebanon War)*. Jerusalem and Tel Aviv: Schocken Publishing House, 1984.

Schiffer, Shimon. *Snowball: The Story Behind the Lebanon War*. Tel Aviv: Idanim, 1984.

Shapiro, Yonatan. *Chosen to Command*. Tel Aviv: Am-Oved, 1989.

Sharon, Ariel, with David Chanoff. *Warrior: The Autobiography of Ariel Sharon*. New York: Simon & Schuster, 2001.

Shavit, Maty. *Arik: The Commandos' Commander*. Tel Aviv: Madin, n.d.

Tamir, Shmuel. *Son of This Land*. Israel: Zmora-Bitan, 2002.

Teveth, Shabtai. *Moshe Dayan*. Jerusalem, Tel Aviv: Schocken Publishing House, 1971.

Vardi, Ronit. *Bibi: Mi Ata Adoni Rosh Ha'memshala?* Jerusalem: Keter Press, 1997.

Weizman, Ezer. *The Battle for Peace*. Jerusalem and Tel Aviv: Yedioth Ahronoth Books and Idanim, 1981.

Ya'akovovitch, Mordechai. *Adam Ve'lohem: Sipur Hayav Shel Yitzhak Ben-Menachem*. Tel Aviv: Amihai, n.d.

Yenuka, Moshe. *From Kibiya to the Mitleh*. Tel Aviv: Bitan, 1967.

Zeira, Eli. *Myth versus Reality: The October 1973 War, Failures and Lessons*. Israel: Yedioth Ahronoth Books and Hemed Books, 2004.

Zipori, Mordechai. *In a Straight Line*. Israel: Yedioth Ahronoth Books and Hemed Books, 1997.

PRIMARY SOURCE DOCUMENTS

Agranat Commission Report. Report of the Commission of Inquiry
   into the Yom Kippur War. Tel Aviv, Am-Oved, 1975.
The Disengagement Plan. June 2004.
Kahan Commission Report, Report of the Commission of Inquiry
   into the Events at the Refugee Camps in Beirut, February 1983.
The Lebanon War: Ariel Sharon's Version of Events. Tel Aviv
   University, Institute for Strategic Studies, August 1987.
*A Performance-Based Roadmap to a Permanent Two-State Solution to
   the Israeli-Palestinian Conflict.* Washington, D.C., April 2003.
Ruling of the Attorney General, Menachem Mazuz, Greek Island
   Affair, June 2004.
State Comptroller Report, Miriam Ben-Porat, January 1992.

ABOUT THE AUTHORS

NIR HEFEZ, a graduate of Tel Aviv University, is a senior editor of the daily newspaper *Yedioth Ahronoth* and editor in chief of *7 Days, Yedioth Ahronoth*'s magazine. He has filled a wide range of posts in journalism, including editor in chief of *Yedioth Tikshoret,* a nationwide chain of weekly newspapers, and editor in chief of the weekly *Tel Aviv.* He serves as a major in the Israel Defense Forces reserves.

GADI BLOOM, a graduate of the Beit Zvi School of Stage and Cinematic Art, is the managing editor of *Yedioth Tikshoret.* He has written a regular column for the weeklies *Tel Aviv* and *Ha'ir,* as well as numerous investigative features.

ABOUT THE TYPE

This book was set in Fairfield, the first typeface from the hand of the distinguished American artist and engraver Rudolph Ruzicka (1883–1978). Ruzicka was born in Bohemia and came to America in 1894. He set up his own shop, devoted to wood engraving and printing, in New York in 1913 after a varied career working as a wood engraver, in photoengraving and banknote printing plants, and as an art director and freelance artist. He designed and illustrated many books, and was the creator of a considerable list of individual prints—wood engravings, line engravings on copper, and aquatints.

28 DATE DUE *DAYS*

MAR 0 7 2007		
NOV 1 6 2007		

GAYLORD | | | PRINTED IN U.S.A.